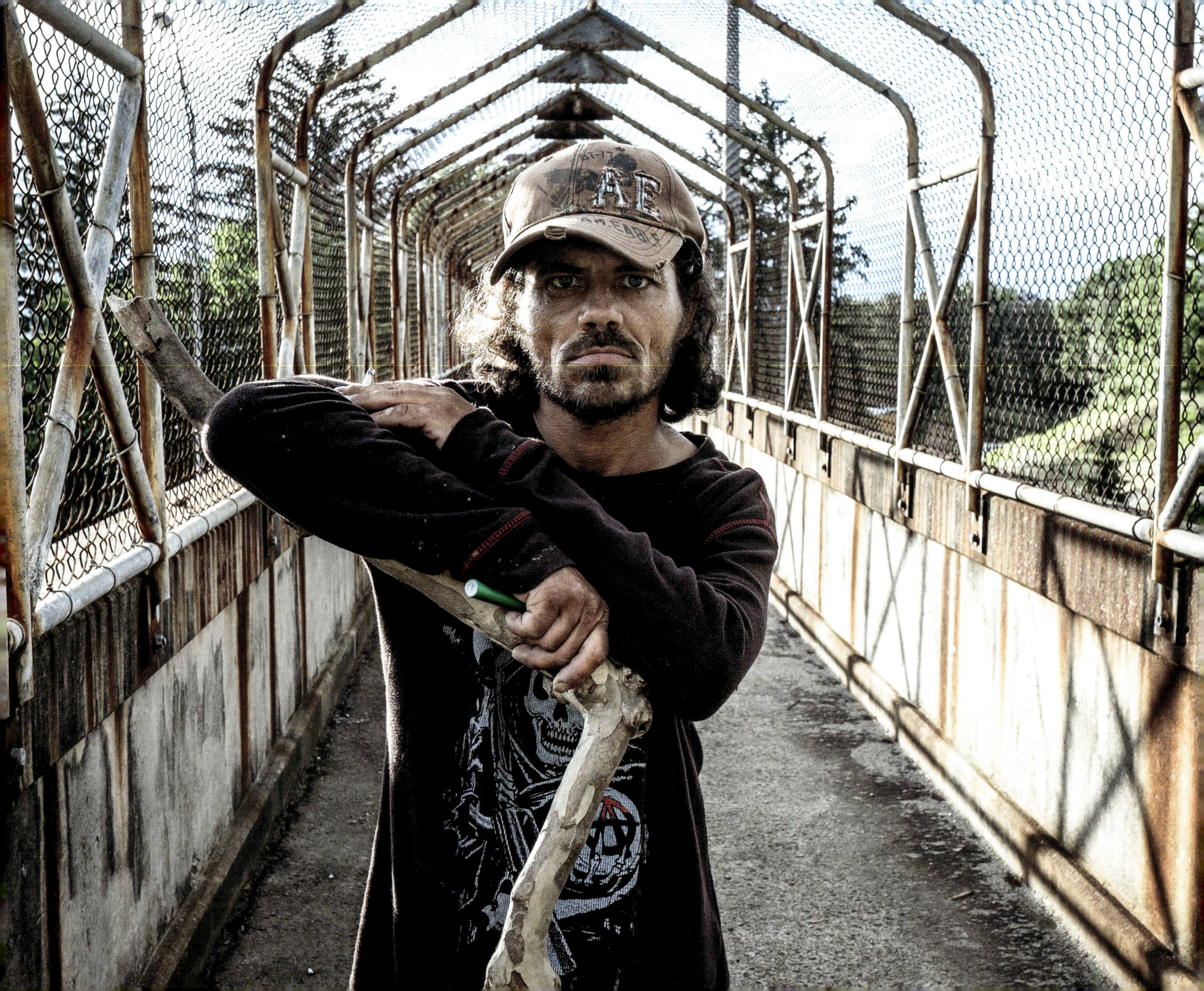
AE

THE HIDDEN SOUTH

Come Home

Edited by Angela Wiechmann
Proofread by Hanna Kjeldbjerg
ISBN 13: 978-1-59298-835-8
Library of Congress Catalog Number: 2015918341
Printed in the United States of America
Second Printing: 2016
20 19 18 17 16   6 5 4 3 2
Book design and typesetting by Brent Walker

For more information or to order, visit TheHiddenSouth.com/book or call (800) 901-3480. Reseller discounts available.

Contact the author at ths@TheHiddenSouth.com
60 Postal Pkwy, #71921, Newnan, GA 30271

Join the conversation at **TheHiddenSouth.com**

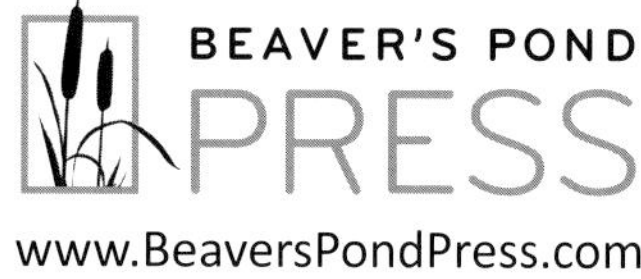

www.BeaversPondPress.com

To my mother, Phyllis Walker. Thank you for teaching me what it means to love unconditionally.

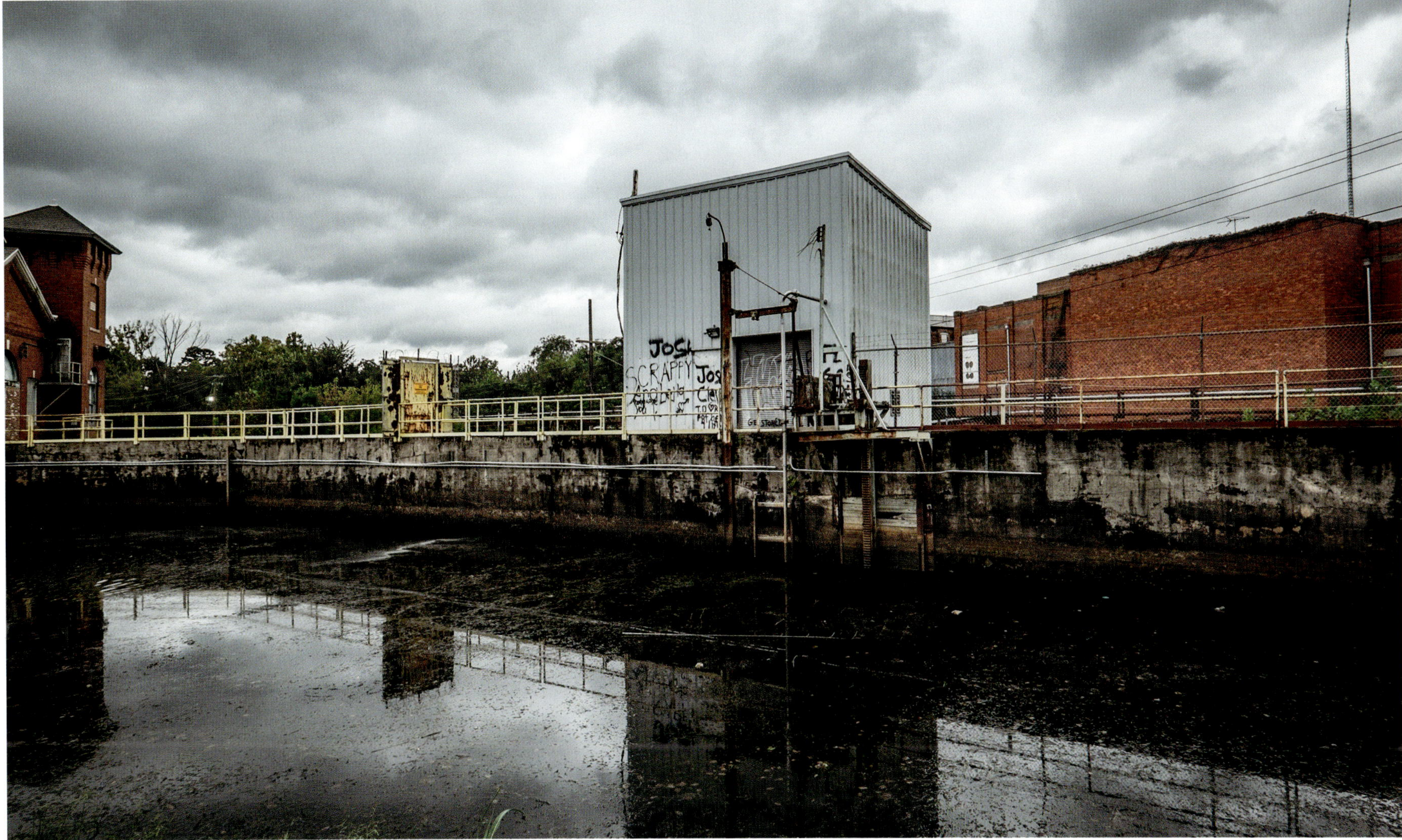

We come into this world with a clean slate and are thrown into the waters of life. For some, the waters are calm and peaceful. But for others, they are turbulent and littered with the debris of a harsher reality. For those of us who find it too painful to survive on the surface, going under seems to be the only option, the only place where we can truly seek refuge. Many of us never return from the bottom. But for some, there is hope. There is light. There is an opportunity to learn to manage the obstacles swirling around us and move forward toward healing.

I designed this book around the questions, attitudes, and values inherent to that journey—feelings and frustrations we all share as humans—to allow readers to experience that journey with the people in the book. I wanted to show our obvious, and not so obvious connections—connections we wouldn't otherwise make.

I also allowed for easy navigation that encourages readers to move in a nonsequential way through the book, so they can easily find the stories that interest them most.

I used comments from Facebook to not only highlight the gaps in how we address these issues as a society, but also show how we shine as humans.

In some cases, it was necessary to modify conversations and comments for clarity and brevity.

While most of the teachings in this book surface from the stories, pictures, and comments, I have chosen to add referenced facts and quotes that provide additional context.

"You're only as sick as your secrets." That's one of the many infuriating things they said to me when I first began showing up at A.A. meetings at age seventeen. If I knew anything, it was secrets. I had plenty. I didn't really care when the recovery people said sharing those secrets would help heal me. They were too scary to say. How could anybody love me who knew the truth?

So for the next thirteen-plus years, I was in and out of recovery. I'd have brief periods of sobriety followed by completely defeating relapses.

It was during one of these attempts at getting clean in my early thirties that I finally told my mother about being molested at the park when I was twelve.

It was a difficult conversation. Even though she couldn't have known what happened that day at Will's Park, she felt guilty and hurt. I too had remorse for not trusting her enough to tell her years before. But I think both of us walked away with a sense of relief: me, because the weight on my shoulders felt a little lighter, and her, because it explained a lot about my actions as a teen that were hurtful to her and the rest of my family.

I didn't realize it at the time, but the act of letting go of that and other secrets was the beginning of the healing journey I'm on today. It didn't fix everything, but it did give me the chance to begin the process of recovery. I noticed that every time I shared secrets, they had less and less power over my life. And it turned out that all the fears about telling secrets I had carried around for years were complete and utter bullshit.

Long before I had the idea for this project, before I even picked up a camera for the first time, I had an understanding of the power of sharing secrets and stories. During the years leading up to *The Hidden South*, I came across incredibly powerful projects like PostSecret and StoryCorps. Postsecret in particular caused me to really consider the power of a picture with a secret. I couldn't wait to see the new posts every week. I loved the brevity and raw punch of blunt honesty that I'd get when I read the postcards.

I knew it would be powerful if I could tie that type of honesty to a portrait. But how do you do something like that? You can't just walk up to people and ask them to tell you such intimate things. Why would they share anything with me, a stranger? It was hard enough just asking to take someone's picture on the street, much less asking someone to share a personal story. I wrestled with it for years.

The first stranger who told me her story was a prostitute less than a mile from my studio in West Georgia. At the time, I was working on another project called *Grey State*, and I was putting together a zine issue called "Instant Gratification," in which I used an instant camera to photograph random people posing sexy.

We had our brief photo session on the train tracks. I loved the rawness of the pictures—Caucasian girl, blond, in her mid to late twenties. There was something special about those images. They were desperate to tell a story. The best part was when she got back in the car and started telling me about her life.

Alice: I only been with like ten or fifteen white guys. Been with hundreds of black guys. I don't know . . . white guys . . . I drift off when I get high wit 'em. When I was thirteen, I got high for the first time with this old black guy. He was like sixty or somethin'. I liked brothers ever since. That wasn't my first time, though. My first sex was with a little black girl when I's like seven.

BW: I guess we all like what we like for a reason.

Alice: Drop me at the dope man. Can you wait on me and take me home?

BW: No, darlin', I can't do that. I don't go around that shit anymore. I thought you were gonna take that money home to your old man?

Alice: I'll just spend $5 and take the rest home.

BW: You know that shit ain't happening.

Alice: You're right. Fuck it.

I dropped her off at her dealer's house and went on my way. But I was hooked.

I realized that my anxiety about this project was one I created on my own. I was worried about "interviewing" people. But I didn't need to interview people—I just needed to have a conversation with them. When you interview people, you're on one level and they are on another. It's not equal. But when you have a conversation, you are on the same level. You create an opportunity to connect.

And that's what this book is about: connection. Connecting with people. Connecting with problems. Connecting with solutions. Connecting with *The Hidden South.*

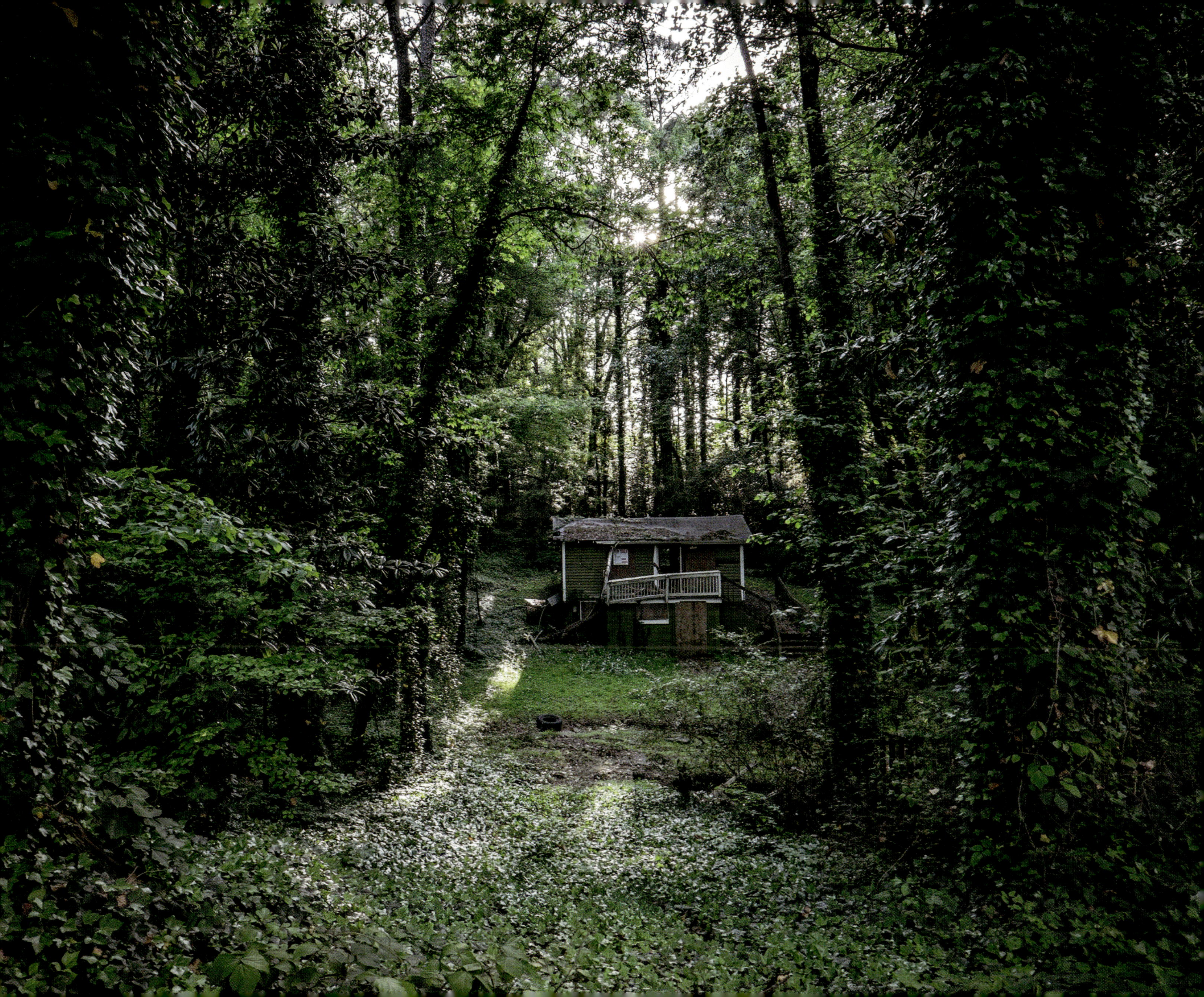

Daniel: I forgave her a while ago . . . I mean, I lost a full-ride scholarship to Oklahoma State University for wrestling because she decided she wanted to smoke crack and be a prostitute instead of working a job and being a mother. I had to drop out of school and sell drugs to keep a roof over our head. It cost me everything.

BW: Do you really think you forgave her?

Daniel: No, I don't.

—*Daniel (p. 10)*

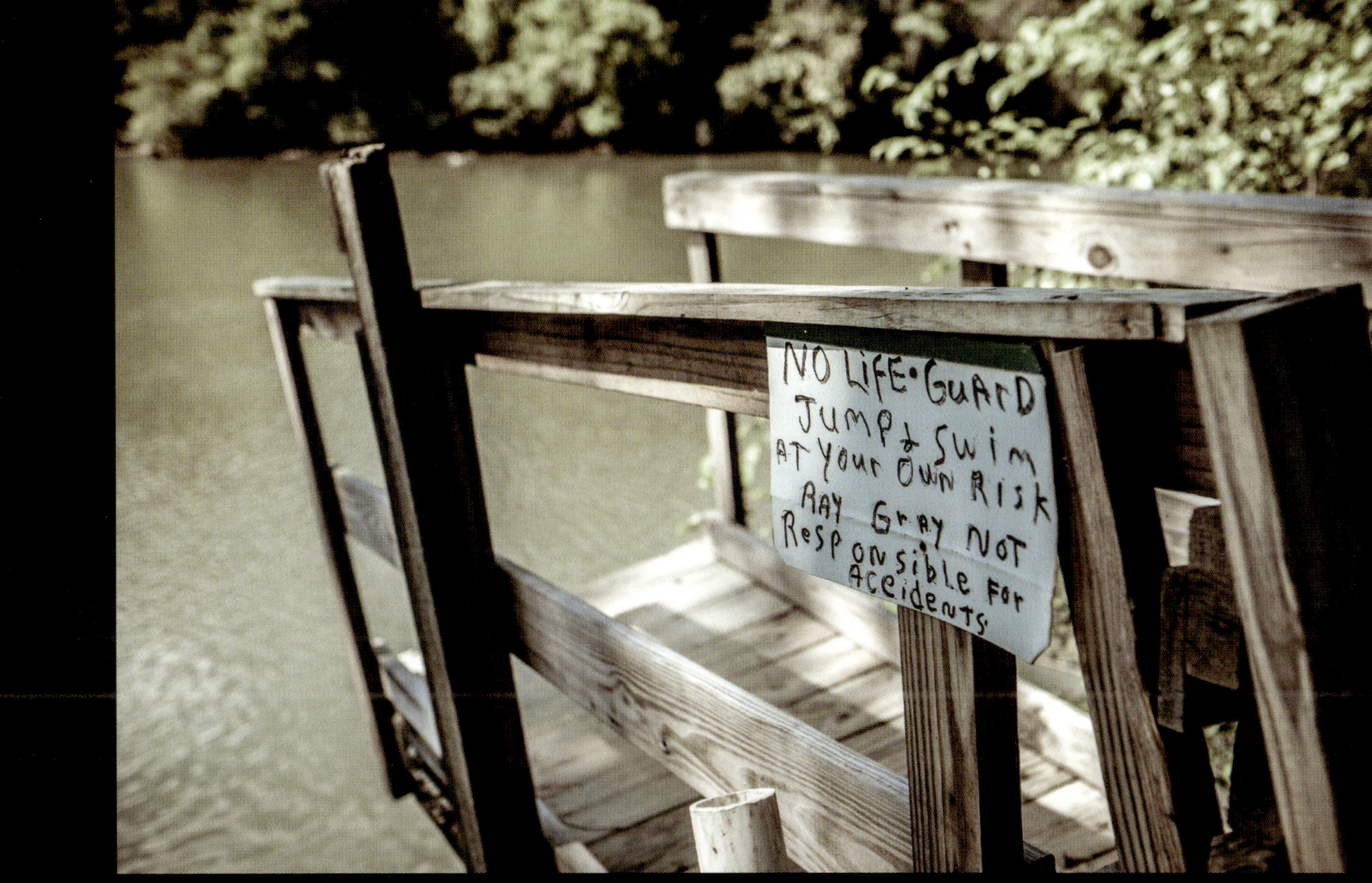
NO LIFE•GUARD
Jump & Swim
AT your OWN RISK
RAY Gray NOT
Responsible For
Accidents

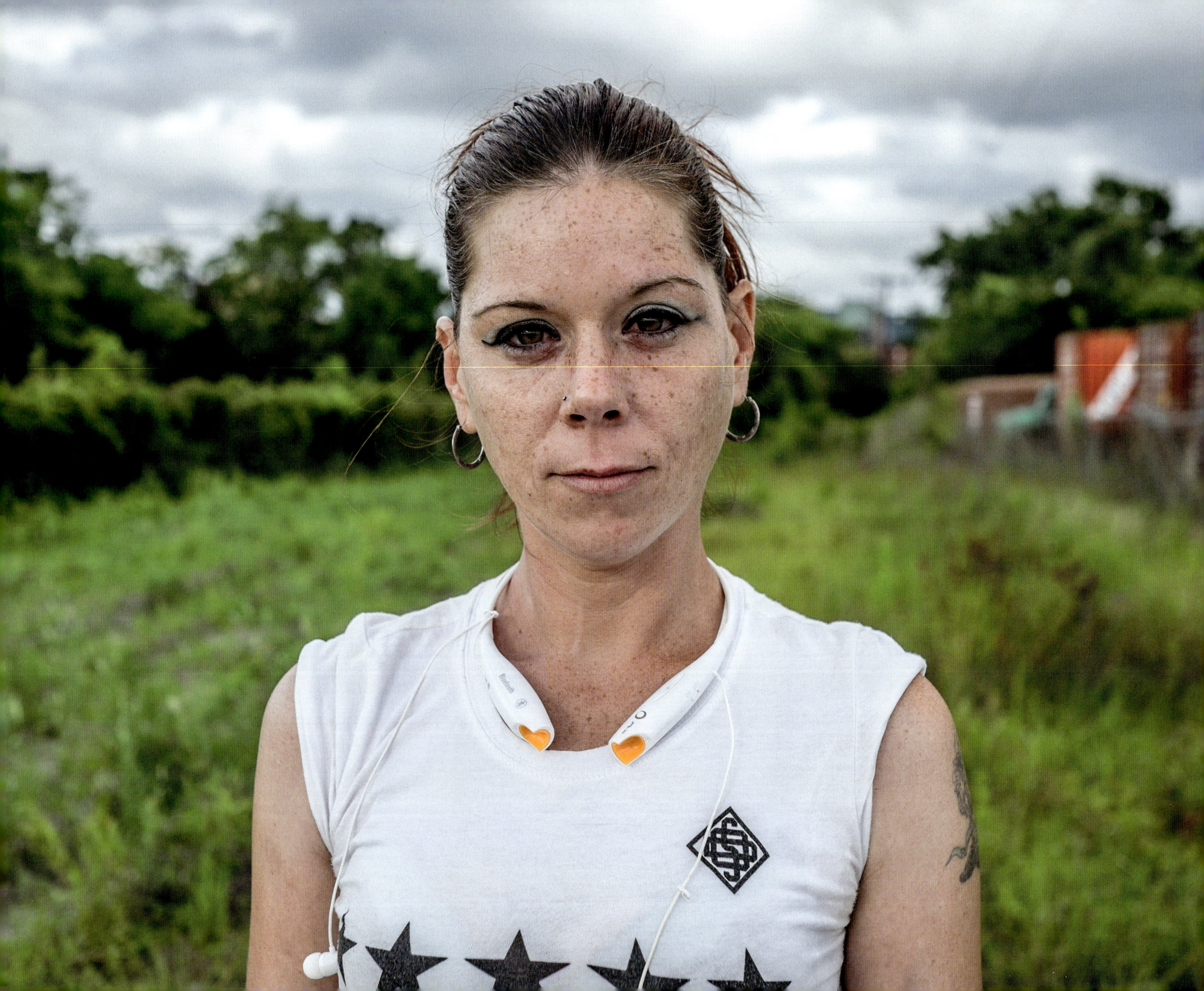

SAVANNAH, GA – 2015-05-24

Amy: I grew up in a KKK family. I was made to drink beer at age six. I was made to smoke my first blunt at the age of eight. I've been abused with electric cattle prods, thrown into a stove, electrical cords . . . Most of the abuse was by my brother's father.

My mom decided to leave him, so she did. We went to a bar, and we were staying in a room at the end of the bar. I was nine years old, so I was in the room waiting on her to get back from the bar. She came back later that night with a man. They were on one bed messing around, and I was on the other bed watching TV or whatever, trying not to watch them.

Then, out of nowhere, my stepdad busts in the door. He takes my mom and beats her to a bloody, naked pulp. She was completely red. I drug my mama down the stairs to the manager's office. I drug her in there and told him to call 911.

I went back upstairs to get my mama's dog. By the time I got there, my stepdad was gone, and the man my mama was with was in the tub—bloody, shaking, and flopping around. I crawled into the tub and was trying to hold him. But by the time the ambulance arrived, he had died in my arms.

[About twenty years later] I was addicted to cocaine, extremely bad. I've got three kids. The first two are girls, and the third is my son. When I was pregnant with him, I was really messed up on drugs. I was using real bad with him. Something in my mind was playing like I was gonna give him up for adoption. I had the people picked out and everything, but I didn't follow through with it. I went into labor with him two weeks early on Super Bowl Sunday. Unfortunately, I'd done $700 worth of cocaine the day before.

My life was crazy at the time. I was going through a bunch of stuff with my family, and I was getting a divorce from my husband. I should have stopped and realized what I was doing to my kid. Everything in life just overpowered me at the same time.

I gave birth in Chatham County, and they tested for drugs, so I never got to take him home. The worst feeling as a mom is to walk away from the hospital without your baby.

I fought really hard to get all my kids back. I was going through a court program and everything. But I started thinking a lot about how my family is and how I didn't want them to grow up like that. The only way the family chain could be broken was allowing them to be adopted.

So they were. They were all adopted by the foster lady who picked my son up from the hospital. All three of my kids have been together since my son was born.

The hardest thing I ever had to do was leave my kids at that DFCS [Division of Family and Children Services] office five years ago. I was crushed. I was devastated. I didn't leave the house for about six months.

BW: Are you able to stay in touch with them?

Amy: It's not an open adoption, but me and the foster mom had an agreement with each other. For like the first three years, I couldn't see them. Finally we got to a point where she'd let me see them periodically for birthdays and things like that.

I understand completely. I'm the biological mom, but she's the mama. She does everything for them, and I'm grateful for her. My kids can be anything they want to be right now instead of being a statistic. My two girls are straight-A students, and my son is doing really well.

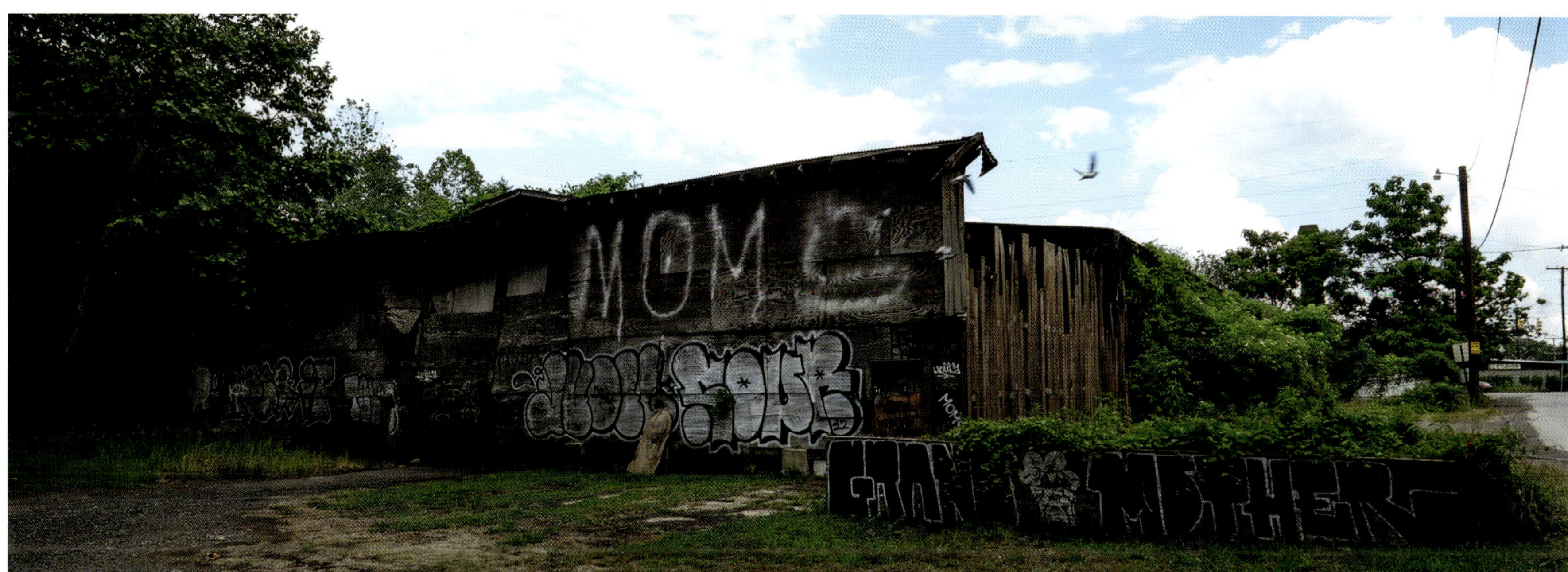

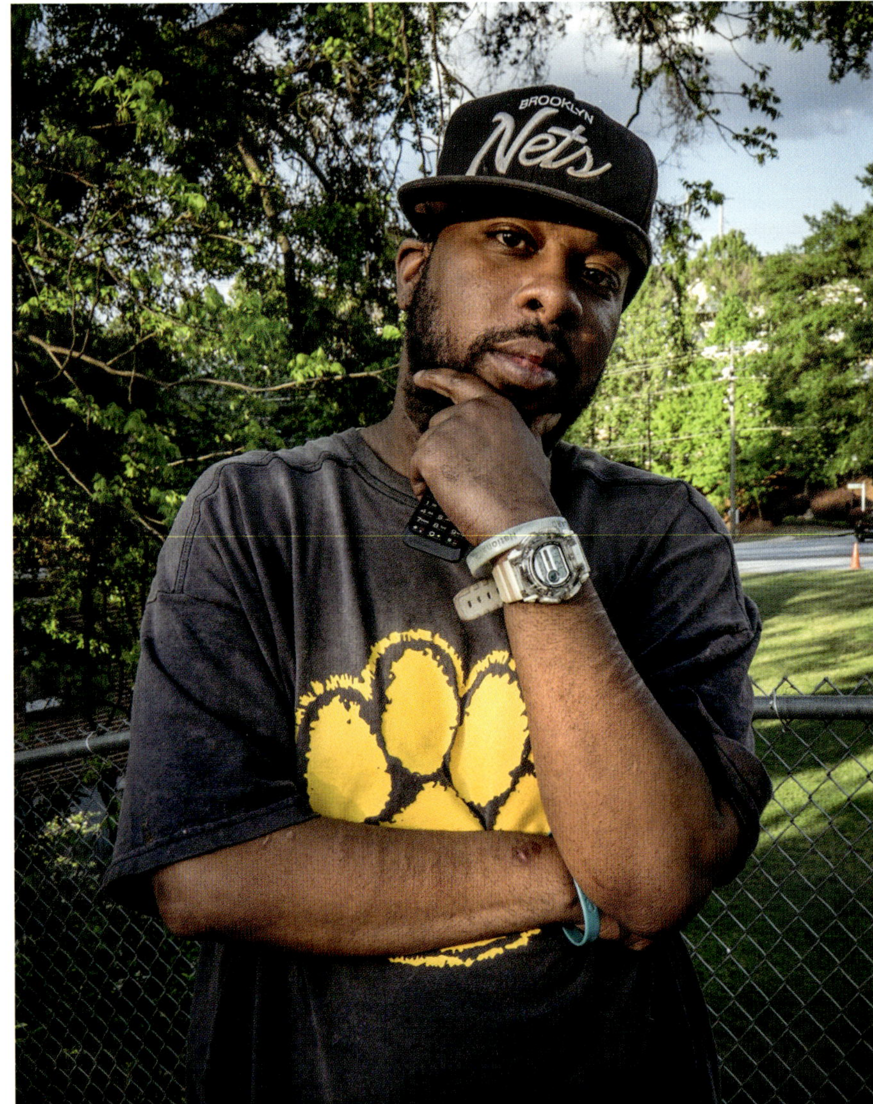

ATLANTA, GA – 2015-05-03

Mike: I'm from Homer, Alaska. I grew up in a drug-infested family. When I say drug-infested, I mean that they were selling dope and my mama was on crack. She used to beat me and abuse me when I was growing up 'cause of that crack . . . She couldn't get what she wanted, so she would take it out on me. She used to lock me in the closet. She'd feed me bread and milk in the closet. Sometimes she would handcuff me to the bed and beat me, buck naked.

The system took me away from my mother when I was eight or nine. The abuse was going on all the time. When she smoked, she'd beat me. When she couldn't get none, she'd beat me. I had cigarette burns. I had scars all over my body from extension cords.

One day I went to school. They was wondering why I wouldn't take a shower at school with the rest of the guys. One of the teachers saw the whip marks on my arm. She asked where it came from. I said, "I can't tell you, 'cause if I do, I get in trouble." She was like, "We're not gonna let that happen, so just tell us what happened." So I did. I told them everything. When they seen all the whips all over my body, they were disgusted, so they called DFCS.

DFCS took me from my home and made my sisters go live with my grandma. Sometime around the age of twelve, the whole family moved from Homer to Atlanta. My mom was doing federal time for selling drugs. I wound up back in the system when I got to Atlanta.

BW: So you were in DFCS most of your childhood?

Mike: Yeah. The majority of my life until I was about twenty-one. I was in group homes and institutions . . . The group homes were worse than the institutions. They abused and beat me when I was in a group home too. This white family—no offense.

BW: None taken.

Mike: I hated eating, and they used to force me to eat bananas and mayonnaise.

BW: Banana and mayonnaise sandwich on white bread?

Mike: Yep. Man, I used to hate that shit. To this day, I can't eat bananas. They use to beat on us for not eating. There was this older guy that lived there that would try to have sex with the girls in the house. Try to feel and touch on them. His wife knew about it, but she didn't give a damn as long as she got paid at the first of the month.

BW: Did anyone ever try that with you?

Mike: Nah, they didn't fuck with me 'cause I'd go get knives and stuff out of the kitchen. You ain't gonna sexually harass me. They used to beat me, though. Used to lock two or three of us in a small closet and leave us for hours and hours, not feeding us and shit. We might go a whole day without eating.

BW: Do you ever talk to your mom anymore?

Mike: Yeah, we're close now. In 2010, we had a powwow. We sat down and argued, we cried, we forgave each other, and we moved on from that. I still love her. She's my mother, you know? But I let her know in 2010 how all that made me feel. And I also let her know . . . how can I put this? How it affected me as a man, growing up, because I have issues when it comes to relationships with women.

BW: Forgiveness is powerful. Nothing heals like it. But do you feel like you really forgave her for all that?

Mike: Sometimes I don't, to be honest. When I sit back and think about it, it's really fucked up . . .

> Veterans of the US foster-care system are twice as likely to have PTSD than veterans of the Iraq War.[1]

ATLANTA, GA – 2015-02-10

> *I got molested by my grandmother's man. I told my grandmother, and she told me she believed me. Then about a week after I told her, me and my brother were being shipped off . . .*

I met twenty-four-year-old Kizzy close to a homeless shelter in Atlanta. She had arrived three weeks prior from Ohio to escape from the drama of her life there.

Kizzy: I was seven or eight when I got molested by my grandmother's man. I told my grandmother, and she told me she believed me. Then about a week after I told her, me and my brother were being shipped off to live with my mom in Detroit. My grandmother knew my mom was still on drugs. Shortly after going to Detroit, we were sent to foster care.

BW: Did your grandmother stay with the man who molested you?

Kizzy: She did, yeah. She stayed with him till he died. She knew the situation, and she just didn't give a fuck.

When I was eighteen, I got with a man who was older. He acted like he had money, but he didn't. I was naive and dumb, and I got knocked up twice by him. I had a job in the medical field, but I lost it. I was very dependent on my family to look after my kids for a bit so I could go to work, but they wouldn't. There wasn't a reason for it. They just didn't want to help me. I got behind on my rent, and I got evicted. I feel like my family was trying to sabotage me, because after I got evicted, they called child services on me. My kids got taken away from me.

The last little bit of money that I had, I spent on a bus ticket to Atlanta. I left everything that had value to me in Ohio. Everything that was good is shattered to me right now.

BW: Is there anything you want to tell your kids?

Kizzy: I would tell them that I love them from the bottom of my heart, no matter what. I hope where they're at is where they need to be.

BW: Where are your kids now?

Kizzy: They're in foster care **. . .** I would imagine. I haven't called because I'm not in a position where I can say anything or do anything.

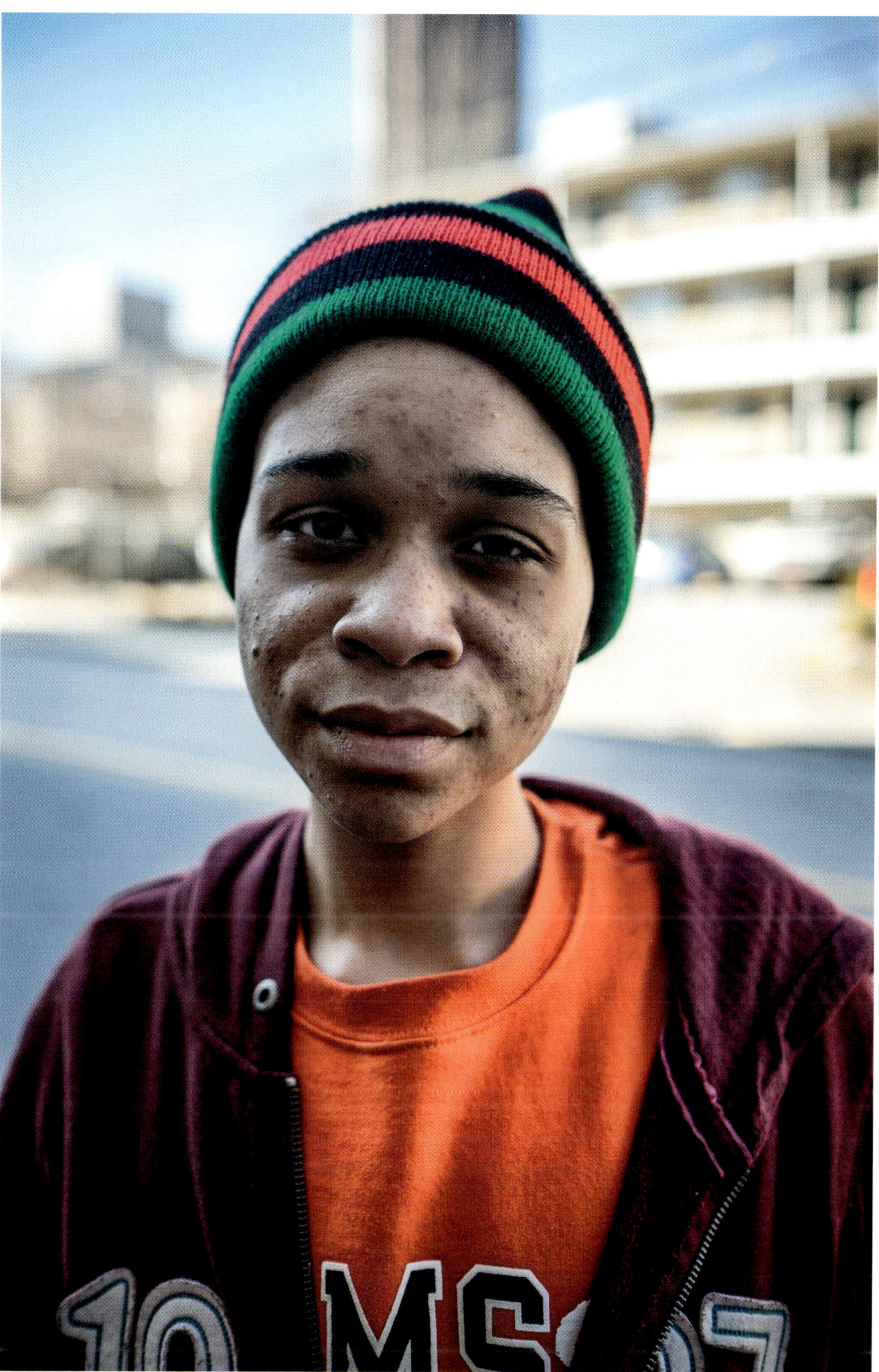

#Molestation #FamilyBetrayal #Alone

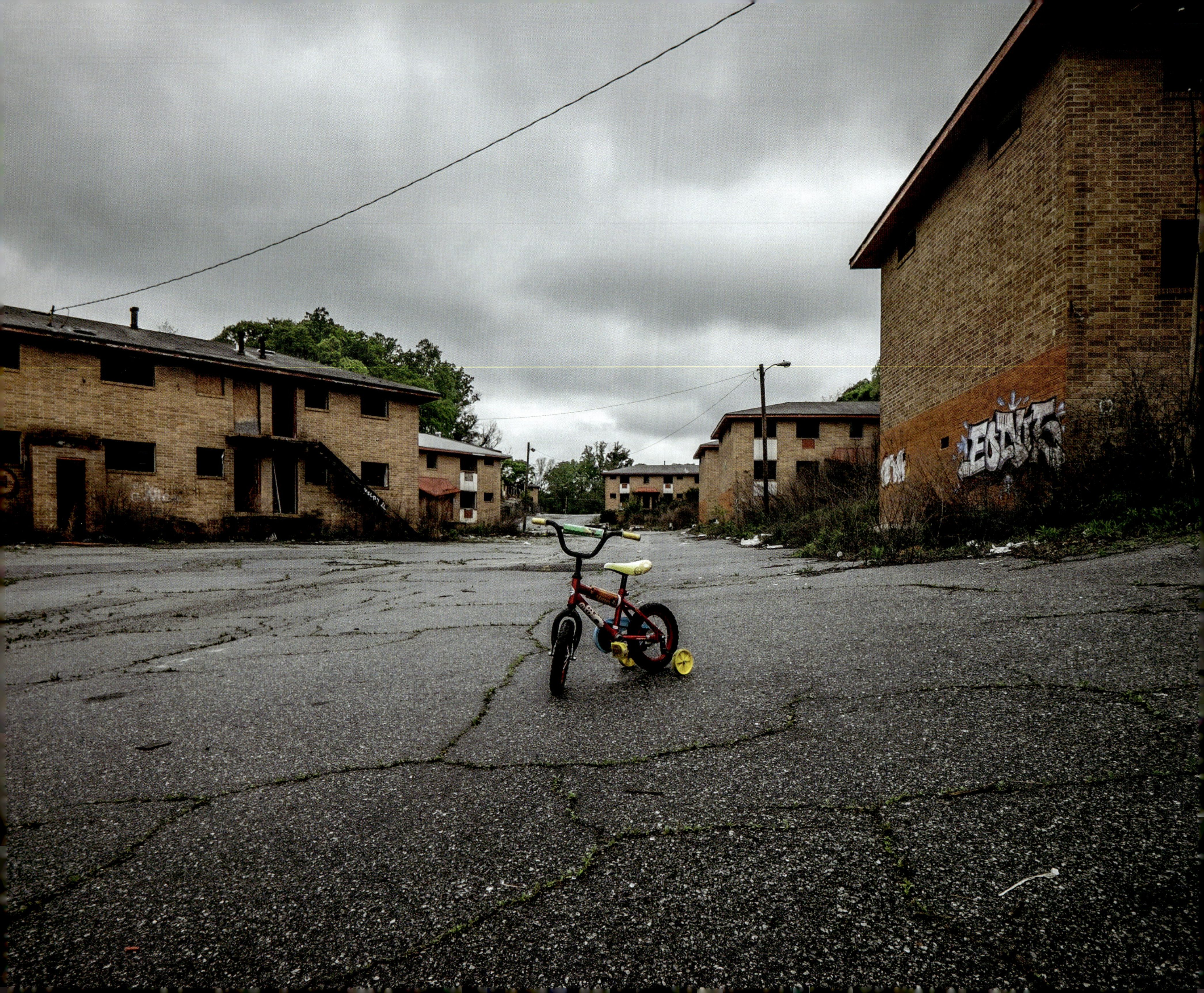

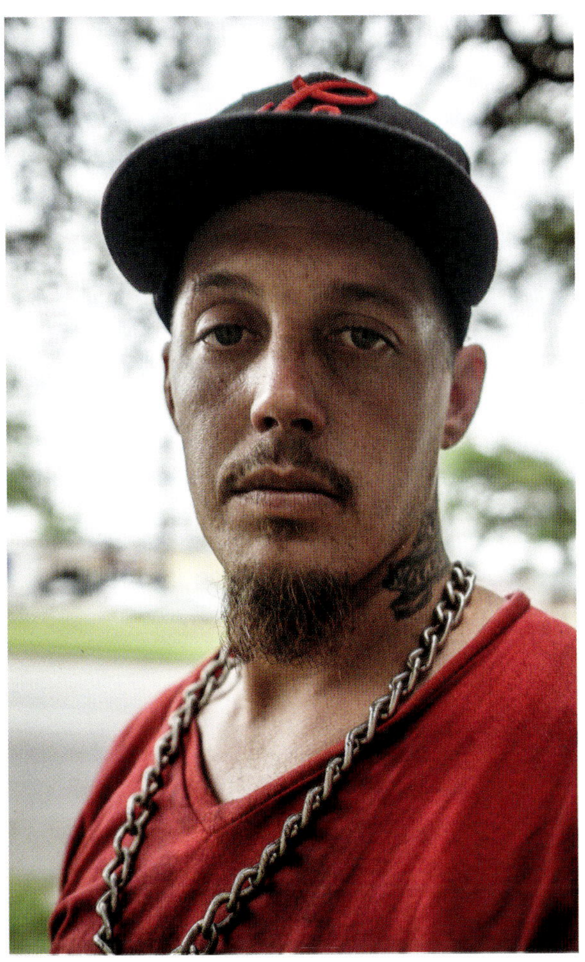

NEW ORLEANS, LA – 2015-05-11

Daniel: When I went to prison the first time, I was eighteen years old. Basically, when you go to prison, man, you gotta stick with your own people. Like, Florida isn't as bad as Texas. Texas is segregated real bad. Like, when you go to the chow hall or you go to the yard, you talk to white people only. You don't talk to the blacks. You don't talk to the Mexicans. You stick with your own.

Basically, man, you gotta get down with something. Know what I'm saying? 'Cause if you don't, you're gonna get run over, and you're not gonna be able to have anything. Gang members will come and take it from you. I didn't really want to join a gang or anything of that nature because I knew the bullshit that was gonna come behind it. You gotta do certain things. But as I was there a little bit longer, I was approached by the Aryan Brotherhood. They basically explained to me how they feel and what they do—the laws of what it is and what it's about. It made sense to me. I was kind of lost at the time. Being that young, I'd have to fight all the fuckin' time. I mean, hell—I'd have to fight just to be able to drink the damn milk I got for lunch.

I ended up at a level-seven disciplinary camp, which is the highest you can go in the state of Florida. Out of 1,800 inmates, 968 of them were lifers. They are never gonna see the light of day again outside of prison walls. These people do not care. They will fuckin' kill you over a dollar—just for looking at someone the wrong way. I seen a black dude get his whole face sliced open just for saying something stupid.

BW: What was the hardest thing about being in prison. Is there one day that stands out?

Daniel: The hardest day I had, out of all the years on and off, was this last time. It was my twenty-eighth birthday. And on my twenty-eighth birthday, at six in the morning, I got sent to solitary confinement over a cigarette. And it wasn't even the cigarette that he locked me up for. He said I had an attitude.

BW: What was solitary like?

Daniel: You're in an eight-by-ten box for twenty-four hours a day. You do not come out of that damn box. You know what I'm saying? The only time you come out is to go take a shower, and you go right back in.

BW: How long did they keep you in there for that one?

Daniel: I did pretty much the last five months of prison in that box. When I came back home here, September 21 of 2014, I couldn't even walk down Bourbon Street. Could not do it. Too many people. It freaked me out bad. I'd been in a box by myself for five months. Oh man, it'd fuckin' wig you out. I'd have to run up to the river and sit there for a while, collect my thoughts.

BW: I think the average person in America thinks that there's some type of rehabilitation that goes on in prisons. But what they do is mess you up worse and put you back out there and expect you to act different. So how is putting someone in a box for five months, by himself, helping him adjust to reenter society? I don't mean to get preachy, but it seems completely backward.

Daniel: Exactly. It doesn't make any sense.

BW: It sounds like you've spent a lot of your life incarcerated. What I'm curious about is what set you on that path.

Daniel: When I was in second grade and third grade . . . you know, I never really had a structure as far as parenting because my mother was a hardcore alcoholic and my father wasn't there. So if she would ground me or something like that, I'd come home from school, and she'd be passed out drunk. So I'd be like, "Grounded, my ass. I'm doing what I want to do." So that set me on a path of not following rules—doing whatever I wanted to do, whenever I wanted to do it.

BW: Do you ever talk to your mom anymore?

Daniel: My mom passed away on October 8 of last year. When I got back here, I seen her one time on Bourbon Street. I didn't even recognize her at first. The next thing I heard was she was dead.

BW: Were y'all talking at the time?

Daniel: I mean, I had just got out of prison, but yeah, we were really, really close. I forgave her a while ago . . . I mean, I lost a full-ride scholarship to Oklahoma State University for wrestling because she decided she wanted to smoke crack and be a prostitute instead of working a job and being a mother. I had to drop out of school and sell drugs to keep a roof over our head. It cost me everything.

BW: Do you really think you forgave her?

Daniel: No, I don't.

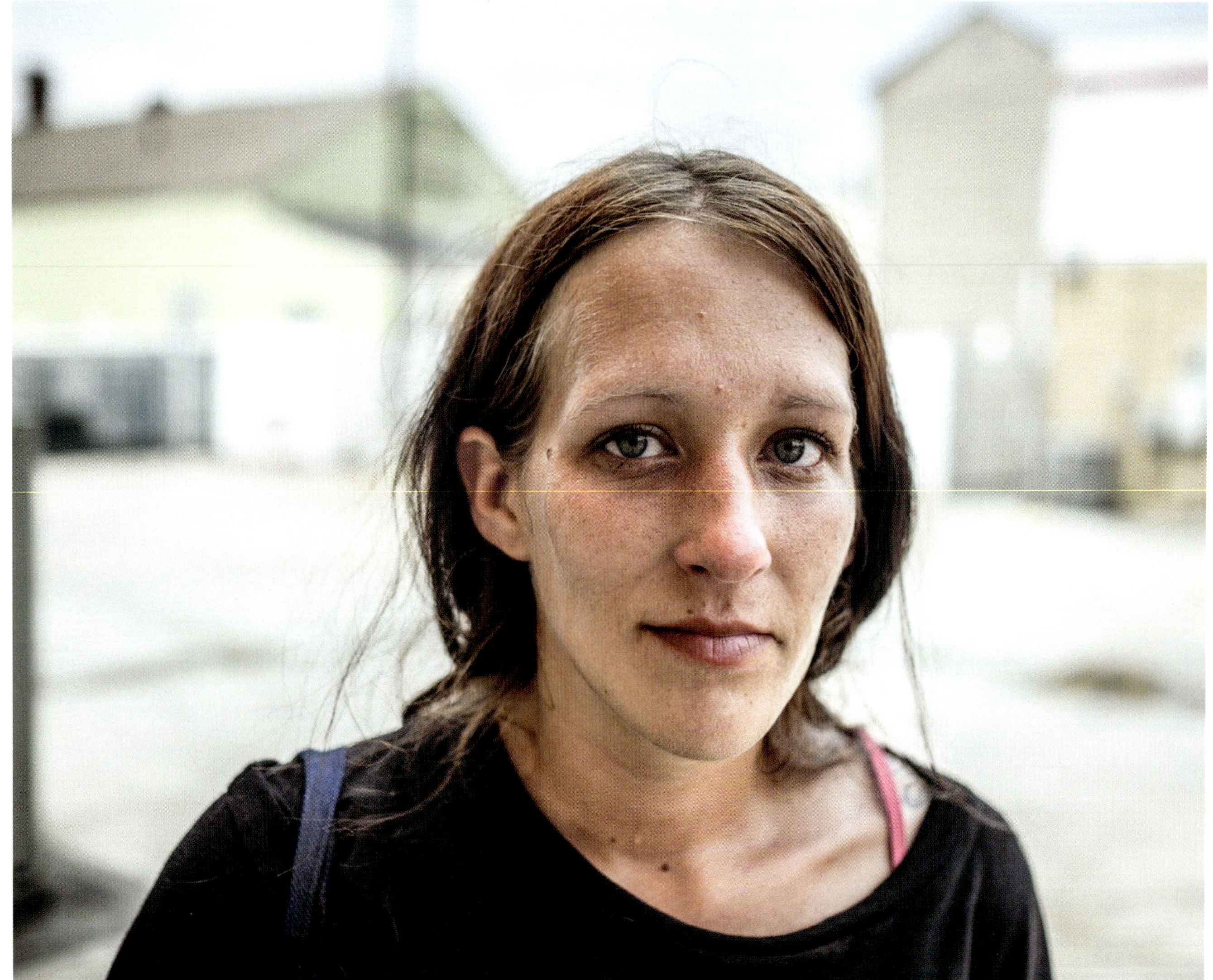

NEW ORLEANS, LA – 2015-05-11

Melissa: I've unfortunately been shooting heroin for about ten years now. Trying to get off the streets while you're shooting heroin is next to impossible.

BW: What led up to you using heroin?

Melissa: I have a daughter. [Crying.] She's thirteen now. I lost custody of her. And when I lost custody of her, that's when I started using. Just trying to cover up that pain, you know? 'Cause that'll kill you.

BW: How'd you lose custody?

Melissa: I didn't have a job. I didn't have anything. I couldn't provide for her because I was dependent on him [the daughter's father]. When we split up, there wasn't anything I could offer her.

BW: Where's she at now?

Melissa: She's with her dad in Oklahoma.

BW: Do you ever get to talk to her?

Melissa: [Tears.] No. For her birthday and Christmas, I send her money, but I can't talk to her. I know they don't give her the cards I send. He says he's saving them and he'll give them to her when she's older.

BW: Do you ever see pictures of her?

Melissa: Yeah. I go on Facebook, and I'll look at her pictures.

BW: Does she look like you?

Melissa: Yeah, a lot.

BW: If you could give her a message what would the message be?

Melissa: That I'm sorry that I didn't step up and be the mom I should have been.

ATLANTA, GA – 2015-02-15

Kristy: Being pregnant on the streets was the hardest thing I've ever been through in my life. It's very dangerous as a woman out here. There are so many more opportunities for men than there are for women. Did you know that there's twenty something shelters for men, but there's only four for women and they're always full?

The father didn't want to have anything to do with us. But I had one friend, James, who really protected me when I was pregnant. This guy swung a metal rod at me while I was asleep at four o'clock in the morning, and James went after him. He was my savior out here.

So I had my daughter and gave her up a month ago to a beautiful family that couldn't have children. She only weighed five pounds, eight ounces.

BW: Was she premature?

Kristy: No, she wasn't. But out here on the streets, it's a very hard thing to take care of yourself. I didn't eat right or sleep well out here, so she was very small. She's doing well now, though. Fortunately, the people at the lesbian bookstore are really sweet and let me sleep on the front porch. It's sort of a neutral territory, where the police can't mess with you.

BW: Do you get updates on your daughter?

Kristy: Yes, it was an open adoption. I get to see her for the first time next week. [Smiling.] Her name is Emily Rose.

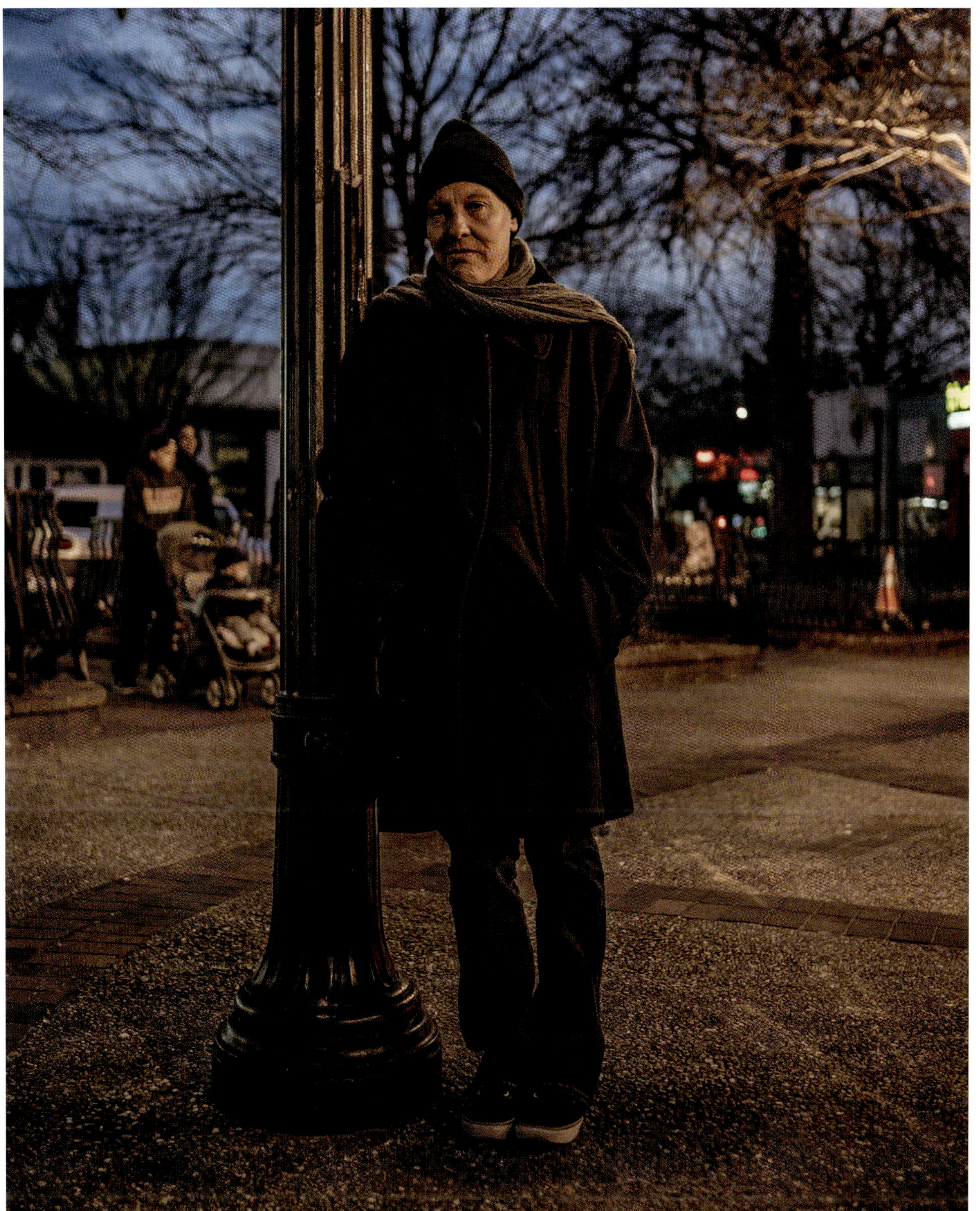

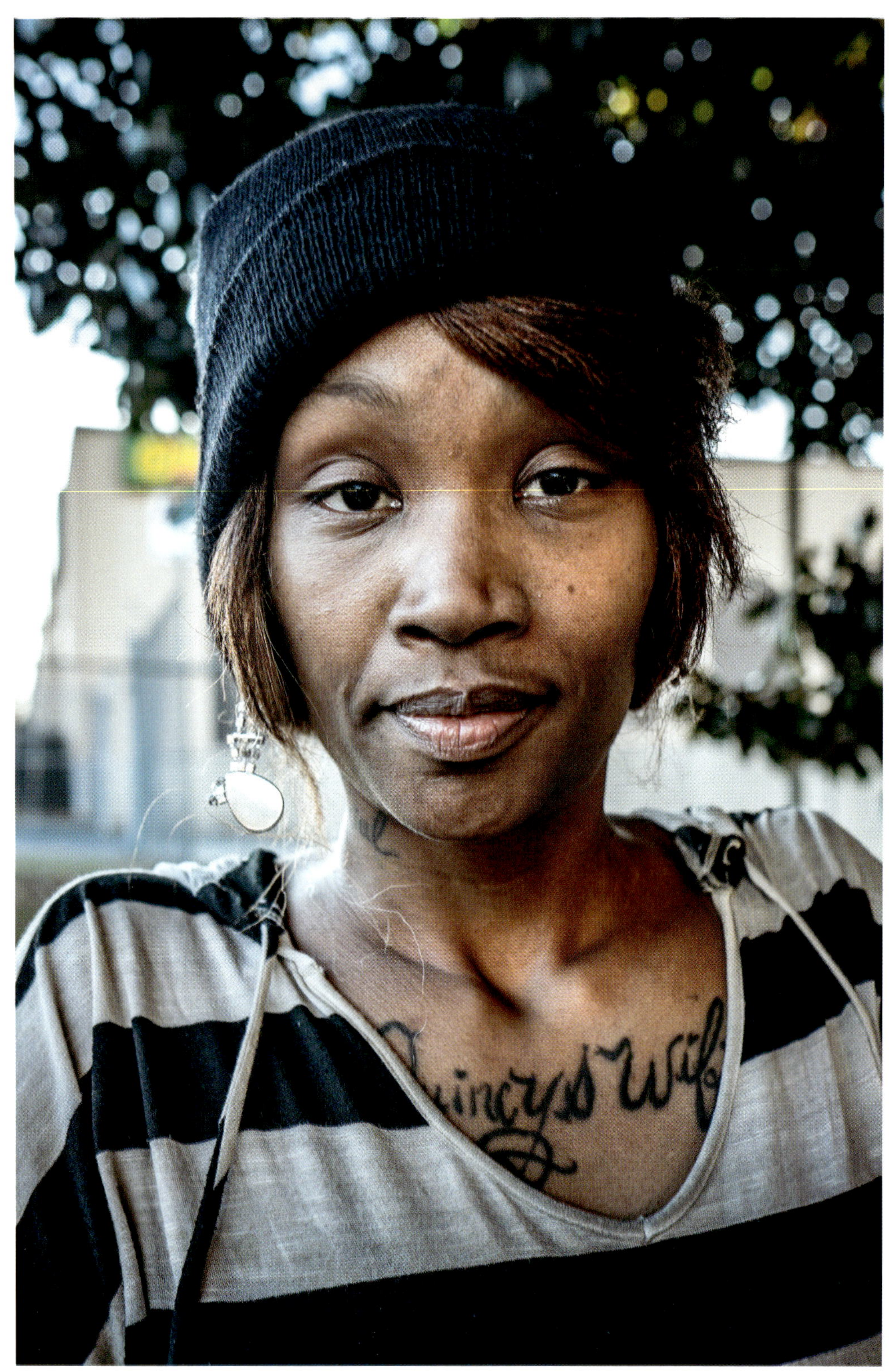

ATLANTA, GA – 2015-01-25

Queen: My mom passed when I was nine. She was really sick. She had been addicted to crack cocaine, but she got her life together. The last three years of her life she spent with us, clean. She had always been sick. She had lupus, arthritis, enlarged heart, and sickle cell. She always tried to hide it from us 'cause she didn't want us to see her hurting and stuff. But I always was the one that knew and took care of her.

When she passed, I wasn't that sad because I didn't want my mom to hurt no more. I know now that she's in a better place.

BW: Do you think you'd be out here if she were still alive?

Queen: No, I wouldn't. For sure, I know that.

BW: Why?

Queen: Because whether she was on drugs or not, she took good care of us. We always had the finest things—nice, clean, new clothes. She was on drugs, but like I said, we were never neglected or abused. We went out to eat and skating. She was never like a crackhead mom.

BW: Who did you live with after she passed?

Queen: Foster family. They were abusive to me. They used to beat me and pull my hair. I ran away and was sent to another foster home, where I was raped by the dad. I was eleven then. When I was thirteen, I ran away and never looked back.

BW: How did you survive?

Queen: I went to my aunt's house—my mother's sister—in the middle of the night. I found out where she was at. She started crying when she opened the door and said that the people wouldn't tell her where I was at. She said, "You don't have to go back, never," so I never went back.

BW: So she kind of saved your life.

Queen: Yeah. She put me in school and bought me clothes and stuff. She had her own kids, but she always made time for me.

Part 2 of Queen's story can be found on p. 137.

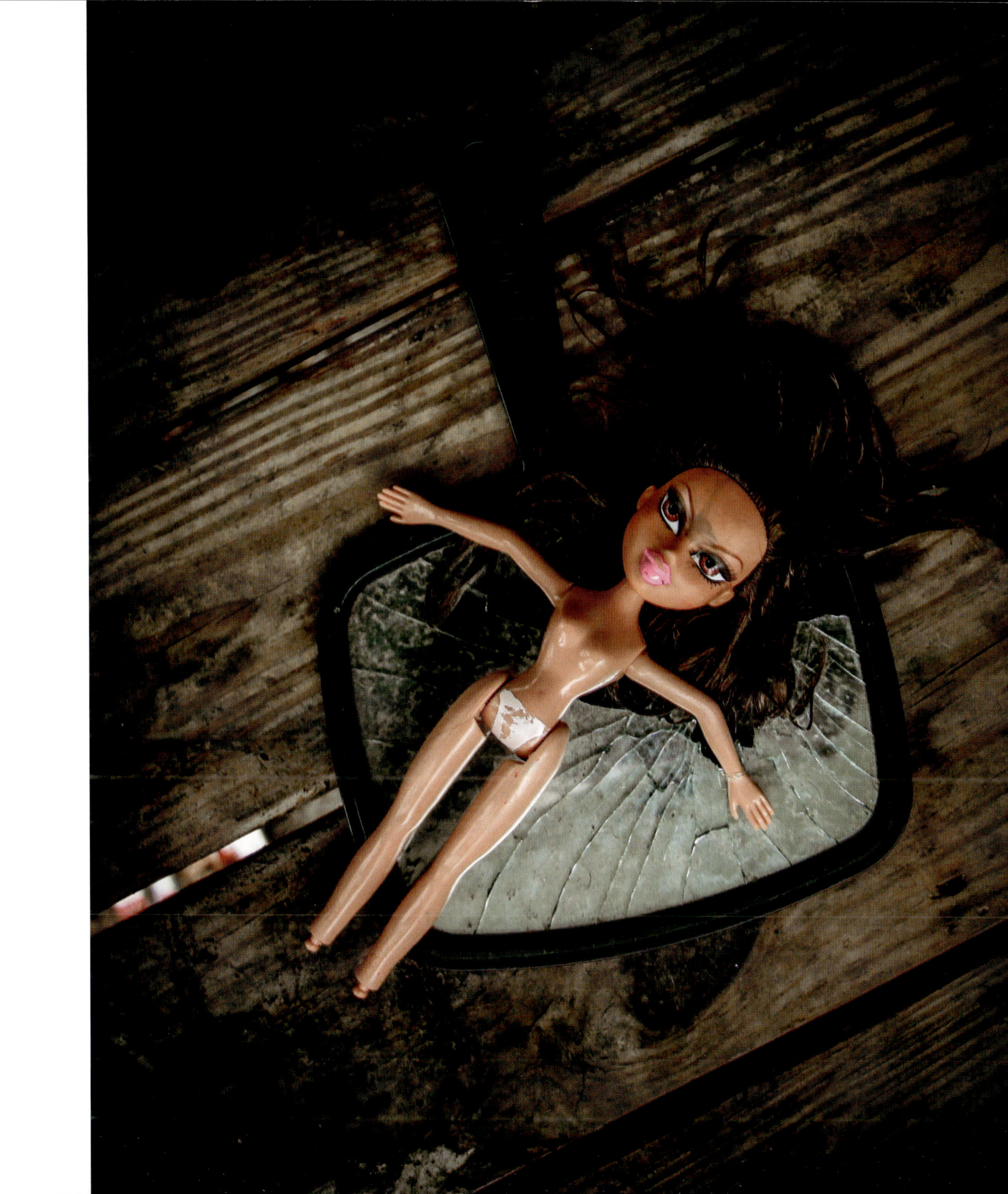

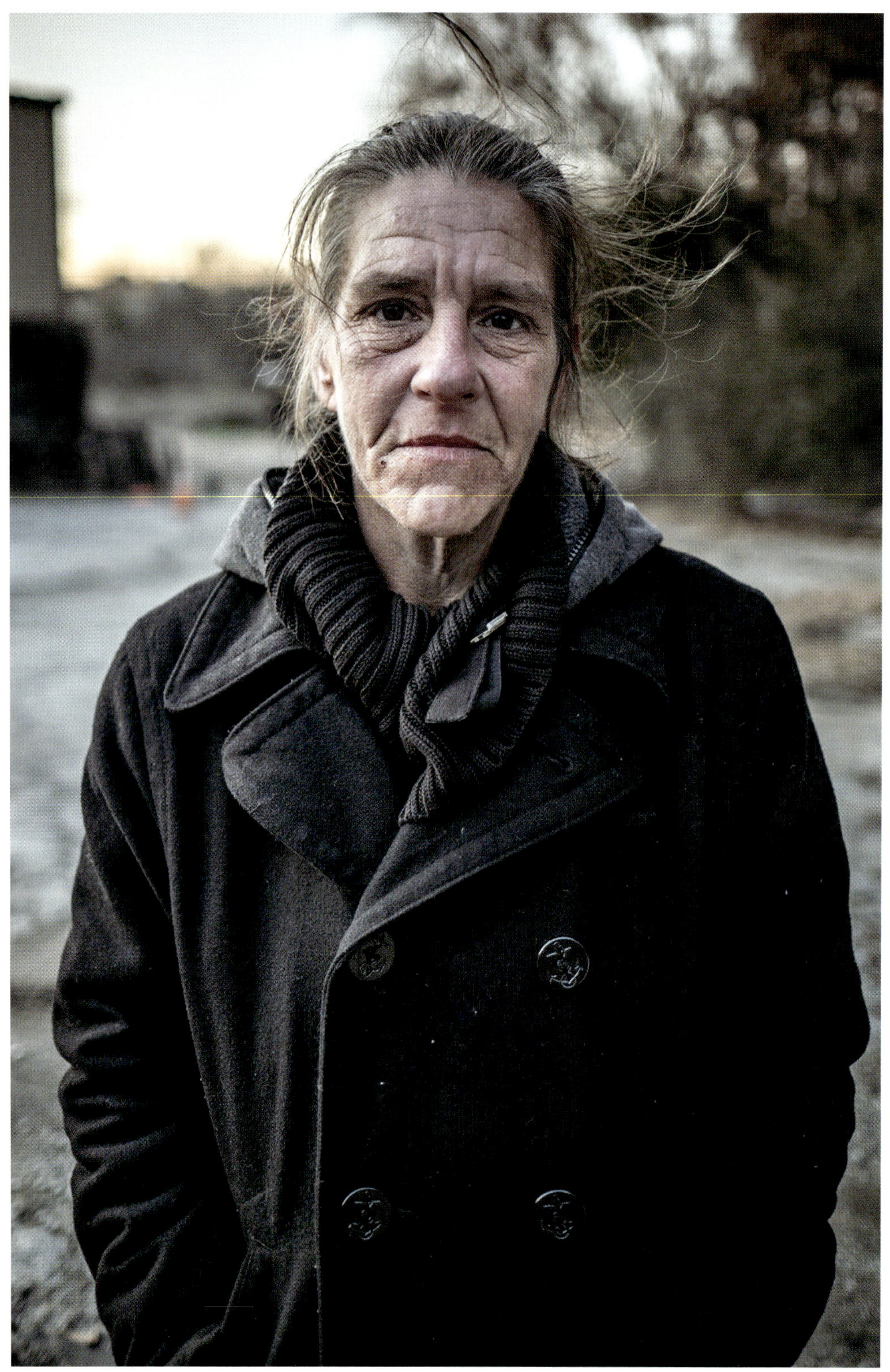

ATLANTA, GA – 2015-02-02

Wanda: I was married for twenty-seven years. And I could have said no, but my husband got me hooked on crack. We moved down here from Virginia to Georgia because he had a job transfer. The drugs got worse. I ended up returning to Virginia because I was getting brutally beat by my husband. My daughter stayed here, and she got pregnant at sixteen.

So I moved back to Atlanta to be with her. I found the crack again after being clean for nine months. It felt so good when I was sober.

My daughter became ill with diabetes real bad, and she moved home to be with my mother. My parents are poor and couldn't afford to take care of both of us, so I stayed in Atlanta. I had to learn how to date—prostitute and stuff. I was still doing the drugs, looking like a zombie.

So I got a call about a year ago. It was when we had that ice storm. It was a call telling me that my daughter had passed away.

I went home for the funeral, and there was a letter my daughter had never mailed to me. She had written it three days before she died. It said, "Mom, if something happens to me, know that I still love you. I just want you to change your life. Don't do no more prostitution or drugs."

I ended up coming back to Atlanta. I stayed awake for nine days smoking crack, mourning my daughter's death. I was almost dead. I had a friend, Lele, that stays here, come up and tell me she had a dream. In the dream, my daughter asked her to tell me to stop doing what I was doing. It was really weird because she never knew my daughter.

Lele prostituted and did drugs too. We chose to look at each other and say, "We're not gonna do it anymore." From that day on, the Lord has blessed me. He gave me a job, and I worked for almost a year. It closed down last week, or I'd still be working there. I've been clean now for eleven months. [Tearful smile.]

BW: Congratulations.

Wanda: I guess the reason I'm telling you this is because I want my daughter to hear that I'm telling this story. God is good. He has helped me, and I'm still struggling.

Lele really helped change my life. She didn't even know my daughter, and she came to me with that dream. She's still doing really good too. She's a beautiful person. She knows that if she needs something, I'll give her anything I have, and she'll do the same for me. There's been times when one of us really wanted crack, and we sit there and cry together and help each other get through it. It's a struggle. I wish other people could find each other like we did.

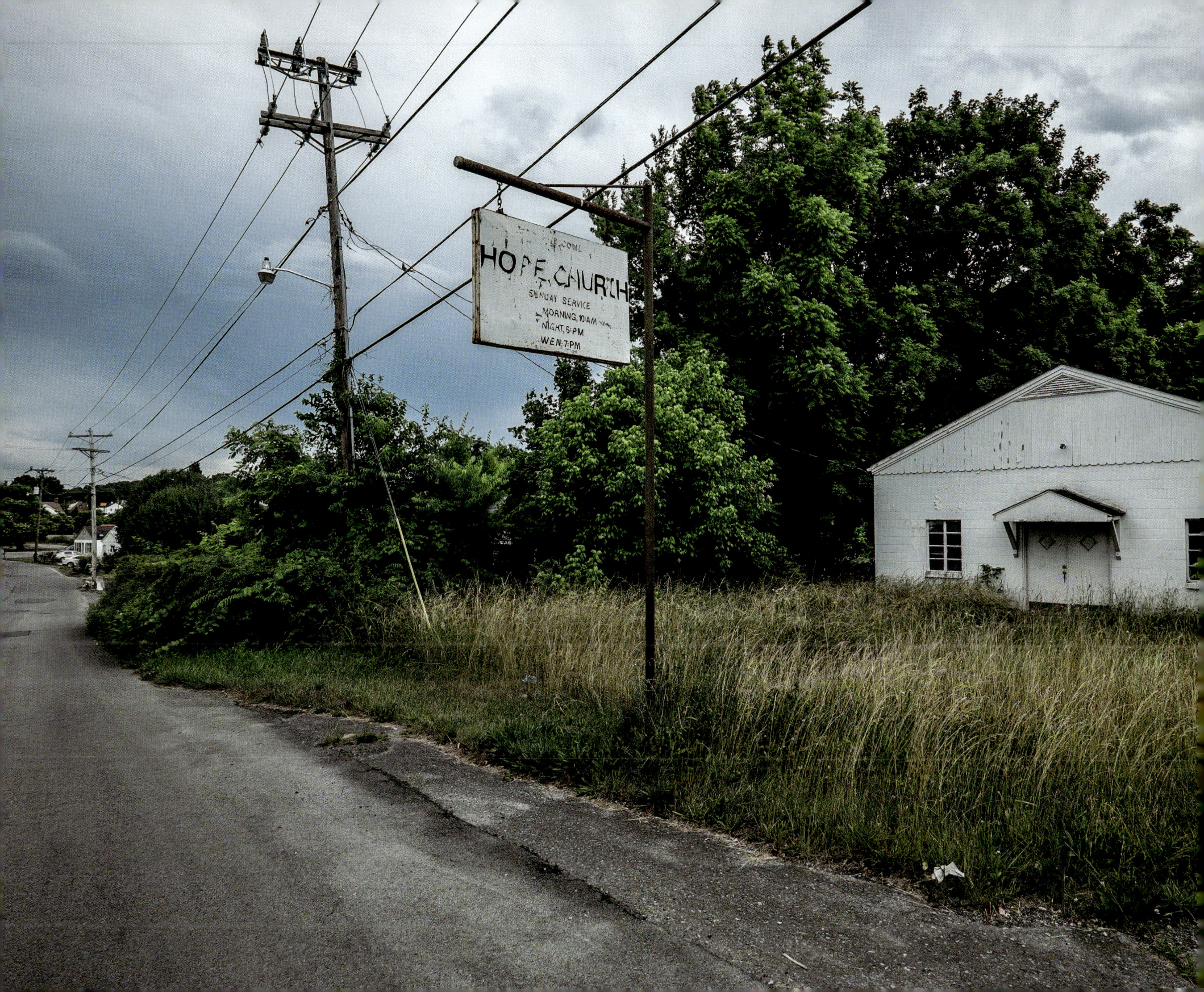
HOPE CHURCH
SUNDAY SERVICE
MORNING, 10:AM
NIGHT, 6:PM
WEN 7:PM

The bottom is dark and desolate. Family and what few friends I had left weren't allowed in because of the tremendous shame of what I'd become and the threat that they posed to the constructs of my addiction. Many days I woke up desperately vowing it would be different and praying for freedom from consuming any more of the poison. Within the day—often within the hour—I'd be back at it. I simply couldn't stop. Towards the end, the only thing I prayed for was death. I was drowning in demons, but it was better than what I perceived awaited me on the surface.

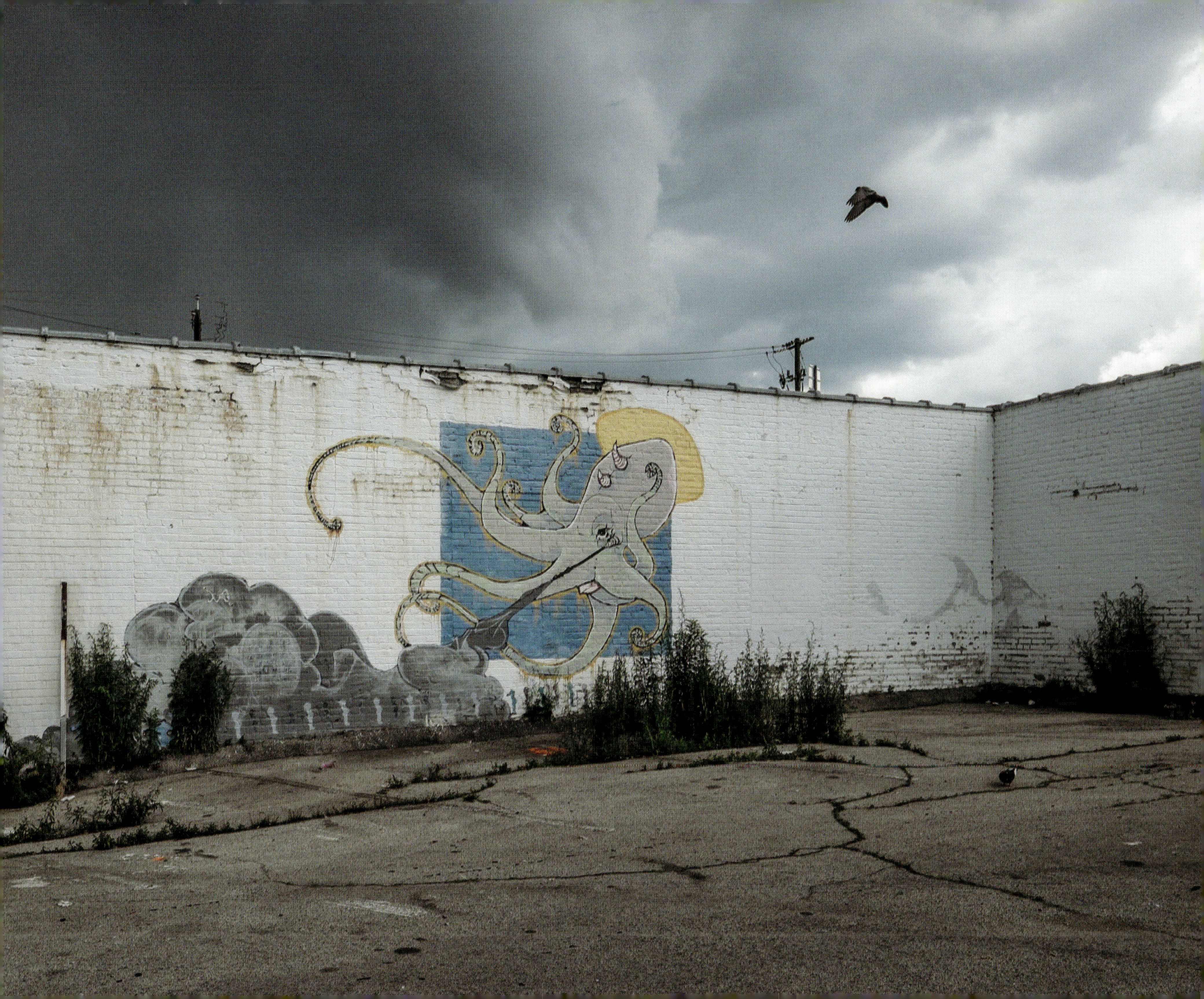

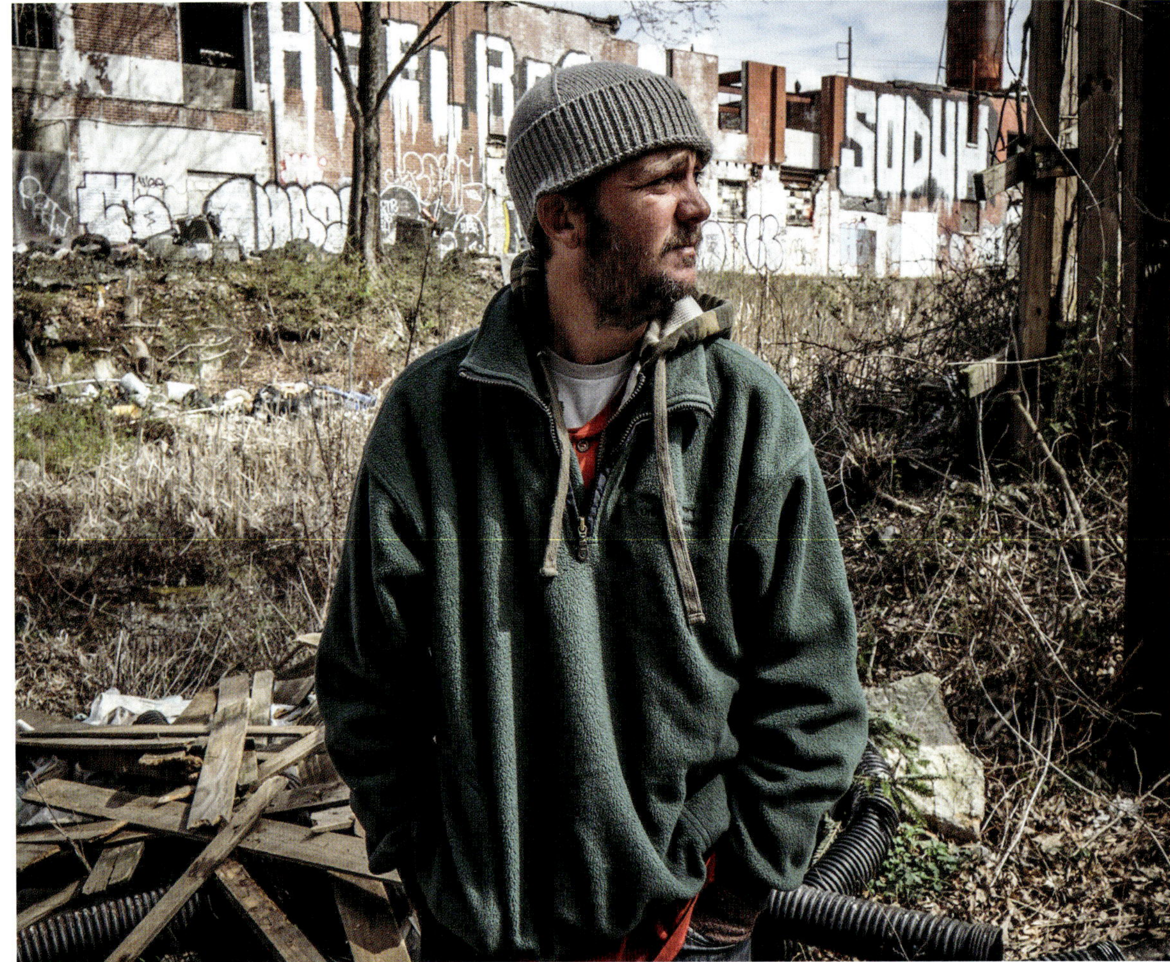

ATLANTA, GA – 2015-03-06

Nick: My mom had an addiction to cocaine. They actually let her out of jail because she was pregnant with me. She left me with some babysitters when I was about eighteen months old and told them that she was going to the hospital—she never came back. So they took me to an orphanage or whatever. I was adopted by two Christian people when I was like three. They're really good people. They love me. At this point, they're sick and they're older, and they really don't want me around because of my addiction.

BW: Heroin?

Nick: Yeah.

BW: When did you find out you were adopted?

Nick: I was probably eight or nine. My mom came in while I was taking a bath and sat on the side of the tub and told me. At the time, it didn't really bother me. It didn't really mean that much to me. As I got older, it bothered me more.

BW: Did you ever try to find your real mom?

Nick: No, no, no.

BW: You aren't curious?

Nick: Yeah, I am. I just . . . I don't know.

BW: If you could tell your real mom anything, what would you tell her?

Nick: Phew, man. I'd probably . . . Man, that's a hard one.

BW: Do you think you'd be pissed? Do you think you'd be more sympathetic of her addiction because of your own addiction?

Nick: I mean, I feel like I was an addict before I ever did drugs.

BW: You think you were born addicted, with drugs in your system?

Nick: Yeah, I definitely think so. I don't know it to be fact, but I'm pretty sure she was using with me while she was pregnant. I always had a strong curiosity about drugs before I even tried anything.

BW: How did you start using heroin?

Nick: I started in 2000. Me and my girlfriend decided to get off meth. We locked ourselves in our apartment, and we slept for two or three days. When I woke up, I turned my cell phone on, and immediately it was ringing. It was a friend of mine who'd been trying to get ahold of me. I told him we were gonna quit. He said, "I got something for you to make you feel better." I said, "What's that?" He said, "OxyContin."

So he comes over, and he has this bag full of white powder. I asked him where the pills were, and he said that he'd already crushed them up and that they were the powder. I snorted a little line of it, and I knew within ten minutes that it was something else. It just hit me so hard. That was the first time I did heroin, and I haven't stopped since.

I don't think I'll ever quit doing opiates. I just . . . I just don't see myself quitting.

ATLANTA, GA – 2015-03-23

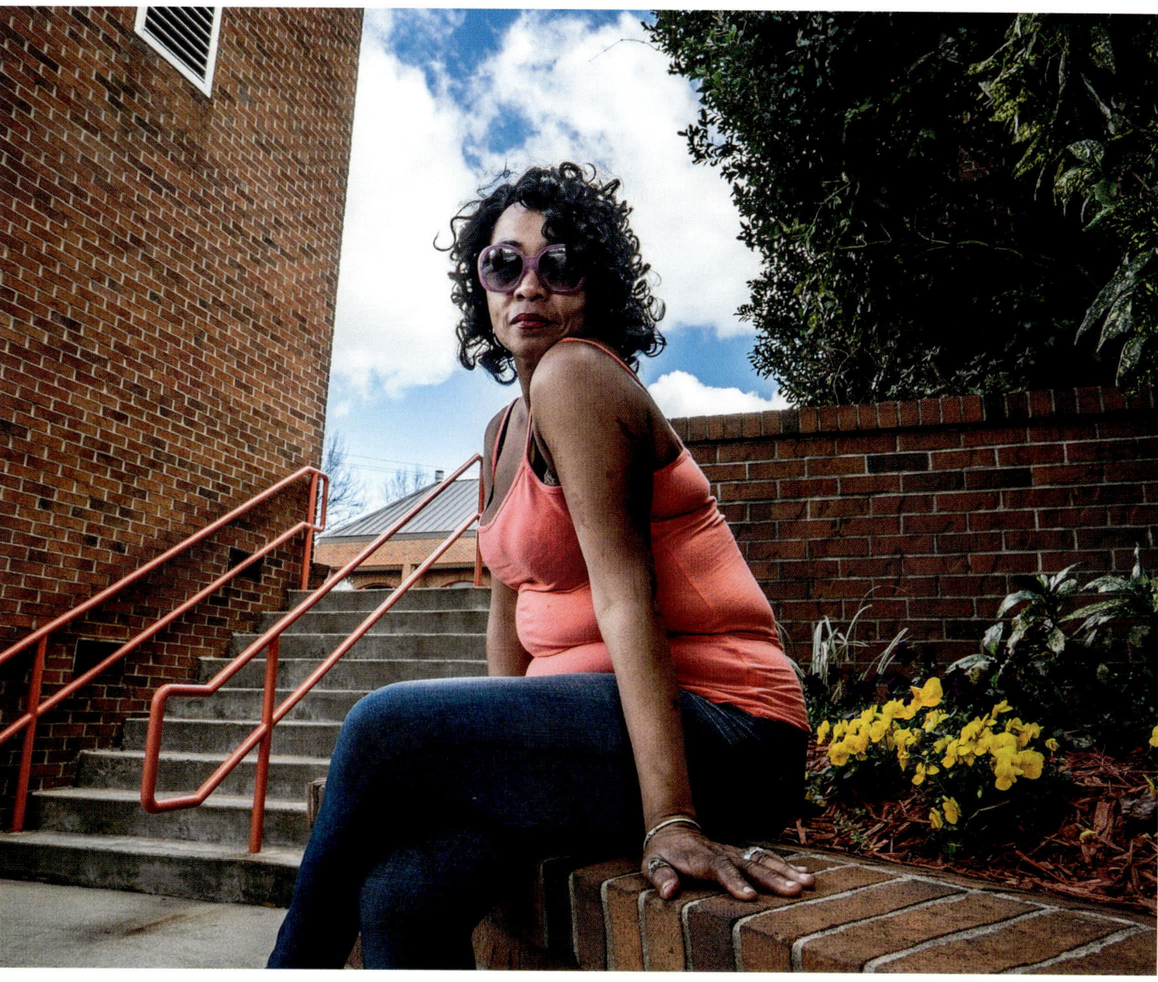

Judy: I was born in Jacksonville, Florida, in 1963. My mom was a heroin addict and an alcoholic, but she was also one of the first black registered nurses. I don't know her. I never met her. Me and my older brother, Henry, were adopted by her brother and brought to Cobb County, Georgia. We lived in a big, giant old house. I had good parents that worked really hard.

I was about three when I went to live with them. I can remember my first Christmas—it was like a dream. Everything I ever wanted.

I had a great life till one night I woke up and found out my brother was a child molester. I would wait on him every night, like the boogeyman was coming. Know what I'm saying? I would tuck myself in so tight every night that it felt like I was suffocating myself. I'd try to cover every inch of me from my feet to my head 'cause I knew he was coming. He used to tell me, "Don't tell nobody, 'cause if you do, we'll be sent back to that bad place." I used to have dreams where people would be passing my body around.

Now that I'm older, I can say that my brother didn't mean what he was doing. He was doing what somebody had taught him to do. But he died before I could forgive him.

BW: Was your brother a lot older?

Judy: I was about three, so he was about ten.

BW: How did you wind up working out here?

Judy: Well, I been married twice. I really loved my second husband a lot. When that marriage dissolved, it hurt me real, real bad. I just said, "Fuck it," and I went into a really bad state of depression. I ran away. I have no idea how I got to New York or how I got the money. I didn't snap out of it until I woke up and I was sleeping on the ground in front of Port Authority. That's when I found out I was schizophrenic. That's also where I met my real dad.

BW: Really? How did that happen?

Judy: I had tried to kill myself about four or five times, and I was on suicide watch. They told me the only way I could get out of there is if a family member came and got me. I guess the hospital searched, and they found him. When he came, he brought a picture, and sure enough, it was me. He got me out, and we are still close. We talked just yesterday.

Around that time, I started stripping. I went out one night, and I couldn't find no powder. I had about $2,000 in my pocket. I went into the bathroom, and there was a girl in one of the stalls. I thought she was smoking a woolie. I went in the stall and said, "Bitch, what you smoking? I'll give you a hundred dollar bill for what you got on that pipe." She gave [crack] to me, and it was over with. Been addicted ever since.

I'm not a junkie. I'm an addict. I don't like that word *junkie*. I'm addicted to something I can't control right now, but I don't want to be judged.

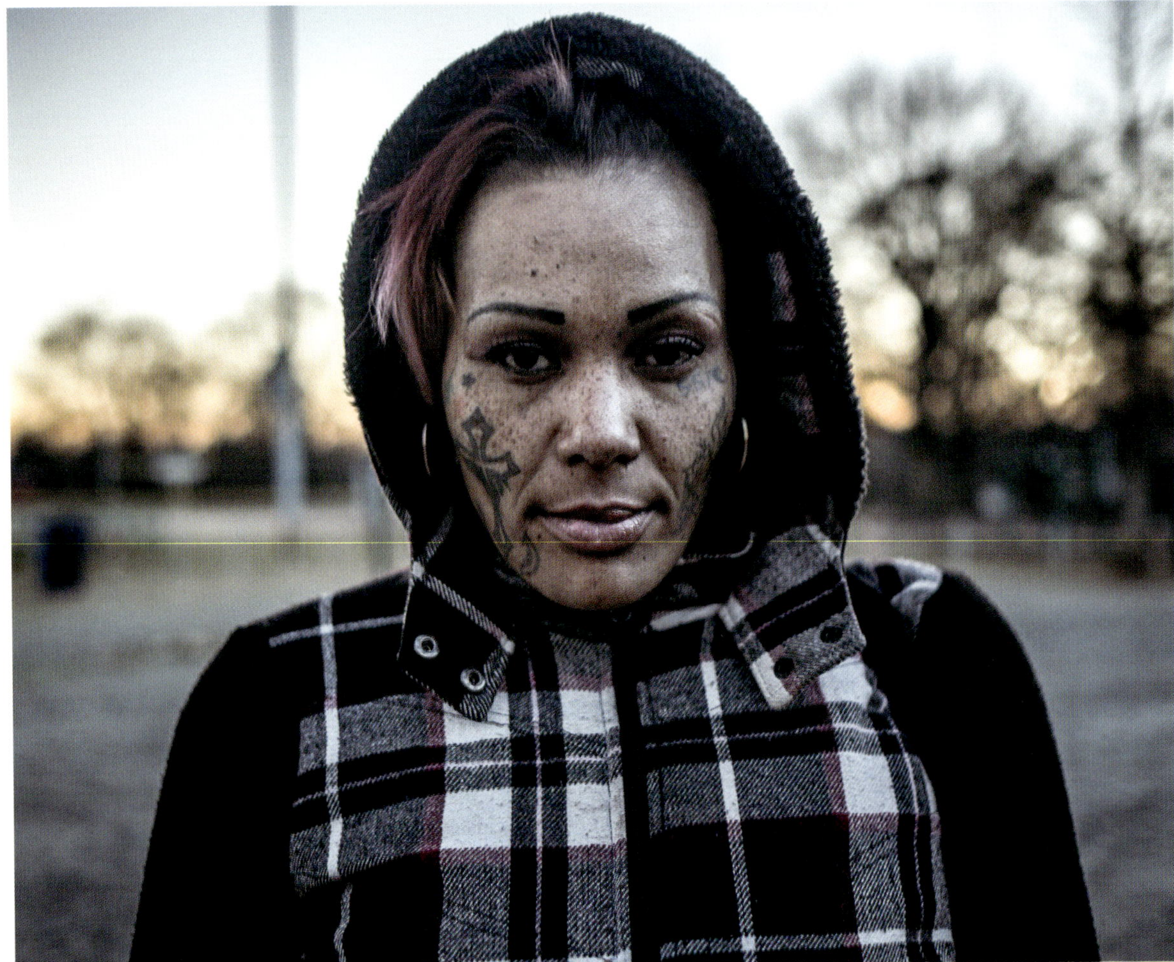

ATLANTA, GA – 2015-02-10

*When I first explained the project, Jennifer teared up and told me she couldn't believe I stopped to ask about her life, because no one had ever done that before. She proceeded to share the experience of her childhood in the DFCS [*Division of Family and Children Services*] system in Atlanta.*

Jennifer: I went into DFCS custody when I was five, and I didn't get out until a few days before my eighteenth birthday. I was in a number of DFCS facilities. I was literally raised by the state. When they released me from custody, they put me in handcuffs and called the police. They put me in the back of the police car and took me to Georgia Regional [Hospital].

BW: Why?

Jennifer: I became defiant. I was over DFCS. I was pissed off because they would never get punished for the stuff they did to us—and those people did a lot of stuff to those kids. At the end of the day, these kids are still human beings. Ninety percent of the time, kids in DFCS facilities are ignored. They don't have foster families or any family at all. I was one of them.

Growing up as a kid, sometimes you would get into fights here and there. Well, if two kids get in a fight while they were in a DFCS facility, they get abused all over again. They're restrained by four or five heavyset adults. Sometimes they would be put into safety coats, which were like full-body straitjackets. Most of the time, they're tied to beds by nonambulatory restraints. There are restraints on both ankles, on both wrists, and across the waist. Once they restrained you, they would inject you in the buttocks with either Thorazine or Vistaril. If you're too out of control, then they give you a high dosage, and you'll be knocked out within ten to fifteen minutes.

Once you wake up, you have to be quiet for a certain amount of time in regards to the restraints coming off. After you're quiet for that specific amount of time, they only unlock one of your wrist restraints. Then you have to wait fifteen to thirty more minutes for them to take off the second restraint, which would be one of the ankle restraints. This would continue in fifteen-to-thirty-minute intervals. Sometimes they'd take all of them off the third time, but sometimes they would be assholes and they'd make you wait another thirty minutes.

After you come off that bed, you would have to go into what they called a behavior control room, which was worse than a jail cell. There are concrete walls and a hole in the concrete floor. It is completely empty. They feed you through the door, and you have to eat with your hands because you aren't allowed any silverware. Sometimes if they felt a child was just out of control verbally, they would make the child drink the Vistaril or Thorazine.

It's abuse. What if a parent did that to their child inside of a home? They'd be locked up.

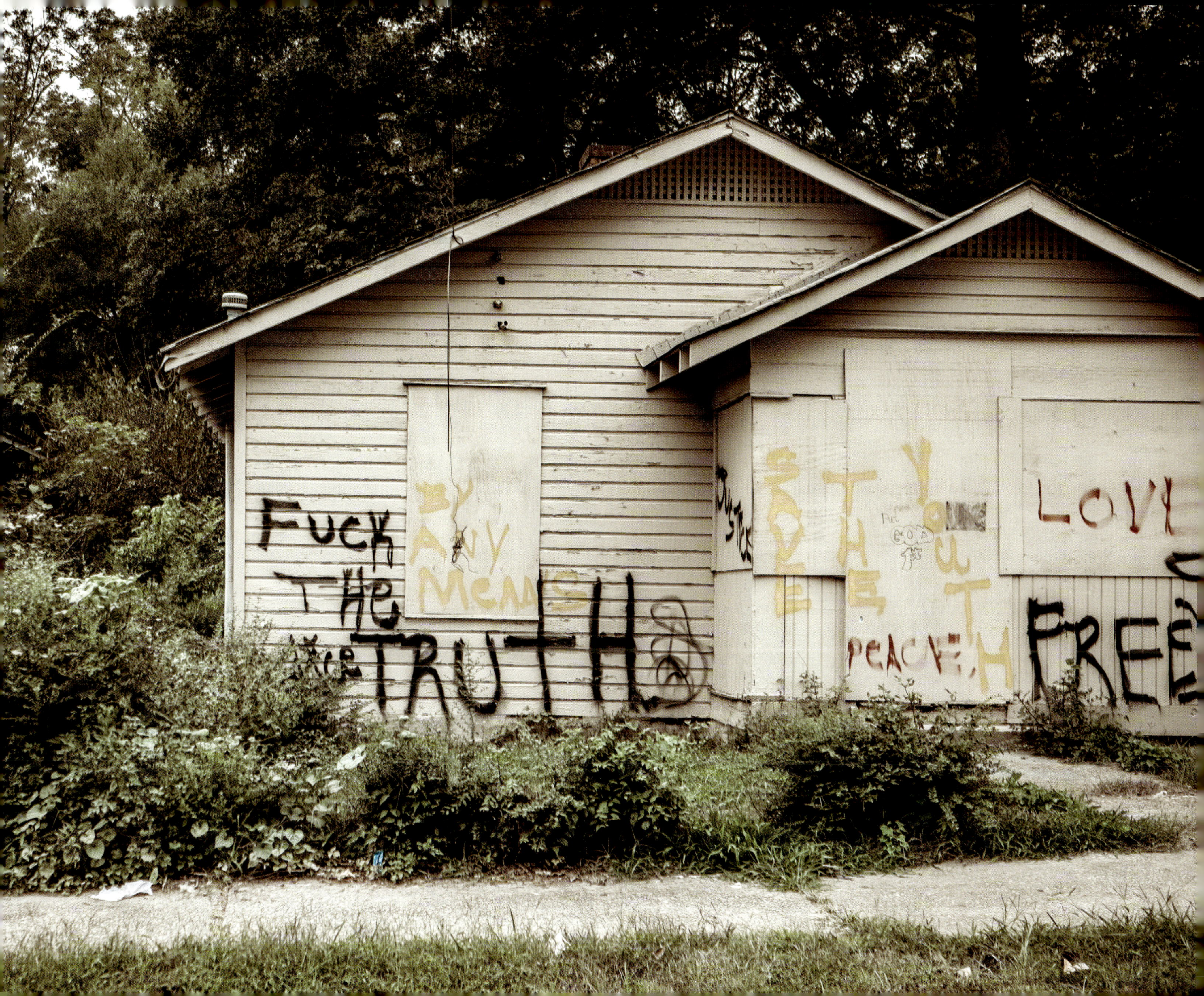
FUCK THE TRUTH
BY ANY MEANS
SAVE THE YOUTH
PEACE
LOV
FREE

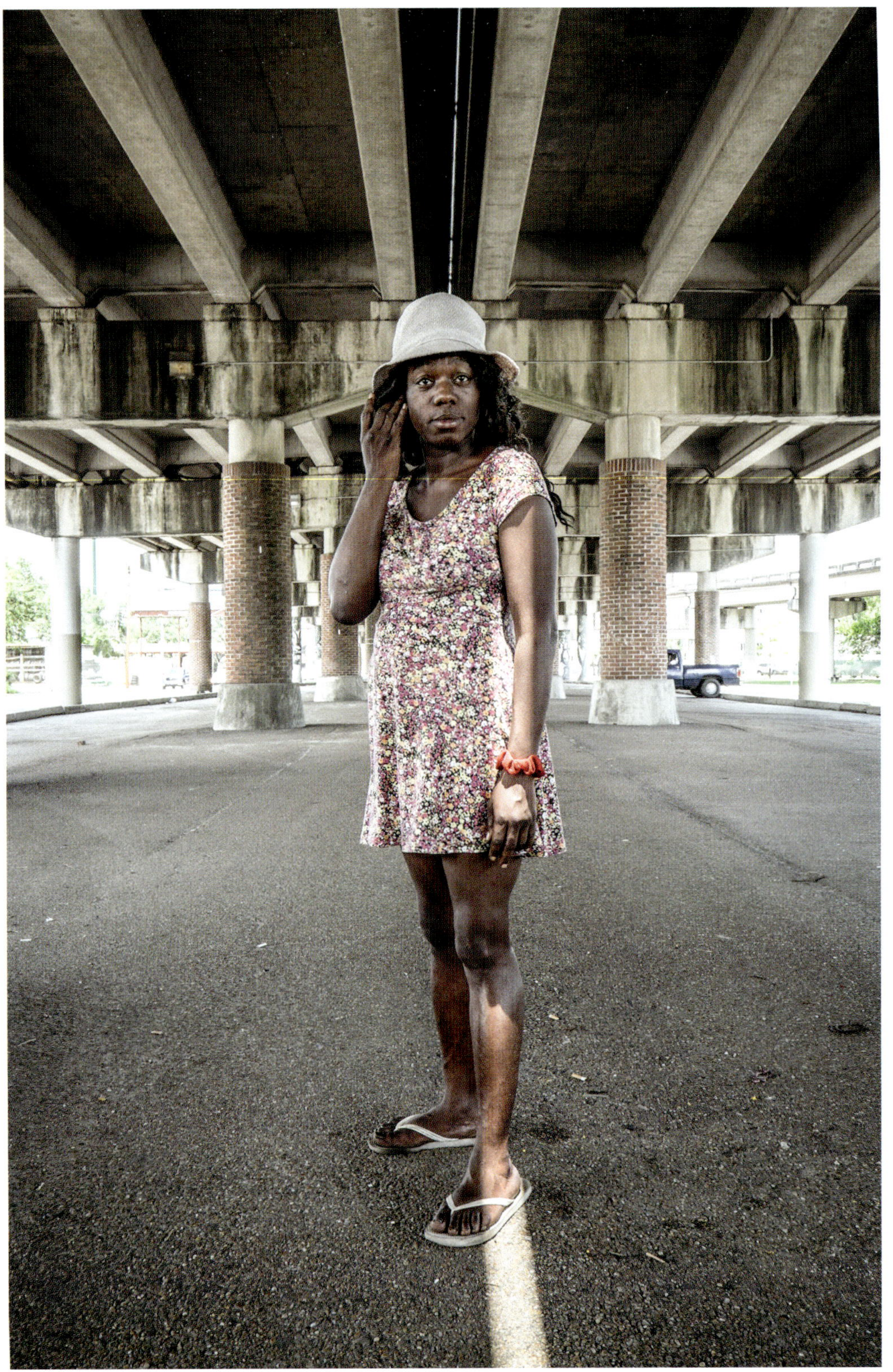

NEW ORLEANS, LA – 2015-05-08

Sheena was the first person I met when I pulled into New Orleans. She warned me about staying safe in the neighborhood and then agreed to tell me her story.

Sheena: I was in foster homes from two months until I was thirteen. After that I moved around to group homes until I was twenty. It was really rough growing up in group homes.

BW: Tell me about one of the hardest days.

Sheena: The hardest day was in April of 1999. I went and got baptized, and when I got home, my foster mother wasn't there, but the next-door neighbor and her son were there. Twenty minutes after I got home, I got raped by the next-door neighbor's son.

Nobody believed me 'cause they didn't like the way I dressed, but that was just me. I was a young girl. That really changed my life because I signed myself out of custody. I didn't trust anybody, and I don't trust black men especially. It kinda put me in a loop and put me on drugs. Life has been rough since then.

BW: So you literally got baptized and raped on the same day? How did that make you feel about God?

Sheena: Oh, it didn't stop it [relationship with God] at all. It made it stronger. 'Cause I know it was not his fault. I knew some people are just evil and they do things 'cause they want to do it. Just being cruel. So it made me closer to God, but hate men more.

BW: Surely you've wondered how did it happen on the same day? Why did that happen? Your life-changing moment was supposed to be the baptism, and instead you get raped that day.

Sheena: Yeah, it was hard.

BW: Did you turn him in?

Sheena: No, I lied. I told them it was somebody else. He ended up giving me an STD. But [tears] it didn't matter, you know? Because even if I would have told the authorities, he had already left.

BW: He fled after he raped you?

Sheena: Yeah.

BW: I'm really sorry that happened.

Sheena: Most people think that when we women end up on drugs, we have a choice, but . . . even though we try to bury the truth, the past replays over and over like a camera.

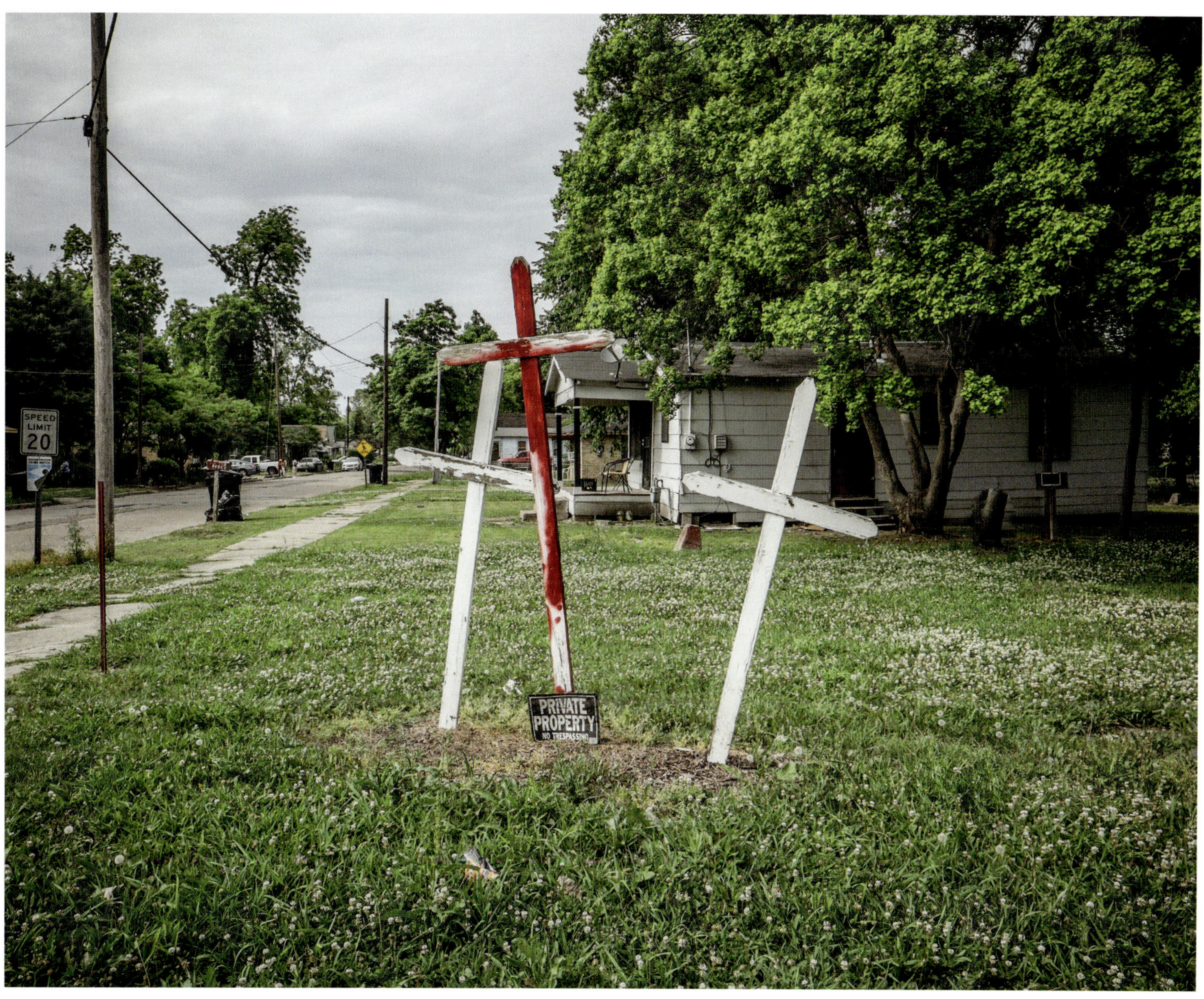
SPEED LIMIT 20
PRIVATE PROPERTY
NO TRESPASSING

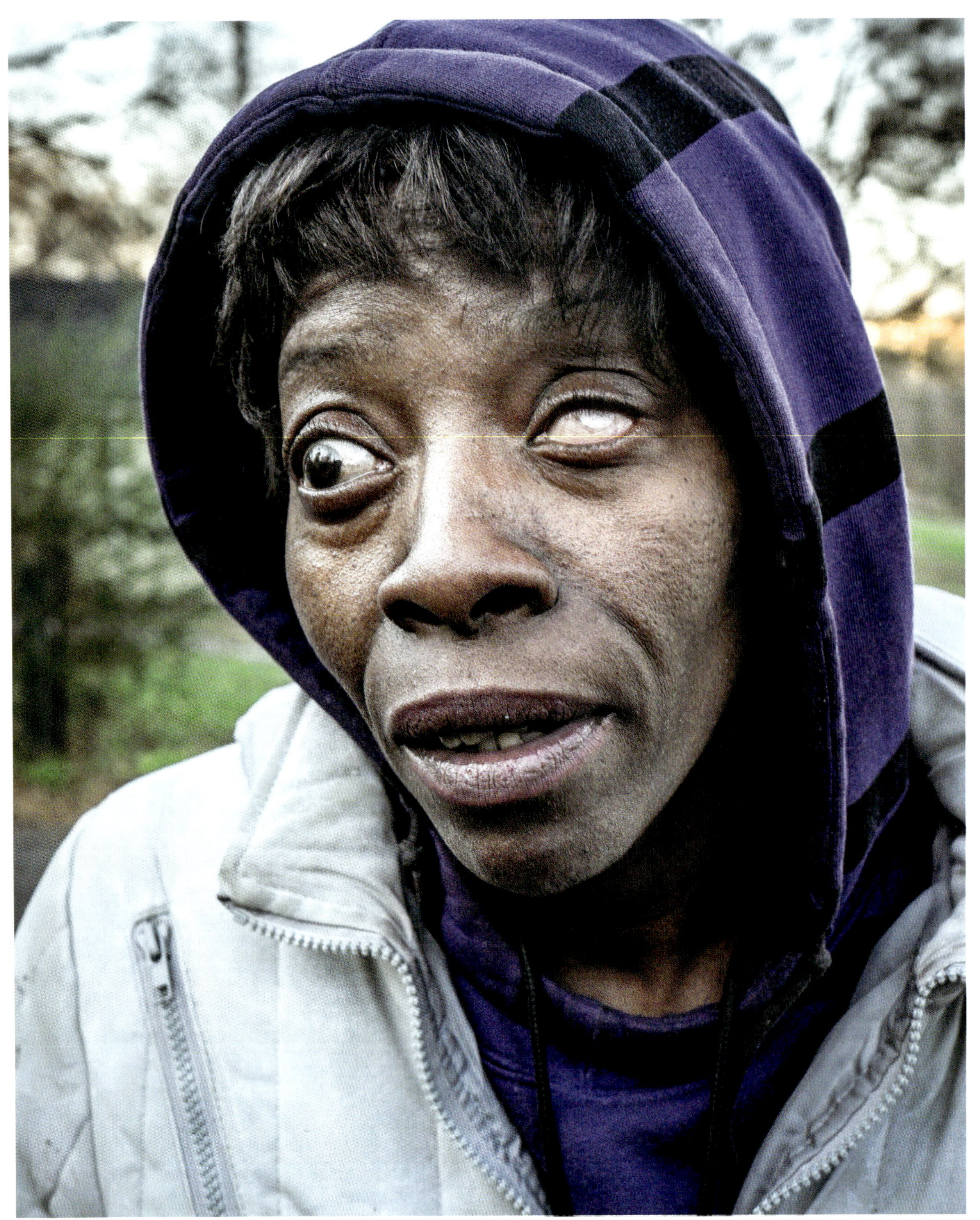

ATLANTA, GA – 2014-12-10

Barbara: I lost my mom when I was six years old. We were in a car crash, and they pronounced my mom and my brother dead, but I survived.

I stayed with my sister and was molested most of my life by different men. Since I came back to Atlanta, I've been raped twice.

Right down there, this guy grabbed me from behind, smothered me, and when I fell, I hit my eye on a bottle. Glass went in my eye. I went to the hospital, and the doctor gave me a shot, bandaged it, and told me to put ice on it for three days. Mold got in my eye, and I can't see out of that eye anymore.

I went back to the hospital, and they told me it would cost twenty-five to thirty-five thousand to get a fake eye. How can I do that when I'm homeless?

SAVANNAH, GA – 2015-05-24

Diamond: I came to Savannah because I was doing a lot of things in Augusta, and my mom wanted me to go to a new environment. When I got here, I met this Jamaican. He was a bootlegger, and he was very old.

So me and my sister had been going to him for about nine months to get sodas and stuff. He was like a candy man, you know? Every time I'd try to pay for something, he'd say "No, no—you keep." My sister told me, "You better start paying because you don't want to owe that man." So I stopped going around so much because he was always trying to give me things.

One day I saw him, and he asked if I want to smoke a blunt, so I said yeah. I'd seen other women there, so I thought it was okay. I was like eight months pregnant at the time. He left and came back from another room. When he came back, he had a machete. He saw I had some money, so he started accusing me of stealing from him.

It was me and another lady in this room when he started acting crazy. I started crying, and the other lady kept telling him I was pregnant. He let the other lady leave and told her, "If you tell, I'm gonna kill both of y'all." [Tears.] She left out the door.

He started throwing plates and stuff like that. He was snorting coke. He started taking off his clothes, looking at me, playing with himself. He made me take off all my clothes, and he tried to rape me.

I was in there for a couple of hours. Finally I got a chance to get out. I ran out of the house butt naked. I stayed right there till the police come. They took him away, but I was so scared.

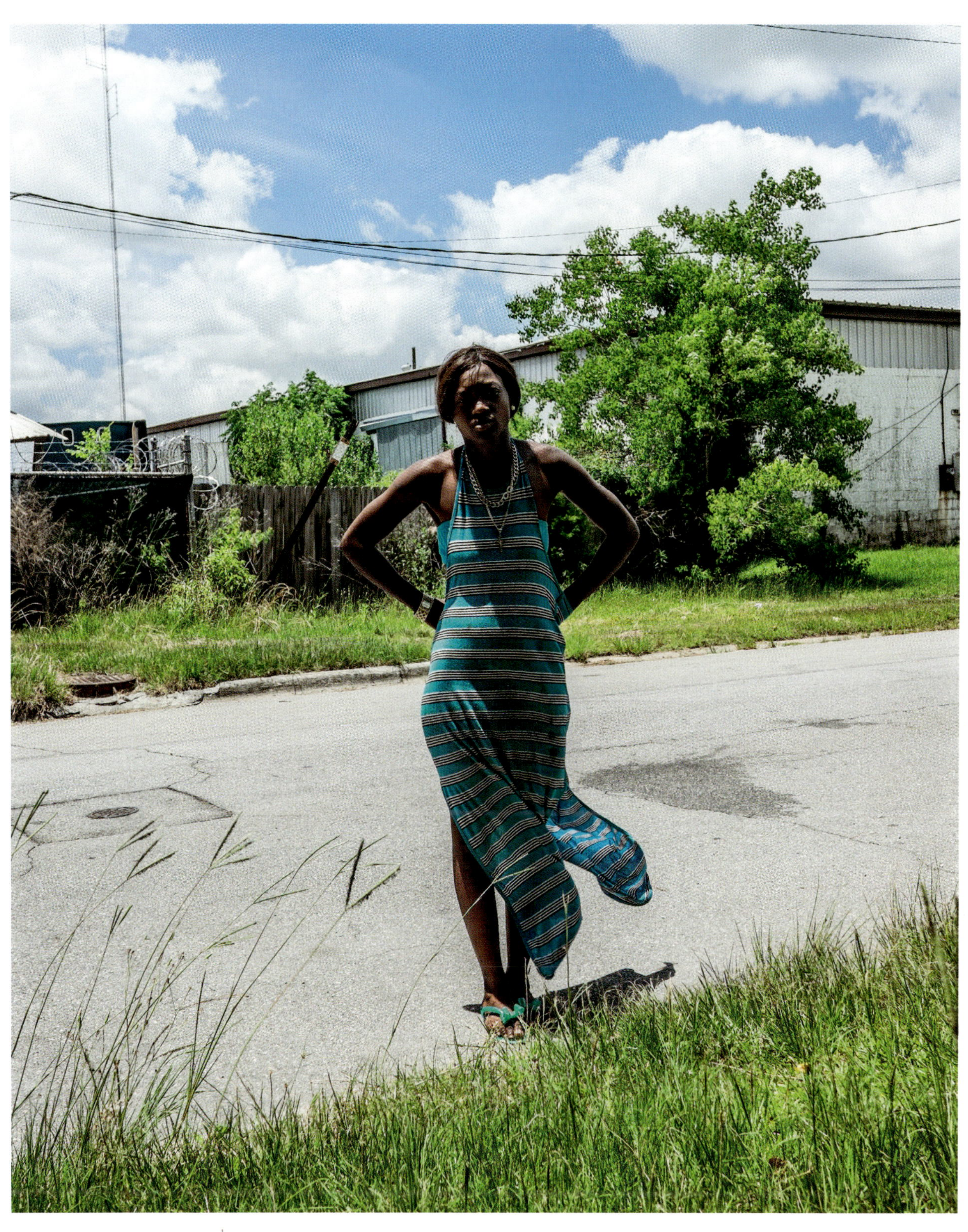

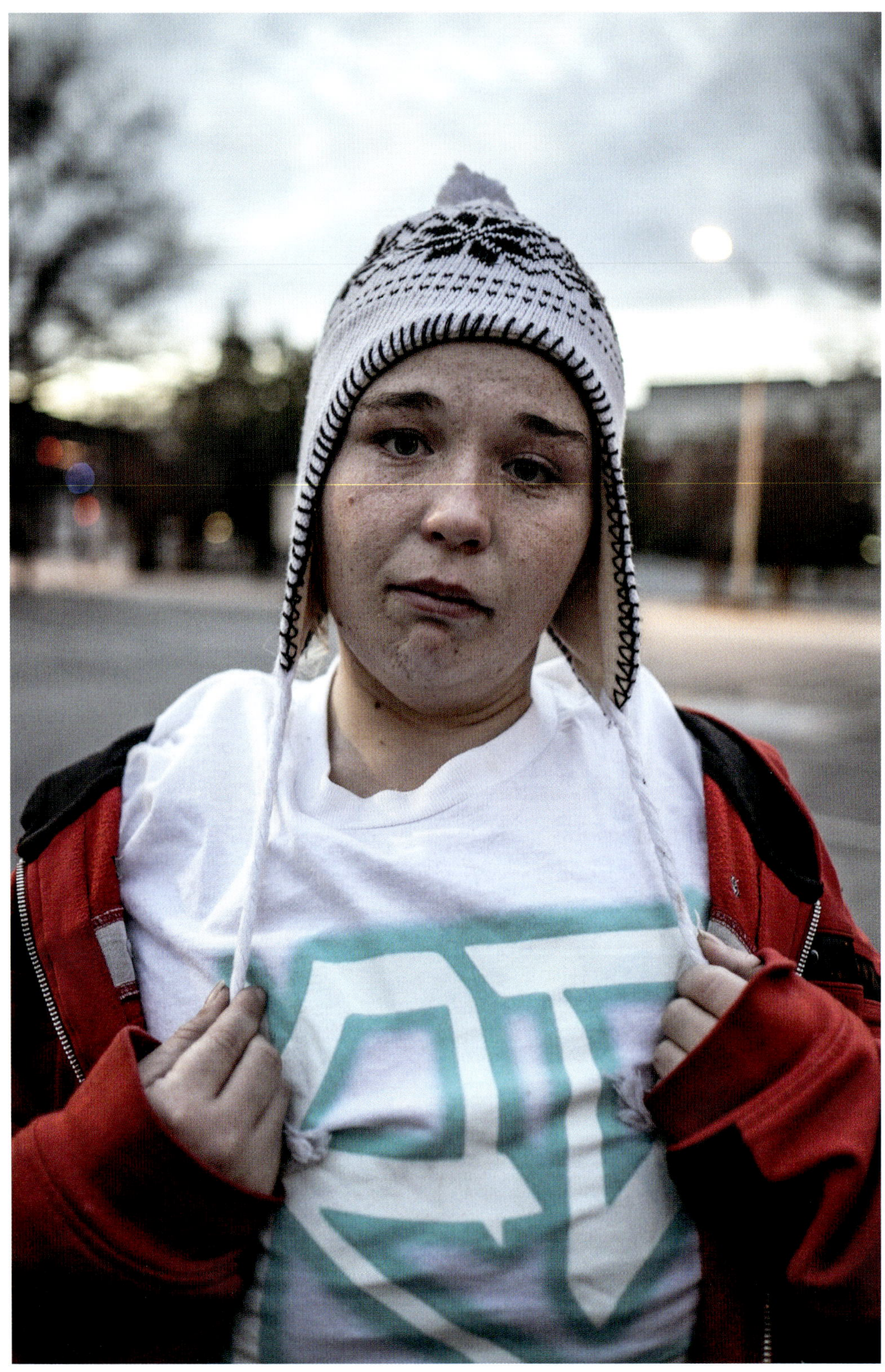

ATLANTA, GA — 2015-01-04

Lydia: I left Florida last year and went to New Orleans. I got diagnosed with cancer, and I got diagnosed with heart failure and liver failure. My mom lost my little sister when I was sixteen, so . . . this is a big change. I don't want to go. I know the man might say I only got nine months, but the Lord is the only one who can tell me when it's my time.

BW: What kind of cancer did they diagnose you with?

Lydia: Leukemia.

BW: And they said you only have nine months?

Lydia: Yeah. They said my liver is looking really bad.

BW: Is there treatment they can do for it?

Lydia: Well, I left New Orleans because I'm just tired. I'm an addict. I smoke crack cocaine. I guess you could say I been running the streets more than taking care of my health.

BW: Are you close to your mom?

Lydia: We are, but we've been growing apart because of my addiction and because I'm not close to home.

BW: What's the nicest thing anyone's ever done for you?

Lydia: Um . . . when I overdosed on methamphetamine, my mama came to the hospital, and she brought me dinner. She sat with me for hours and hours. It was really nice because I finally got to be with her, without her being upset and her taking it out on me emotionally because I usually get in the way.

BW: Is there any message you want to tell your mom?

Lydia: [Tears.] I love you, Mom, and I'm sorry.

BW: What are you sorry for?

Lydia: I'm sorry about hurting you emotionally and physically. And I just want you to know I'm trying. I know I'm fucking up hard, but I'm trying to get everything situated. And I want to see my little brother and little sister and my twin sisters. I hope to see you guys soon.

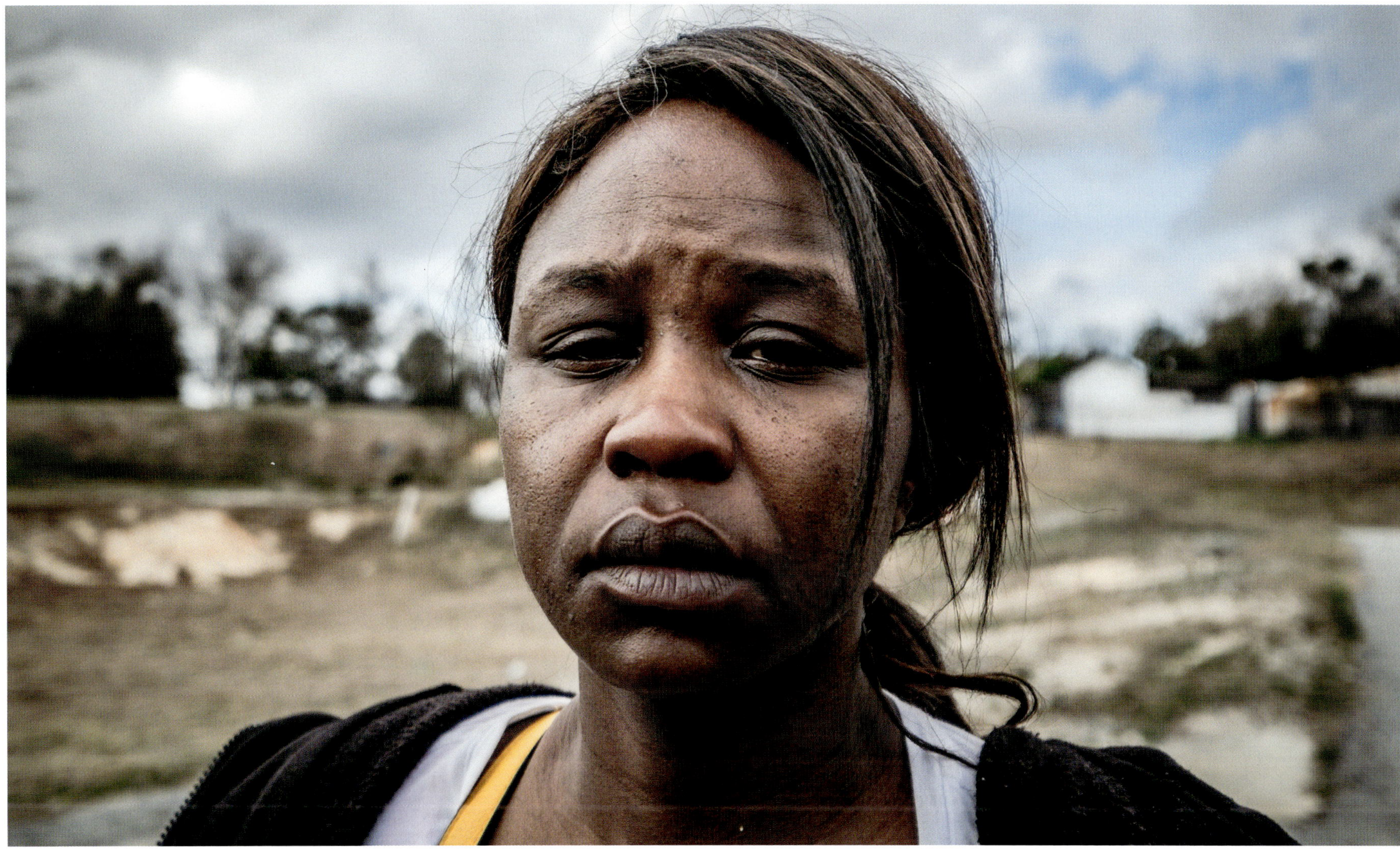

MACON, GA – 2015-03-04

Amanda: Every day on the streets is the worst day of my life, 'cause you lose so much. [Tears.] You lose your loved ones, your self-esteem, your dignity . . . It's rough.

BW: How long have you been out here?

Amanda: About seven or eight years.

BW: Have you ever stayed clean for any length of time?

Amanda: Yeah, I done got clean and stayed clean for five years. I can do it. But every time something happens in my life that's hard, I go back to the streets.

BW: What do you think keeps bringing you back?

Amanda: Just trying to escape reality . . .

BW: You mentioned losing your loved ones. Do you have any kids?

Amanda: Yes, I have five children.

BW: Who do they stay with?

Amanda: [Tears.] Three are in foster care, one is grown, and one lives with his daddy.

BW: Do you have regrets with your kids?

Amanda: Yes, all the time. All the time . . . I love them. I just wish we could be together.

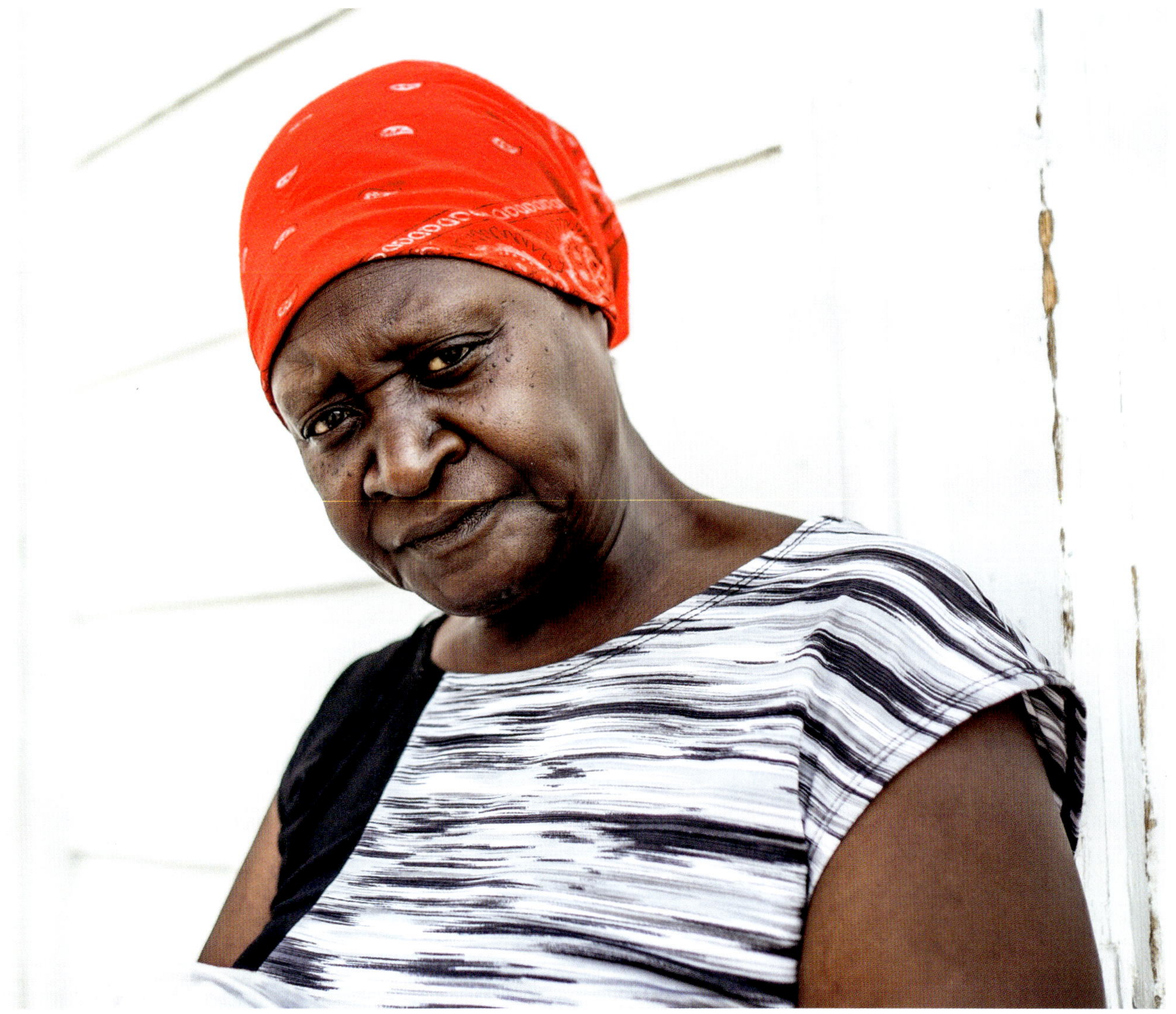

NEW ORLEANS, LA – 2015-05-11

Lou Anna: It's like a lifelong story. I used to do drugs. One day I was high, and I heard a voice that said, "Get a knife," so I had a knife in each hand. The voice told me I could fly, so I jumped from the fifth floor. I fell to the second floor. Didn't make it to the first. This was God, because the direction I was going in, I didn't go that way. It was like something caught my right foot. I was hanging from the second-story balcony, head down towards the ground.

There were a lot of people standing around. It was like a movie. Firetrucks and everything else.

They put me in cuffs and brought me to Charity Hospital. When the doctors came in and talked to me, they said, "You're one lucky person. You should be dead, bruised, fractured, or something."

BW: Five-story fall, and you didn't break anything?

Lou Anna: Nothing. It was God.

I continued to use drugs until I was just so tired. Just got tired of giving the dope man my money. I prayed to God to take this habit away from me.

One day, I bought some dope to take home. I went to take that hit. After I took that hit, I had to run straight to the bathroom, and it came back up. From that day until this day, I haven't done any more drugs.

BW: So you didn't get Twelve Step help or any of that?

Lou Anna: Yeah, I have been to Twelve Step meetings. But see, when you yearn for something, that's what the Lord will do. He will step in.

BW: How long has it been since then?

Lou Anna: Three and a half years. I feel very close to God. From that fall, it had to be God. With that jump, I was headed down. Who was there? It was that sin that made me do that, and it was God who saved me.

This was God, because the direction I was going in, I didn't go that way. It was like something caught my right foot. I was hanging from the second-story balcony, head down towards the ground.

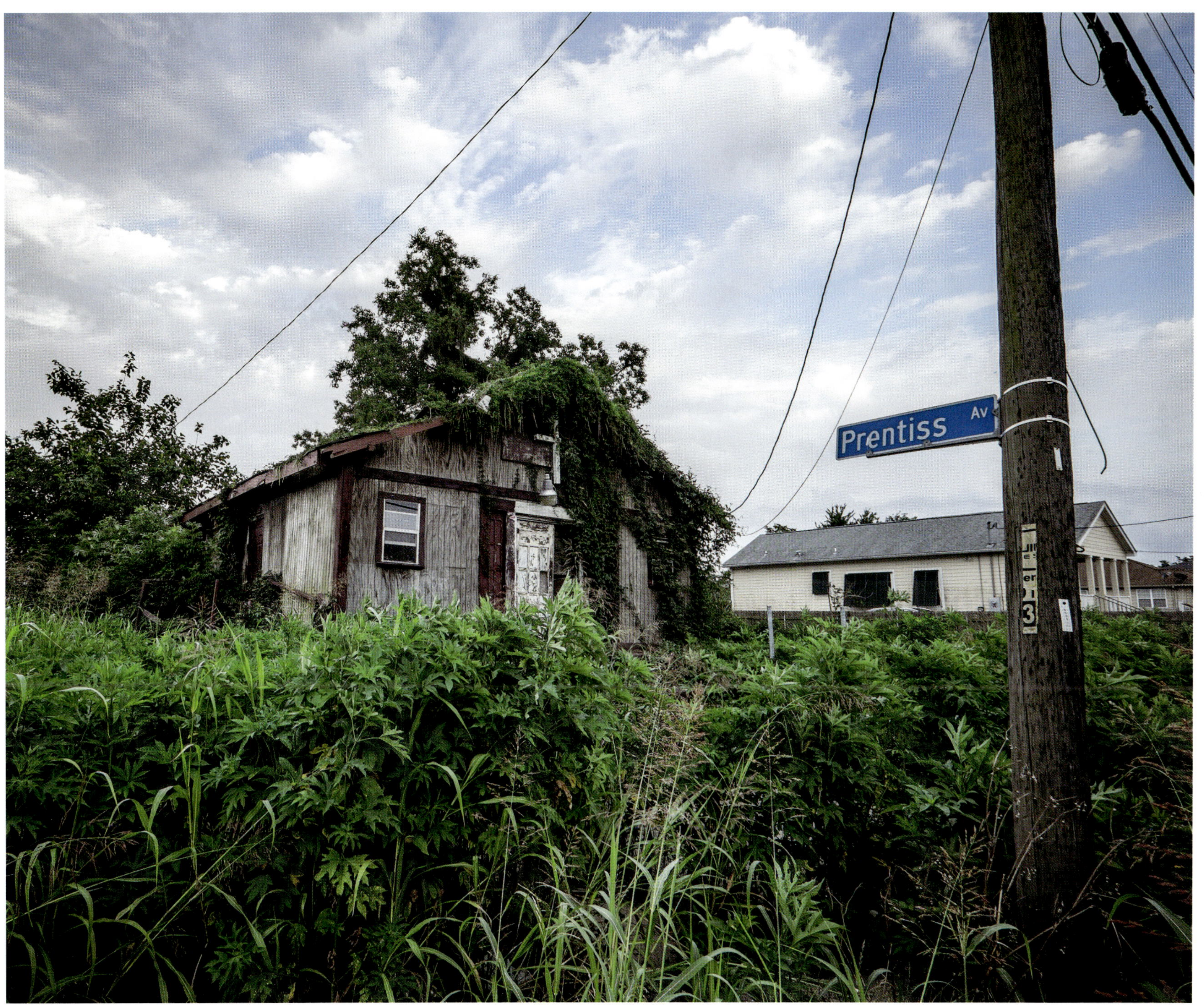
Prentiss Av

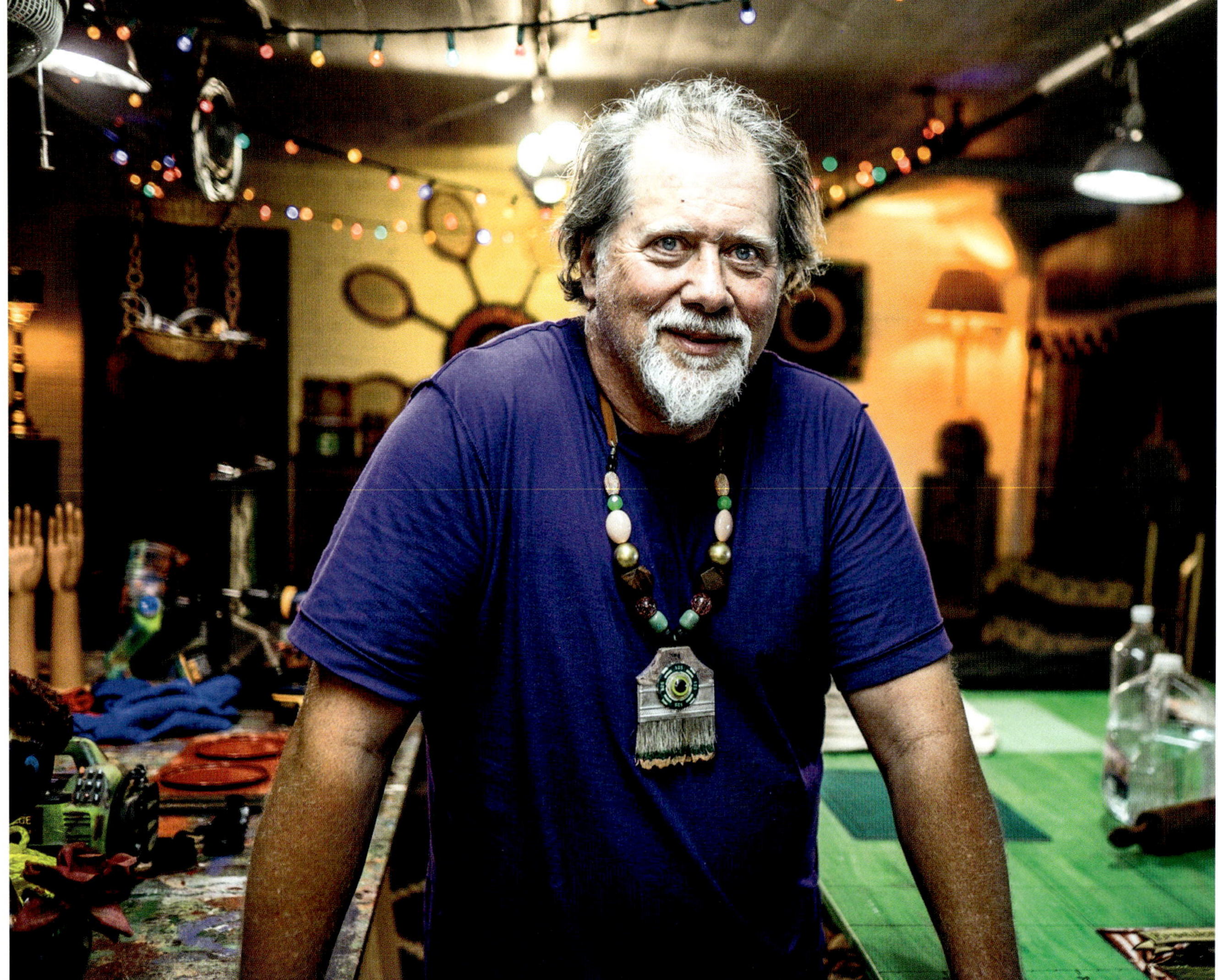

ASHEVILLE, NC – 2015-06-01

I spoke with Rob, a folk artist based out of Asheville, North Carolina. I asked him how he became a working artist and was amazed at how similar our stories were.

Rob: My last real job was as a computer operator for the Department of Commerce in Charlotte—in a windowless, fluorescent-lit room with lots of buzzing noises. Very artificial. Felt very much like you were stuck in the Matrix.

For me, it was such a transformative thing that happened that I resisted it. I was sitting with my mom while she was dying in the hospital. I'd see all these people in poor shape up and down the hall, and I realized that it's rarely one thing that gets you. It's like something weakens you, and then something else comes in and finishes the job.

Sometimes life changes are that way too, you know? It can just be normal things—like, for me, a divorce, my mom passing, a couple of job layoffs. But when all those things happen within a few months, it can really leave you kinda raked over the coals.

During that time, I was listening to a teacher who said, "You always have to have some breakdown to have a breakthrough." When I heard that, it made the hair on my arms stand up. It goes all the way back to birth. The baby's not comfortable when it's leaving its comfort space, and it's being pushed through violent contractions to who-knows-where. So I sorta developed that into my own saying: "Birth always looks like death from the other side."

So for me during that time period—when jobs weren't working, my mom passed after months in the hospital, and my marriage split up—I was like, "Dammit!" [Shaking head.] You know? But this thing just kinda came out of the middle of it. I'd look for old soup spoons, and I'd join them together—tape them up and join them with leather. Kinda make them look nice, and play spoons with them. When they were joined together, they were easier to play. One day I was out buying spoons, and I decided to buy a whole box to see if I could make rings. I did. But it was just like opening up a Pandora's box. I went and bought a little torch to solder with. Kinda taught myself.

Next thing I know, I have a living room full of little people and animals and things. This lady came over and said, "You should take some of these to a show." I had that moment I see so many people have—where they're skeptical, scared to make the jump. But within a few weeks, I was starting to say to myself, "Well, I should take this stuff somewhere." So I just started. At the time, I had no idea there was an entire country full of art shows and festivals and that type of thing.

As fate would have it, the very first time I took some pieces to a show, a man named Joe Adams, who was a folk art dealer and collector, came through and bought a whole armload of stuff. Didn't haggle or anything. I came home from that event with cash. It wasn't like working somewhere and a couple weeks later you get a check, but an actual face-to-face exchange. It felt real. He and I became good friends, and through him I discovered this whole world of folk art, or outsider art. The first time they invited me down to do a show at one of their galleries, that was another in a series of epiphanic moments for me. I walked in and saw all these great paintings. It wasn't like a lot of galleries, where they had paintings every twelve feet. They had paintings from floor to ceiling. I was like, "Holy shit. I've painted stuff like this before." Before that, I didn't know there was a name for it or anything. But it sort of gave me permission. After that, if I felt like doing a painting, I just did a painting. I didn't worry about if I could paint or not.

That's the way kids do it. They don't worry about what people think; they just do it. The most important part about rediscovering the inner child is letting go of our fear of outcome.

BW: Growing up in the South, you hear a lot about being born again. Art was kind of my savior. I believe I'd be dead, or wishing I was, if I wouldn't have found a way to express myself and a way to support myself outside of a corporation. The experience you talk about is very similar to mine, and it's like being born again.

Rob: And again and again. Seven or eight times a day sometimes.

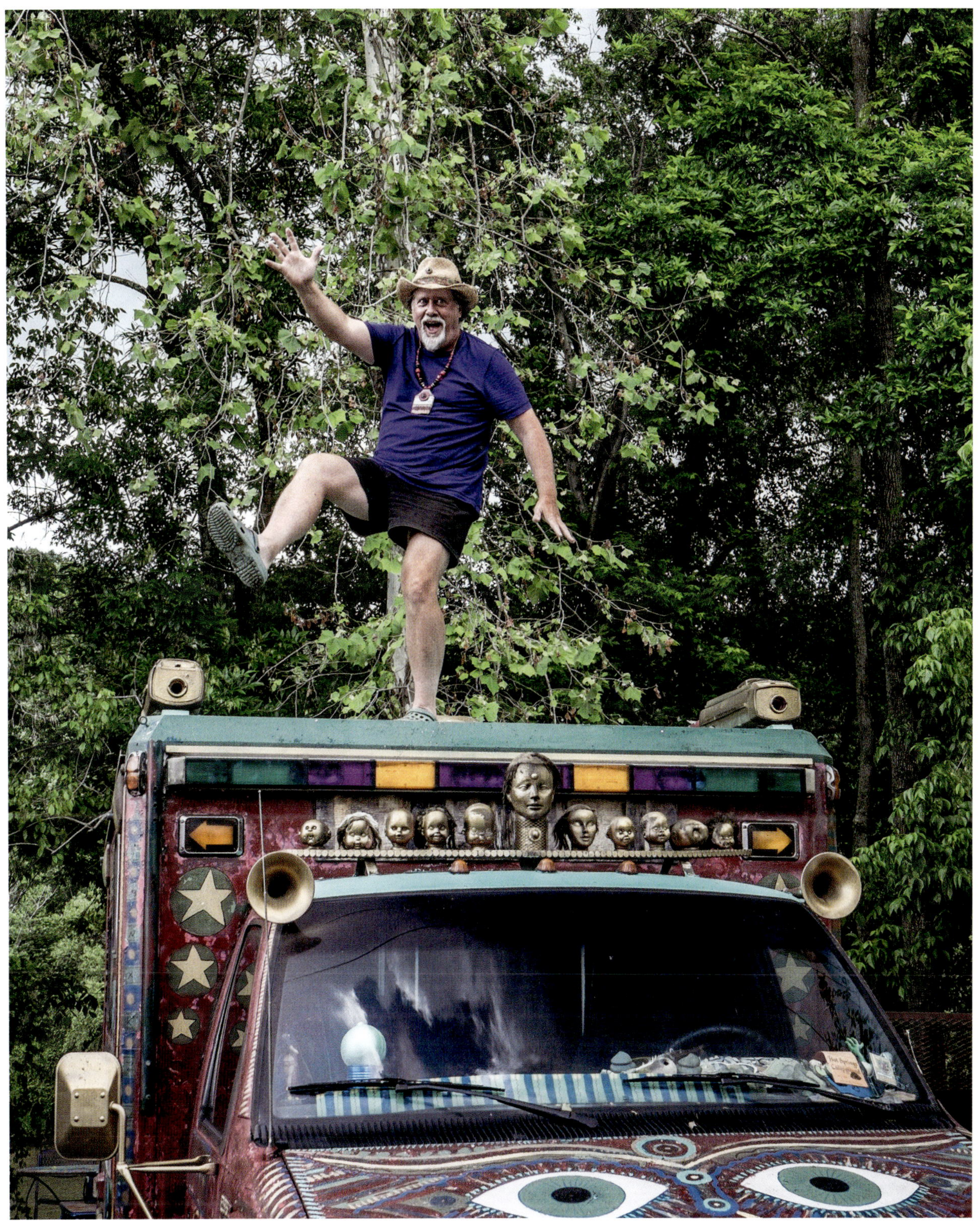

I've come through many hard trials
Through temptations on every hand
Though Satan tries to stop me
And to place my feet on sinking sand
Through the pain and all of my sorrows
He was there to catch me when I fall, yes He was
He was there, always to protect me
For He's kept me . . . (2)

—*Sung by Dominique* *(p. 41)*

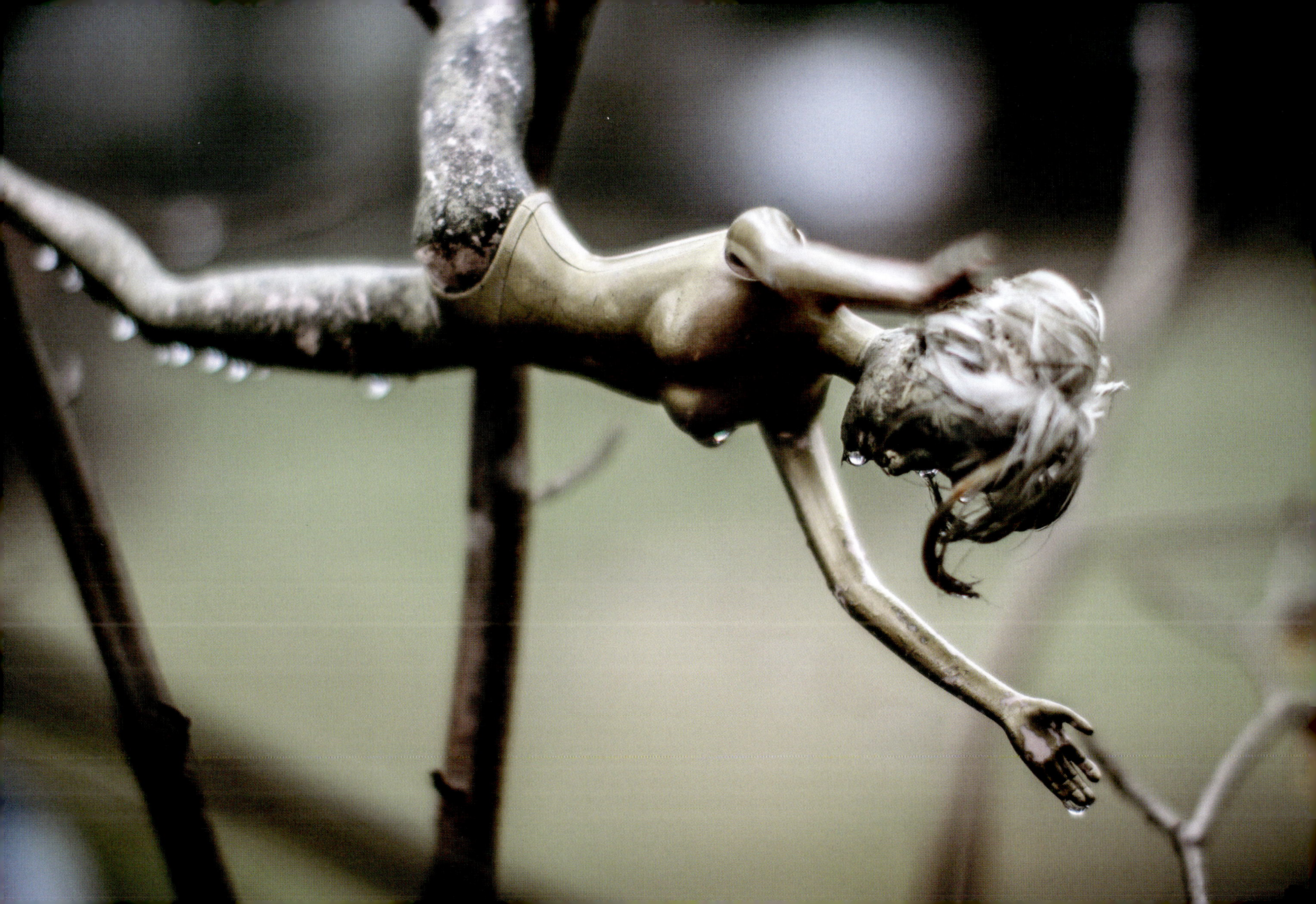

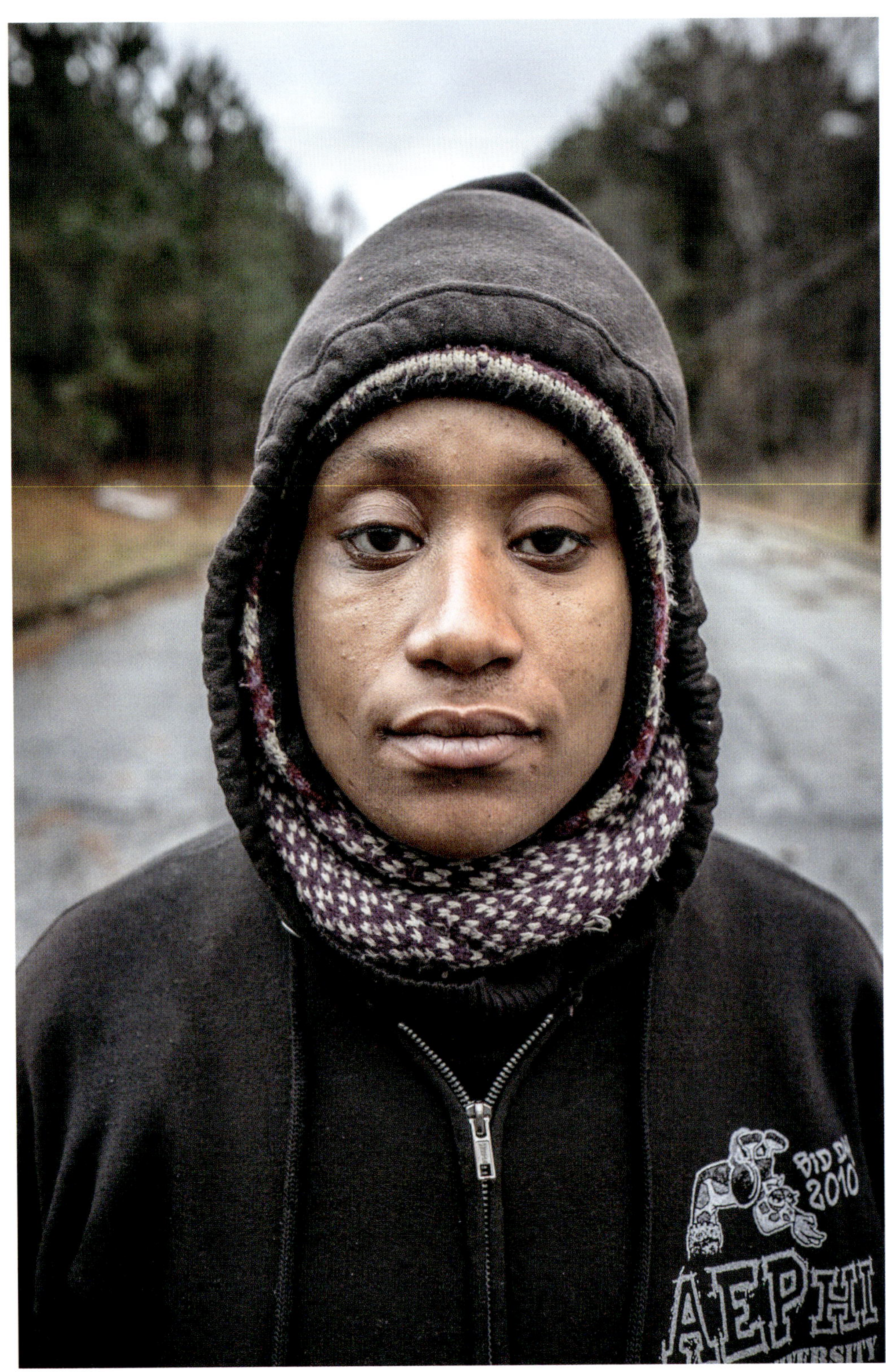

ATLANTA, GA – 2014-12-24

Ursula: When I was eight years old, I was shot up with cocaine and raped by my father.

BW: What? He shot you up with a needle?

Ursula: Yes, he shot me up and raped me. That was the first and last time I seen my father.

BW: You didn't know him before that?

Ursula: No. He was sent to jail because he was trying to hurt my mom when she was pregnant with me. He got out of jail when I was eight. The night before it happened, he came over, and they were arguing about him coming back into my mom's life and stuff.

My mom was at work the next day, and my brother and I were at home by ourselves. My brother had snuck out of the house while I was taking my nap. When I woke up, my father was sitting there in my room. He had a rope. He tied me to my bed. I remember specifically thinking, "This is not no kids game."

BW: Did you know he was your dad at the time?

Ursula: Yes. My mom had shown me pictures of the bastard when I was growing up.

It changed my life. I really still can't let it go. I try my best not to think about it. I try to put it deep in my head. The only people that know it happened—until now—is my family.

BW: I can't imagine.

Ursula: [Nodding.] Right after that, my brother's father started molesting me. He molested me from the time I was eight until I was sixteen. My brother found out about it when I was sixteen and shot his father twice.

BW: Damn . . . What happened after that?

Ursula: I'm gonna tell you what happened after that. He [brother's father] went to rehab to try to change his life, right? And then tried to come to me and apologize for what he did . . .

I know I'm out here doing crack. When I saw that it took my memory away, I really took advantage of it. There are too many things I don't want to remember.

BW: If you could do anything, what would you do?

Ursula: I would sit here and thank God for his grace. Seriously, I've been through it out here for six and a half years. I been hit four times by a car. I done been gang-raped three times. I've been shot, stabbed, burnt.

BW: How can you thank God for his grace when your life has been so hard? To be honest, I'd be pissed.

Ursula: Believe me, through all that I have been through, I should be shot out and crazy. I let go and let God and put everything in his hands.

BW: Thanks for telling me your story. You're like a little walking miracle.

Ursula: [Smiling.] Whoa, man—I can't believe that just came out of your mouth! That's so cool you said that!

SAVANNAH, GA – 2015-05-24

BW: When did your dad start molesting you?

Darlene: Well, from age three, up. He'd take my brother coon hunting and beat him in the head with stuff. He beat me with the horsewhip so bad that I'd have to tell the people at school I fell down the stairs. It wasn't like now. I didn't have any help. My mom was scared to death. She didn't know what was going on. He had her all messed up.

I got married at fifteen to get away from him. I got pregnant. The guy I married got put in jail for breaking and entering, so I had to go back home. I ended up getting pregnant and married again at seventeen to get out of there.

It took a long time to put my dad in prison. I couldn't tell anyone about what he'd done to me until later, but he'd molested cousins and other people too. He was a real nut.

BW: Have you forgiven him?

Darlene: *Me*? I'll never forgive him! I had his ashes in a black box. I was gonna put him in the sewer or something, but I ended up giving them to his sister to bury him.

BW: Are you close to anyone in your family?

Darlene: I didn't answer my son's call for Mother's Day.

BW: Why?

Darlene: I'm too upset. [Crying.] My daughter was murdered after the sheriff dropped her off in a motel room, then my husband divorced me, and my brother was murdered three months later in New Mexico. All that happened in a year. They don't know how I'm not on a bunch of pills and stuff.

BW: That's a lot for anyone to live through. Have you ever been diagnosed with anything?

Darlene: I know I have PTSD. I know I'm probably bipolar, and I have anxiety. I need an advocate to get me back on SSI. Then I could get me a truck with a camper. At least then I'd have a place to stay.

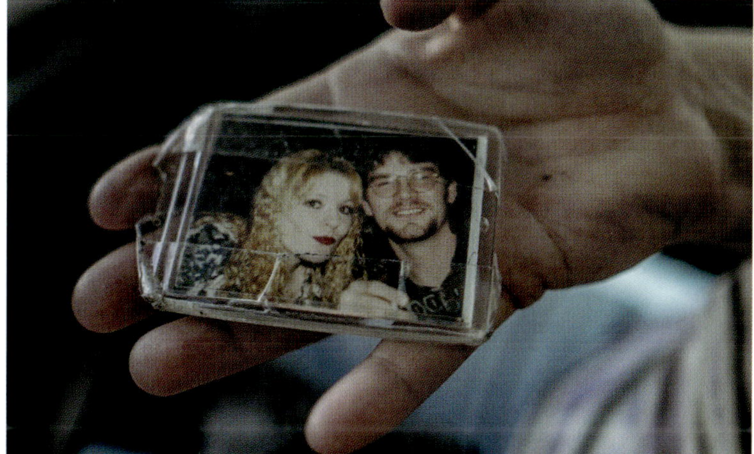

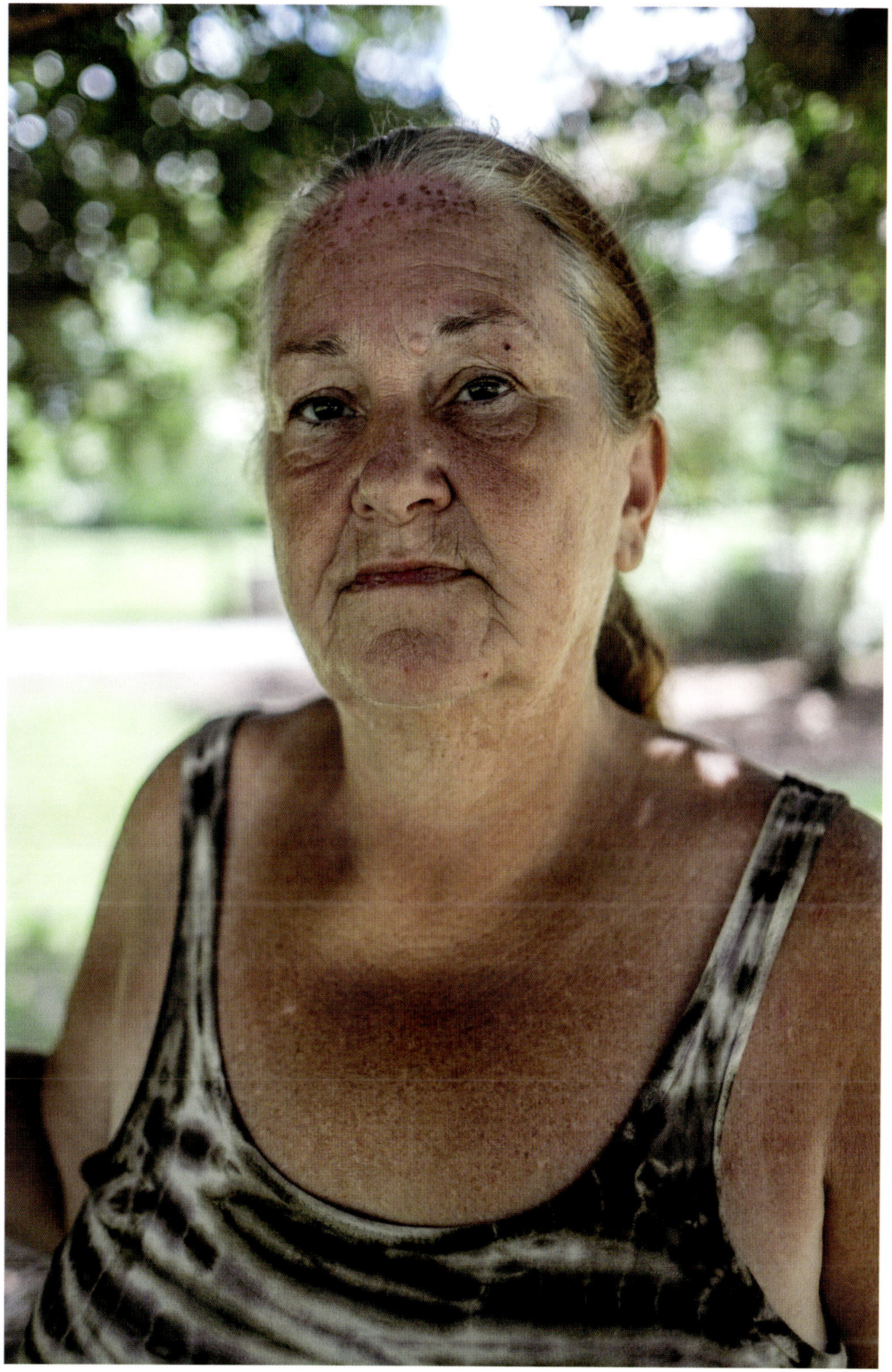

#Incest #Disbelief #DeathOfChild

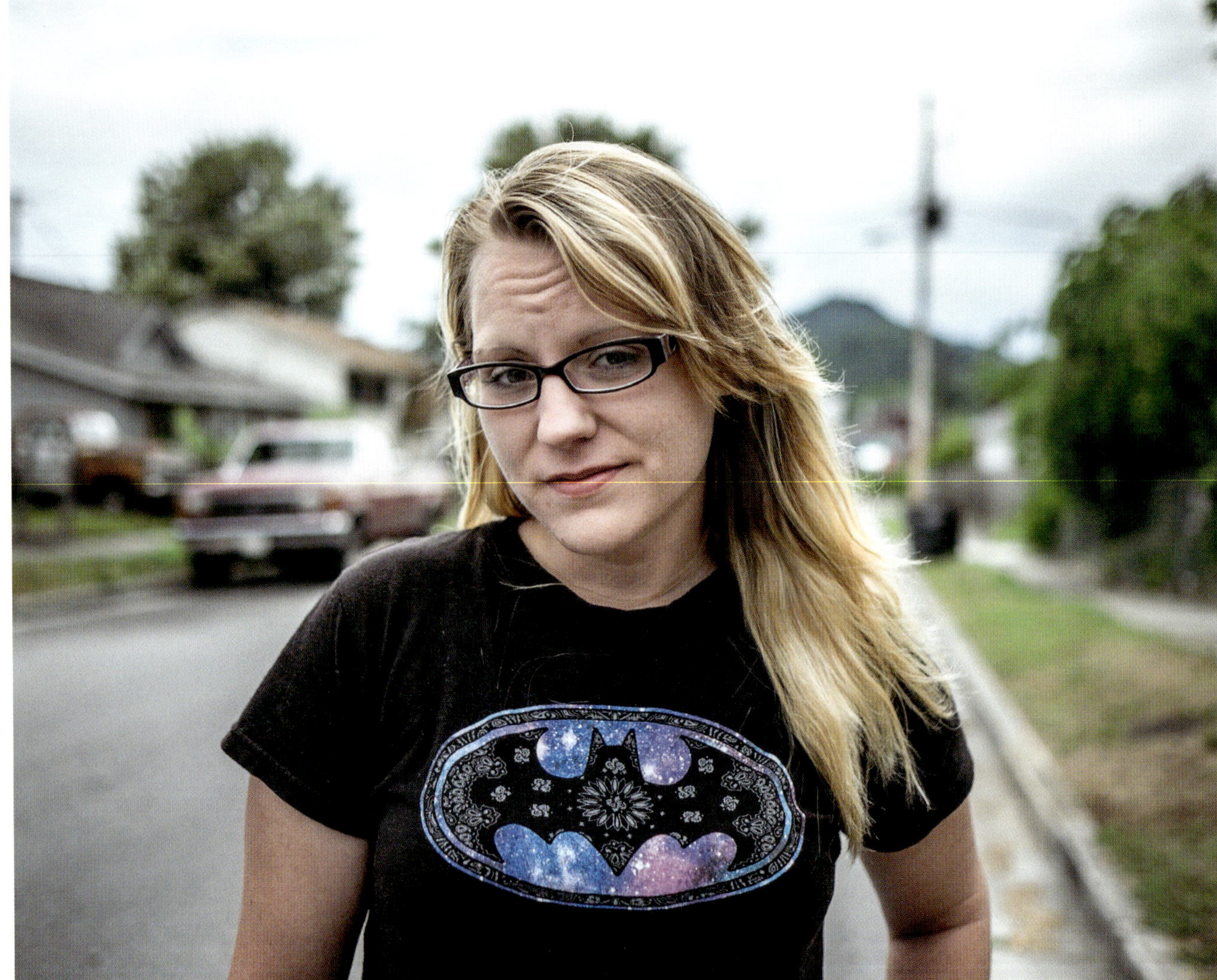

KINGSPORT, TN – 2015-06-03

Melissa: Last year on the Fourth of July, my older brother murdered my baby brother, Stephen. He stabbed him seven times.

Me and my baby brother were best friends. He was 6'2" and about 250 pounds. He was tall and muscular. We went out together that night. He drank a whole bottle of Jäger and several forties. He was staggering. He kept saying, "Sis, I need some female attention."

He wanted to go see his ex-girlfriend, Chayanne. She lived in an apartment above my grandma's. Chayanne's mom said Stephen could spend the night. My older brother, David, was downstairs in my grandma's apartment. He had his baby's mama there. She wasn't supposed to be there because he acts like a psycho when she's around.

So, I watched him stagger off.

My older brother murdered him, and he didn't get no time.

BW: Why didn't he get any time?

Melissa: They said it was self-defense, but he didn't have a mark on him.

David's got anger issues. He's either really happy, or he's really angry. There's no in-between for him. He's about an inch shorter than me and has a hip disease. Stephen was a lot bigger, and David was always scared of him. It was a lot of fear, anger, and jealousy. It all clashed together, and he couldn't control it.

BW: Do you still talk to your older brother?

Melissa: Yeah. He lives here with my parents. I'm staying with a friend right now because I can't take looking at him.

BW: What do you miss most about Stephen?

Melissa: His shit-eating grin and his big blue eyes. The bluest that the sky could get is how blue his eyes was. He was the one that brought everyone happiness and laughter. When a good song would come on, he'd be the first one dancing to it.

I know we're all supposed to forgive, but right now, I just can't. He took a lot from us.

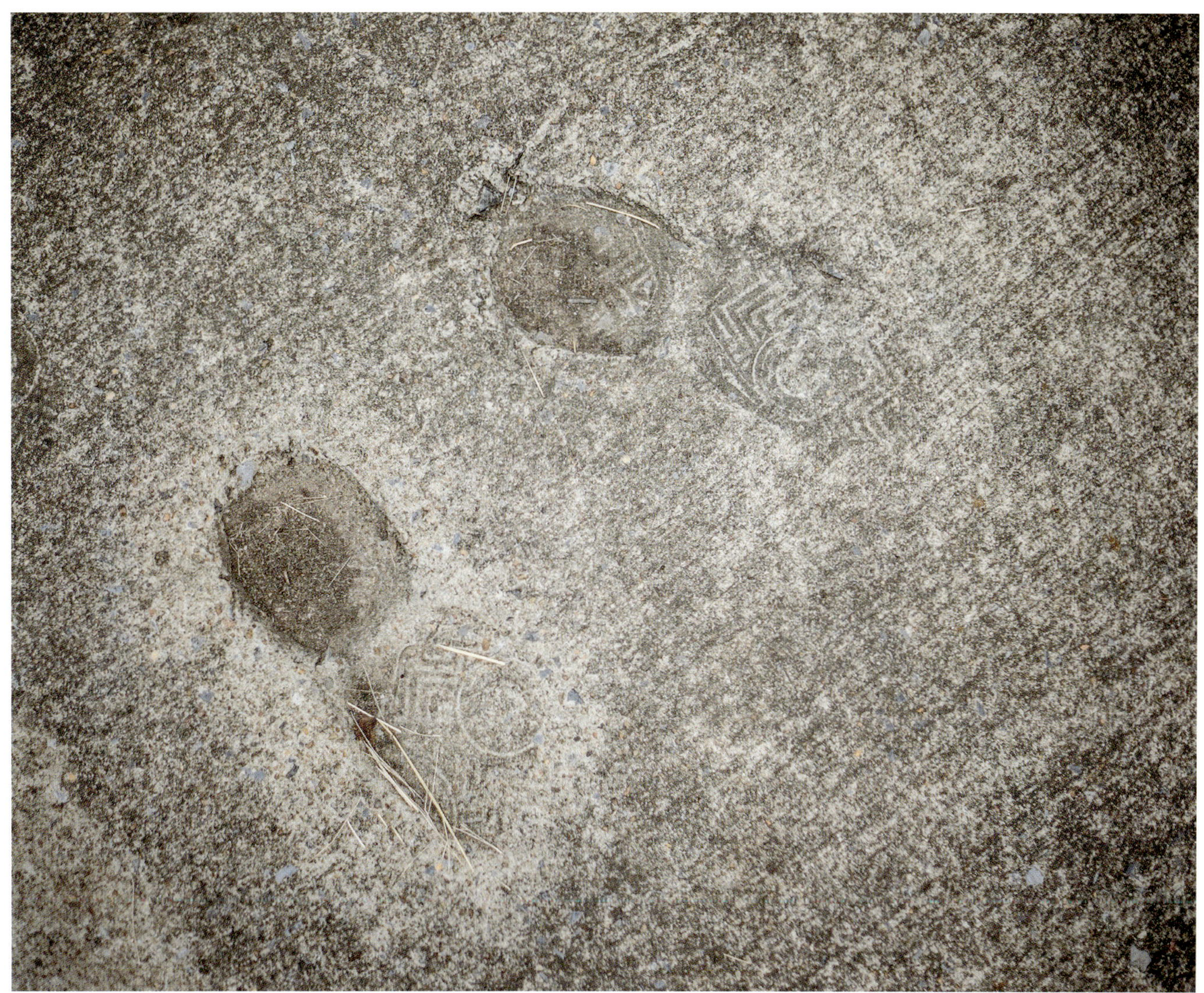

Stephen's footprints in front of the family home

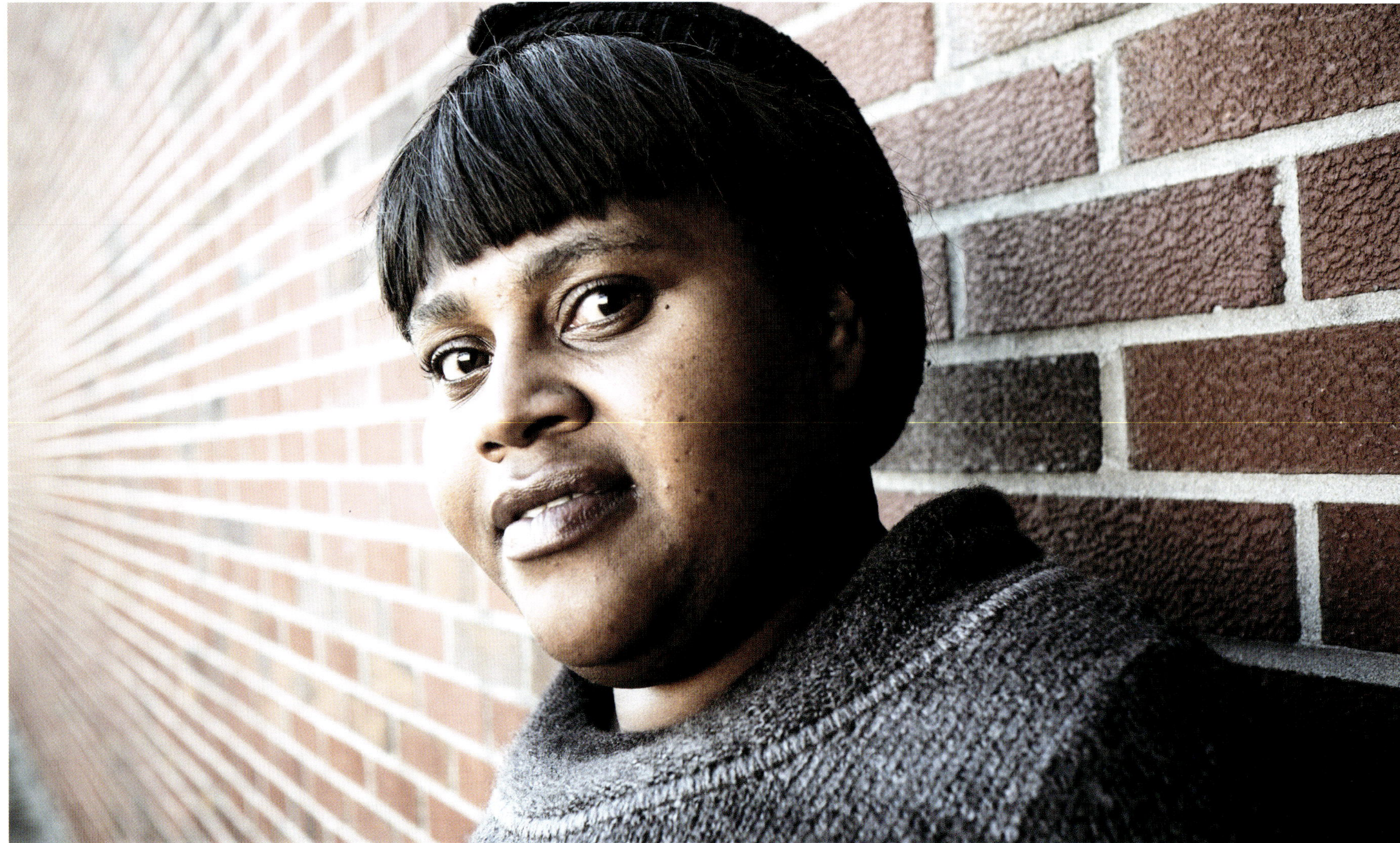

ATLANTA, GA – 2014-11-26

Shante: When I found my mom deceased in her bed, January the eighth of 2011, that's when a "fuck it" attitude just came over me. I was just like, "Okay, I'm Superwoman. I can do anything I want to do."

I went to prison twice for selling drugs. My dad passed away four days after I got out of prison, the second time. After that, I didn't have anyone but my brothers and my ten-year-old son.

BW: A lot happened pretty quick. What are your hopes for the future?

Shante: Honestly, I have two years of college. I'm a licensed massage therapist. I'm going back to school starting January the seventh for business management.

BW: Have you ever had a job as a massage therapist?

Shante: Yeah. At a nursing home. It was like massage therapy and rehabilitation.

BW: Would you like to do that again?

Shante: Yeah. I'd like to open up my own business doing massage therapy. But . . . I think . . . I don't want to do old people anymore. Some of them old people are, like, freaks.

BW: [Laughing.] How are they freaks?

Shante: Because! Some of them old guys want you to touch them in places . . . You know what I'm sayin'?

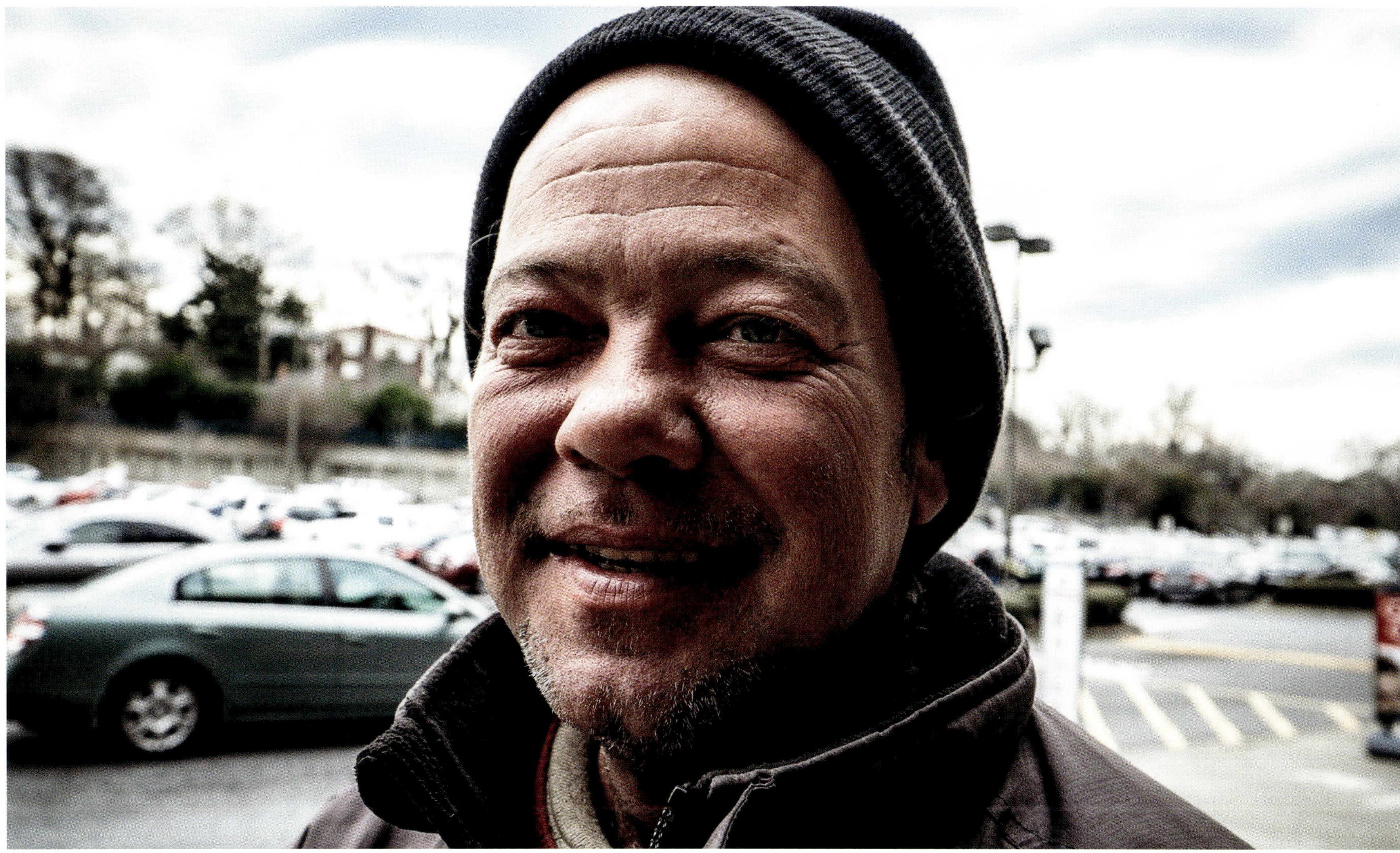

ATLANTA, GA – 2015-01-29

When I met Randy, he was looking for a hand in front of Home Depot on Ponce. He grew up in Wynne, Arkansas, and told me he'd always dreamed of moving to Atlanta. So he did, many years ago.

Randy: I moved here and got involved with a guy named Matt. We were together for nine years.

BW: That's a long time.

Randy: In gay years, that's like fifty-something years. [Laughing hard.] We used to live right over there by the Fox Theater.

He eventually died.

BW: How did he die?

Randy: He had HIV. He didn't have to die of it, though. They had health care up there on Ponce for free. He just didn't take care of himself.

BW: When did he pass away?

Randy: He died in 2006. It's been a while, but I still think about him 'cause it was the happiest time of my life. I wish he was here right now. I really did love the guy. I did. After all these years, I still love him.

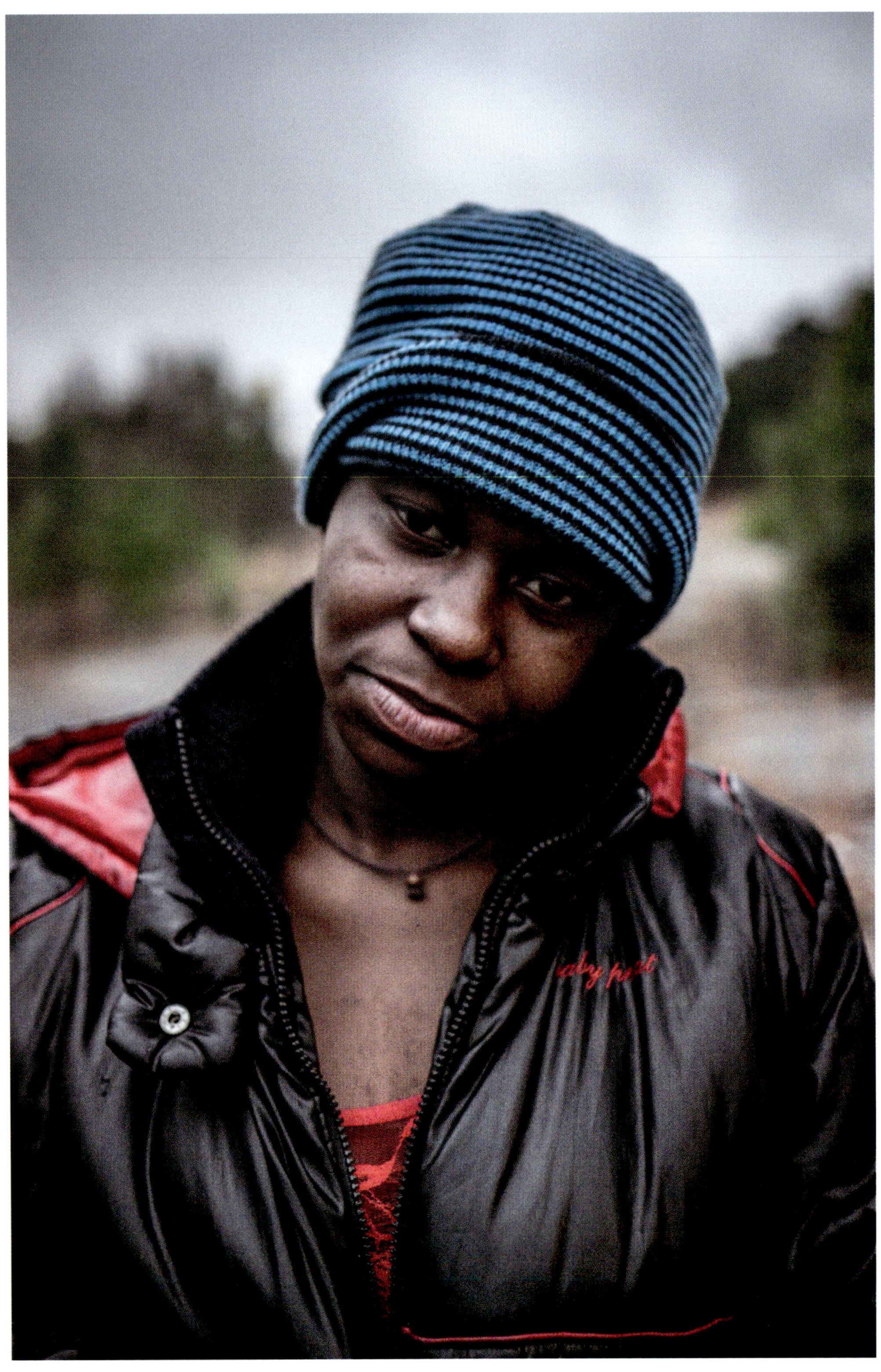

ATLANTA, GA – 2014-12-28

Dominique: My father and my auntie were on drugs. Now my father is a preacher. They are both clean. I guess it's just a test that the Lord sends us through. I know if my auntie and father can overcome it, I will too.

I've been on the street since I was twelve, and I've been on drugs since I was fourteen. I'm twenty-eight now.

BW: Why were you out of the house when you were twelve?

Dominique: I was getting molested by my stepdaddy from the time I was ten, eleven. My grandma looked in my eyes, and she knew something was wrong. I kept denying it. She kept asking me, and I started crying. She asked, "Has that man done anything to you?" I kept denying it, but I ended up telling her the truth.

My mama was standing there, and my mama asked me again. My grandma threatened her. She said, "Either you get him locked up, or I'm gonna get both of y'all locked up." She ended up getting him locked up, and he's still in prison to this day.

I took it out on my mama. I felt like she was against me 'cause I was the baby girl. She didn't believe me. Now that I'm older, I'm like, why would a child lie to you about something like that?

We were staying in the hood. I used to see girls walk by wearing heels and stuff with short pants or whatever. I got introduced to it [prostitution], so I ran away. They [tricks] used to ask me how old I was when I was twelve, and I would lie and say I was eighteen years old.

BW: So you've been a prostitute since you were twelve?

Dominique: Yeah. Metropolitan, Stewart Avenue, Chocolate City.

BW: Damn . . . What would you like to do if you could do anything?

Dominique: I like to sing.

BW: You should sing me something.

Dominique: Okay. (See p. 33.)

ATLANTA, GA – 2015-04-14

Meshell: I was a straight-up nympho from the time I was fourteen. I met my [now] ex-husband, and it was crazy, though. I would sneak out the house, steal the car, drive over to his house, do what we do, and come back home. Like, it was an everyday thing.

BW: Was he older than you?

Meshell: Yeah, he was twenty-one years older than me.

BW: Damn . . . What are you doing out here?

Meshell: I'm not gonna lie—I'm out here trying to make some money. I just got out of prison about five weeks ago.

BW: What were you in prison for?

Meshell: Violation of probation.

BW: Right, but what did you do?

Meshell: I was running an ad on Backpage and was dating out of the hotels.

BW: How'd they bust you?

Meshell: Another girl that does this had come and asked if she could rent my room during the day. I rented it to her, and I sold the dude dope and all that. Come to find out he was undercover. They got me for manufacturing and sales of crack cocaine, escortin' without a license, running a house of prostitution, paraphernalia.

BW: So they got you for pimping?

Meshell: Basically, yeah. Running a house of prostitution is basically just renting out a date house.

BW: Got it. How'd you get started as a prostitute?

Meshell: When I first started using [drugs], I was taking some friends back and forth to the truck stops. They'd pay me to sit there and watch for them. A truck driver walked up to me one day and said, "Hey, wanna make some money?" I said, "I don't do that." He said, "What if I gave you $100 just to give me some head?" I was like, "Let's do it!"

And from there, I thought, "If it's that easy, I can do this again."

Read part 2 of Meshell's story on p. 150.

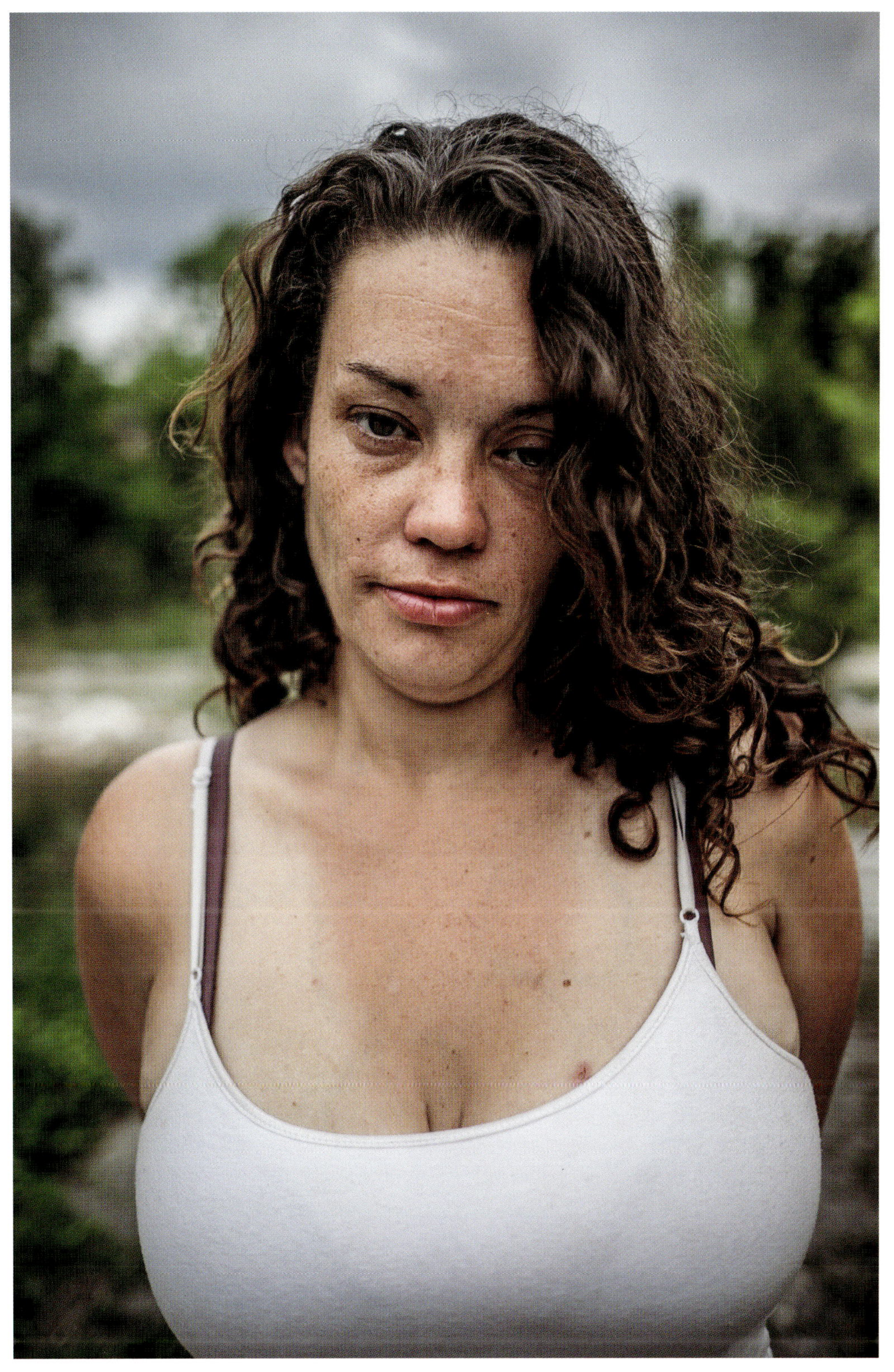

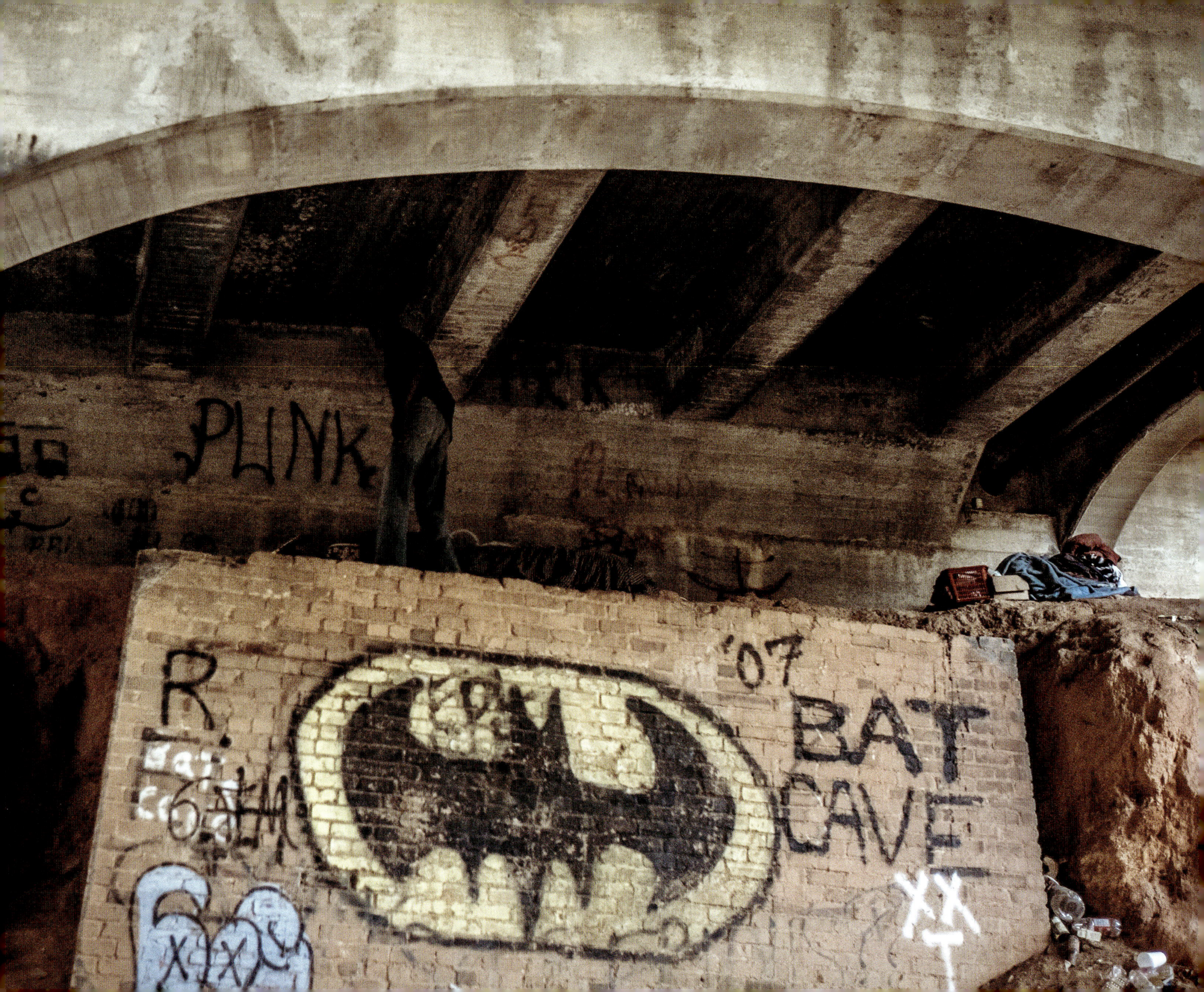
PUNK
R.
'07
BAT
CAVE

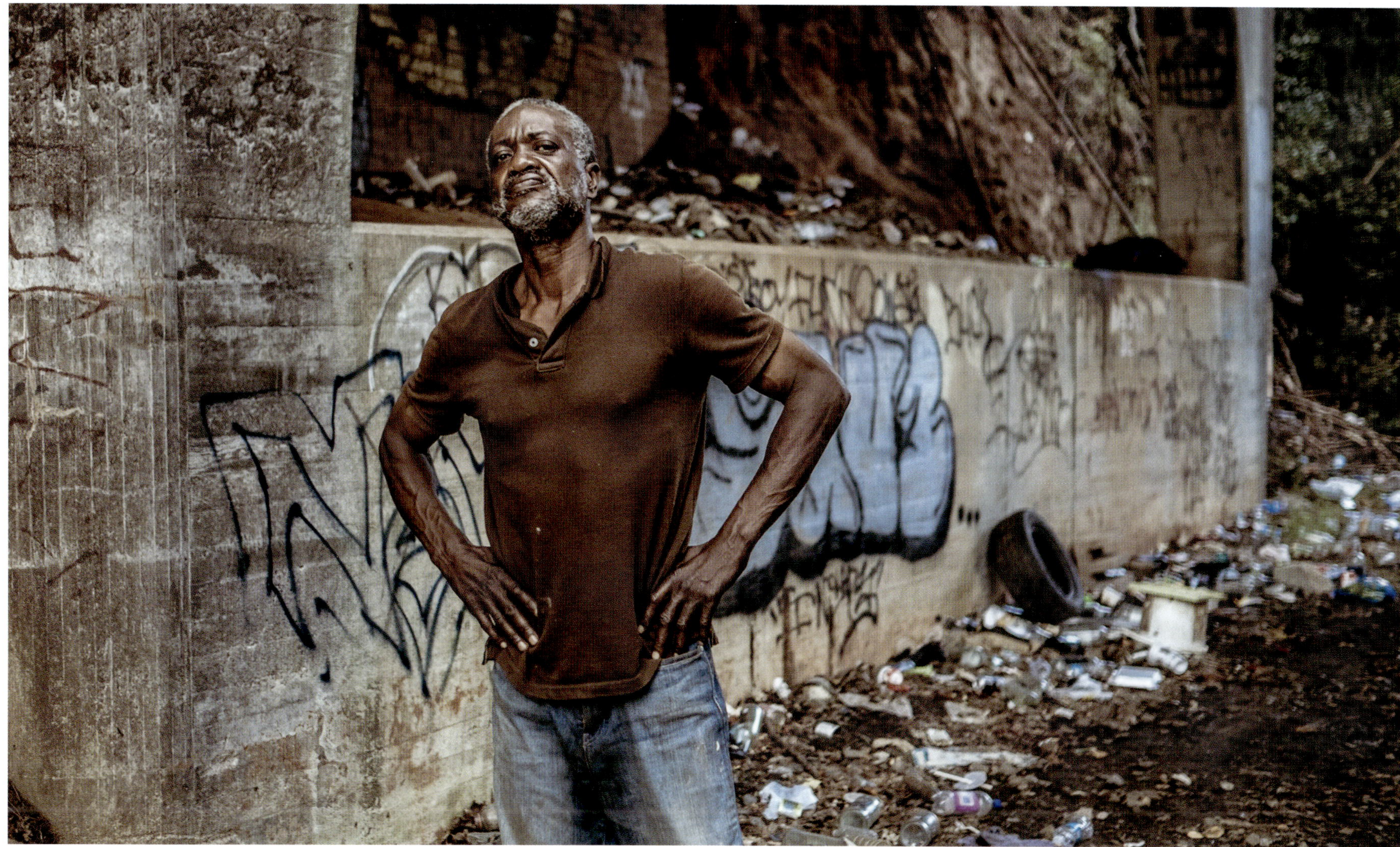

NEWNAN, GA – 2014-09-03

I was walking down some tracks by our place early one morning and came to a bridge I'd visited quite a few times. I started taking pictures of the graffiti and saw some movement in the shadows. I looked up, and there was Rambo.

BW: Mornin'.

Rambo: Hey, what you taking pictures for?

BW: My name's Brent, and I'm working on a book about people I meet in the South.

Rambo: I'll be right down. Let me take a piss. Rambo's got a story to tell you.

BW: Take your time.

Rambo: In 1996, a bullet came through the living room window and killed my mama dead. I found her. It made my mind different.

My aunt died ten years ago, and you're looking at the last person in my family. I ain't got nobody.

BW: That's tough. How long have you been outdoors?

Rambo: I been in the Batcave about ten years. That's ten years of summers and winters out here. That's why they call me Rambo, 'cause I can survive. People ask me, "Rambo, how you make it?" And I say, "With Jesus in your heart, you can survive anything."

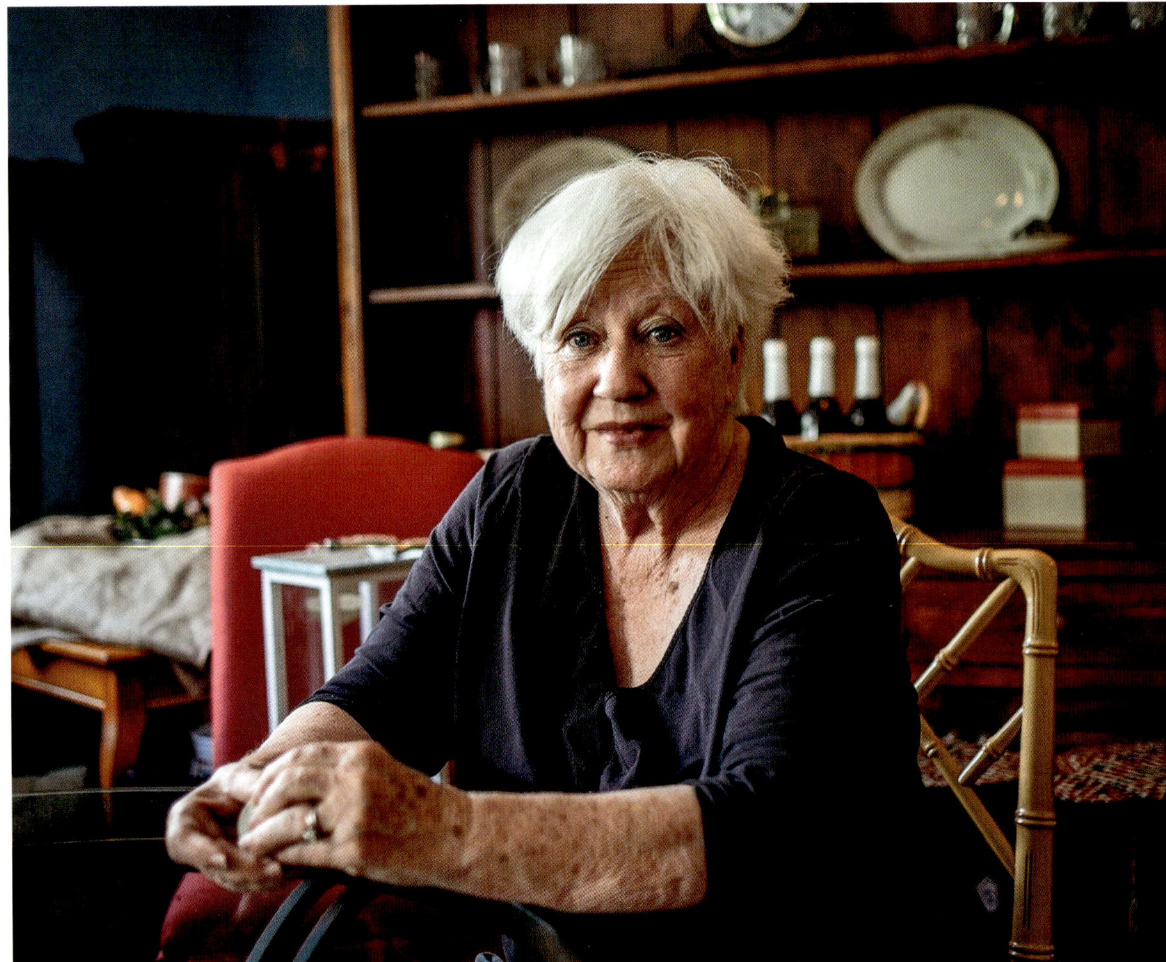

MORGANTON, NC – 2015-06-05

Sylvia: I met [my husband] when I was a senior in high school, and we were together for sixty years. I get lonely for my husband because there are little things that happen, and I'll say to myself, "Wait till he hears this. I've got to tell him that." And then, of course, I don't get to tell him, and I don't get to vent. My son will listen, but it's just not the same. My husband and I were on the same wavelength.

And we worked together too. People would say, "How do you manage that?" We just got along. We were in the antique business for many years together.

There's an old adage that says, "You don't know what you've got till you lose it." I always knew I had a good husband, but I always thought he depended on me more than I depended on him. That was the thing that was so surprising because I found out that wasn't true. I did depend on him a lot more than I thought I did.

Even though I had assumed a lot of the responsibilities in our old age, it was hard to get used to not having him to bounce things off of. Having to make single decisions is not good. I don't like it.

It was Thanksgiving Day, and my husband was so thrilled we were getting settled in our new apartment. He came out of the kitchen and leaned over. He looked like he was going to pick up a television to put it in the cabinet. I said, "Tommy, don't do that!" And he just keeled over on the floor, faceup. I thought he'd hit the back of his head, but he'd had a massive heart attack. We were living only three minutes away from the hospital, so they arrived very quickly. They flew him by helicopter to the hospital in Charlotte.

He was there five days. He never really came back again. Those people at that hospital were so good to me and my husband. They let me stay in the room with him the entire time.

He was on life support, and he was having constant seizures. When it came time, they finally told me I had to make a decision. They had tried everything they could, and nothing helped. So I finally told them when I was ready. The chaplain came and wanted to know if he could stay with me while they took the life support off. I told the chaplain no. It was a very private thing.

I didn't . . . I didn't know if I could do it or not. I figured I'd lose it completely, but some kind of strength came over me. The doctors told me it could take days after they took him off, but it only took about six minutes, and he was gone. But I sat there and held his hand while he passed.

It was the best thing I could have done, and I was glad I made that decision. It had been him and me for sixty years, and it was just me and him at the end. It was very peaceful.

As much as I miss him, and as much as his passing has changed my life, I know things worked out the way they should have, because I wouldn't want him to be where I am now without me. Not that I'm that valuable a person, but to him I was. I don't know that he could have managed or survived. I just think he would have been lost.

Read part 2 of Sylvia's story on p. 88.

Hallie: Bless her. That decision is so hard to make and watch. You don't want to let go, but you know it's best for your loved one. Glad there is an inner peace. My heart goes out to her.

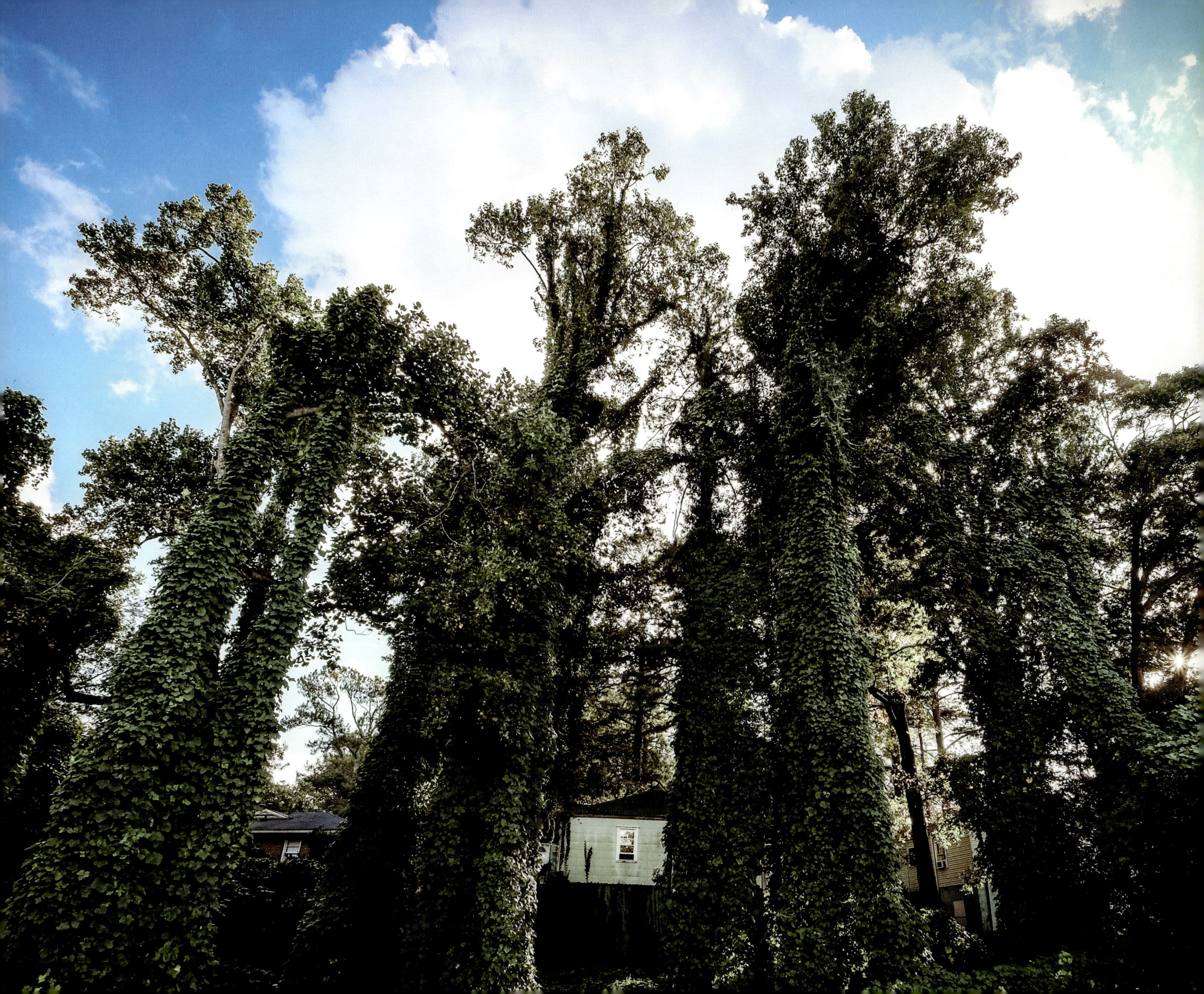

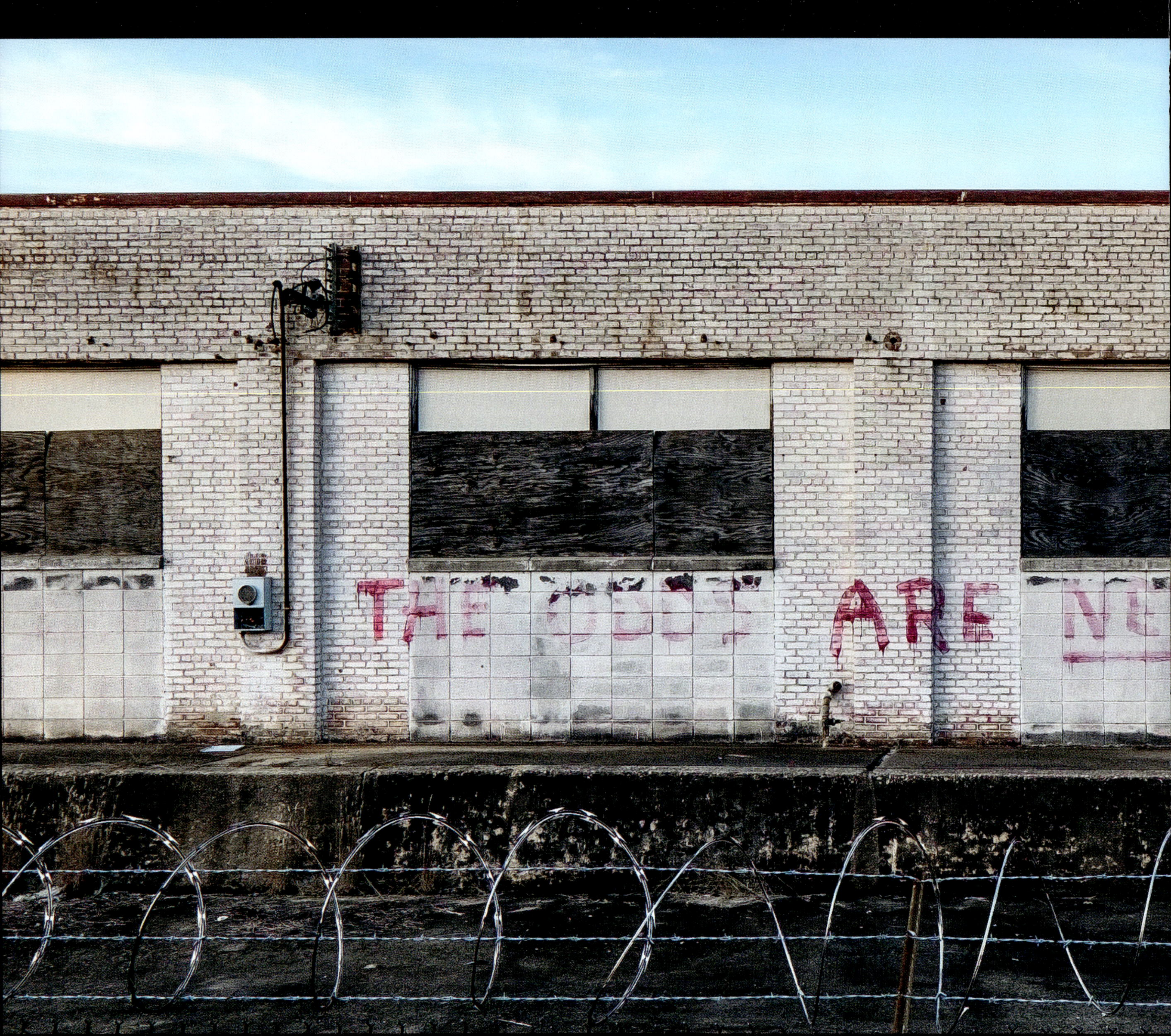
THE ODDS ARE

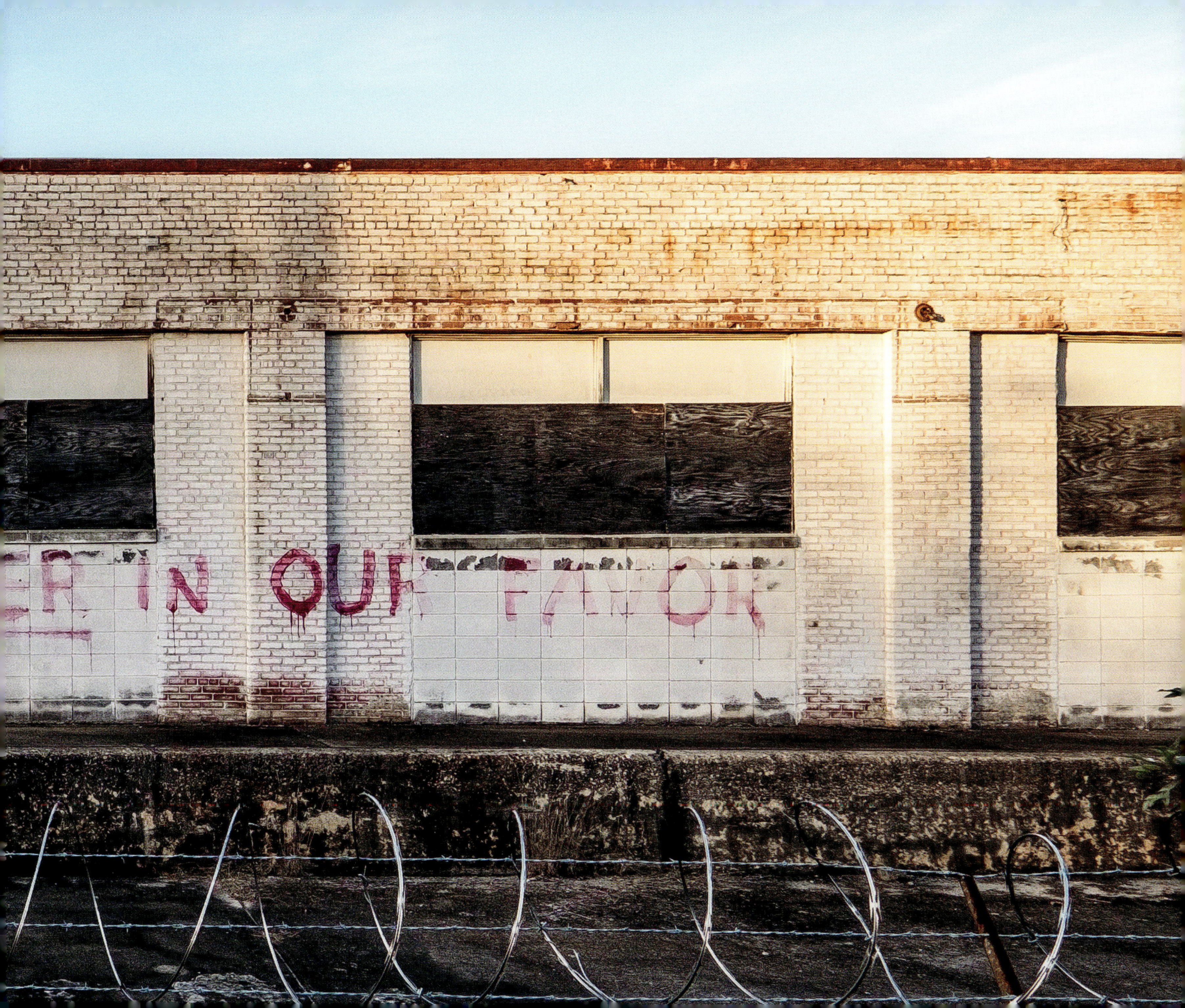
IN OUR FAVOR

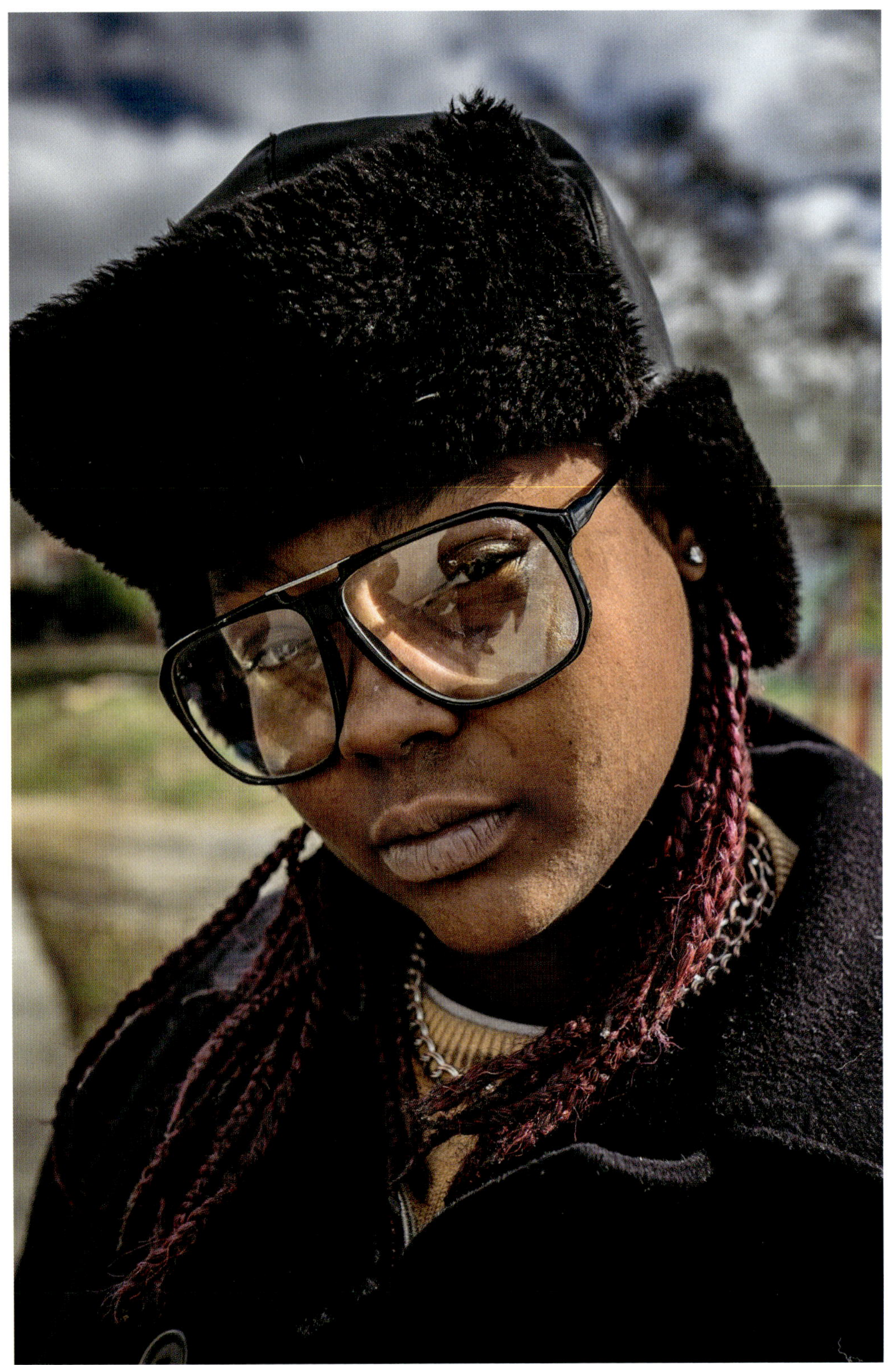

ATLANTA, GA — 2015-02-02

Michelle: I used to be a sex slave.

BW: When you were a kid?

Michelle: Yeah, in the Dominican Republic. I was sold into it by my father when I was six months old.

BW: Damn . . . So when did they make you start working?

Michelle: They would make girls start working between eight and twelve.

BW: How did you get away?

Michelle: I ran away when I was sixteen. I met an old white dude. He asked me what I wanted to do with my life. I told him I wanted to cook, and he took me away. And they killed him.

BW: They killed him?

Michelle: Yeah, he's dead. They found him over here. He used to be a big trick around here. Can we talk about something else?

BW: Sure. What do you want to talk about?

Michelle: You know what people think about you in this neighborhood? They think you full of shit. To be honest, it's known that when a white man comes over here, he's paying to be in control. He's paying to be dominant. He's not paying for my ass. He's paying for me to be his black slave. Yeah, you gonna pay me to do all the shit your wife refuses to do. So a lot of white men that come over here have black girlfriends.

That's just how we were trained. We were trained to get out here and sexually satisfy a man. That's the Dominican Republic. Regardless of what he want to do—if he want to stick his toes in your ass—you trained to do that. You are built, broken down, and rebuilt mentally from a child to an adult to tolerate that.

BW: You were brainwashed from the time you were a little kid until you came here, but you seem like a strong, independent woman. How did that happen?

Michelle: I'm a survivor and I'm skilled. Any more questions?

ATLANTA, GA – 2015-02-10

Barbara: I went through a lot of childhood stuff. I was the youngest of five and the only girl. I guess I was a trick baby, because she was getting high with the dope man when I was conceived.

Because of my mom's addiction, I was left alone with four brothers. I'm not able to have kids because I have scar tissue where they used to mess with me. I used to sleep with all my brothers because it was cold and we wouldn't have no heat. I used to do stuff with them for food.

BW: What do you mean?

Barbara: I mean . . . we didn't have shit. My mom was on dope real bad. My older brothers were able to go out and get food. They had girlfriends and friends they could get food from. So I was hungry, and I'd let them do stuff with me for food. That's why I hate being hungry so much now. I cry sometimes when I can't get money for food.

When I was a little older, my mom would let the dope man stay at our house. I think there were times when she would let them come upstairs and mess with me for a couple of hits. My room was right above hers, and I know she could hear everything that happened up there.

BW: How old were you when that happened?

Barbara: Ten, eleven, twelve. Then I started getting high when I was fourteen. There were a lot of things my mom and I never talked about. By the time I came down here to take care of her, she was clean. I just didn't want her to feel guilty and stuff. She used to brag about how well my brothers took care of me. She'd say, "Your brothers took good care of you. By the time I got home, they'd have so much [baby] powder on you. They gave you your bath and put you to bed." The truth is, they put powder on me to cover up all the bruises.

So I was hungry, and I'd let them do stuff with me for food. That's why I hate being hungry so much now. I cry sometimes when I can't get money for food.

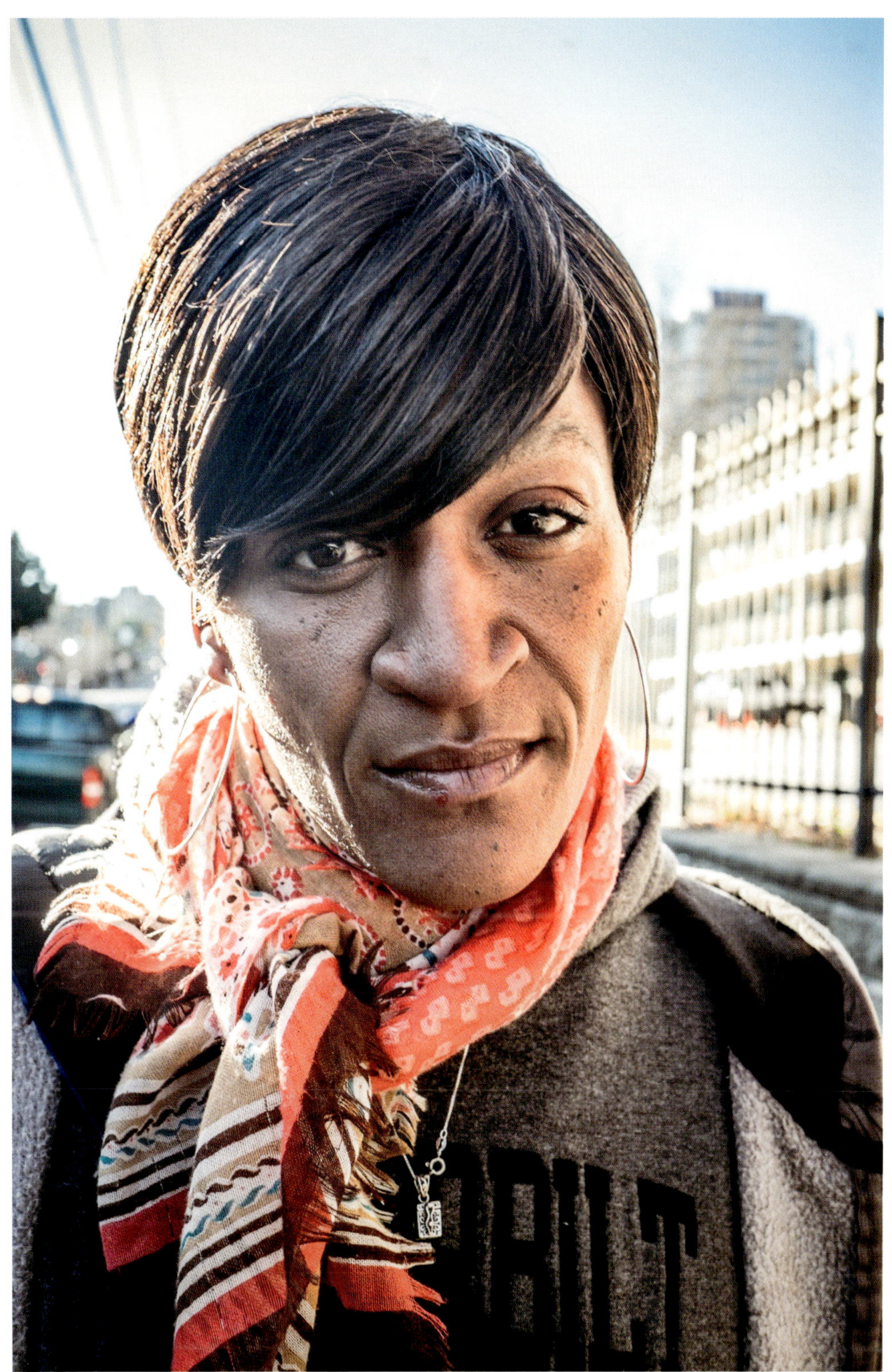

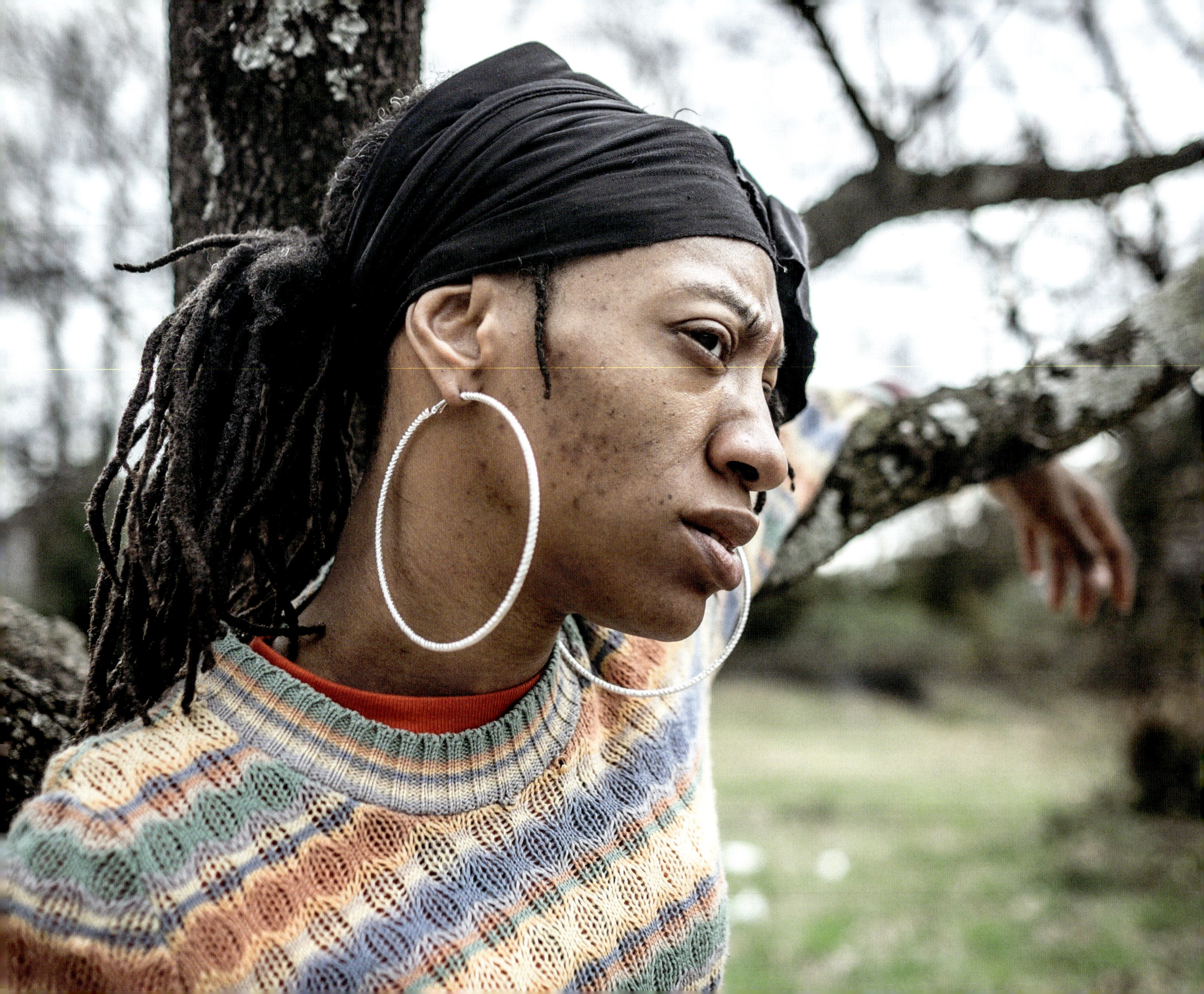

ATLANTA, GA – 2015-03-10

Tanyesa: I'm thirty-eight years old. I moved to Atlanta when I was twelve.

BW: What was it like growing up?

Tanyesa: Oh, I was super spoiled. My first recollection of Santa Claus was my [step] dad in a Santa Claus suit. So if my daddy's Santa Claus, you know I'm spoiled.

BW: So what happened when you moved to Atlanta?

Tanyesa: My mom and [step] dad were gonna get back together, but they didn't. She came to Atlanta to find a job and a place to stay. We moved to Austell, and I went to South Cobb High School.

I ended up getting my GED because I brought a gun to school when I was in ninth grade. People kept messing with me, and I kept getting suspended 'cause I kept getting in fights.

BW: How did you end up in this neighborhood?

Tanyesa: I've been in Pittsburgh [Atlanta neighborhood] since I was like twenty-five. I had started out dancing when I was twenty-one. Started snorting powder and drinking alcohol. I was a hot mess, honey. A hot one. But I made money.

One night I was dehydrated, and I'd been snorting too much powder and had to go to Grady Hospital. When I got out, I couldn't find my phone, my credit cards, or nothing. This guy came up to me and said he had somewhere for me to stay for the night. He took me up under the bridge. There was a little community there. They had everything you needed: bubble gum, condoms, everything. I ended up smoking crack for the first time that night.

BW: Rock changed everything?

Tanyesa: Yeah, pretty much. I used to cry when I couldn't get it.

BW: Has any day since you've been out here really impacted your life?

Tanyesa: Yeah, when my [step] dad passed a few years ago. Um . . . that shook me up a little bit.

Right after that, I found out about my biological father. When I did, it explained a lot to me. It explained my addiction a little bit. It explained why when things are going good I go off to the left somewhere and all hell breaks loose. My biological dad is schizophrenic.

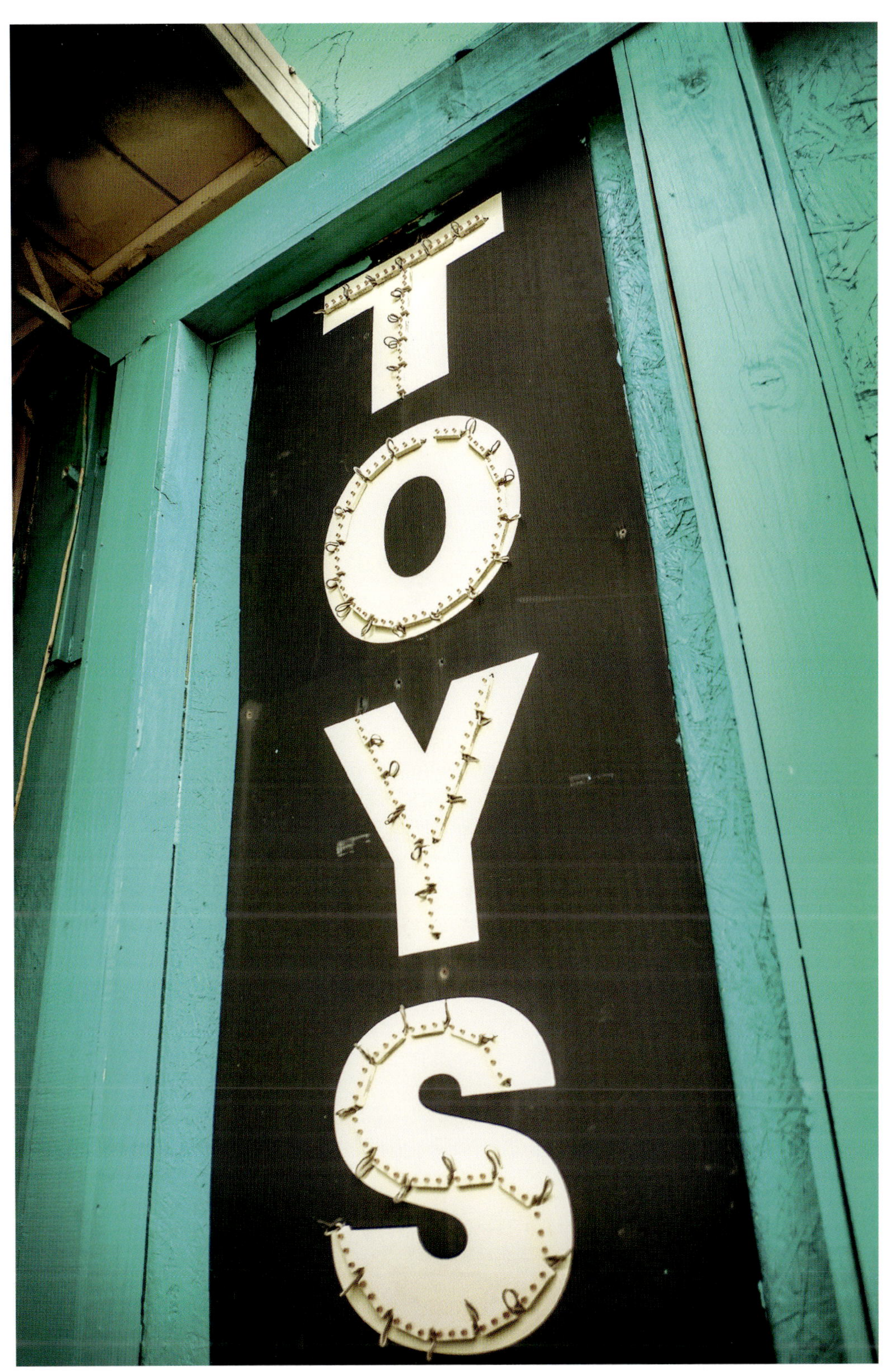

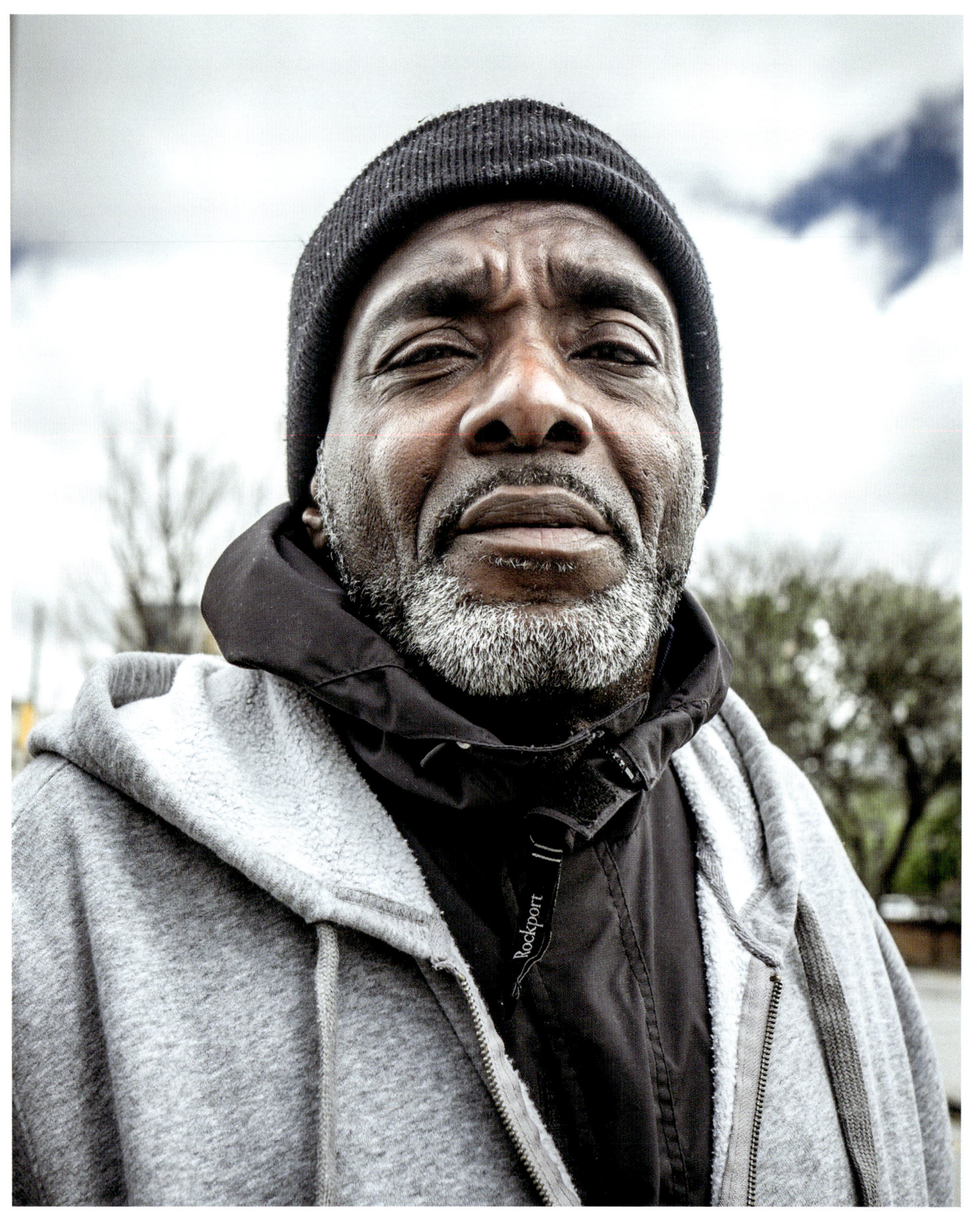

ATLANTA, GA – 2015-03-27

I met Jerome in front of the Greyhound station in Atlanta. That's where the hustlers hang out—seasoned pros who will tell you whatever it takes to get another hit. So when Jerome approached me with that desperate need in his eyes, I didn't have much hope that our conversation would yield anything real. But I did notice something about him, almost immediately, that indicated he was new to this life. I told him about the project, and he agreed to tell me an honest story.

Jerome: I'm just coming out of a nine-year marriage. I'd been wanting out for about five years, but I wouldn't leave until my daughter was out of the house. She turned eighteen, and she's in her first year of Alabama State.

It's very depressing when you're with someone you really love from the beginning, and then things happen that pull you apart, and the financial struggles come in. And, you know, you just can't find common ground.

BW: What do you think caused the breakup?

Jerome: Well . . . there was a number of things. First . . . our sexual relations. I'm hot-blooded, and she's cold. She had some things that transpired when she was a child that I think probably had an effect on her.

For the first four or five years, we were really focused on business. We ran two different businesses. We had a property management company and a residential remodeling company. We focused on that and maintaining our own rental properties. [The lack of intimacy] bothered me, but it wasn't as bad because we were busy.

But the more time we had to spend together, when things kind of slowed down, it just wasn't there. I made a lot of sacrifices, and I felt like I wasn't appreciated.

BW: It sounds like you were really well-off financially for a while there.

Jerome: Oh, very. Very well-off. Add that on to it—the crash of the housing market! You go from making in the $300s for about four or five years . . . We had the company doing $1.8 million at its peak, and then it all goes down the tubes.

BW: So we talked a little earlier about addiction . . .

Jerome: Yeah, I wouldn't wish this on nobody. I really wouldn't. It's formed a wedge between myself and everybody else. You don't let nobody get close to you. Me personally, I'm shame based, and I have a lot of guilt associated with it. It's a perpetual cycle. Just knowing that you're really out of character and that you can't be free.

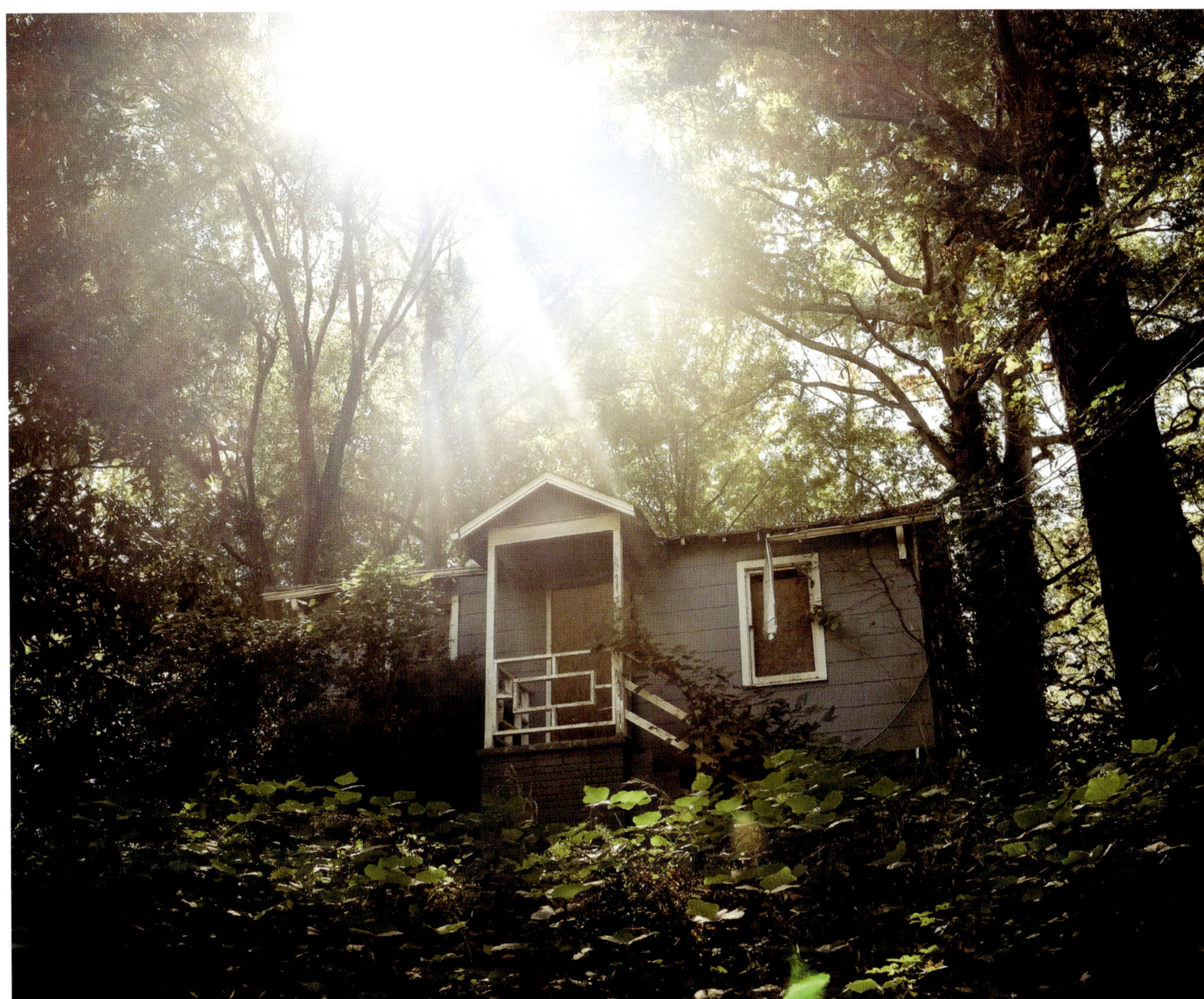

BW: When did that start for you? During the marriage?

Jerome: Well, it actually started before we got married. I told her about it one day. We were riding down the street, right before we got married, and we were looking at some guys who were homeless. She made some comment about him, and I said, "There but for the grace of God go I." I told her about my past. She didn't want [to know]. She said she didn't see any of that in my character or how I presented myself.

So it was about eight or nine years in, after we started going through struggles, that I started using again. My dishonesty from cheating . . . You know, you're cheating on a woman who you really love, and then you got to come home and look at her . . . the guilt . . . Phew, it's a hell of a thing, and you don't get it out. It took me back. It got to the point where I felt so bad, to where hitting a piece of crack was a relief for the weight on my shoulders. In reality, it just opened a door for a hell of a lot worse to come in.

Jerome and I talked for a while longer. I asked him what would help, and he said that just talking about it was helpful. I felt a strong connection to him and his story. I gave him a few bucks for his time, and he immediately shot behind the building to get his fix. As I left, I couldn't help but think, "There but for the grace of God go I."

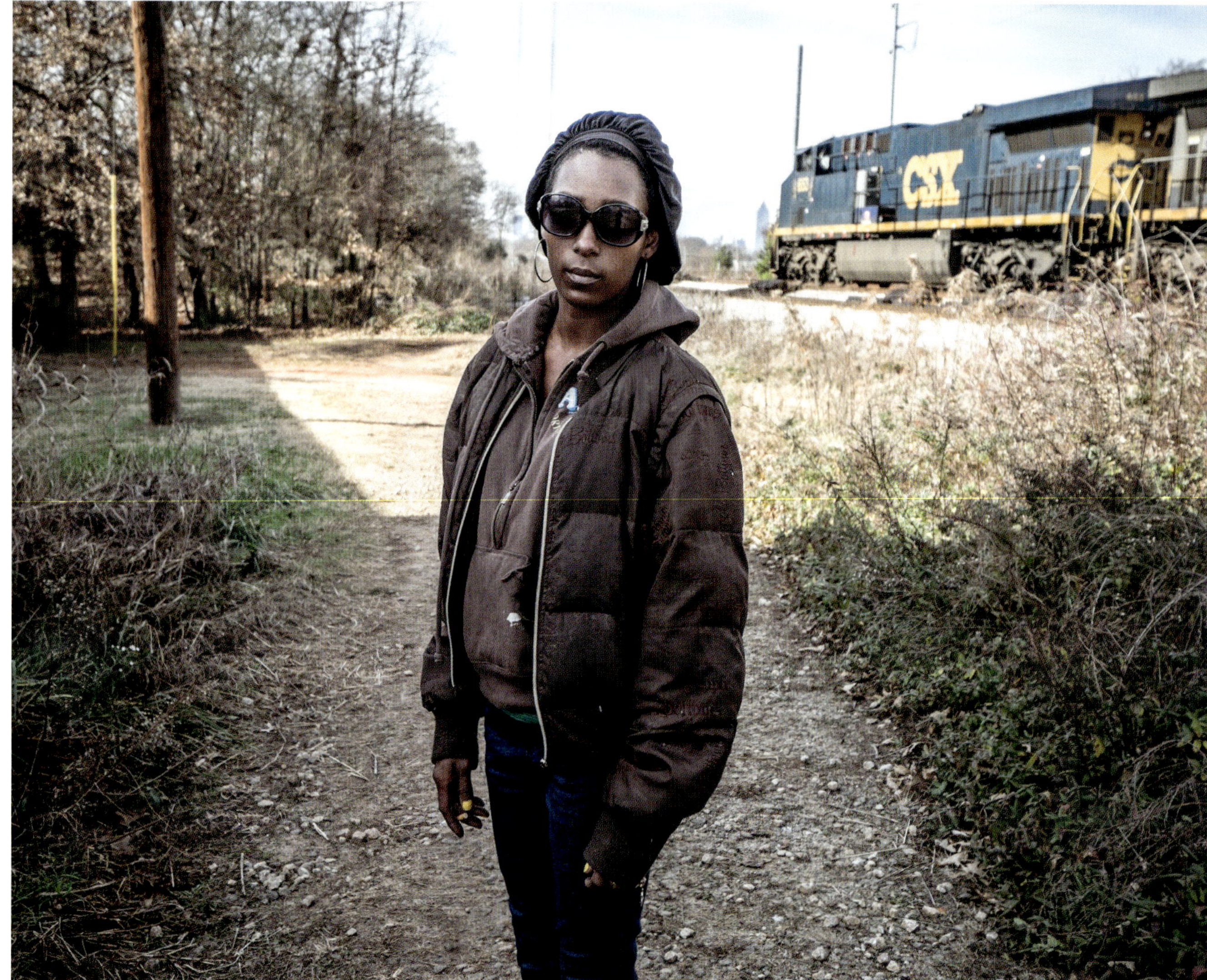

ATLANTA, GA – 2014-12-17

BW: How did you get started using heroin?

Tory: I've been on it for four years. My ex-boyfriend put me on heroin. We were dating, and he had been on it. He just introduced me to it, and I ended up liking it. After liking it, my body became addicted to it. Now I need it so I don't get sick.

I used it on my own free will [tears], but how could you possibly put someone you care about on that shit? It's very selfish if someone does. You know? I wouldn't do that to anyone.

It destroys your mind, and you have to work ten times harder to get your mind back. You play yourself the whole time, thinking your mind's still the same. But you're really in a delusion. It's very selfish when you do drugs.

BW: You mentioned you have two children. Do you think your addiction affects your kids?

Tory: I know it does. [Tears.] Like right now, I'm supposed to be checking myself into treatment.

BW: Huh . . . Why don't we just go now? It's no coincidence that I show up today and am willing to take you. This is your chance.

Tory: [Pausing.] Okay. I'll do it.

We started driving to the treatment center.

BW: What's the scariest part about going to treatment?

Tory: Just not being able to do drugs. Know what I mean? Sometimes it's stronger than my will and my want to stop. Even though [tears] at the end of the day, you don't really know what you're chasing. Like right now, I just keep thinking about one more hit. But I'll never get there. I'll always just want one more hit.

We pulled over before we got to the treatment center.

Tory: Can I push my stem and hit it one more time while we're here?

BW: Rock?

Tory: Yeah . . .

BW: You can do whatever you want.

Tory: [After the hit.] Do you think you could help me write my own book?

BW: I'll help you in any way I can. What do you want to do?

Tory: I want to write a book about my life—how I went from the "it" girl to an addict.

We stopped and picked up some notebooks so she could start writing her story. When I left her at the facility, she was rapidly jotting it all down. I hope to see her book someday or even just hear that things are better.

About 15 years ago, Portugal had one of the worst drug problems in Europe. Instead of continuing a failed war on drugs, they chose to decriminalize. Funds that would have otherwise been used to arrest and jail addicts are now being used to reconnect them with society. This approach has resulted in a 50% reduction in intravenous drug use. [3]

"The opposite of addiction is not sobriety. It is human connection."

—Johann Hari

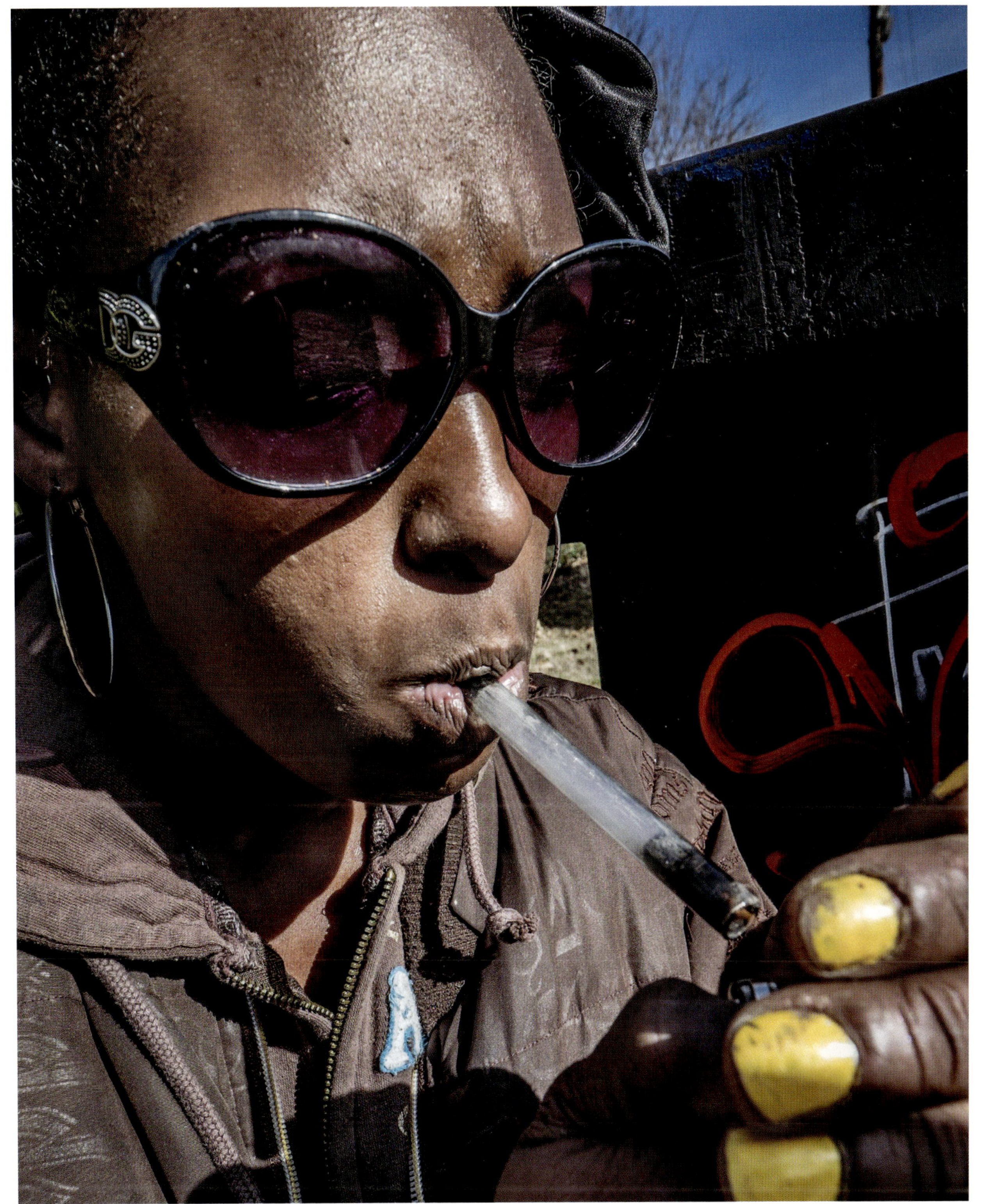

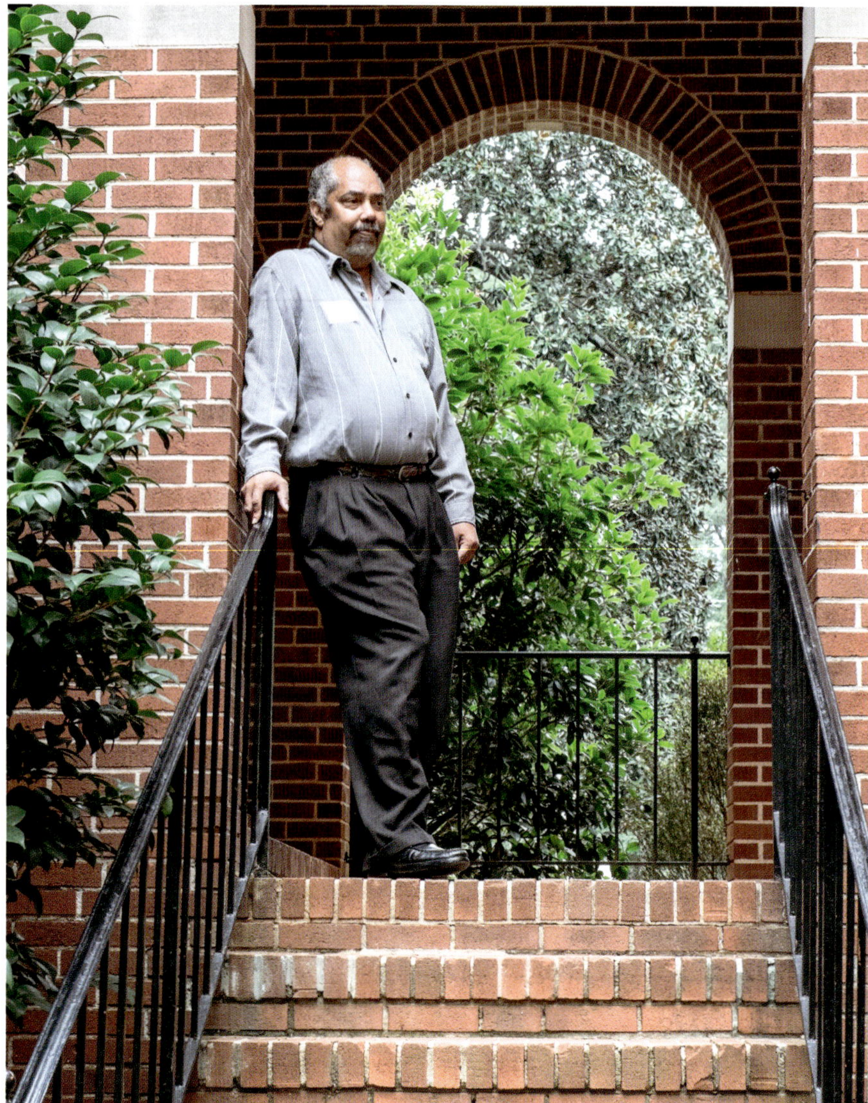

ATLANTA, GA – 2015-08-29

Marshall: I used to be an addict. When I got to treatment, I was taking my first shower in about six weeks. When I came out of the shower, this guy who had been in treatment for a while had this boom box. He had a Michael Jackson song playing. I had heard this song a thousand times when I was getting high but never listened to the words. The song was "Man in the Mirror." I just started crying. I made a promise to God that day that if he helped me get my life back I would dedicate my life to helping people out of bad situations. I've lived my life to keep that promise ever since I made it.

BW: How long ago was that?

Marshall: [It was] 1998. The place that helped me get off the streets was Central Presbyterian. All the other churches around English Avenue told me they didn't have any programs to help me—twenty-three different churches.

These people stopped to talk to me one day. They knew just from looking at me I was an addict. They told me about this lady named Carol—said she could help me. They told me I had to get there early to be seen, so I made it my business to walk from the Bluff to downtown and be the first person in line at 5:00 a.m.

BW: What got you there? What made you want to stop?

Marshall: I got sick and tired of being sick and tired. At one point, I thought I was gonna die. I was ready to commit suicide.

I don't share this with many people, but my mother committed suicide in active alcoholism. I had to identify her body. She jumped from that white apartment building across from the Arts Center train station. You know, they have the glassed-in patios. They glassed them in after she jumped from the seventeenth floor. She just got tired, like I was.

When I went to Central Presbyterian that morning to see Carol, I had a .38 strapped to my ankle. I told her if she couldn't help me that day I was gonna walk out back of that church and shoot myself in the head 'cause I just couldn't do it no more.

I'd been sleeping on the streets at that time for three weeks in abandoned houses. One of the houses was right next to the drug dealer. There was feces and piss all over the floor, but I ended up staying in that house through outpatient treatment. They tried to put me in some shelters, but they were getting high at the shelters. So I stayed in that house. The drug dealer was actually happy for me. He said, "I'm really happy you getting clean 'cause you helped me buy my new Cadillac." He even fed me.

I knew I had to stay clean. I looked like a skeleton. I weighed 127 pounds when I went to treatment. I hadn't looked in a mirror in six months, and when I did, I didn't recognize myself.

BW: I know you do a lot of work with people on the streets. Can you tell me about what you do when you're out there?

Marshall: HIV testing, [and] I have overdose-reversal kits with me. I just got an organization to donate some pregnancy test kits. I offer them a way off the streets, if they want it. I use the harm reduction approach. I don't try to make anybody do anything. I just let them know that when they're ready, give me a call—no matter what time, day or night. I meet people right where they're at and have frank conversations with them. I don't force my views or my values on anybody. I just treat them with unconditional love. I don't try to save nobody, but I'm there when they're ready to save themselves.

People know that I really care. I talk to them, hug them. I don't care what they been doing or what they smell like or what drugs they been doing. I hug everybody, and they know when I hug them it's a hug of love. I don't judge them. It's unconditional. I'll love them whether they get clean or not.

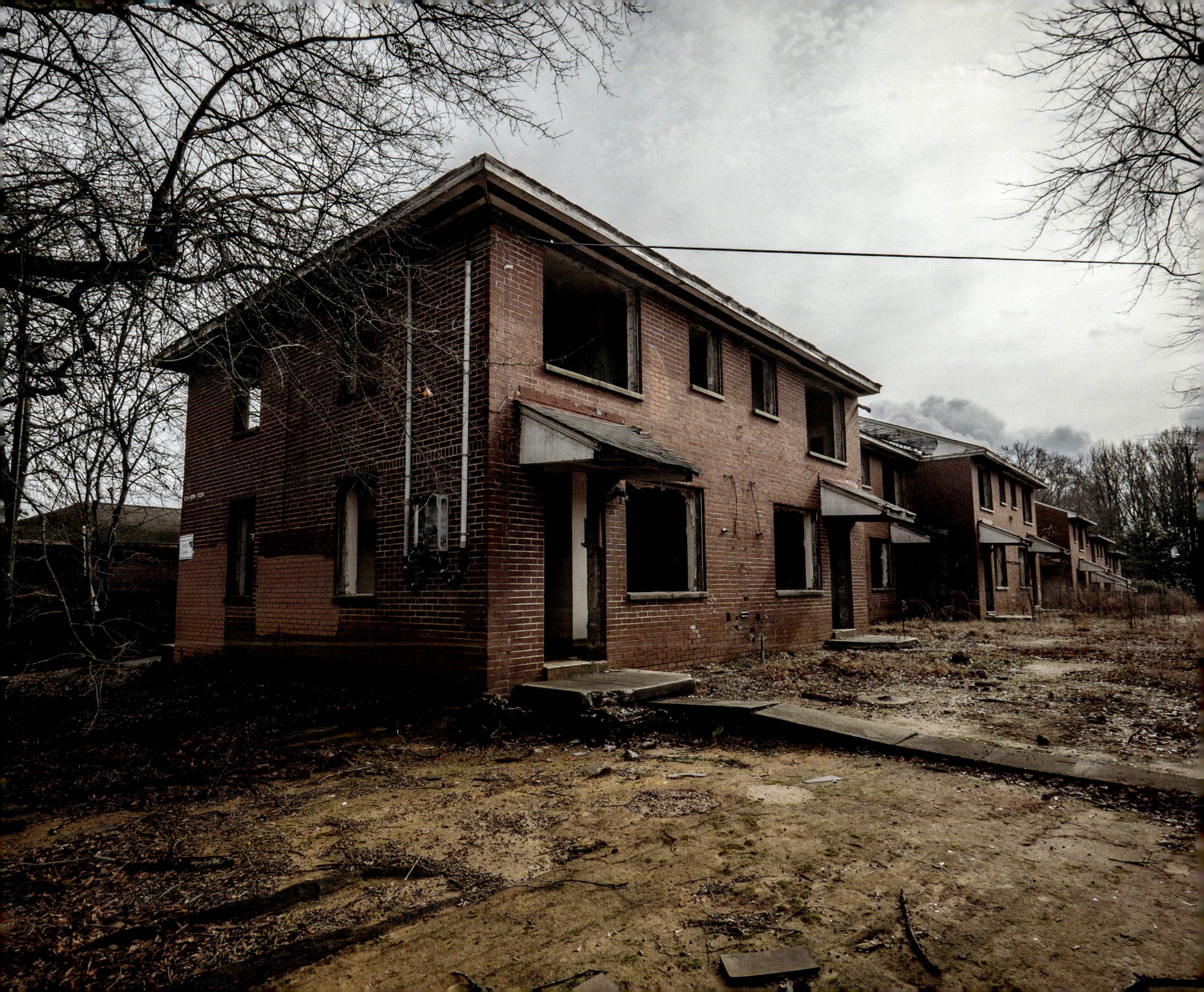

God, grant me the serenity to accept the things I cannot change,
The courage to change the things I can,
And the wisdom to know the difference.

—*The Serenity Prayer, Reinhold Niebuhr*

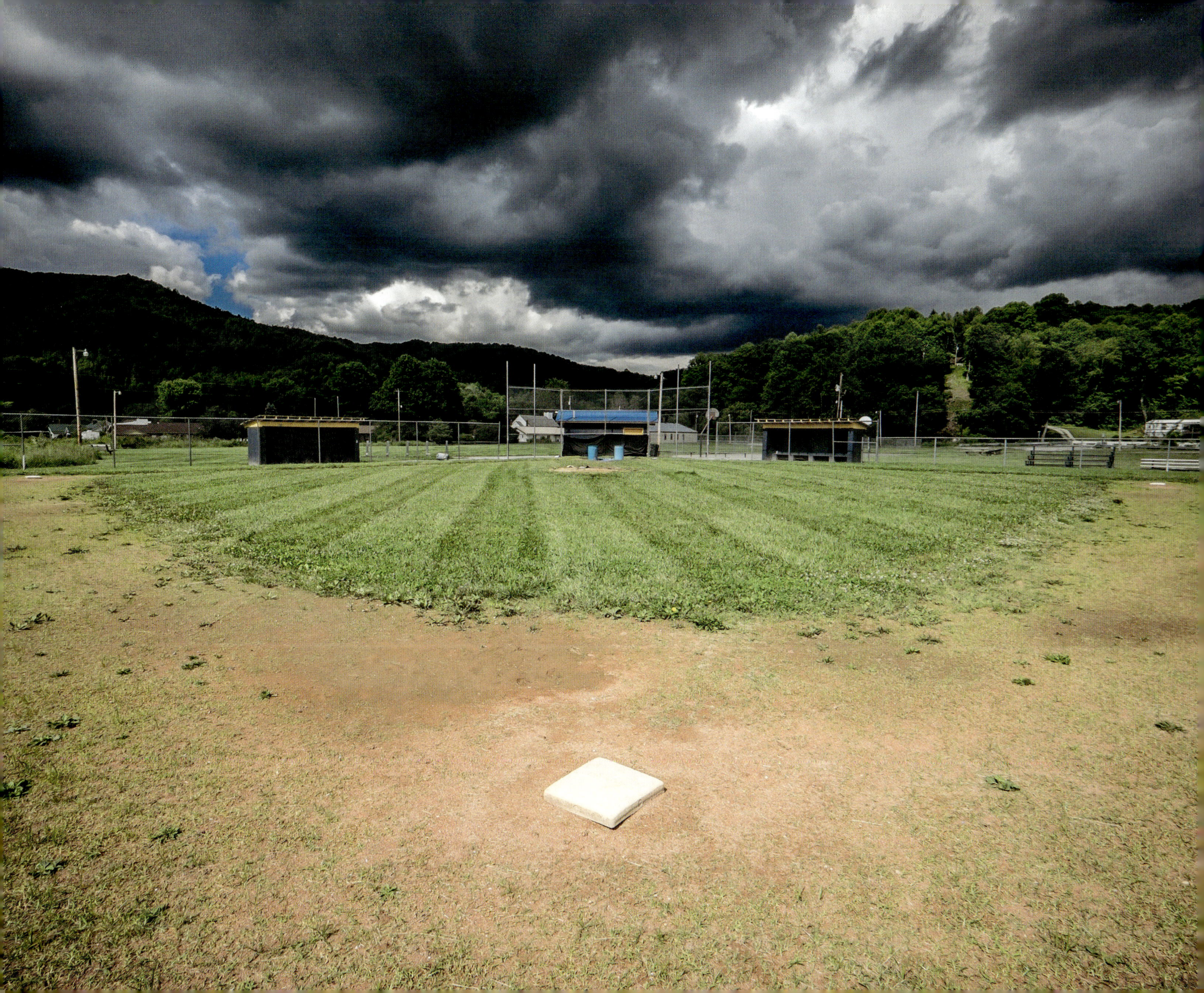

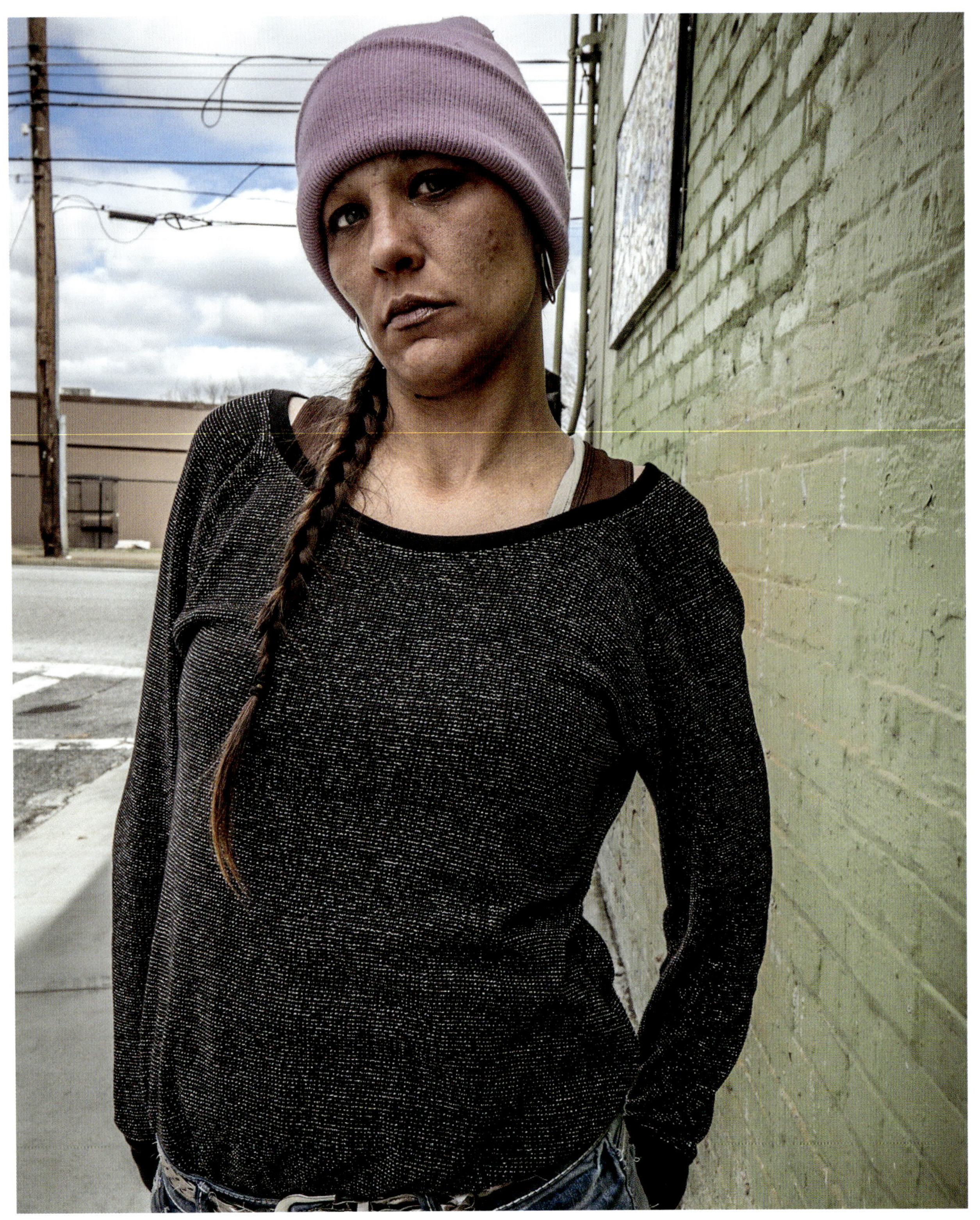

ATLANTA, GA – 2015-03-06

Lydia: I've been through hell since I moved to Georgia [from Birmingham].

BW: Why did you move here?

Lydia: Honestly . . . to detox and get clean off heroin.

BW: Judging by the neighborhood you're in, I'm guessing it didn't work out.

Lydia: It worked for a little while, and I'm actually in the process of trying to get back off of it. I'm working on getting together a deposit to get a room at a boarding house.

There's a person that's making me want to change my life, and that's my son.

BW: How old is he?

Lydia: [Sobbing.] He'll be five months old at the end of this month. I didn't even know I could have kids. I'm thirty-one years old. I mean, I've gotten pregnant before but haven't ever successfully held a child past three months.

When I came here in September, I was clean for ninety days, and then I relapsed. Then right after my relapse, I found out I was pregnant. I wasn't able to completely get myself back off the dope, so I ended up having to sign my son over to my mom in order to keep him out of foster care.

So it's kind of been a hectic thing. But God kind of put his hand on Sean, because he wasn't born with anything in his system. He didn't have to be detoxed.

BW: Is your mom in Birmingham?

Lydia: No. She's actually right down the road from here. That's why I stick around this area. Every now and again, I'll see my mom and get a glimpse of my son. She won't let me come and visit him, which is understandable, 'cause I'm not doing right. And . . . I'm trying. It's just hard. People who haven't been in my position wouldn't understand why I do what I do or why it's so hard for me.

BW: What would you like to tell your son?

Lydia: I would want him to know that even though it seems I'm choosing the drugs over him, it's really not the case. [Sobbing.] I don't know . . . I just . . . I don't know where to start to even get right. It's not really stopping using the drugs that I need to deal with as much as why I use the drugs in the first place.

BW: Why is that?

Lydia: Um, I don't know for sure . . . but I'm assuming that it . . . uh . . . probably has something to do with events from my childhood.

BW: Were you molested?

Lydia: Um, yes. But it's not really so much being molested as much as by who it was. That's the hardest thing for me.

My mom was a drug user as well. She started using crack when I was a kid. I have six siblings. They're all younger than me. So I ended up being a mom at a very young age. I didn't want to see my younger brothers put into foster care, so I got emancipated. I was made a legal adult when I was sixteen in the state of Alabama and got custody of my two youngest brothers.

BW: Ironic that your mom has custody of your son now and you had custody of her two kids.

Lydia: Yeah. Different drug but same situation.

BW: Who molested you?

Lydia: I mean, it was more than one person. But it's the first one that's the hardest for me.

BW: I'm sorry. Do you remember when it started?

Lydia: I think I was about three or four, and it went on until I was about ten. At that point, I started rebelling against the situation. I started realizing that what was going on was wrong and that it did not happen to everybody. It wasn't something that should be happening. So once I realized that, I quit being so cooperative, and he stopped. He backed off.

BW: Did you ever tell anybody?

Lydia: Um, no, I didn't. My mom knows now. She kind of had an idea it was happening, but she wasn't for sure. Last year I actually told her myself.

BW: Do you think you'll ever forgive him?

Lydia: I've actually already forgiven him because I understand he is not a well person. He's very sick.

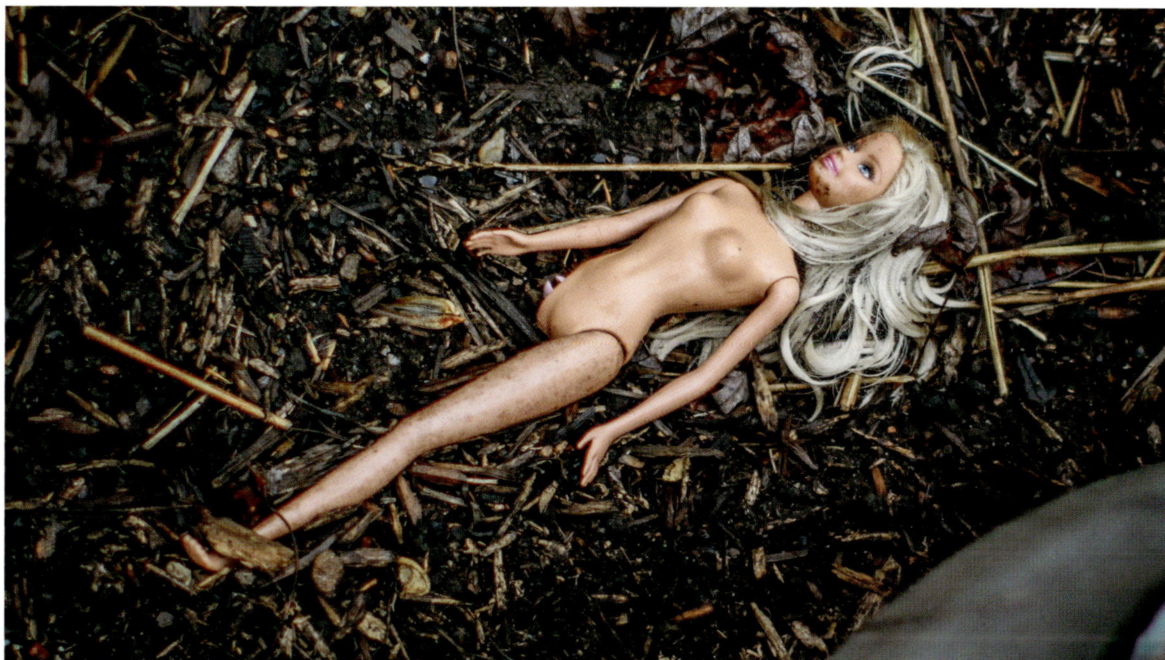

Marissa: You came right out and asked if she was molested? Do you have any experience working with victims of sexual abuse? And it seems like you kept pushing her. By reading this, it's obvious she didn't want to talk to you about it. Please be cautious. You don't want to make matters worse.

BW: I did ask her because I knew. I would have bet anything. She actually did want to discuss it. She brought up that it wasn't the addiction, it was what's behind the addiction, which is true (always). I don't push anyone, ever. I intentionally did not mention the person who she said did it and also left out other intimate details. I take no joy in being right in my assumption, but that is the number one thing that I hear from women that I meet on the street. One of the purposes of this project is to bring these things out of the shadows and in to the light.

One thing that she did say to me before we parted ways was that she didn't expect the conversation to get as deep as it did, but that she felt lighter, like a burden had been lifted. This isn't a magic bullet or a cure, but it certainly can help begin the process of healing.

Ana: A lot of victims go silent until someone asks them about their past and their demons. Sometimes it takes saying it out loud to get it on the right path.

Jessica: Shame is silence. No one asks, ever. Good for you for reaching out to another human being in pain.

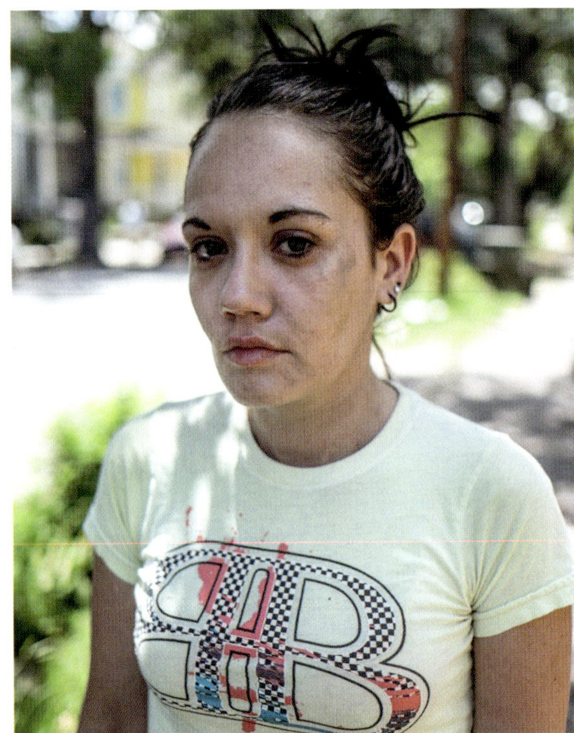

SAVANNAH, GA – 2015-05-23

Lindsey: I'm having a very terrible day. I moved up here like a year ago to be with my dad. He's a crack addict, and he said he was doing good and going to meetings. But, um, he's not doing good.

So I moved in with some other people who weren't the best of people to be around for me. And to be honest with you, like 50 of them just got indicted. One of them was my best friend, my boyfriend's brother . . . So pretty much my whole world was just kinda ripped from me recently. It's just hard right now.

BW: Do you have a place to stay?

Lindsey: Um, I'm staying with a guy just because, honestly, I just needed a place to stay. And he's not a bad guy, he's just . . . I don't love him, and I'm emotionally kind of . . . I mean, he's like sixty years old. Not like that's a bad thing, but I'm thirty, and I just . . .

BW: So what about you? Do you have an addiction?

Lindsey: Opiates and like, I've done the uppers, and I've done everything. You would think that having a dad that kinda showed me what not to do, I wouldn't have done it, but I did. But, um, mostly opiates. Oxys, Dilaudid, all that fun stuff—till it's not fun.

Methadone used to be my thing, but I stopped cold turkey when I moved up here. For two months, I was literally insane. I didn't sleep for fourteen days, and then when I did sleep after that, I was hot, cold. Like, I got agoraphobic. I couldn't go outside the house. It was horrible.

BW: I know when I was using, I was trying to kill pain. Is there pain you're trying to kill?

Lindsey: My dad had a lot to do with it, growing up. He's the type of addict that will have it all together, and he's the funnest, greatest guy in the world. And then he'll disappear in the streets for years at a time or until he gets caught, ends up in prison or jail. Then he does good for a while, gets his shit together, and then . . .

BW: Do you resent your dad?

Lindsey: Honestly? No, because I know he has a disease. I've been in meetings. I know it's cunning and baffling and powerful. And it wasn't about me. But when I was little, I thought, "If only I was funnier, if only I kept Dad's interest more, he wouldn't want to leave me for drugs."

BW: What would you need to get back from being lost? And I don't mean like a specific place, I just mean like . . .

Lindsey: I don't even know what's the first step to take anymore, honestly. Like I don't . . . ugh, I don't know.

BW: You said you've been to meetings before?

Lindsey: It worked when I went. I mean, it really did. It helped me a lot. It's just my willingness isn't there. And then, you know, you fill your thoughts with so many fake people who talk about . . . You know, it's like high school. It's just . . . I know that's not real either. It's just me not wanting to put in the work.

I do believe that was the only way I really stayed clean and happy and content and peaceful. I mean, I know there's a lot to work on—the steps and stuff—but it's the only time I felt good since I ever started using.

BW: How long did you stay sober?

Lindsey: Two and a half years.

BW: That's a long time. How did you start back?

Lindsey: They sent my dad back to prison for something he did four years prior. He was clean with me. We went to a meeting every morning together, and I went to my little nighttime younger-people meeting and hung out with my friends. It had become a way of life for me. Then . . . it tore me up. I mean, it *tore* me up. I think the same night they took him in, they took him from court to jail, then from jail to prison. I just broke down. I got high that same night.

BW: Everything that has to do with your sobriety and your addiction seems to tie back to your dad.

Lindsey: I know.

BW: You love him a lot, don't you?

Lindsey: Yeah.

BW: And he let you down.

Lindsey: [Softly.] Like every guy. But yeah, he did.

BW: I'm sorry.

Jay: There is a quote I once read that said, "A girl has a dad so that she knows not every guy is like the one who breaks her heart." I always found that quote bittersweet because for some of us, it is our dads who break our heart, and we never know or expect any different. Sigh. Chin up, beautiful girl. It will get better someway, somehow, someday.

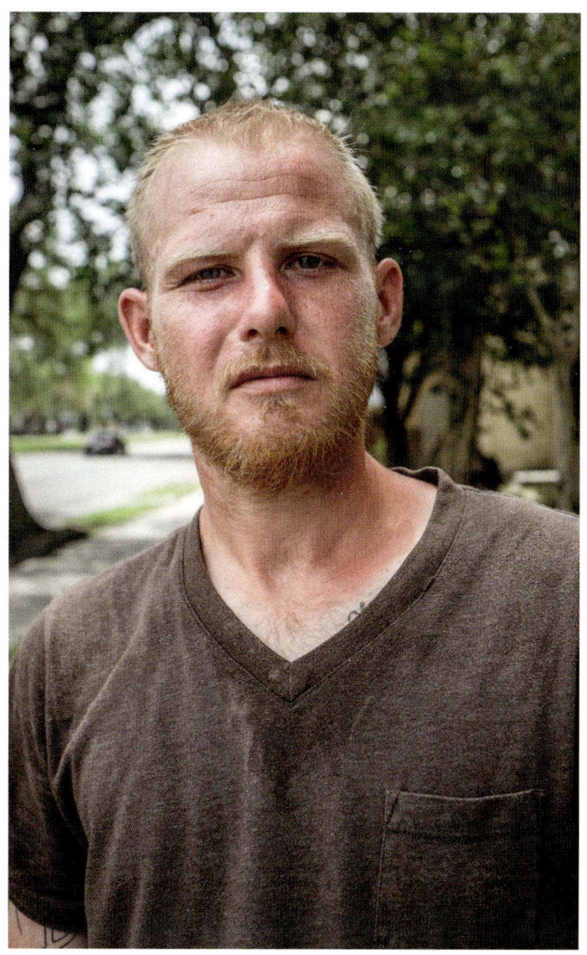

NEW ORLEANS, LA – 2015-05-11

She had absolutely no control over me. I was petrified of my father. I would get away with a lot of shit because my mom was afraid to tell my father because he'd beat the fuck out of me. He only used his fists twice, but you can still abuse a child with a belt.

Lloyd: I've always had a problem with authority. I don't like someone standing over me, telling me what to do and all that. So when I joined the Navy, it didn't go well. I started to get real mad at the world and everything. I was already using drugs, which is a no-no in the military. People found out I was using, and some of them would hit me up on the side and ask me to get them stuff. You're in the military. You're not supposed to know how to get that stuff. Well, I did.

So in the beginning, it was just me helping my friends get their little drugs. Turned out there were a lot of people who wanted drugs. So I said, "Well, fuck—I'm gonna start taxing them." Before I know it, I'm dealing, bad.

I've made twenty to twenty-five grand in a night before. I'm on the Internet for one robbery for $15,000. It took me a few minutes to make that. I robbed people often, a few times a week.

BW: So you were still in the military when you were robbing people?

Lloyd: Well, no . . . The ones I got convicted for were after the military.

BW: Okay, tell me how you used to do it.

Lloyd: I can tell you about one that I got arrested for because I already did my time.

BW: Go for it.

Lloyd: So we're plotting on this night club, and we know the setup and the layout of it. It was on High Street in Portsmouth, Virginia. We got there at like four, and we watch the place. Eventually all the employee vehicles are leaving. We wait until there's one vehicle left. Two guys come out the back door, and when they're turning to lock it, we run up on them, tell them to unlock the door, pull them back in the club. I was in the office with one of the guys. I had my gun out, and it just so happened that they had all the money out, doing the count for the night.

I loaded all of it up. The guy in the office was just devastatingly scared. Man, I felt bad for him. I didn't put much thought into it. I never seriously considered using the gun. The gun just ensured that I wasn't gonna have any kind of problem. I didn't point it at him or nothing. I just held it at my side, making sure nobody did anything stupid. I talked to him and said, "Man, just relax. I got the money. That's what I came for." I like to think I calmed him down, but he probably hates my fucking guts.

BW: What's life like for you now?

Lloyd: Robbery and drug dealing were my life, and I can't do that anymore. Man, it's been so hard. I try to maintain jobs, and I fuck them up. I'm having trouble living the straight life. I refuse to do anything that gets me locked up for ten years or five years. I don't even want to do thirty days . . .

Look, I jumped off the porch when I was young, man. I started doing what I wanted to do when I wanted to do it. I started running the roads. When I was thirteen, I stole my mom's car and drove across the city of Hammond to Ponchatoula and lost my virginity. I just been blow-and-go since then.

BW: Did your mom just not have any control over you?

Lloyd: She had absolutely no control over me. I was petrified of my father. I would get away with a lot of shit because my mom was afraid to tell my father because he'd beat the fuck out of me. He only used his fists twice, but you can still abuse a child with a belt.

Right now, I'm so fucked up. I hate myself. I need to get myself into rehab. I've been on heroin two years straight, and I want to get clean. But every time I take a step forward, I get knocked ten steps back.

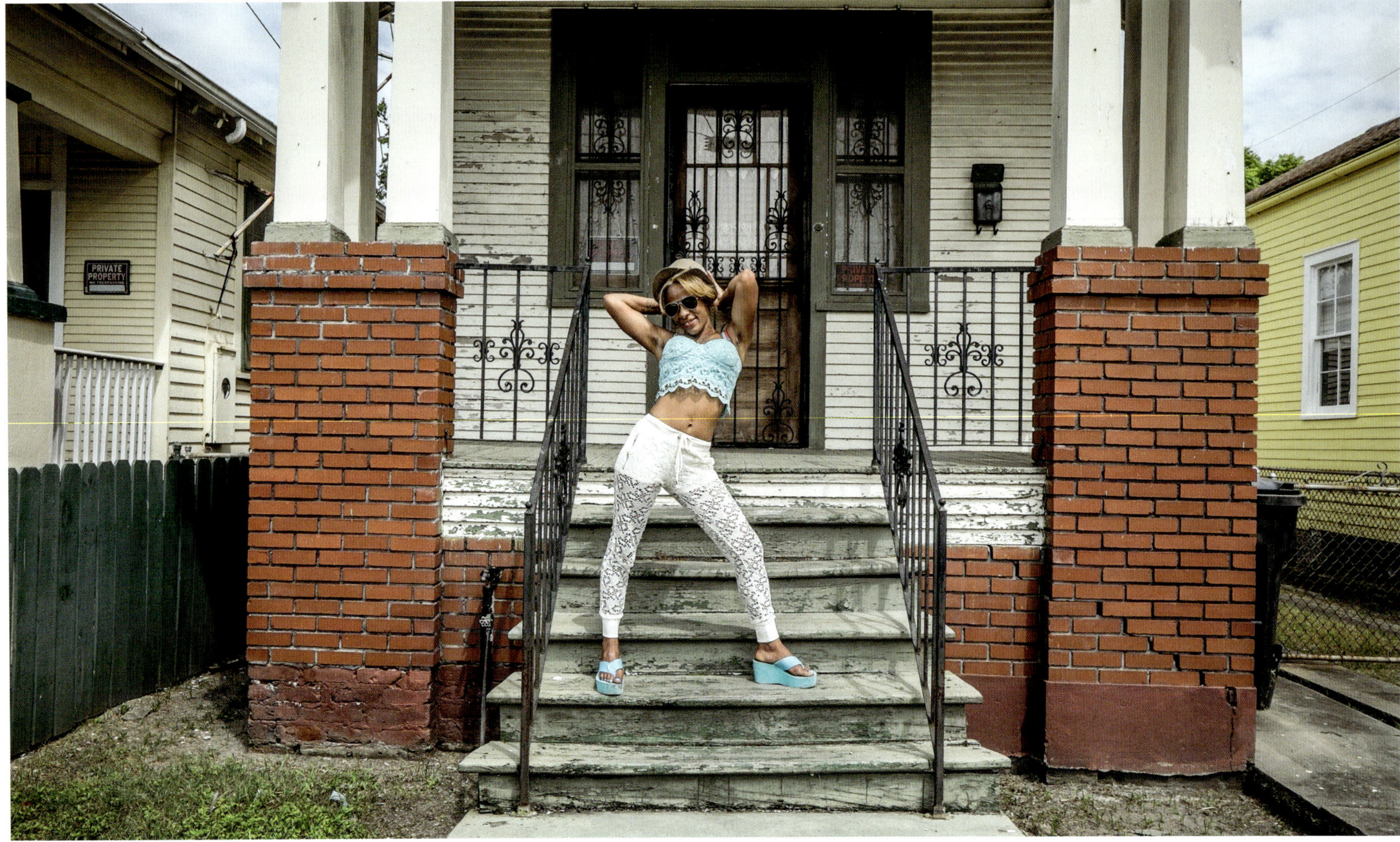

NEW ORLEANS, LA – 2015-05-09

Donetta: The hardest day of my life was the day I got raped by a cop.

BW: How did that happen?

Donetta: He told me to get in the car. He said, "Either you're gonna give me some pussy, or I'm gonna take you to jail." He took my life from me. He messed me up for years.

BW: How old were you?

Donetta: I was twelve, but I had a body like a grown woman. [Tears.] He took everything from me. My dignity, my pride, my everything. I could never love a man.

BW: Did you know who he was when he raped you?

Donetta: I known him all my life. He's the cop who killed my dad. My daddy was messing with his wife. So I guess he was getting revenge by fucking his daughter.

BW: How did he kill your dad?

Donetta: He shot him in the head when I was a baby.

Nicholas: It's hard for me to understand why things like Baltimore, and LA before that, happen. Then I read something like this, and I get it. I don't mean to politicize this, but this project helps illustrate a darker side of our country some of us don't see—word play completely intentional.

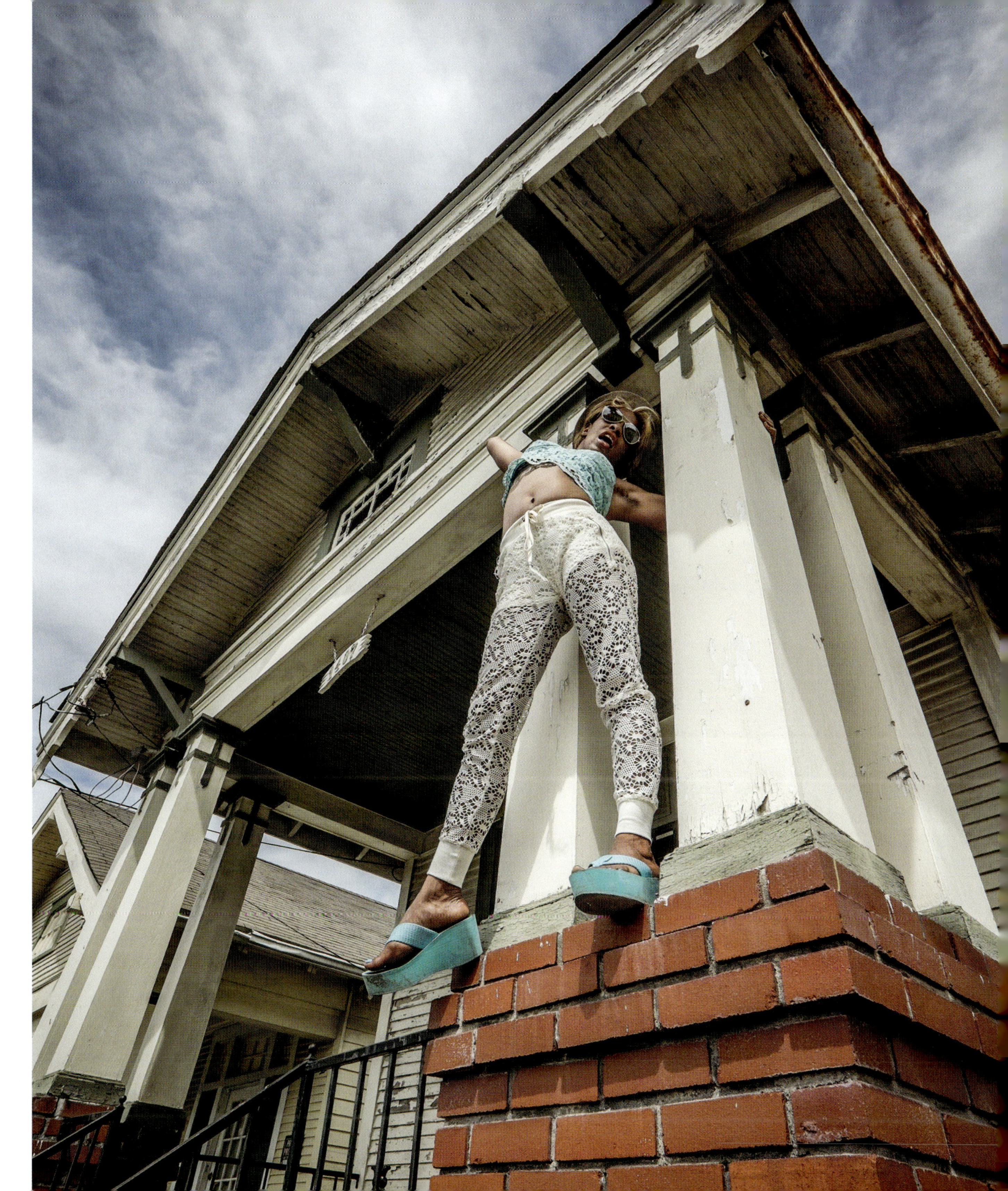

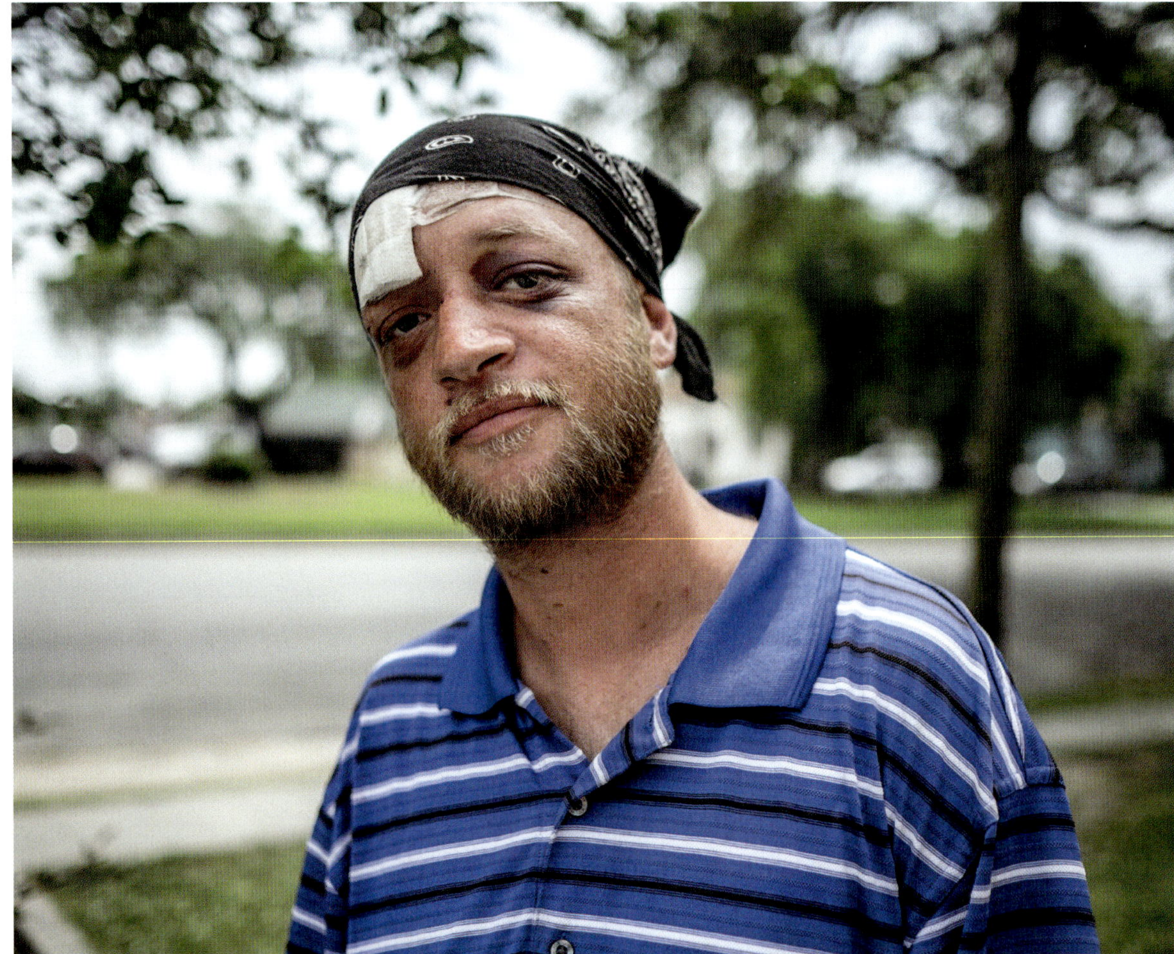

NEW ORLEANS, LA – 2015-05-11

Robert: I was born and raised in New Orleans—Uptown, from the Saint Thomas projects. I got taken away from my mother when I was born because she was addicted to freebase cocaine [crack]. I stayed with my grandma until I was three years old, when they gave me back to my mom.

My parents were alcoholics, so they would always stroll me down onto Bourbon Street. So at about five, six, seven years old, I start seeing how everyone was hustling and making money down there. By the time I was twelve, a lot of my friends had started selling drugs—weed and shit like that. I was like, "Man, I can make money too. Fuck school. I'm smart."

At thirteen years old, I jumped off the porch and ditched school. I started selling crack at this place called Le Roundup down in the French Quarter. Truancy officer came and got me one time. I'm playing the video poker machine at thirteen in a bar. [Laughs.] I had to spend like three months in the juvenile.

At sixteen years old, I was just way to 'bout it. We had this little gang called the Tentmore Block Boys. We was out there slingin' weed, carrying guns. My mom couldn't deal with me anymore, so she threw me out. I was in the streets. I was like, "Oh shit. What am I gonna do?" But I got adopted by Grandma Maggie and my uncle, Dirty Red. They were slingin' weed and crack too, so I said, "Fuck it. I'm gonna still get it in."

I was still too young to buy alcohol, so I was waiting at the store for my homeboy to come out and bring me a beer. There were two dudes arguing in the parking lot across the street. Next thing I know, two shots pop off. I caught the ricochet right here. [Points to leg.]

BW: Is it still in there?

Robert: Yeah. They can't take it out. It's too close to the femoral artery. That's why I walk with a limp. Well, that and the state trooper stuff.

BW: The state trooper stuff?

Robert: Yeah. Two nights ago, I was on Bourbon Street with my girlfriend, dancing. No problem. State troopers pull us apart and throw me against the wall. They run my name. Two warrants popped up, but they'd already been taken care of. But the state police were like, "Whatever—we're taking you to jail anyway." They put me in the back of the squad car. I could hear them on the radio. They were calling Orleans Parish Prison, and the clerk's like, "We're not taking him. Write him a summons." They said over the radio, "Those attachments have already been taken care of."

I can hear the cops bitching, talking about wasting their time and how they were gonna fuck this boy up. I'm like, "Oh shit. I'm gonna get released, but I'm gonna get my ass kicked." They get me out the car. I'm still cuffed, and they put me against the trunk. They uncuff me and hit me in the back of the knees with the baton. They said, "You're banned from Bourbon Street for a month!" I haven't been able to walk right for two days now. I got out of the Quarter real quick.

Their [state cops'] whole job here is to bust heads. The reason they were supposed to come here was to stop the shootings on Bourbon Street, but they're fuckin' with the homeless.

NOPD is cool. It's the state police that are really hurting people. They already have seventy lawsuits on them. It's all because of Governor Jindal sending them in. They were supposed to leave by Mardi Gras, and they haven't. Now they're down in the French Quarter beating up on the homeless.

I got my ribs cracked about a month ago. I had a seizure, and I was on the street passed out. The state police came up and booted me in the ribs.

BW: Just for no reason?

Robert: Because I'm homeless.

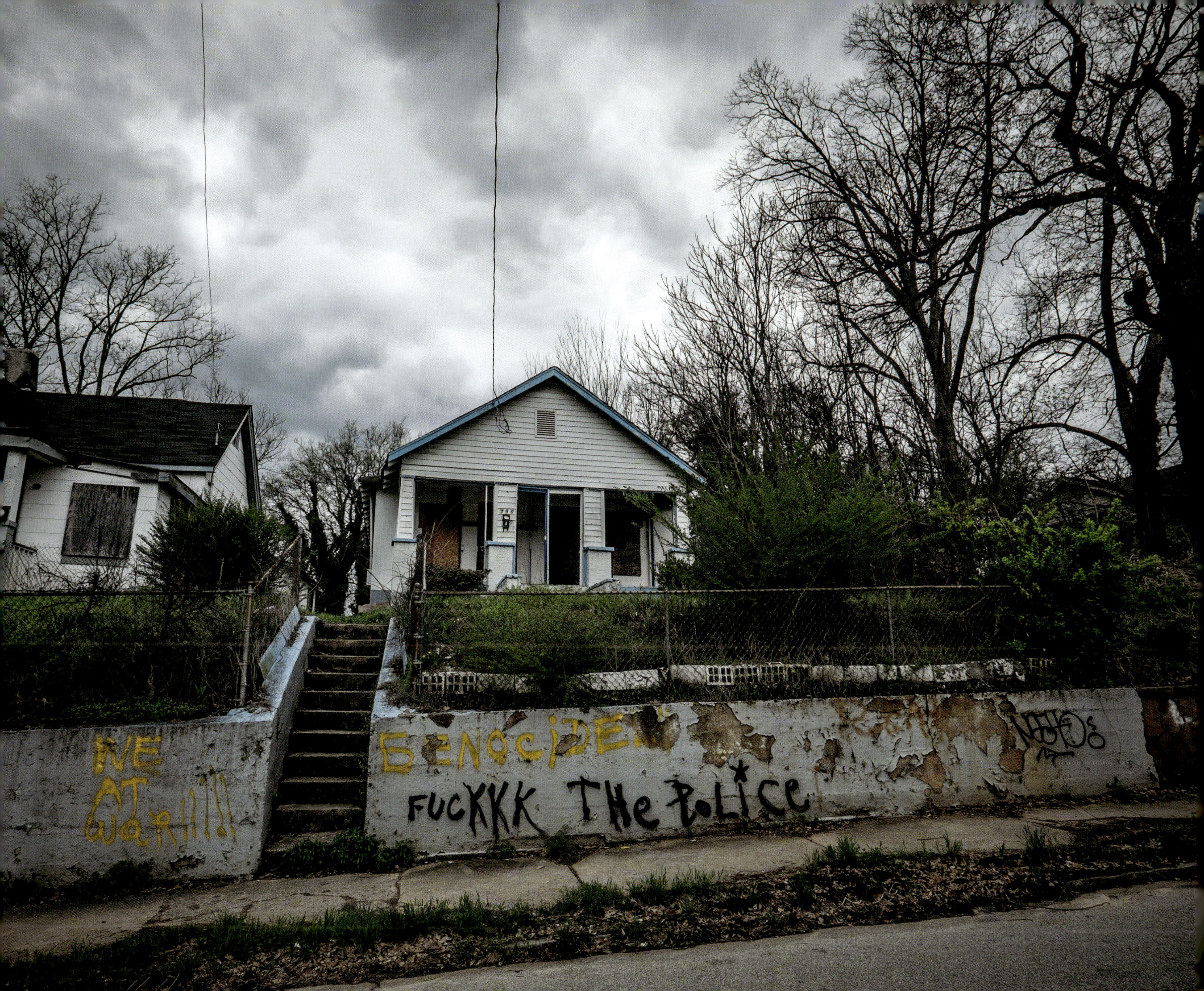
WE AT WAR!!!!
GENOCIDE
FUCKKK THE POLICE

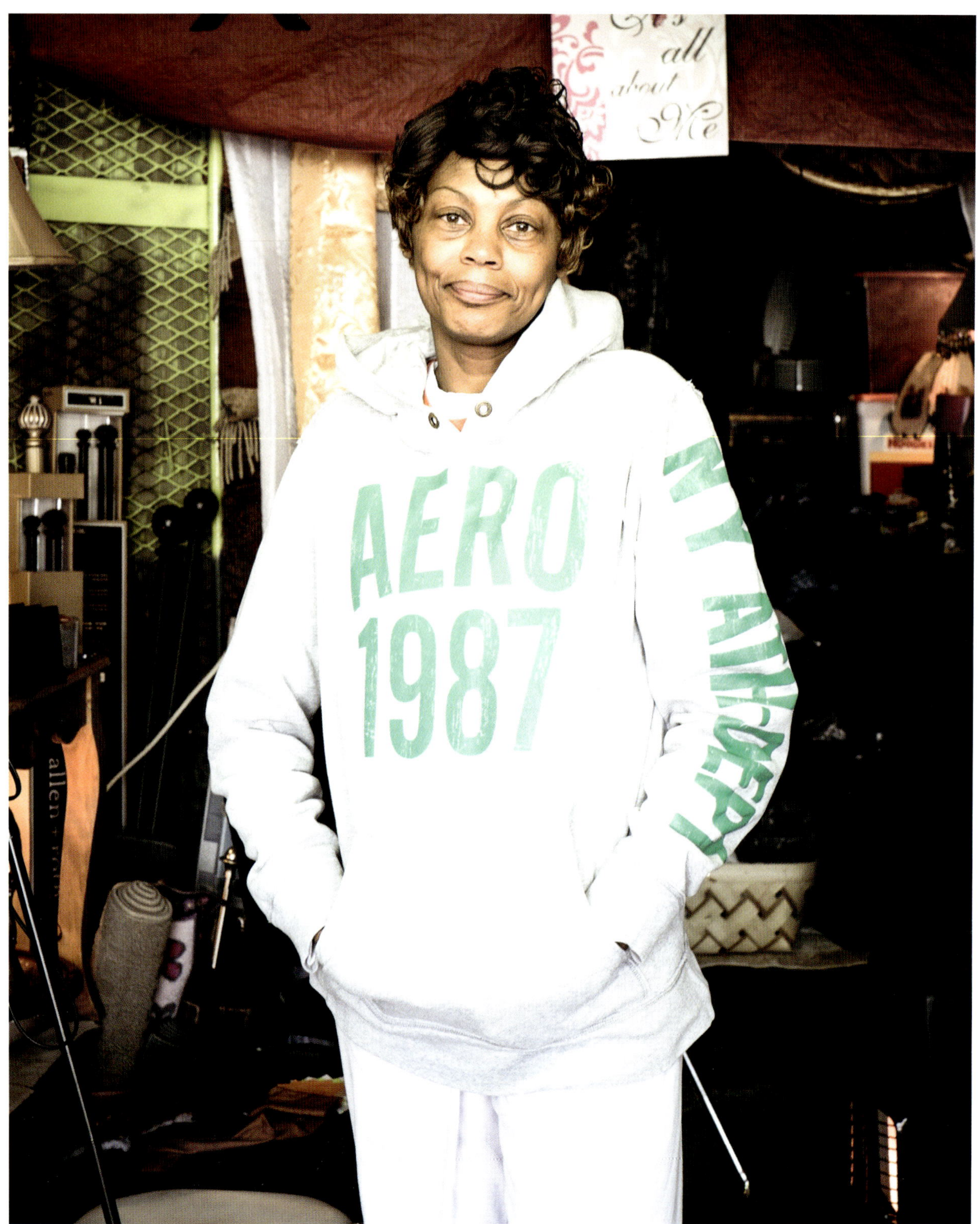

MCDONOUGH, GA – 2014-11-15

Simna: My biggest regret is selling drugs. I did five years in prison. I got out in 1996, and I've been struggling ever since. People don't give second chances. That's why I'm doing this.

I never got the chance to have my real dream.

BW: What was your real dream?

Simna: To be a model. [Tears.]

BW: Have you been back to prison?

Simna: No. I said I wouldn't go back, and I haven't. It's been almost twenty years. I get tired . . .

I found a job last week at Subway making $7.25. Between that and freezing out here on the weekends, I'm trying to make it work for me and my daughter. I just need a break.

The US cages more of its citizens than any other country in the world.(4) Southern states, by far, have the highest rates of incarceration with Louisiana, Mississippi, and Oklahoma leading the pack.(5) At least 65% of inmates are addicts, and only 11% of them receive any kind of treatment while incarcerated.(6)

LAGRANGE, GA – 2015-02-14

Alfred: Basically, Brent, my life is real simple. This is my life, right here. I've been living out here for seven years. I went to prison for selling drugs in '97. I thought I was gonna come back and everything would be all merry.

BW: Have you been able to find work since you've been out?

Alfred: No one wants to give a convicted felon a chance. Everybody's hollering for government assistance. I don't need the government. I got two feets and two hands. I'm capable of doing what I got to do to survive. I live from trash can to trash can. Most of it I sell to make me a few bucks. Get me something to eat.

BW: Are you happy?

Alfred: I'm happy. This is an adventure for me. I have family in LaGrange, and I've stayed with all of them. It just don't work, especially when someone tells you what time you gotta be in the house. [Laughs.]

This is my life, and I love it. I don't allow anyone to just come down here, due to the fact that I like my space. This is my castle, and I am the king of my castle.

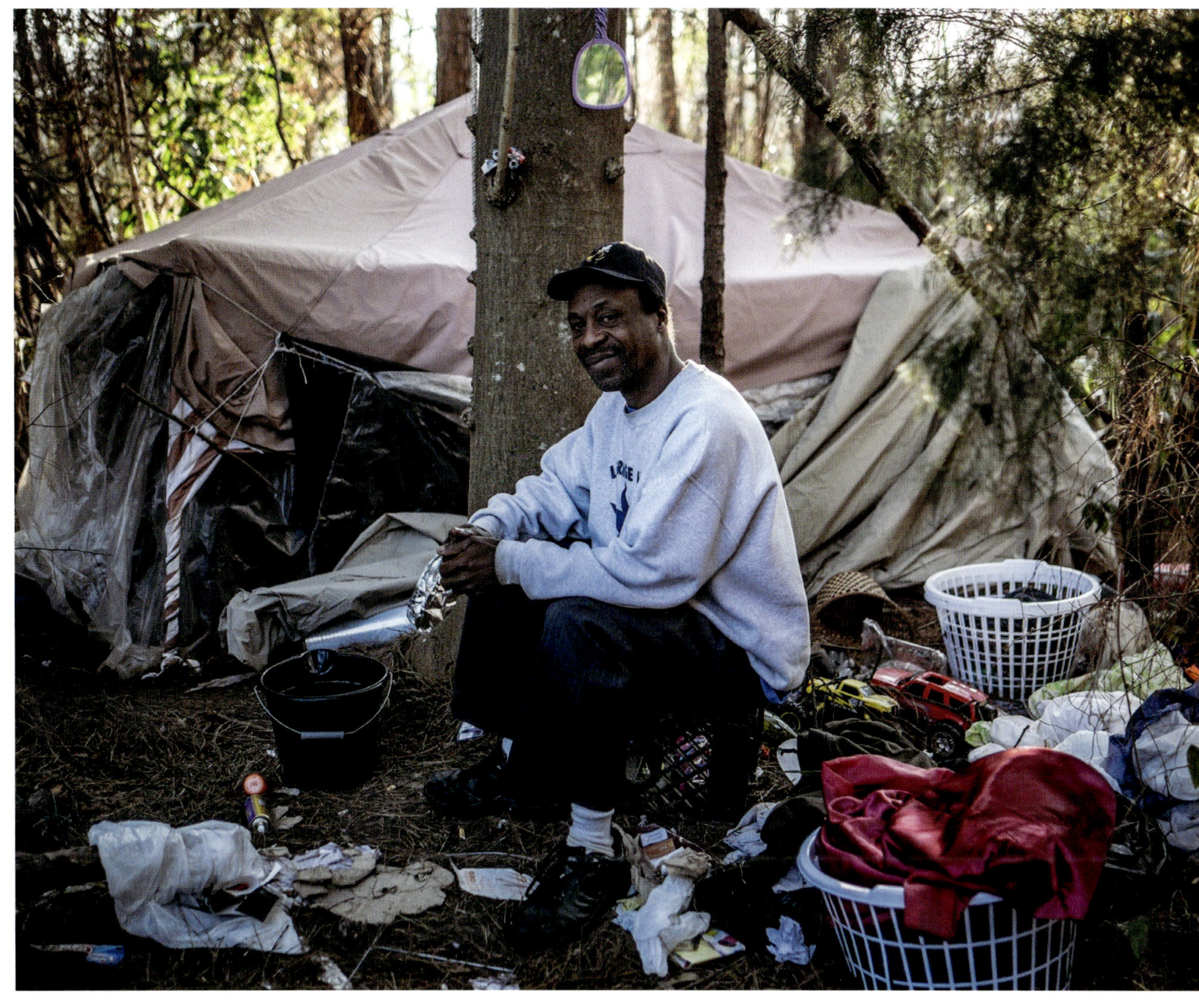

In the past decade, three major private prison companies spent $45 million on campaign donations and lobbying. A 2011 report found that the private prison industry spent millions seeking to increase sentences and incarcerate more people in order to increase the industry's profits.[7]

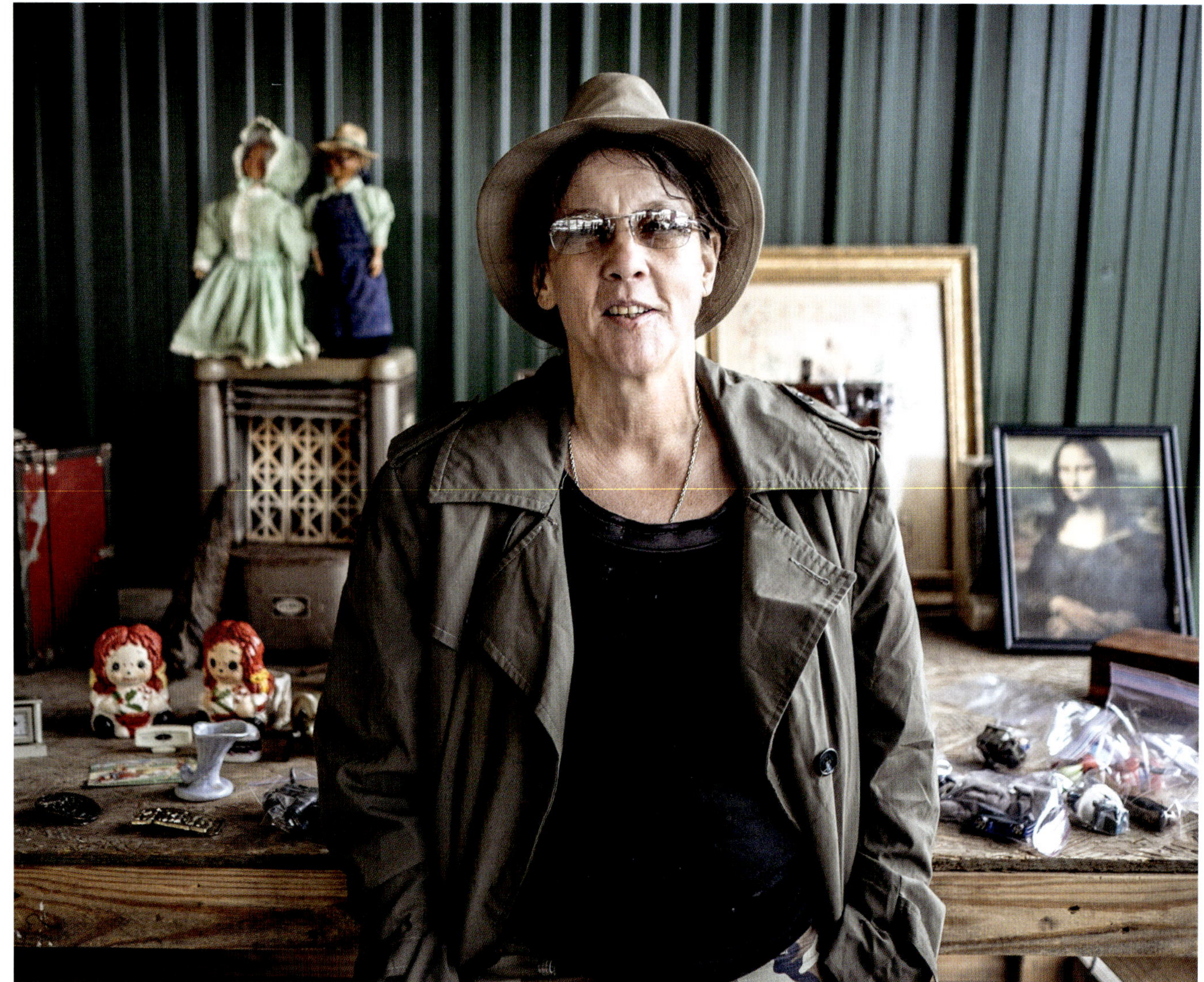

Tiny house villages are popping up all along the West Coast as a way to deal with homelessness. These tiny houses cost about $3,300 each to build.[8] Recently, a megachurch pastor in College Park, Georgia, announced the purchase of a $65 million jet for his ministry.[9] That is about the same amount it would cost to build tiny homes for the entire homeless population of Georgia.[10]

BREMEN, GA – 2014-12-21

Rachel: I had a horrible childhood. I'm from East Point, and we had one of the highest crime rates in the country. All my friends from my childhood are either dead or in prison.

My life has been crazy. Been married five times. I got Camp Jesus out of the last marriage.

BW: Camp Jesus?

Rachel: Yeah. My life was so terrible growing up. I always thought, "If I just had somewhere to go to get my head together . . . and if my friends who wound up in prison just had somewhere to go to get their heads together, it would have been cool." So what I'm doing down here is giving people a place to go and stay.

There is no judging at Camp Jesus. You can come in there all whacked out, and it's okay. Grab you a camper, regroup, then go back out into society, so you don't get in trouble.

BW: Are there rules for staying at Camp Jesus?

Rachel: No cursin' God, and love each other. There's really no other rules. If Jesus were here, he'd be chillin' with people like us. He hung out with sinners.

Camp Jesus is for the rejects. The ones who aren't loved. The ones that people talk about and don't want at Christmas dinner. If that's you, come on down to Camp Jesus.

See, Christianity's all about loving your neighbor, not casting stones.

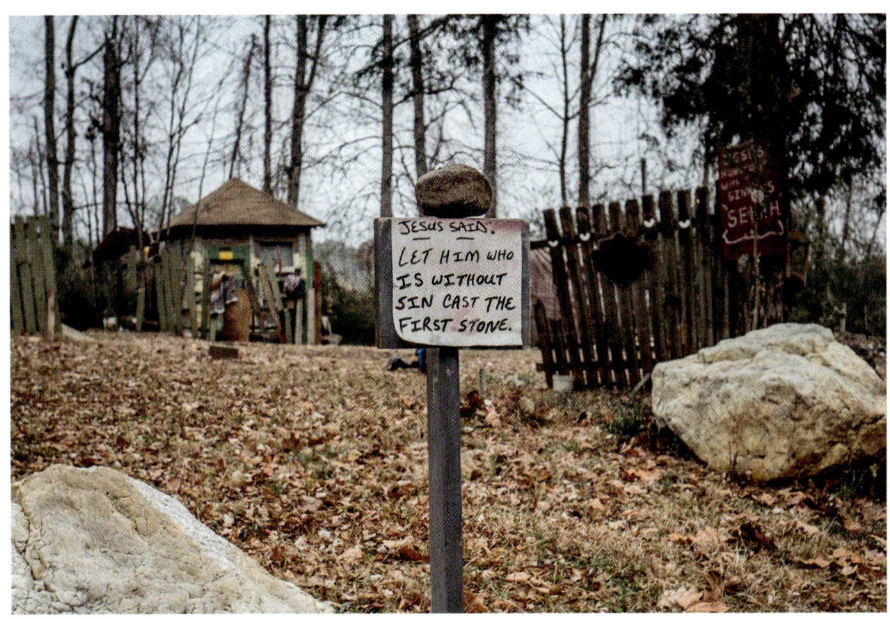
JESUS SAID:
LET HIM WHO
IS WITHOUT
SIN CAST THE
FIRST STONE.

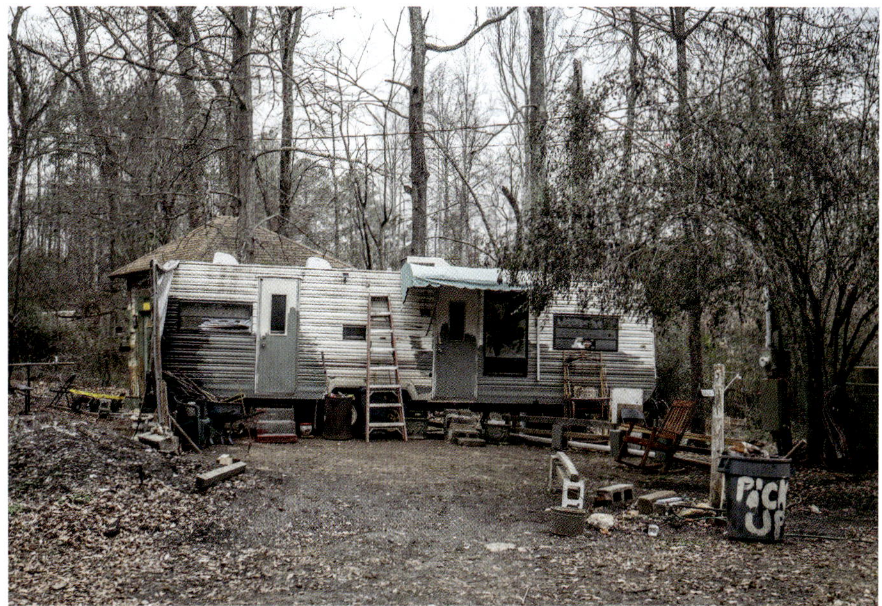
PICK
UP

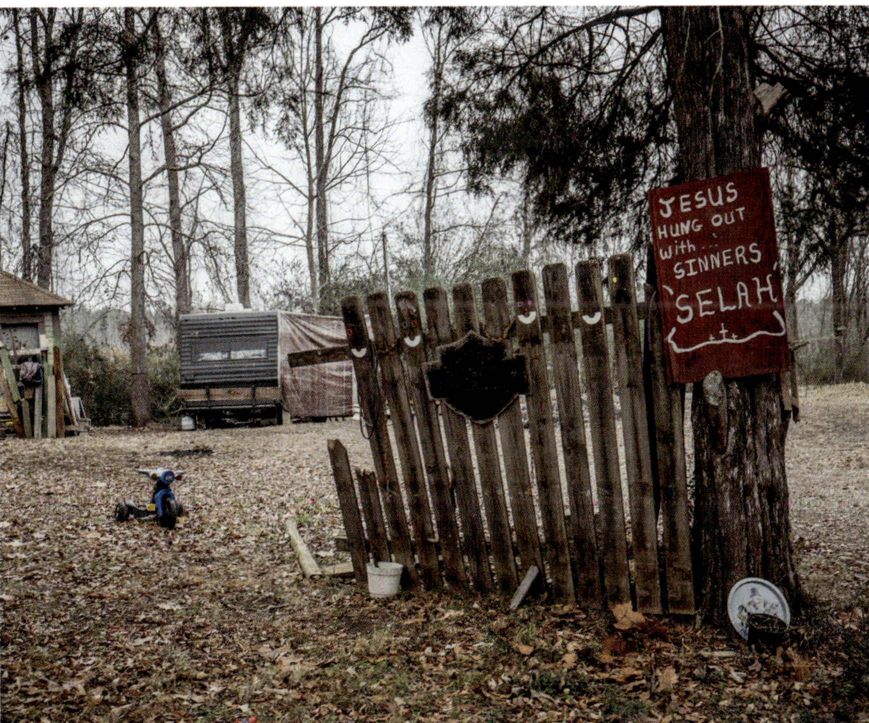
JESUS
HUNG OUT
with...
SINNERS
SELAH

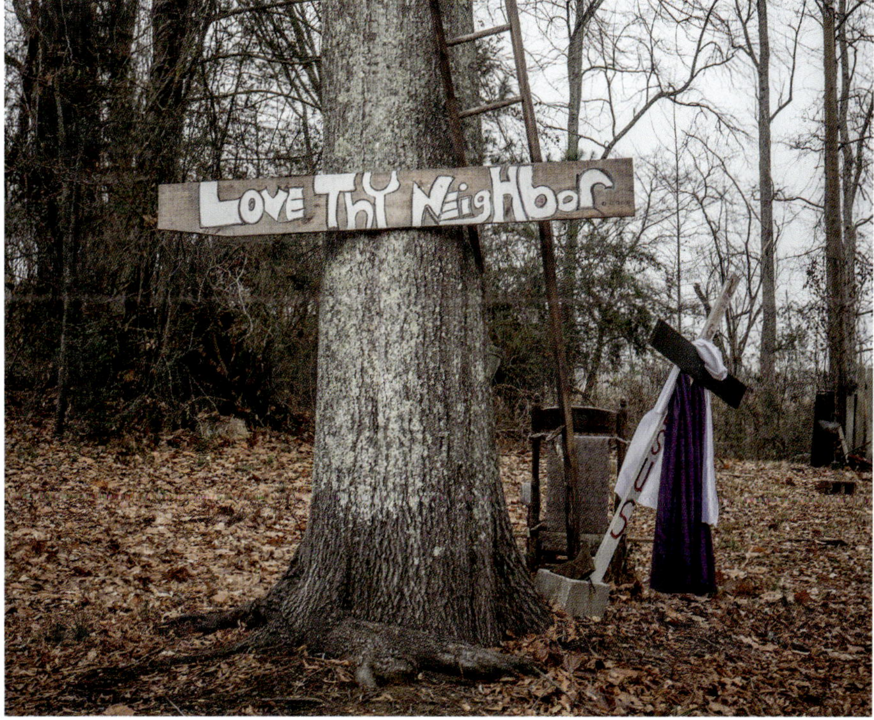
Love Thy Neighbor

I got up with my father at 4:30 every morning. I would get on my bike and go for a ride. I would sit at the top of the hill and watch the morning glories open. They would open so slowly. They were beautiful.

—*Amy (p. 83)*

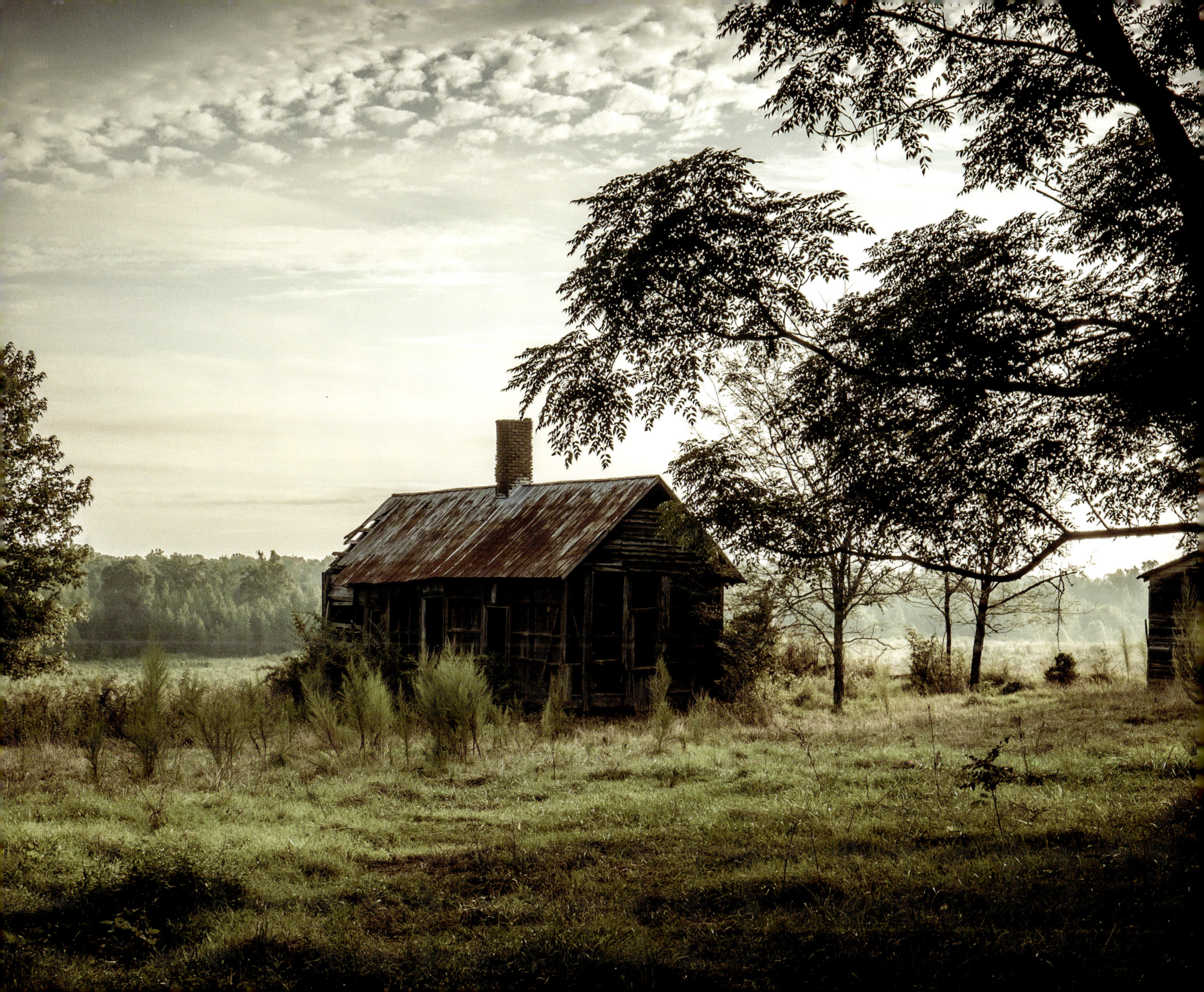

#Incest #Anger #Forgiveness

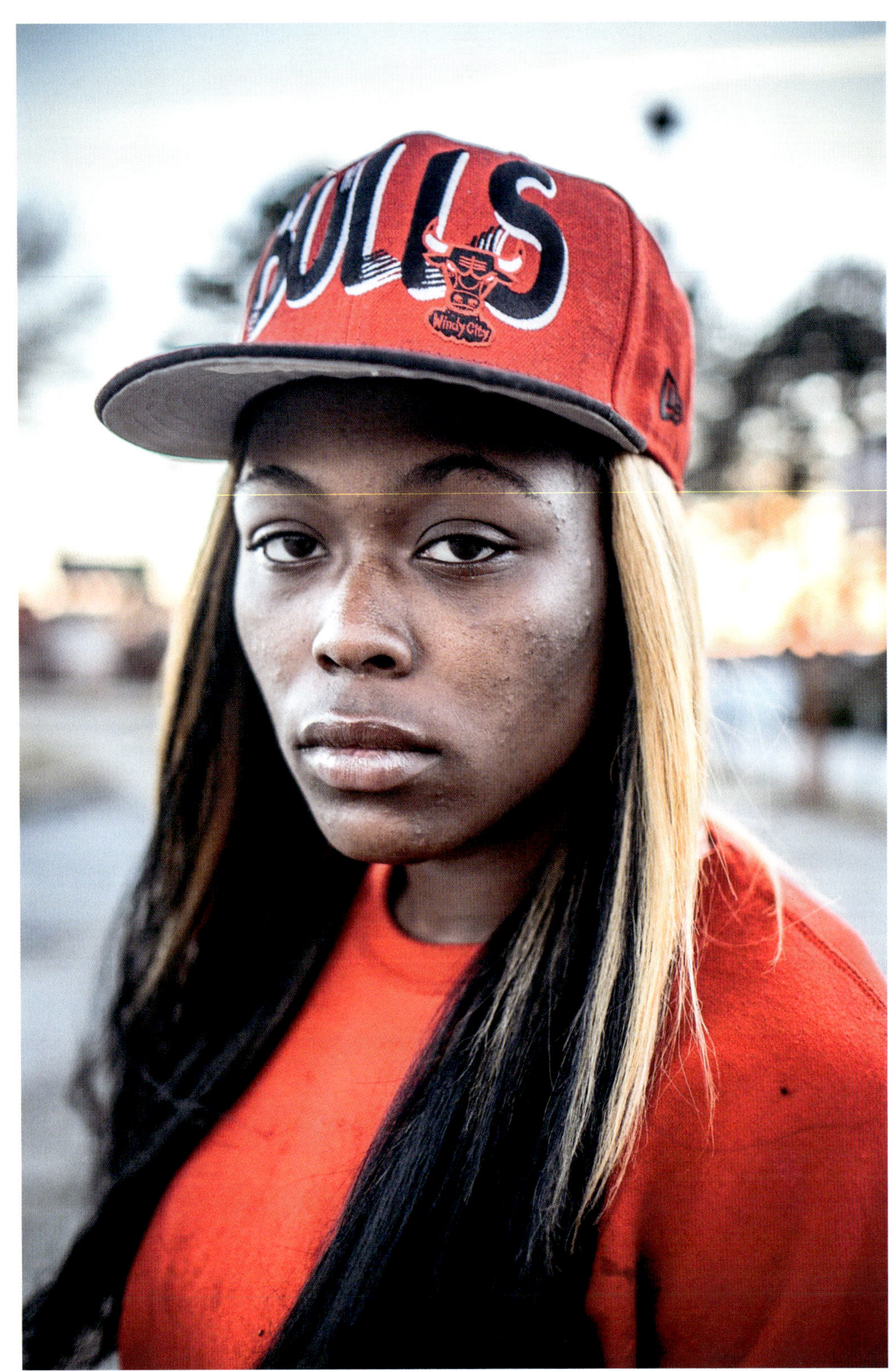

ATLANTA, GA – 2015-02-28

Asia: When I was younger, I had a lot of anger issues toward a certain person. I've been angry for a long, long time, but I've taken anger management classes, and it helped some.

BW: Who's the certain person?

Asia: A family member.

BW: Did someone do something to you?

Asia: [Pausing.] My brother **. . .** he raped me.

BW: I'm sorry. How old were you?

Asia: It started at the age of seven and continued until the age of ten. He was fifteen or sixteen.

BW: Did you ever tell anyone about it?

Asia: Before my mother passed this year, I told her about it. She cried. She was sad that I didn't believe and trust in her enough to tell her.

BW: Why do you think you didn't tell her?

Asia: I was too scared.

BW: Where is your brother now?

Asia: I have no idea.

BW: If you could tell him something, what would you tell him?

Asia: I forgive you. I can't stay mad at him forever. God says everything happens for a reason.

> **Marie:** Forgiveness isn't for him, it's for you. I wish you well on the road you're on in life. No child should have that kind of past.

ATLANTA, GA – 2015-02-15

William: I didn't exactly have the best childhood. My mom left when I was three, and my dad was a long-haul truck driver, but he couldn't do that and watch me and my two sisters. He gave up his parental rights to his mom. My grandma hated me because I was named after my great-grandfather. She hated him, so she hated me. She had all this built-up anger. She hated saying "William" or "Red" or any of the names that reminded her of him.

She lied and said I was a troublemaker and put me in a facility. I was always the runt in the facilities. That meant I got picked on really bad. I have scars from where I was burned repeatedly. You know that knife game where they stab in between your fingers? Well, they stabbed me—three times. I escaped from the boys' home when I was fourteen and have been on my own ever since.

BW: What was the hardest day when you were in the facility?

William: None of them compared to when I was out and having to deal with the family.

BW: So living with your family was harder than being in a boys' home?

William: Yeah. You ever heard of a whistler as a tool of punishment? I'd come home with a bad grade or if my grandma was just having a bad day . . . It was a piece of plywood that had holes drilled into it. My dad made it for her.

When I was seven, I moved to Colorado with my dad because he had met a chick online. She was really abusive. I have scars in places I don't even want to mention. She stripped me of my clothes, hog-tied me, and kicked me repeatedly with steel-toed cowboy boots while my sisters were forced to sit there and watch.

BW: Why?

William: Because I said, "I did it." I didn't even know what I was admitting to. I just knew I didn't want my sisters getting in trouble with her.

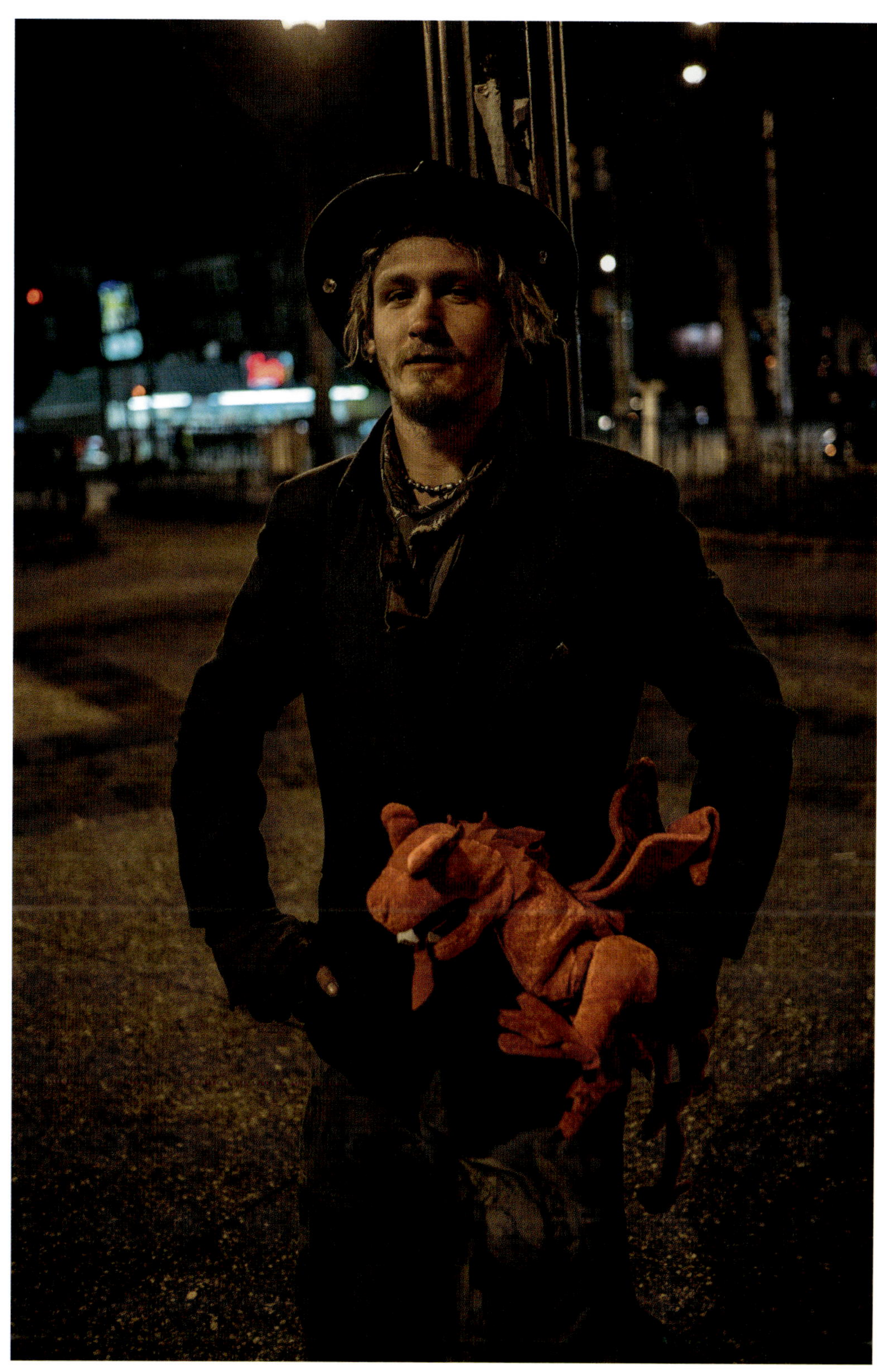

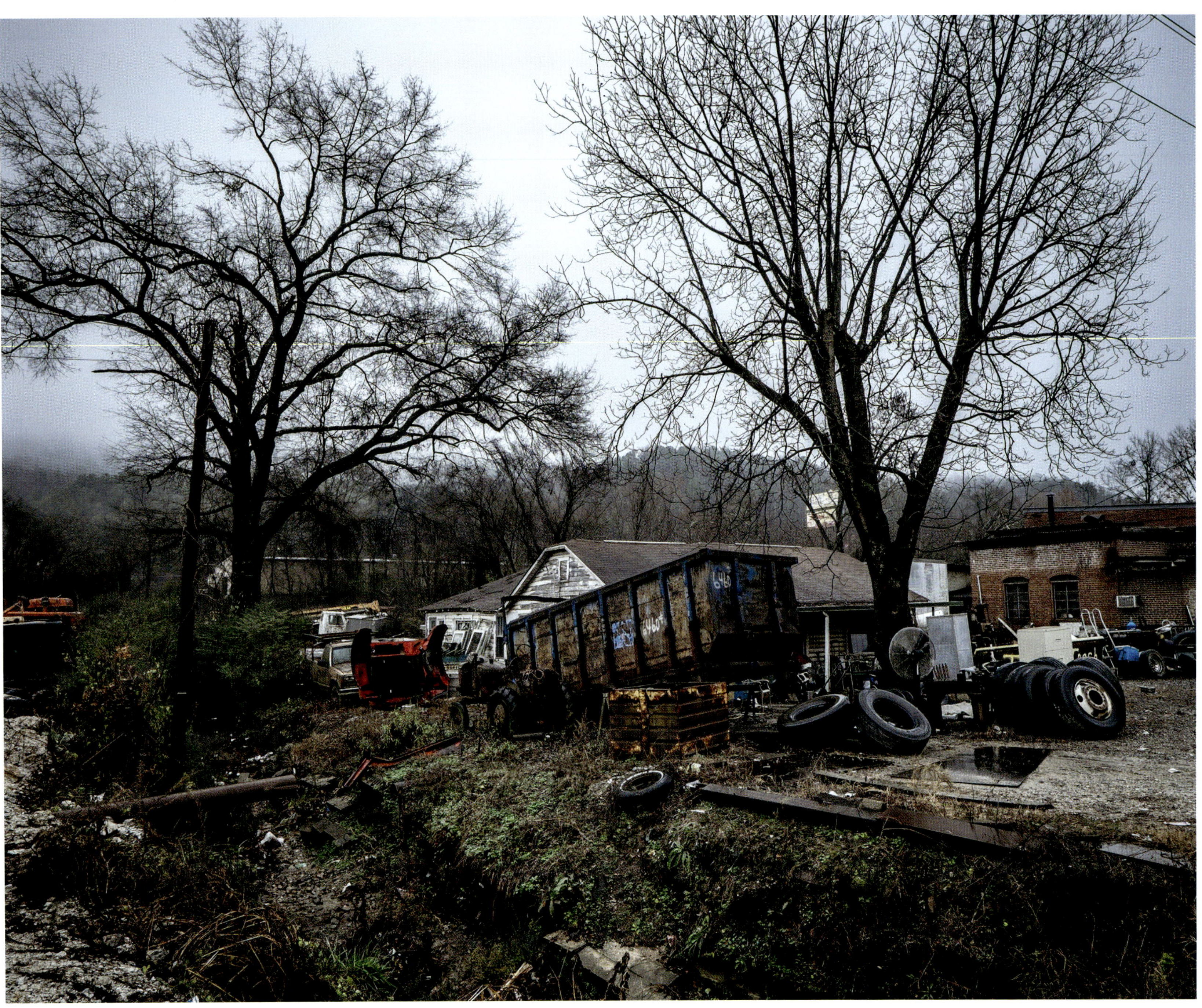

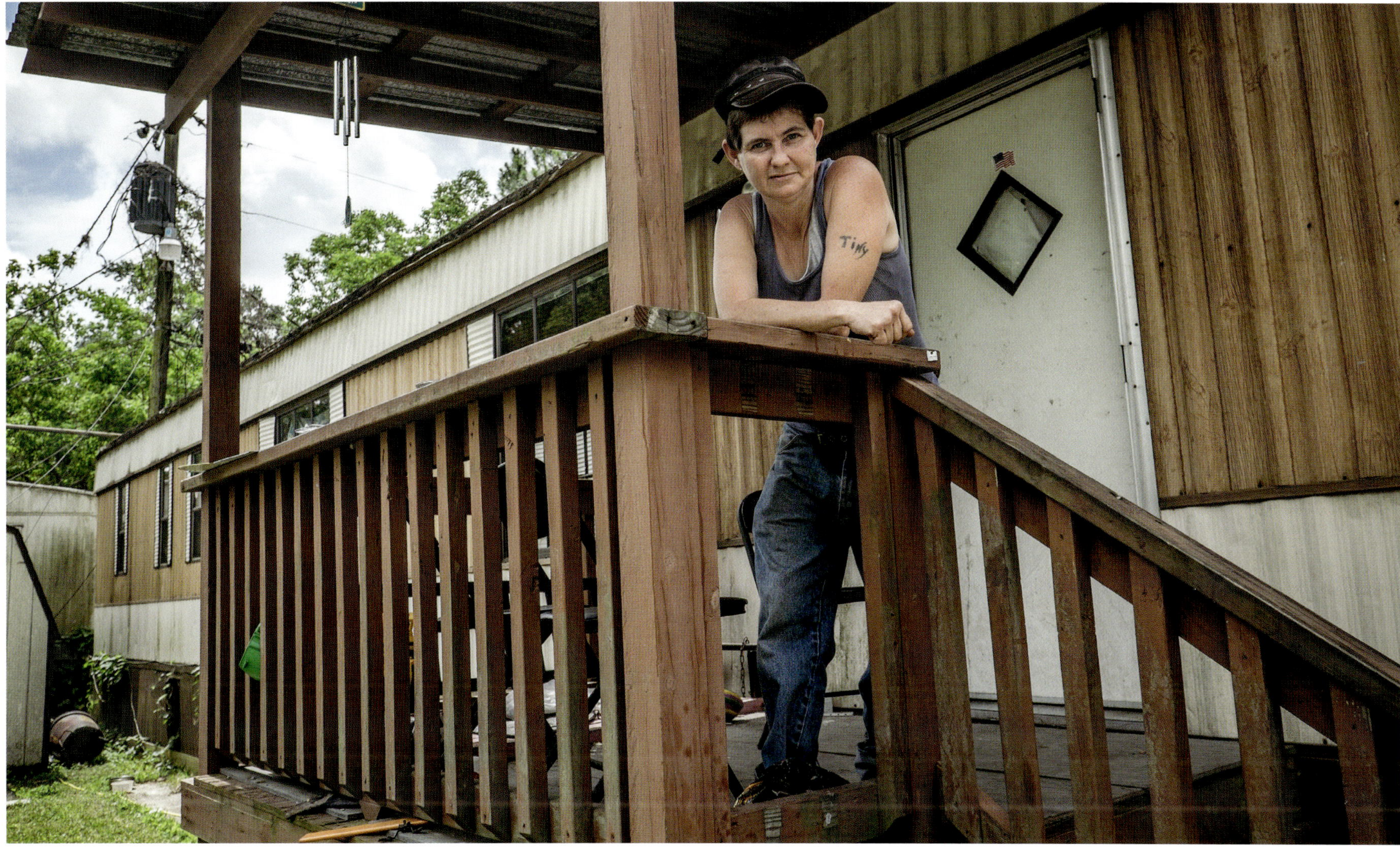

NEW ORLEANS, LA – 2015-05-10

Tina: It was horrible growing up with my mom. What she would let happen to me when I was a child . . . She took in this man from jail who raped and molested me, and then she married him.

BW: How old were you when that happened?

Tina: Well, I was being molested when I was younger, but when this guy came in from prison, I was eleven. He started molesting me when I was eleven and raped me by the time I was thirteen. She married him when I was fifteen. She didn't believe anything I said.

BW: So you told her about it?

Tina: Oh yeah. This one time I even had his handprint across my face, and I had bitten him on the chest, and she believed that I wanted it. That I asked for that at thirteen.

BW: How did it stop?

Tina: My brother started getting violent with him. It made me toughen up too.

BW: Do you think you'll ever forgive your mom?

Tina: No. I walk around with so much anger through my life. It's like having a chip on my shoulder I can never get off.

Read part 2 of Tina's story on p. 145.

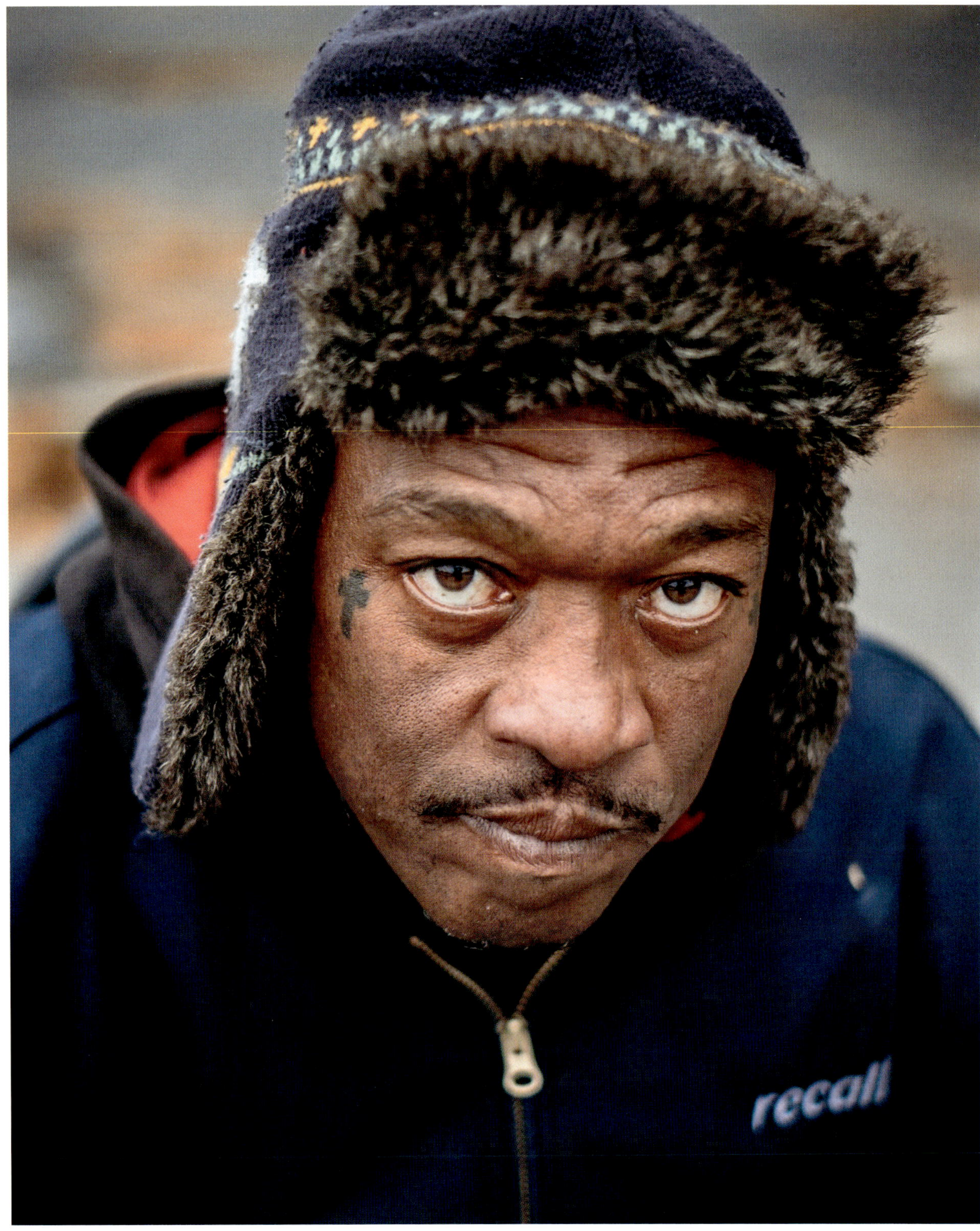

DORAVILLE, GA – 2015-02-26

Victor: I was born in Cincinnati, Ohio. My grandmother had two children by one of the Isley Brothers. So the Isley Brothers always blessed my grandmother's apartment with drums, keyboards, guitars. And that's how I learned how to play.

When I was twelve years old, my mom decided to move to Talladega, Alabama. I kind of quit playing when we moved to Alabama.

There was something that always bothered my mother about me. She never really had love for me, and I wound up in the streets at fourteen. I had an uncle. He grew all this weed in the woods. I'd go and help him and learned all about growing. At fourteen, I'm a pothead and alcoholic.

When I was fifteen, my uncle stuck a needle in my arm for the first time. Shot me up with Ts and blues. I didn't continue to do that, but by the time I was twenty-one, I was living in a drug house in Cobb County, shooting cocaine. I've been to prison five times because of drugs. I was a user and a seller, and that's a bad combination.

The hardest day of my life was the day I called home and found out that my mother had passed. They were burying her the next day, and I didn't have a way to make it home to the funeral. I was living in a van behind the KFC, and I had called home to talk to her. I wanted to ask her why she never loved me as her son. I never got that answer.

BW: Man, I'm sorry. What was the best day of your life?

Victor: The day I decided to pick up the guitar again. Yep, that was the best day of my life.

> **Alan:** He may not be a cop, soldier, fireman, or other person in society we have deemed to be a "hero" . . . but this guy is a frigging hero for still being here and still surviving with that kind of burden. Play on, my brother.

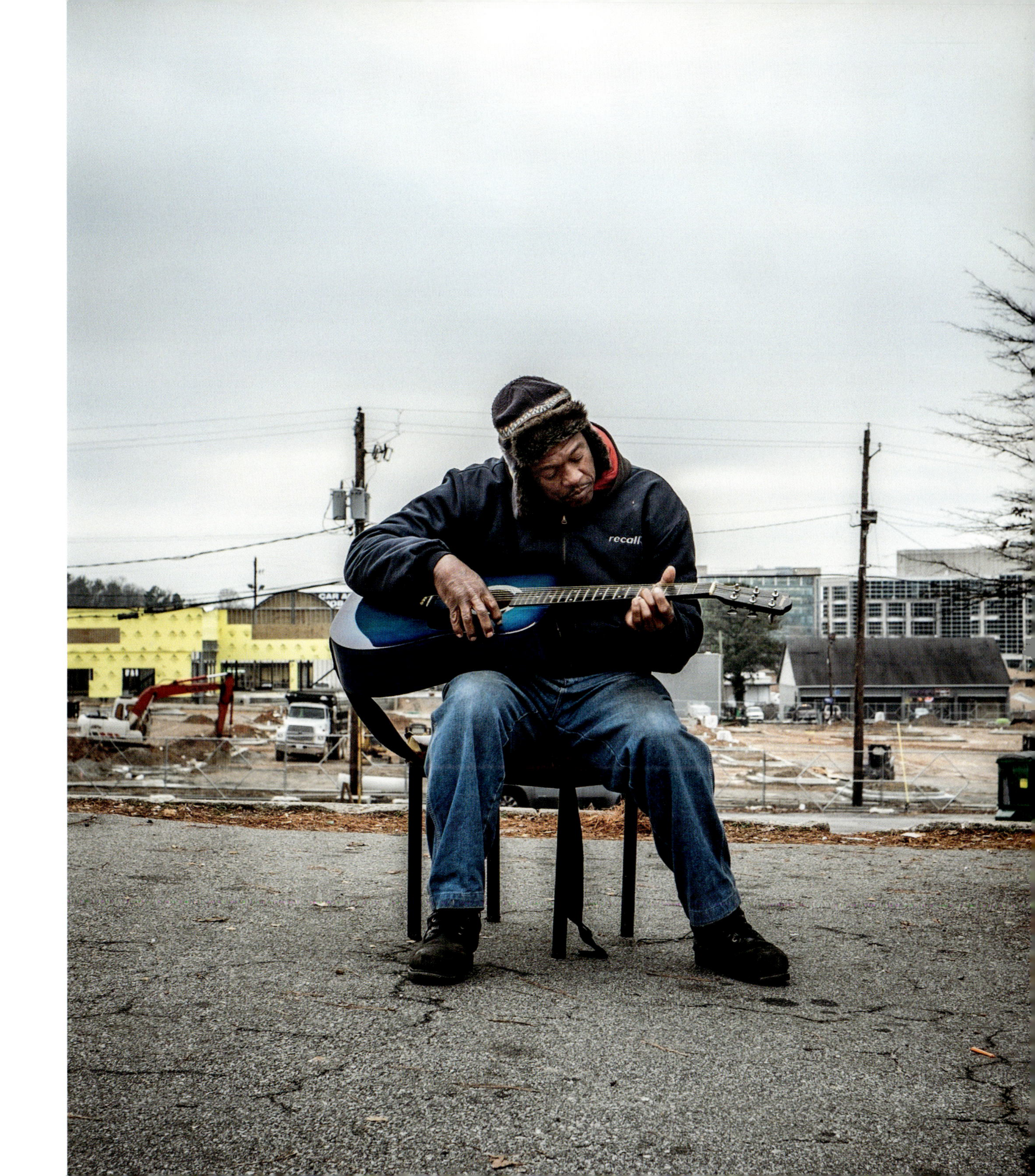
recall

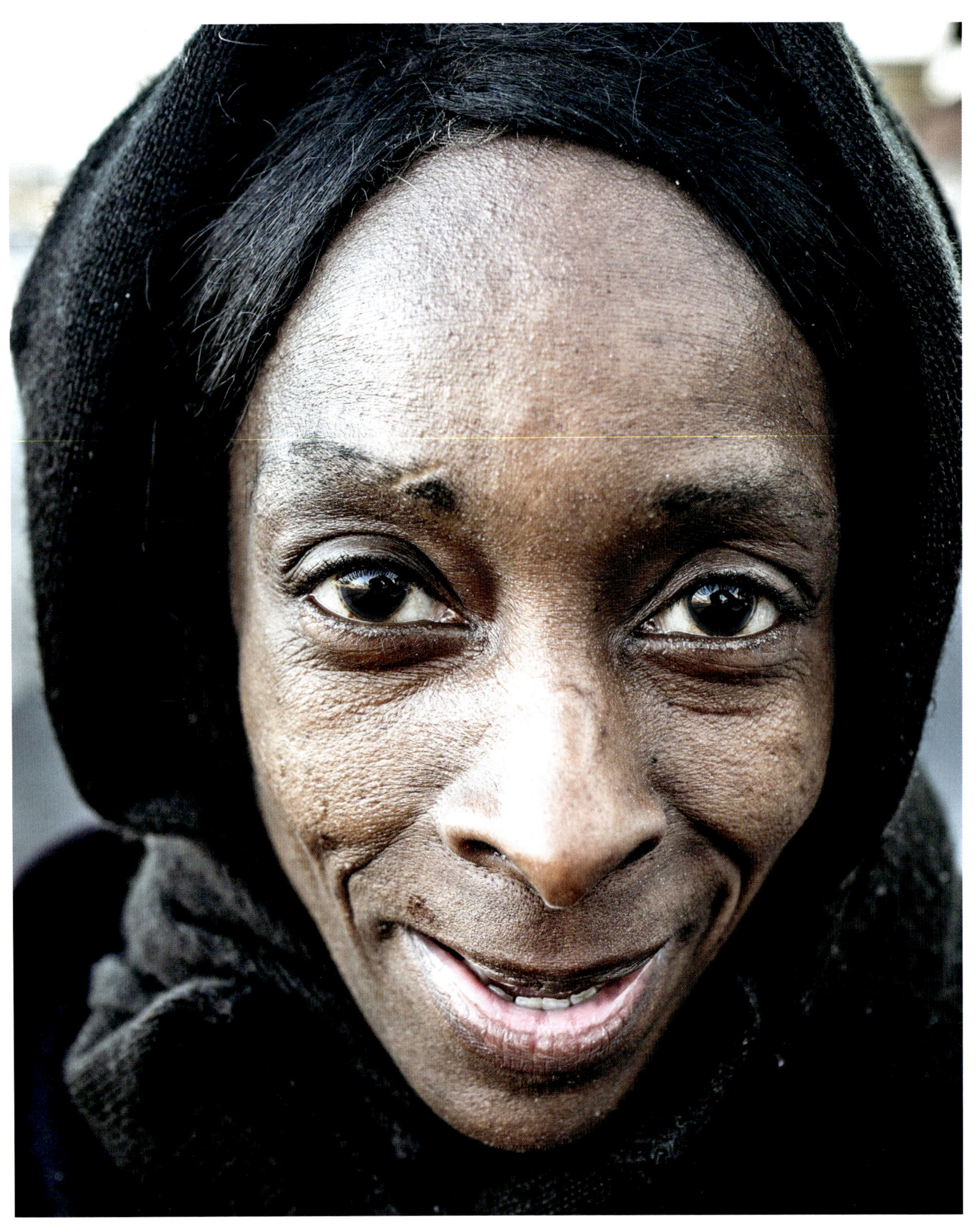

ATLANTA, GA – 2014-12-10

Michelle: My mom put me out at an early age, and the streets took me in. I stayed on the street twenty years waiting on a man to come and fall in love with me.

I stayed clean for five years and worked at Walmart.

BW: Why did you start back?

Michelle: I failed in life, and I medicate to make me feel like I'm somebody.

BW: Crack?

Michelle: Yeah.

BW: Do you know why you started in the first place?

Michelle: When I was in school, they used to talk about how smart I was, but I never fit in. I wasn't accepted. I never had a clique or a best friend. I just didn't fit in. They say I'm bipolar.

BW: Have you ever tried medication?

Michelle: No, 'cause I'm not that bad. I just talk too fast. I can talk nonstop for twenty-four hours.

20–25% of the homeless population in the United States suffers from some form of severe mental illness.[11]

Melanie: It's important to understand that poverty and homelessness are not due to laziness but most often due to trauma. If we could just understand this as a human community, perhaps we could be compelled to do more to support the healing of our fellow persons and lift them up instead of pushing them further down.

ASHEVILLE, NC – 2015-06-01

Flip-Flop: I had a pretty horrible childhood. I grew up with addicts. I'll tell you the truth: I've been in and out of prison and jail. What brought me to prostitution is because I got molested a lot growing up. You lose everything. I'd rather be out here homeless than to go through the shit I went through with them growing up.

BW: Who molested you? Family?

Flip-Flop: Yeah, a lot of my family did. Cousins, uncles . . . My mama was in and out of prison. I had to learn to take care of myself early. That's how I've survived on the streets. But I'm getting older now, and I want something in life. Who wants to wake up in the fucking bushes and wonder what you did? I stay maybe a day or two at the shelter, and I'm ready to go because I get lonely. I don't like to be by myself.

BW: Does prostitution help with the loneliness?

Flip-Flop: Yeah, it does. Sometimes you meet somebody and you're like, "Wow! Is this person really that cool with me, knowing what I do?" I know I need a man all the time, but I think it's just the hurt so deep inside, you know? Anybody that's given me a chance, it's too much for them. I always end up just like I am now, back on the street. They just want pussy all that time, and it's hard for me to have sex, period.

BW: Why is it hard? You think it's hard because you got molested?

Flip-Flop: I think so. And then, I just know what I've done out here. Then I'm thinking I'm worthless. I don't know. Who wants to be with someone who ain't worth a fuck? I mean, look at me now. I've let myself go. What are they gonna say about this girl? "She ain't worth a fuck. She ain't nothin' but a ho. She ain't got nothin'."

It's hard when you love a man, though, and you can't be intimate with that man. I mean, it's gonna take time, especially with a woman like me, coming off the street. But it's like learning how to walk again. I tell this to every man I'm with. You've got to take steps with that woman. You gotta show that woman she's a queen. You gotta help that woman come off that shit.

I just wish I could get somebody in my life that will say, "That's my girl," and they could see me through coming out of this shit. I'm a damn good cook, and I try to keep the house clean.

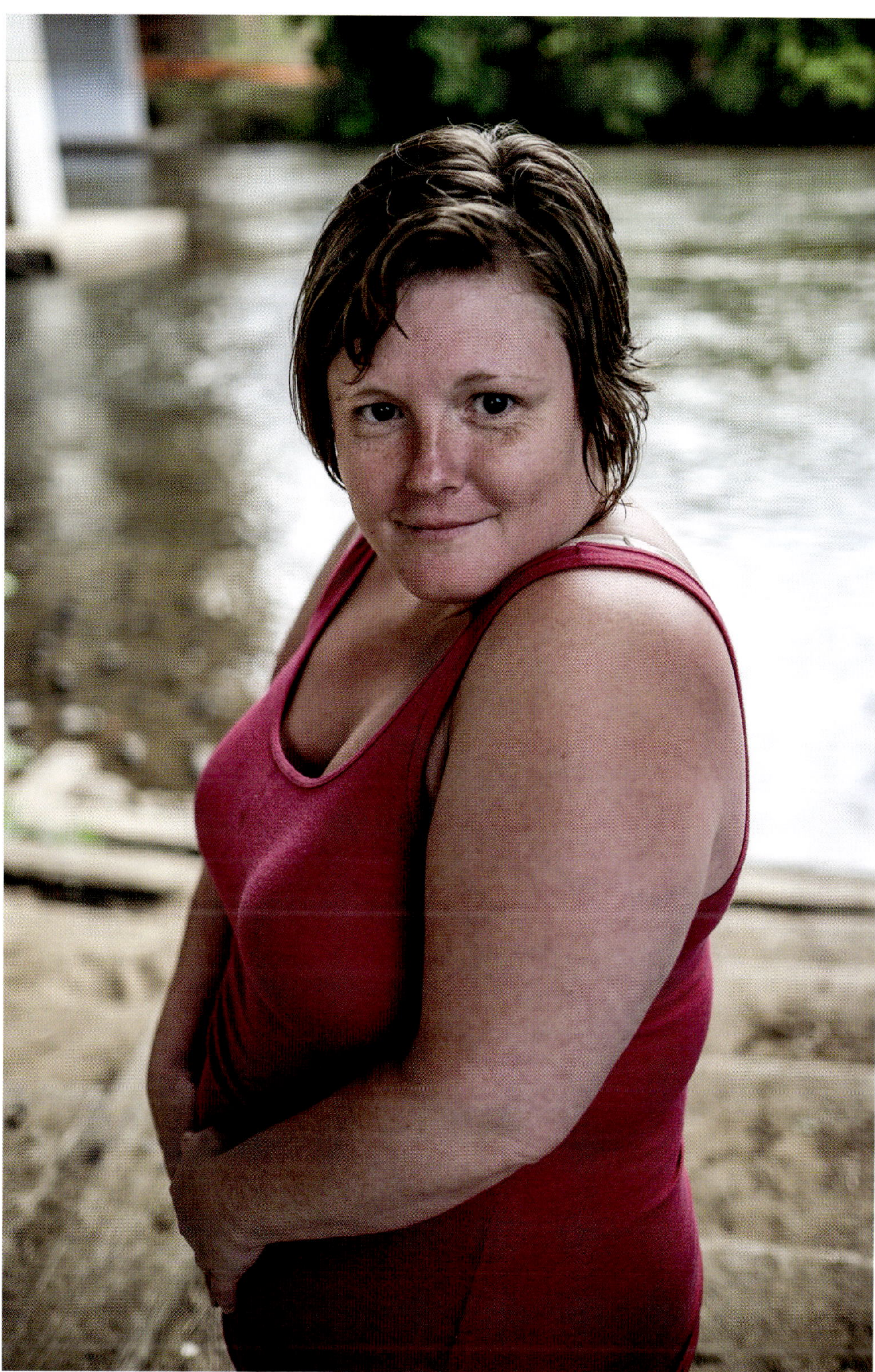

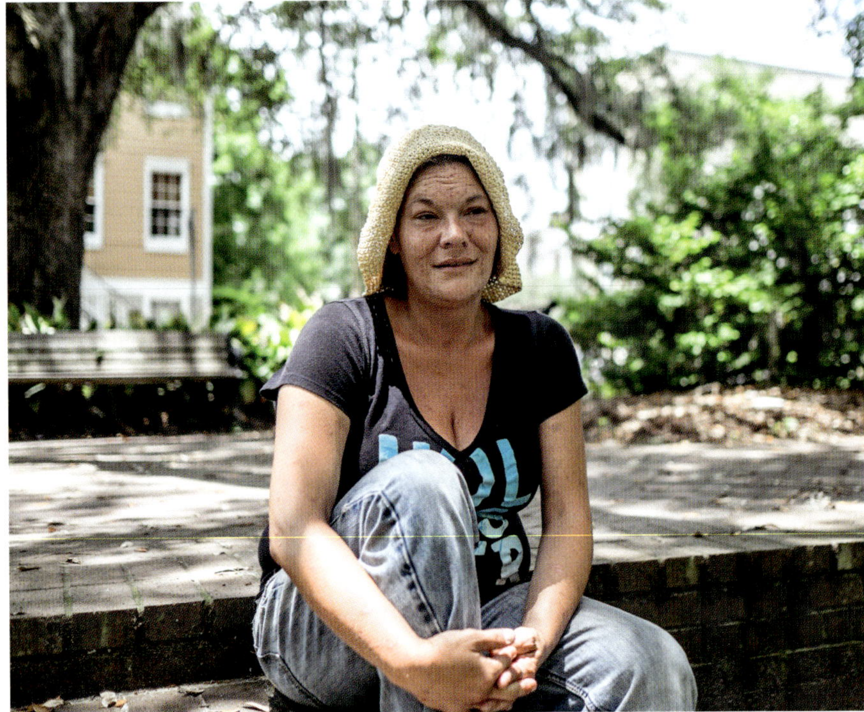

SAVANNAH, GA – 2015-05-22

Amy: It starts out as, "Do you have a cigarette?" or "Can you get me a beer?" and then it's, "I want you." About six times a day, I have to say, "I'm not for sale." That's just how a lot of people live on the streets. I don't belong on the streets. [Tears.] I have a master's degree. I don't belong on the streets! I have cancer. I need medical treatment and a home to live in and a job.

But today I was blessed with my birth certificate, so Tuesday I'll be able to go get my ID and hopefully go to work. [Sobbing.] It sounds stupid, but it's hard to get a bath or shower. I can't go to work if I don't have a way to shower. There are a lot of shelters, but they usually don't have room for women. I'm a victim of violence at least once a week out here, and none of the domestic violence shelters have any room. So I'm left to sleep in a tent or in the outdoors.

BW: I'm really sorry. What do you have a master's in?

Amy: In psychology. I specialized in substance abuse and sex offenders. I worked for the state of Illinois for fifteen years.

BW: Interesting. Why did you get into that line of work?

Amy: My grandfather was an alcoholic, and he was also my favorite person in the world. [Cracks beer open.]

I was taught to drive when I was ten. My grandpa would let me drive his brand new truck because he drank. I thought it was normal. He would say, "Pull over here. I've gotta check the wheel, Amy." He'd get a beer out of the toolbox in the back and pee on the tire. Then I could drive on to the bar.

BW: Did he let you go in the bar?

Amy: Oh yes. All the men in the bar knew me. I was in there from the age of five until he died. They'd give me quarters to play games and buy me potato chips. Then at the end of the night, I'd drive my grandfather home.

BW: So it was kind of a hangout for you.

Amy: It was a great time because my grandpa was my favorite person in the world. He had pins in his legs from the war, and I used to follow him around and try to walk with a limp just like him. He was my biggest hero.

BW: I'd be remiss if I didn't ask . . . Your grandfather was an alcoholic, and you treated people who were addicted. I meet you today, and you're drinking a beer. That doesn't necessarily mean anything, but . . .

Amy: No, I am an alcoholic. I am. I drink to ease the pain. I've been sober for years of my life. When I was raising my daughter, Mya, I didn't drink. I worked and I took care of her. After her father killed himself on his thirtieth birthday, my drinking started again. I took care of her for a year, put her through counseling, and when she was okay, I fell apart. That was my fault.

I found out when Mya was four months old that he was gay. I told him, "I love you with all my heart, but I'm not going to play house with you." But we raised our daughter as best friends. He would take off for years, but he would call me every day. So on his thirtieth birthday, he dropped Mya off. She was eight and had spent the night with her dad in a hotel.

When I told her her dad had died, she said, "Mom, Dad asked me to tell you something." I said, "What is it?" She said, "There's a letter in a wooden box at the head of his bed for you." It was a seven-page suicide letter that said I was the only person who ever accepted him for who he was and that he was simply miserable on this planet and that he had to go.

BW: Who does Mya live with now?

Amy: My parents.

BW: If you could tell your daughter one thing, what would it be?

Amy: [Tears.] You're my best friend. I love you. I'll always be with you.

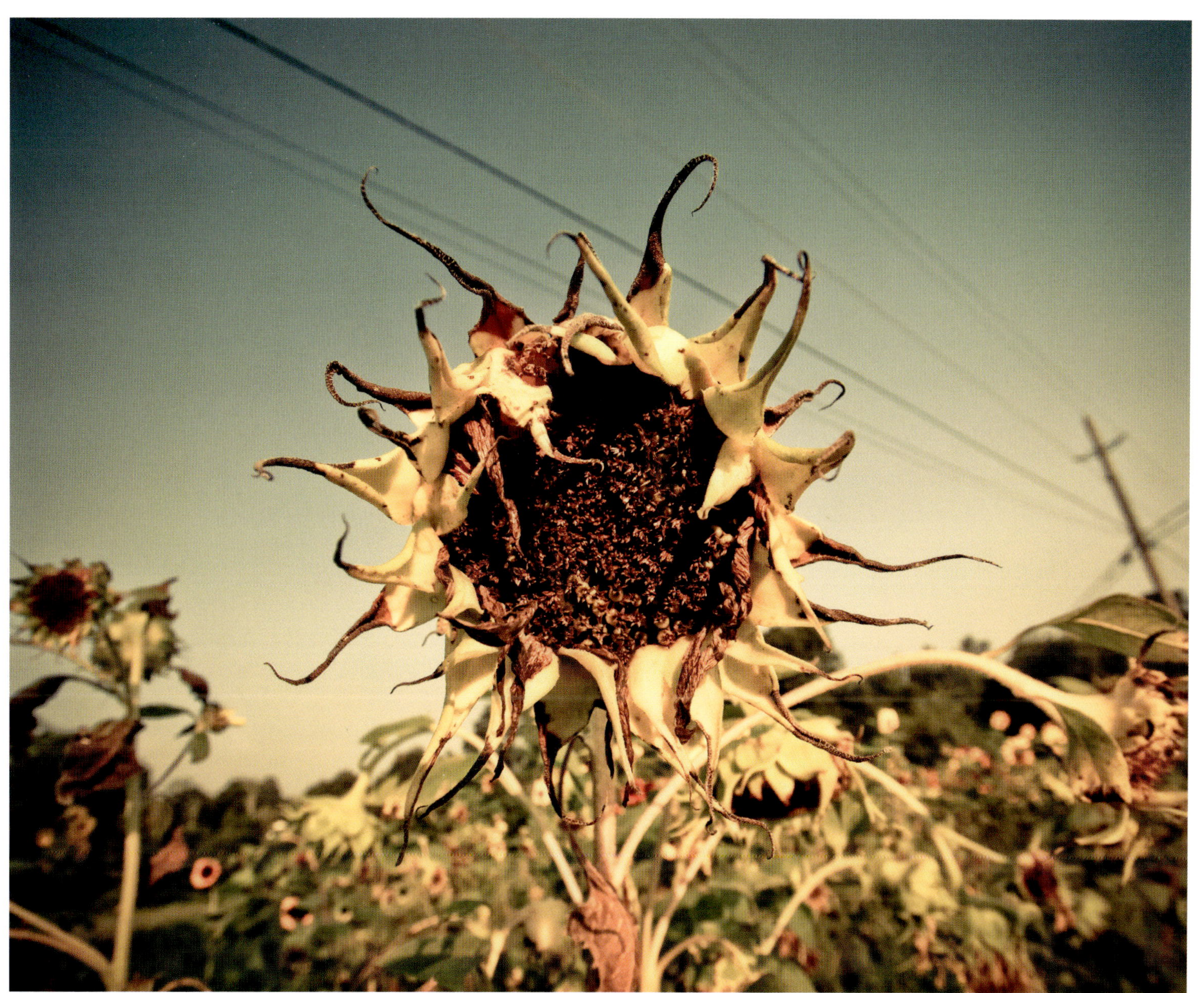

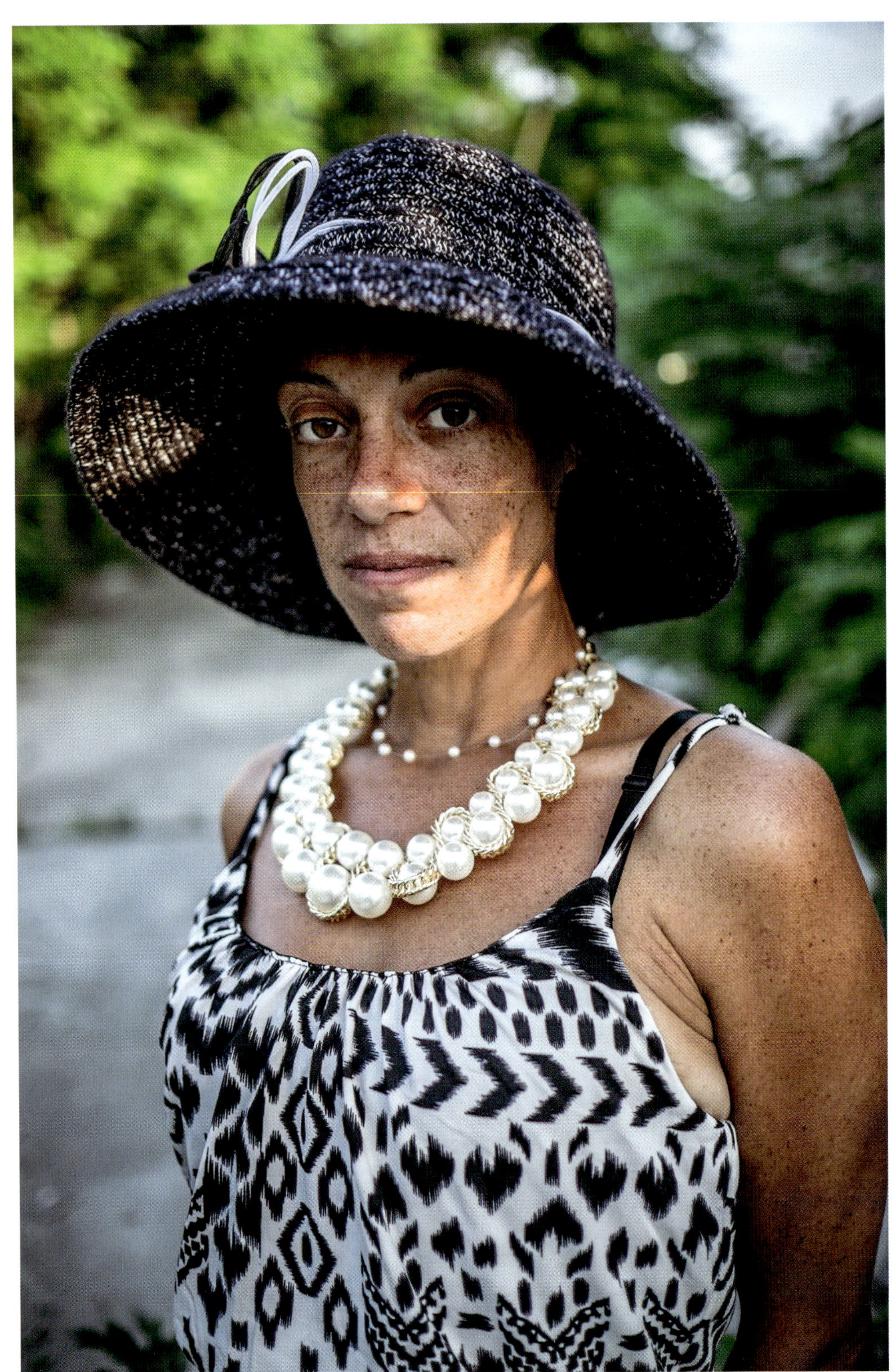

NEW ORLEANS, LA – 2015-05-09

Amber: My son changed my life, for the better. He taught me a lot of things, like responsibility and the true meaning of unconditional love.

BW: Where's your son now?

Amber: My son is in New Hampshire.

BW: Does he live with family?

Amber: He lives with his father at the moment.

BW: Do you mind if I ask why?

Amber: I battled with addiction. My son also taught me that when you love someone, you want what's best for them. I feel I did the most unselfish act I could do by letting him go, you know? [Tears.] We all have to let go at some point. I just had to sooner than I wanted.

BW: What's your addiction?

Amber: Heroin. I'm sober now. A little over a year.

BW: Good job. That's a long time. Do you go to meetings or anything?

Amber: I do. I go to meetings, and I'm involved in a ministry.

BW: What was your bottom?

Amber: My bottom was living in abandoned buildings, eating out of trash barrels. I reduced myself from this beautiful, educated, caring, kind, loving person to someone who was angry, manipulative, shady, disgusting. It's like Dr. Jekyll and Mr. Hyde.

BW: Do you have regrets?

Amber: I used to regret a lot of things. But you know what? It's just such a waste of time. I look at everything now as a learning experience. As long as you learn from it, it's not in vain. You can use that experience to benefit someone else so they don't have to go through the same thing.

BW: How old is your son?

Amber: He's seventeen.

BW: Do you have much of a relationship with him?

Amber: I do. I talk to him every night on the phone. I have a son who is far greater than I deserve. I love him unconditionally.

BW: Do you think he knows that?

Amber: [Tears.] I hope so.

CARROLLTON, MS – 2015-05-14

Cameron: I came out on the first day of high school. I actually had a girlfriend at the time, but . . . fourth period hit, and I saw the most beautiful guy I'd ever seen in my life. Instantly I knew.

BW: Who did you come out to?

Cameron: My mom.

BW: What did she say?

Cameron: She started crying. My family's Mormon, so I had to go to Mormon church counseling. Friends and everything were good. It was home that was not good. I was told not to tell my grandparents or other family members. We just don't talk about it. The whole "it's just a phase" thing.

So ever since that first day of high school, the conflict got bigger and bigger and bigger until I was seventeen. I ended up getting emancipated.

The hardest part for me was them not accepting me for who I am. I feel like the whole reason they weren't accepting is because they were so scared of what everyone else would think. When I actually told family, they either had known for years or it just really didn't matter to them. It was no big deal.

My mom and I hadn't talked for a while after I got emancipated. She called me one day and asked me how I was doing. Then she asked me how my boyfriend was doing . . . That was a big step. After that, we both started trying.

Now I have the best relationship I could ever ask for with my mother and my dad and the rest of my family. I don't have to hide who I am to any of them.

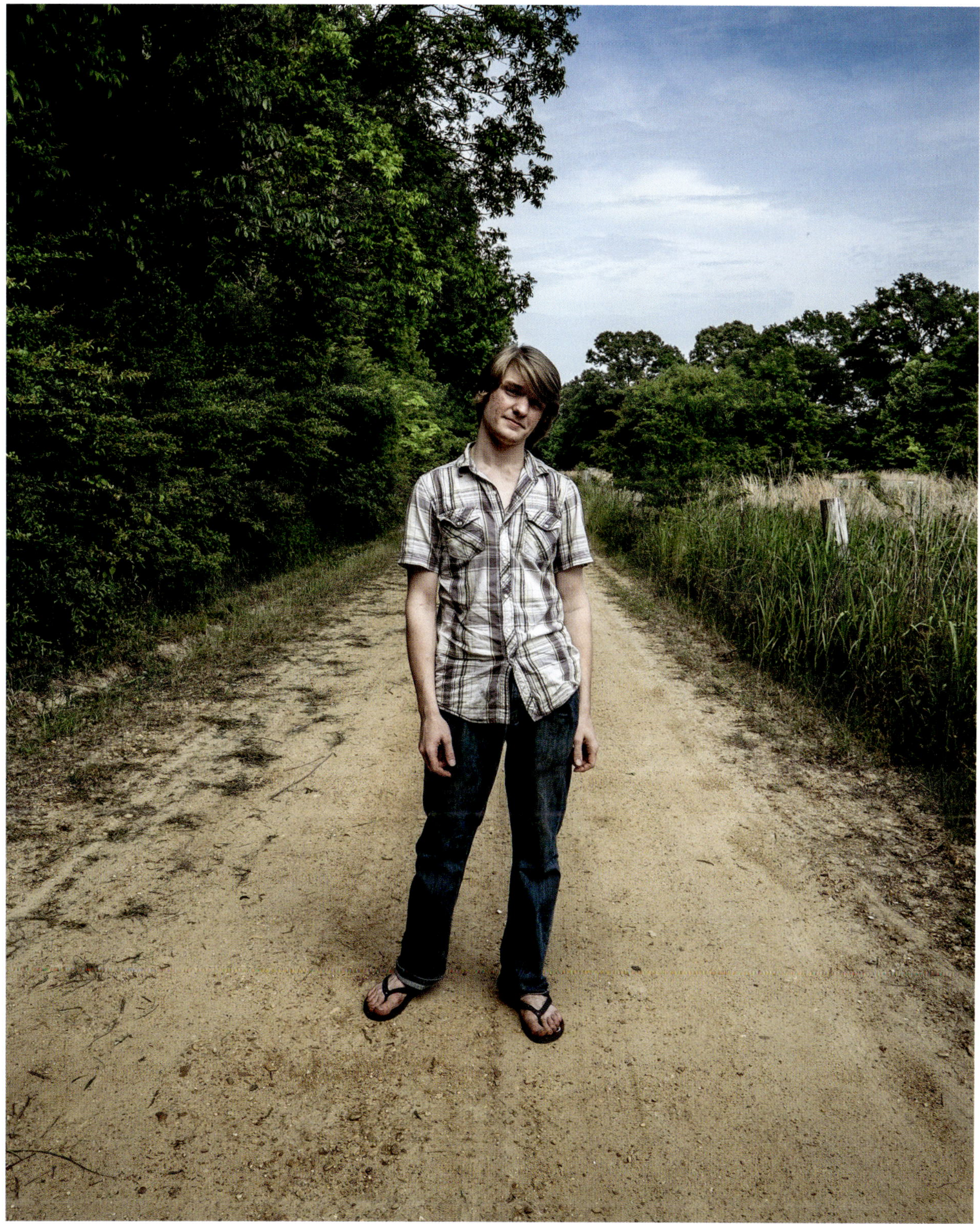

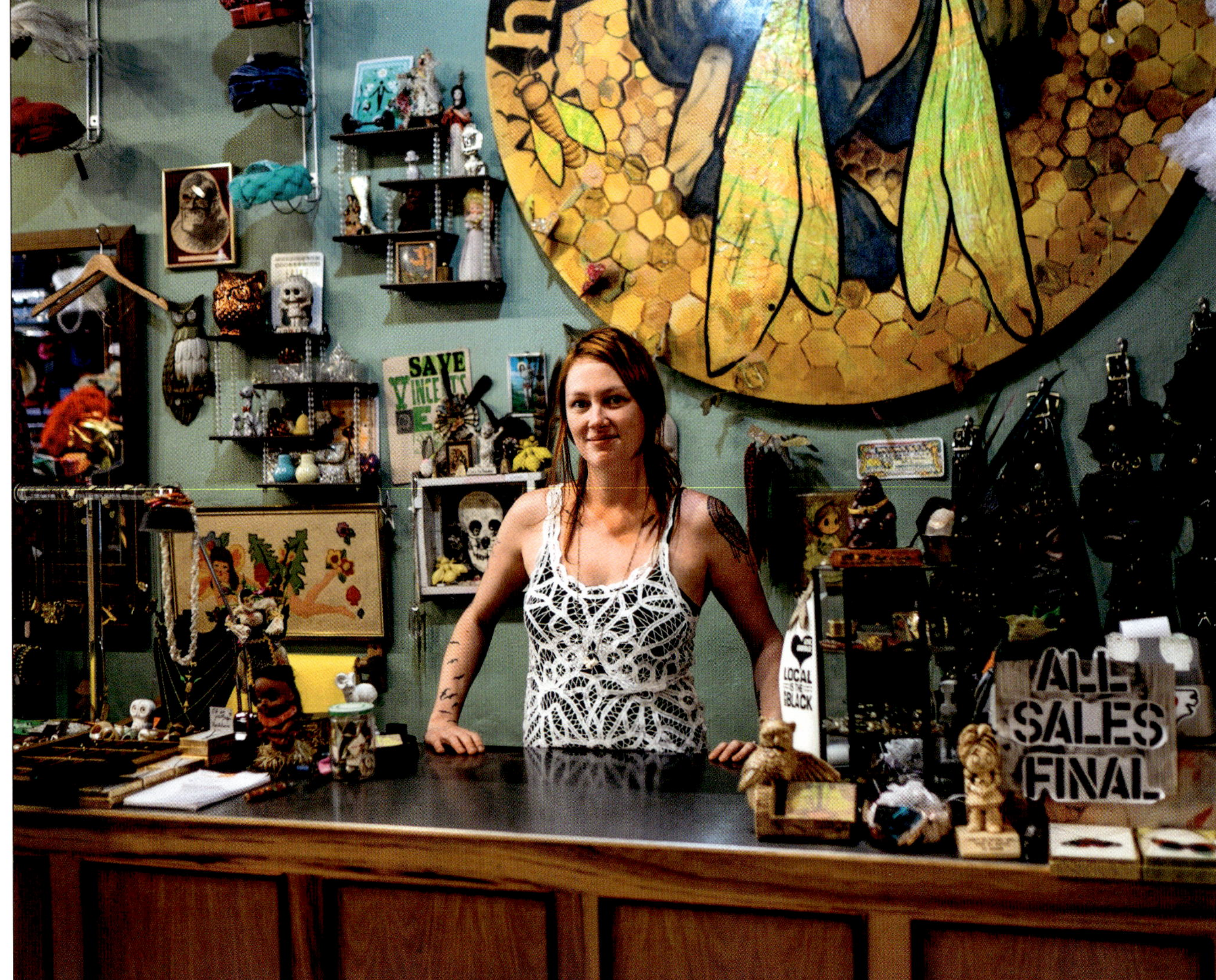

ASHEVILLE, NC – 2015-05-31

BW: What was it like growing up with a mother who was schizophrenic?

Eugenia: Honestly, I didn't know that she was until I was about fifteen. I just thought she was eccentric and quirky, which she was. I took a psychology class when I was fifteen at the community college, and something clicked. I went home and told everyone, and they were like, "Yeah. You didn't know that?"

BW: Was she ever on medication?

Eugenia: No. She married into a very well-to-do family. My two older sisters are from that marriage. During that time, she decided she wanted to be an artist. She got into yoga and meditation and all that. She said that [her in-laws and husband] didn't like that, and they institutionalized her because of it. But I think there's more to the story. But no, she was never medicated. She never went to therapy or anything.

BW: I've talked to other people who grew up with schizophrenic parents, and it could get scary. Was it ever like that with her?

Eugenia: No. My sisters say she calmed down a lot by the time I came along. She was forty-two when she had me. But it really flared up in her late twenties and early thirties. But when I knew her, she just thought the FBI was after us. But it made sense because she was really good friends with Jerry Garcia.

BW: Really? How cool.

Eugenia: Well, she was best friends with Jerry Garcia's baby mama, Manasha Garcia, so we traveled with them a little bit. So she thought that because of his drug connections that the FBI was always after us. It kinda made sense.

She was also obsessed with religion. She would bounce around to different religions and thought that Jesus Christ was walking the earth. She would give every homeless person she saw money because she thought it was God testing her. It was a mixture of Christianity, Hinduism, and Buddhism. She had altars everywhere and crucifixes everywhere. We said the Lord's Prayer every time we got off the phone. A lot of superstition.

But she was super hilarious and really, really intelligent—pianist and tai chi instructor and writer and poet.

BW: Do you see her in you? Some of her quirkiness?

Eugenia: Yeah, for sure. But she was a great mother in a lot of ways. And in a lot of ways it's like, why didn't you teach me how to be a person?

MORGANTON, NC – 2015-06-05

Read part 1 of Sylvia's story on p. 45.

Sylvia and I continued to talk about life and death and she told me this story about the loss of her son.

Sylvia: Everybody experiences death and loss, so I'm not that much different.

BW: Yeah, but not everyone has to bury their child.

Sylvia: That's true. That's true. We had two sons, and he was our youngest. He died one week after his thirty-fifth birthday, very suddenly. He had an abdominal aneurysm.

We were out of town at an antique show. We had a three-story house, and we had to get a ladder to climb in because the house was locked. It was bad. It was horrible. And you know, there are certain images you can't erase. They're ingrained in your memory forever.

My husband tried to keep me from going in the house, and I just about knocked him down getting in there. My son was laying on the sofa. My son had beautiful blue eyes, and of course you die with your eyes open—that's all I saw. I grabbed him up. Later on that night, my husband wouldn't let me go back home. I asked why, and he said there was something he had to clean up. I asked what it was, and he said, "The blood in front of the sofa." I hadn't even seen the blood. I just saw my son.

Sooner or later, the good images come. They kind of envelope you, and you only have those bad images occasionally.

He rode a motorcycle, and he drank beer. I used to worry, of course. He'd say, "Mama, just don't worry about me. I work hard, I party hard, I live hard, but I'm a good person. When it's gonna be my time, there's not gonna be anything you can do to stop it. Everybody's got their time."

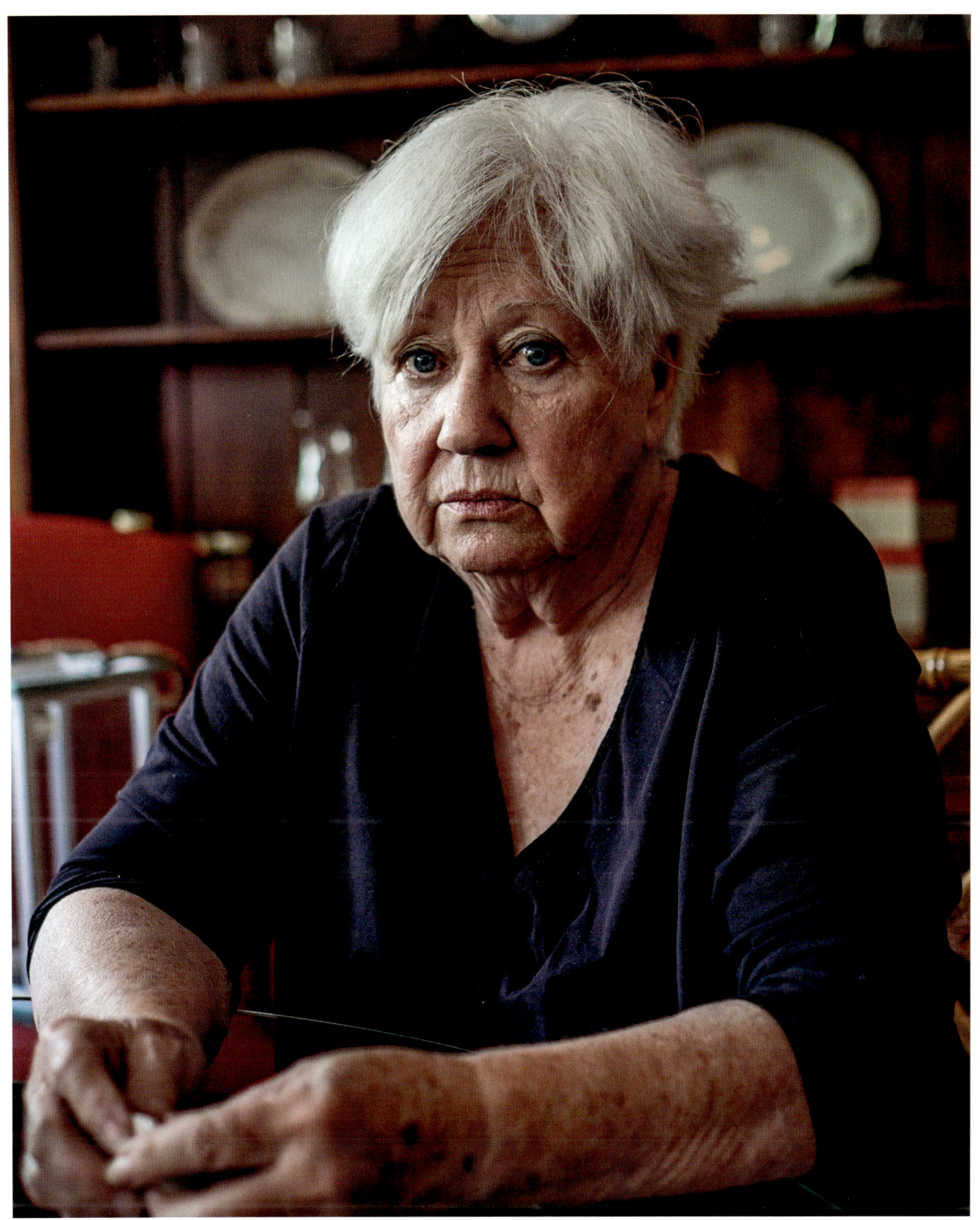

I saw the staffs, and I don't know why I did it, but I reached out for this one. Right before I grabbed it, he said, “It's yours.” I told him I didn't have anything to trade, no money, nothing to offer. He said, “Take it—it's yours.” I still resisted. He looked me in the eyes and said “Take it. You might need it to fend off the wolves.”

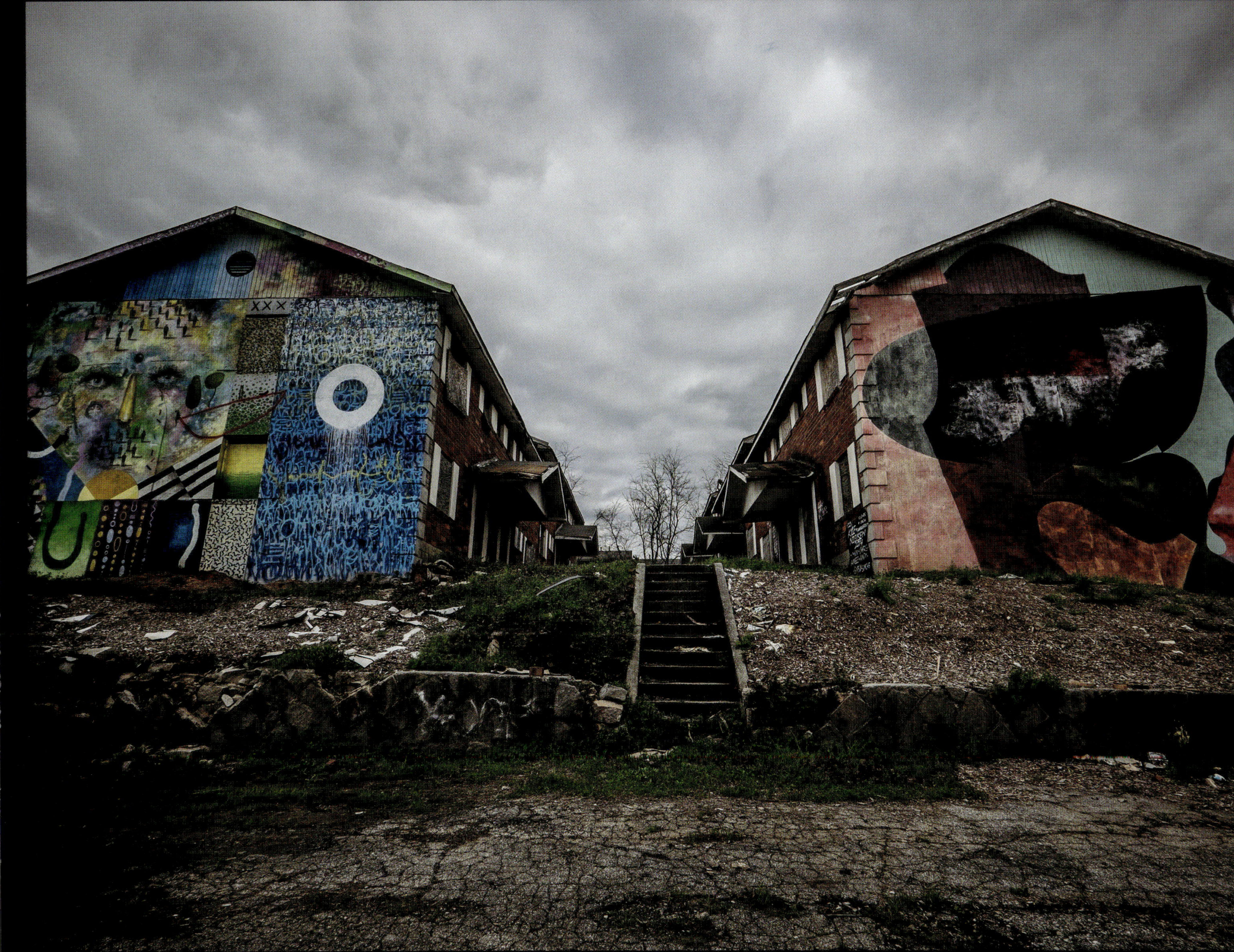

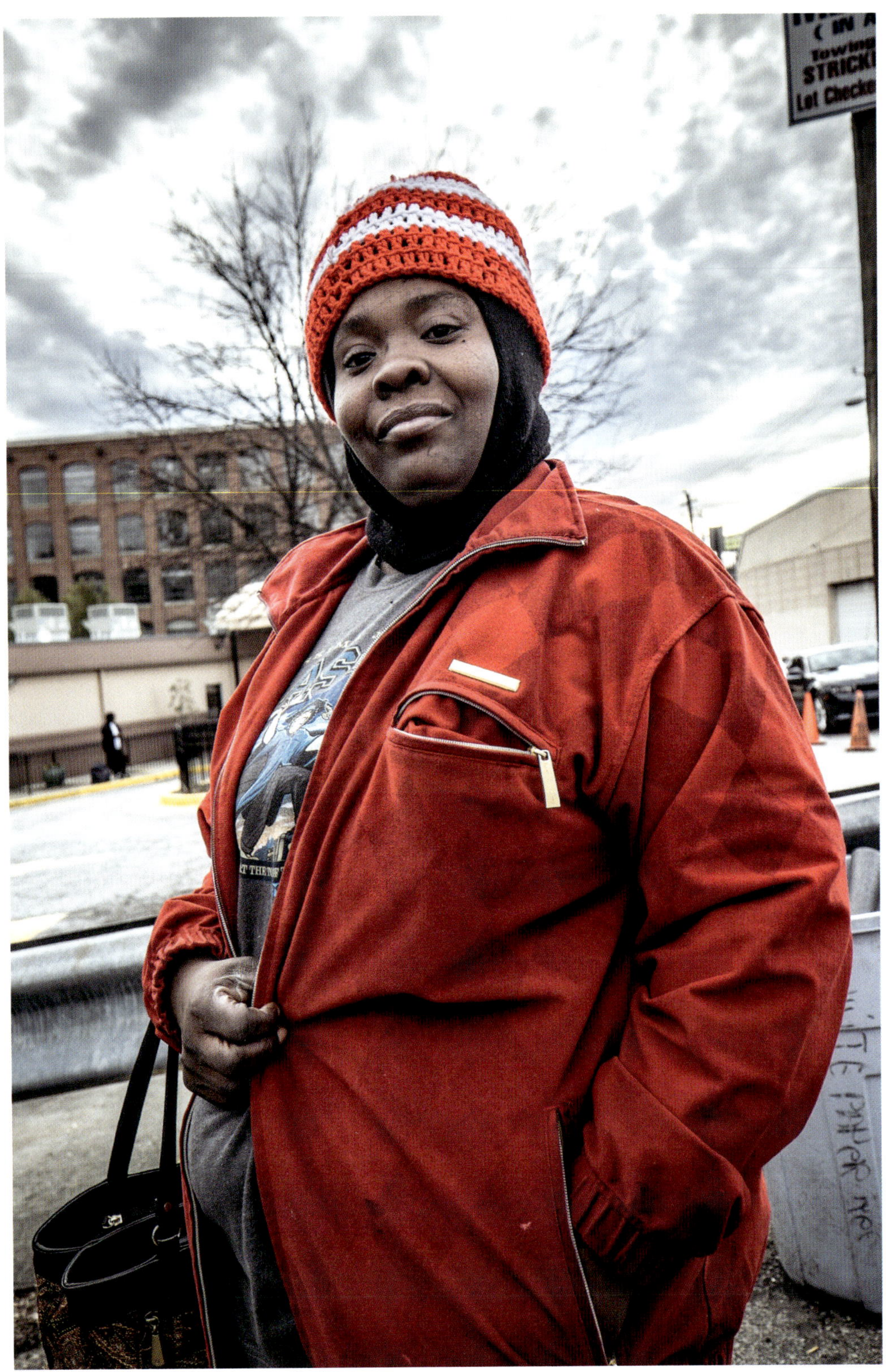

ATLANTA, GA – 2015-01-04

Charlette: When I was young, my mom was an alcoholic, and she had a bunch of abusive boyfriends. She would get drunk and forget I was with her in a liquor house, and a lot of her boyfriends would molest me. One particular boyfriend I told her about molesting me—he shot my mom, in front of me, with a twelve-gauge shotgun. Blew her leg off. I was nine and a half years old.

BW: Why did he do it?

Charlette: Because he didn't want her to go to another liquor house next door, and because she had gotten on to him about touching me.

Catch this **. . .** she testified at his trial on his behalf, and he didn't get but five years. He came out after doing two and a half and stayed with her for six months. But he couldn't deal with her leg being blown off and her being handicapped, so he left.

My mother never recovered. She became worser of an alcoholic. I ended up in foster care, and she died at age forty-two of cancer.

BW: Do you forgive your mom?

Charlette: I do **. . .** She also abused me as a child. When she lost her leg, she took it out on me. That was one of the reasons they put me in a foster home. The only thing I have from my mother is her teeth prints.

BW: She bit you?

Charlette: Yes, she bit me. She threw bottles at me and cut me in the head. She used to lock me in a room. When her alcoholism got real bad, all of her friends left her, and I was the only one for her to take her anger out on.

BW: I'm really sorry that happened.

ATLANTA, GA – 2015-03-26

Angela: I've been through it all. I've been stabbed, ran over, hit in the head with a shotgun, choked unconscious.

BW: Tell me about whatever you want.

Angela: Well, when I was a year old, my grandfather started raping me. I started having bad dreams and couldn't wake up. I would dream that snakes were crawling in and out of me, and I never knew why until I was like seven or eight years old. I went to the psychologist, and they found out that my grandfather was raping me. It went on till I was sixteen.

BW: I thought you said they found out he was raping you when you went to the psychologist at seven.

Angela: Well, my mom knew, but she didn't tell anybody else, and neither did I. It didn't happen again from the time I was seven until I was fourteen, when I ran away and went to my dad's. And that's when it started happening again.

He took me and kept me in a motel for about three years. Held a gun to my head while he raped me . . . He'd sleep in front of the motel door 'cause he didn't want me to leave. Yeah, we were in Donalsonville, Georgia.

BW: How did you get away?

Angela: Well, he bought me this car. We were driving down the road, and he was drinking. He asked me to stop so he could pee. When he got out, I left.

He found me again, and him and my aunt Jeannie stole my car. She signed my name, and they sold it. So I was back around him again. I was seventeen. But this time, I pulled a gun on him and told him, "You'll never touch me again." I think maybe I had a nervous breakdown. I blacked out. You know how it looks when you're in between channels? Like the fuzz in the TV? That's all I could see.

So they ended up taking me to the hospital. I never would tell them what he had done or anything. They just knew I'd wigged out. And boy, did I.

BW: Did he ever get in trouble for what he did to you?

Angela: No, but he died a horrible death. He had a massive heart attack, and they put him in the hospital. They took half his bowel out and moved him to rehab. The day he was supposed to get out, he had another massive heart attack and died. But look—he didn't like black people, and God made sure that every single person who took care of him was black.

BW: [Laughing.] It's ironic that I meet you in the middle of an almost-all black neighborhood. I wonder if there's anything to that?

Angela: [Laughing.] I don't know . . . I just get along with black women better. Every white friend I've ever had has tried to screw me over, steal my clothes, fuck my old man. And so I just don't trust them.

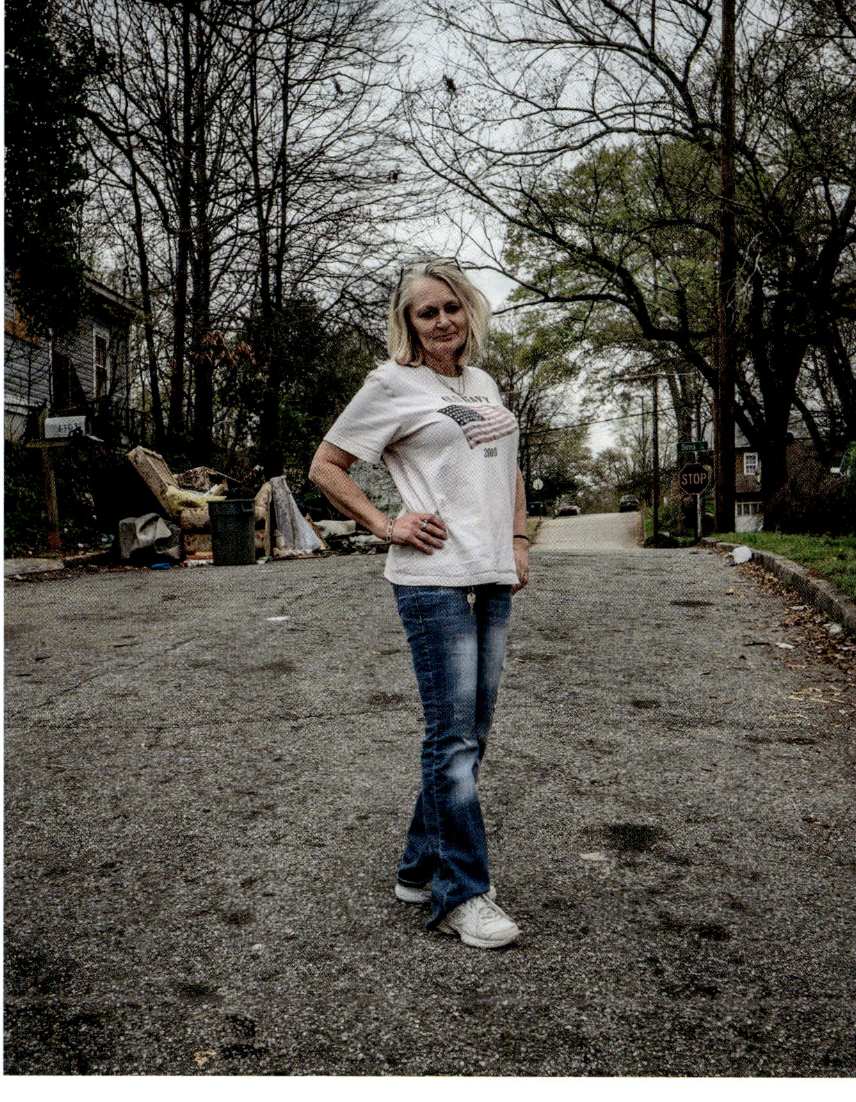

BW: But you trust black women?

Angela: Yep. They stick with you, buddy.

BW: Well, what was the best day of your life?

Angela: Hell if I know . . . When I got baptized. My cousin said I had a gold ring around me, and I was talking to God in tongues. It was pretty cool. It's gonna make me cry . . . But you talk about the best feeling. Your body's so light . . . it's unreal.

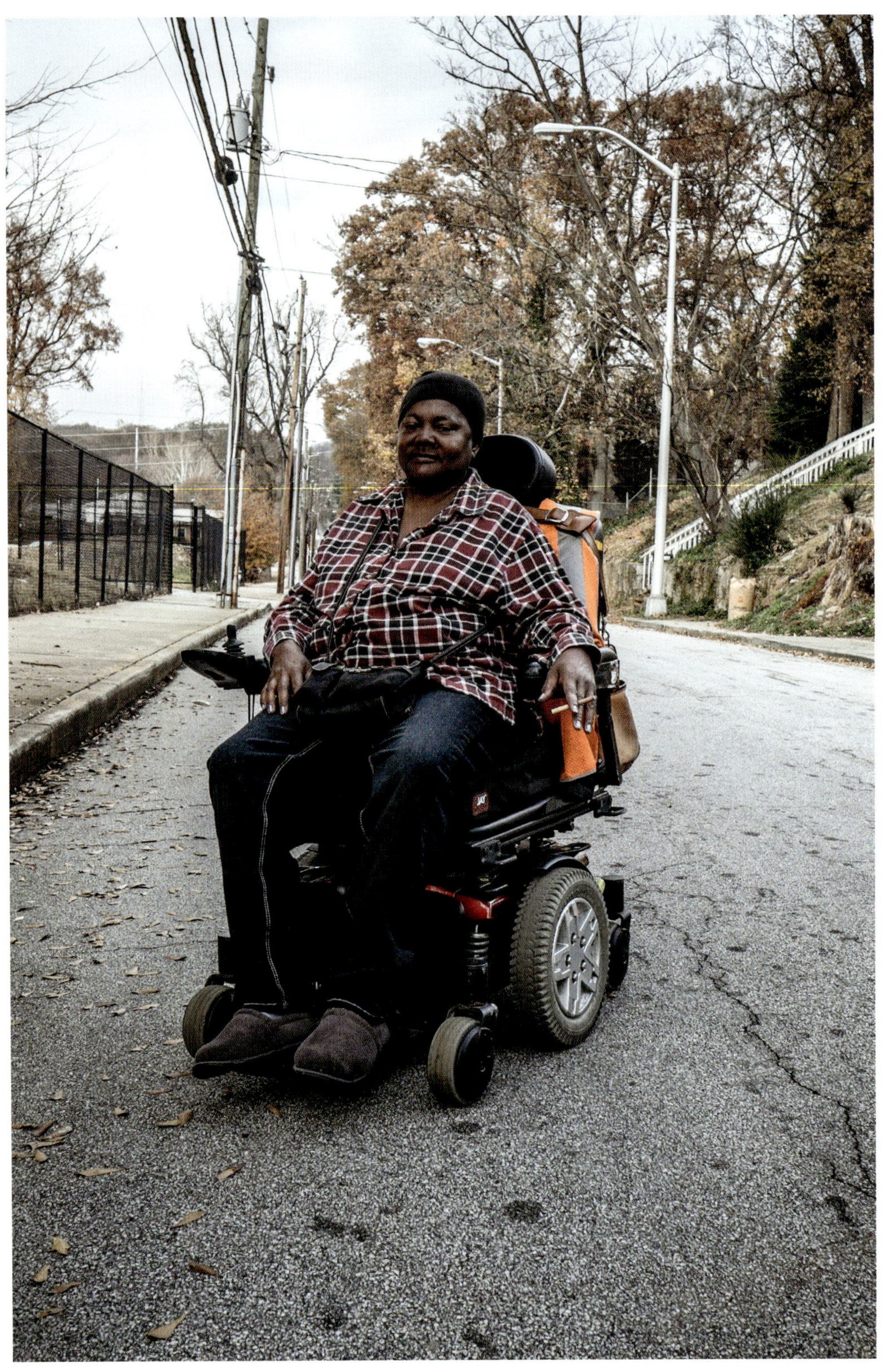

ATLANTA, GA – 2014-12-03

Myrtle: Men . . . I cut 'em out. I came home from the hospital and found a woman in my bed with my boyfriend that I was with for nineteen years. I cut him loose, cold turkey.

BW: I'm sorry. Guess he didn't know you were coming home?

Myrtle: Nuh-uh. Something told me to come home, and I did. I was fixin' to throw him out the window. She ran out the door.

BW: When did that happen?

Myrtle: Oh, that's been about eighteen years ago now

BW: And you still haven't had anything to do with men in all that time?

Myrtle: No. I won't now. I'm fine just like I am.

BW: If you don't have a man in your life, do you have anyone?

Myrtle: Yeah, alcohol. It makes me feel a little bit better.

BW: Are you an alcoholic?

Myrtle: No, I just like to drink.

BW: [Smiling.] That used to be my line. What was life like when you were a kid?

Myrtle: I ran track when I was going to school. I ran the mile. And I was good. Played basketball too.

BW: What did you want to be when you grew up?

Myrtle: A ballerina.

BW: A ballerina?

Myrtle: [Giggling.] Yeah, I love ballet and classical music.

BW: You never got a chance to be a ballerina?

Myrtle: No. Never got a chance to finish running either. This hit me when I was thirty-five years old.

BW: You've been in a chair ever since?

Myrtle: Yes. I have MS . . . multiple sclerosis. Constant pain. I just have to deal with it.

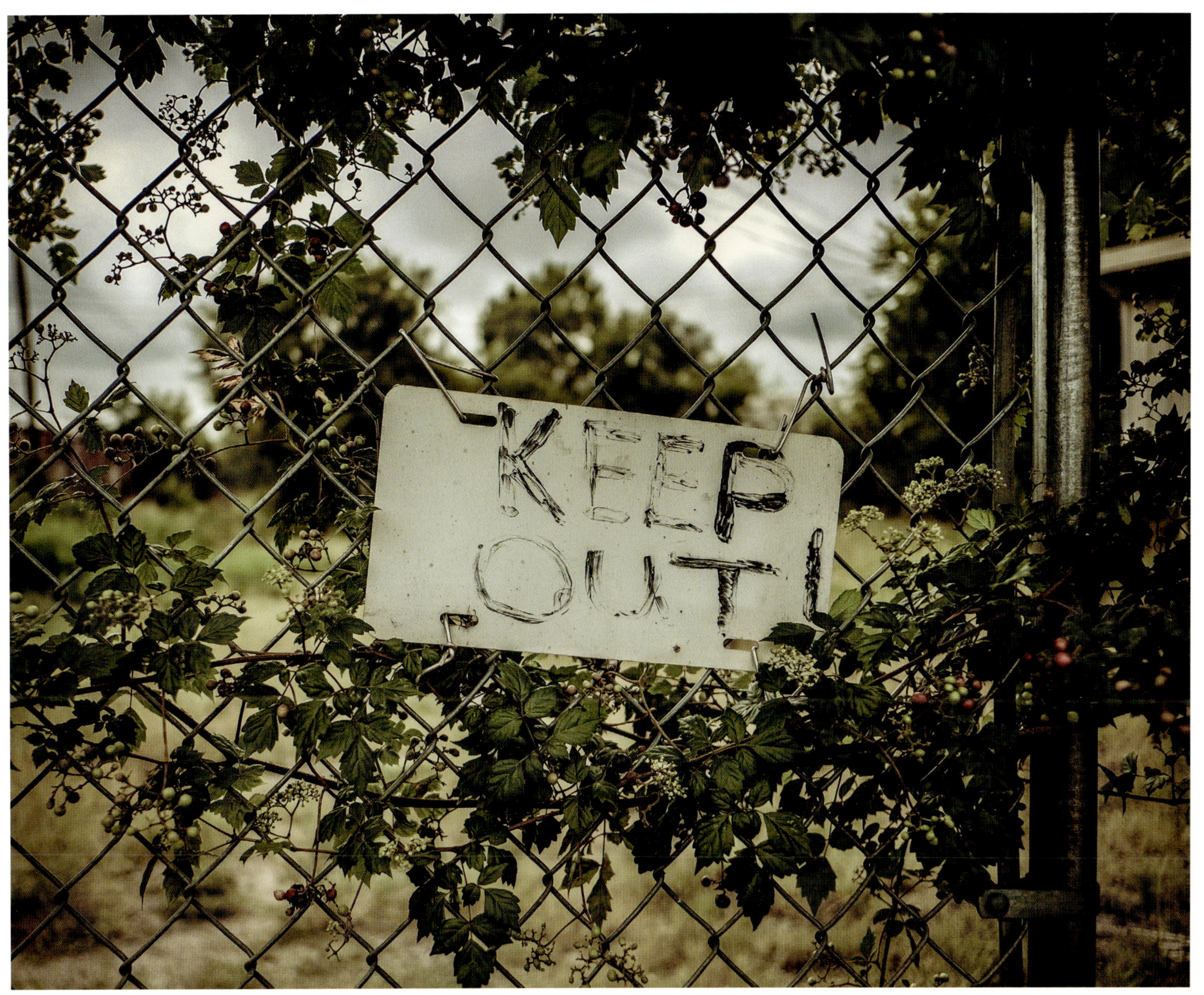
KEEP
OUT!

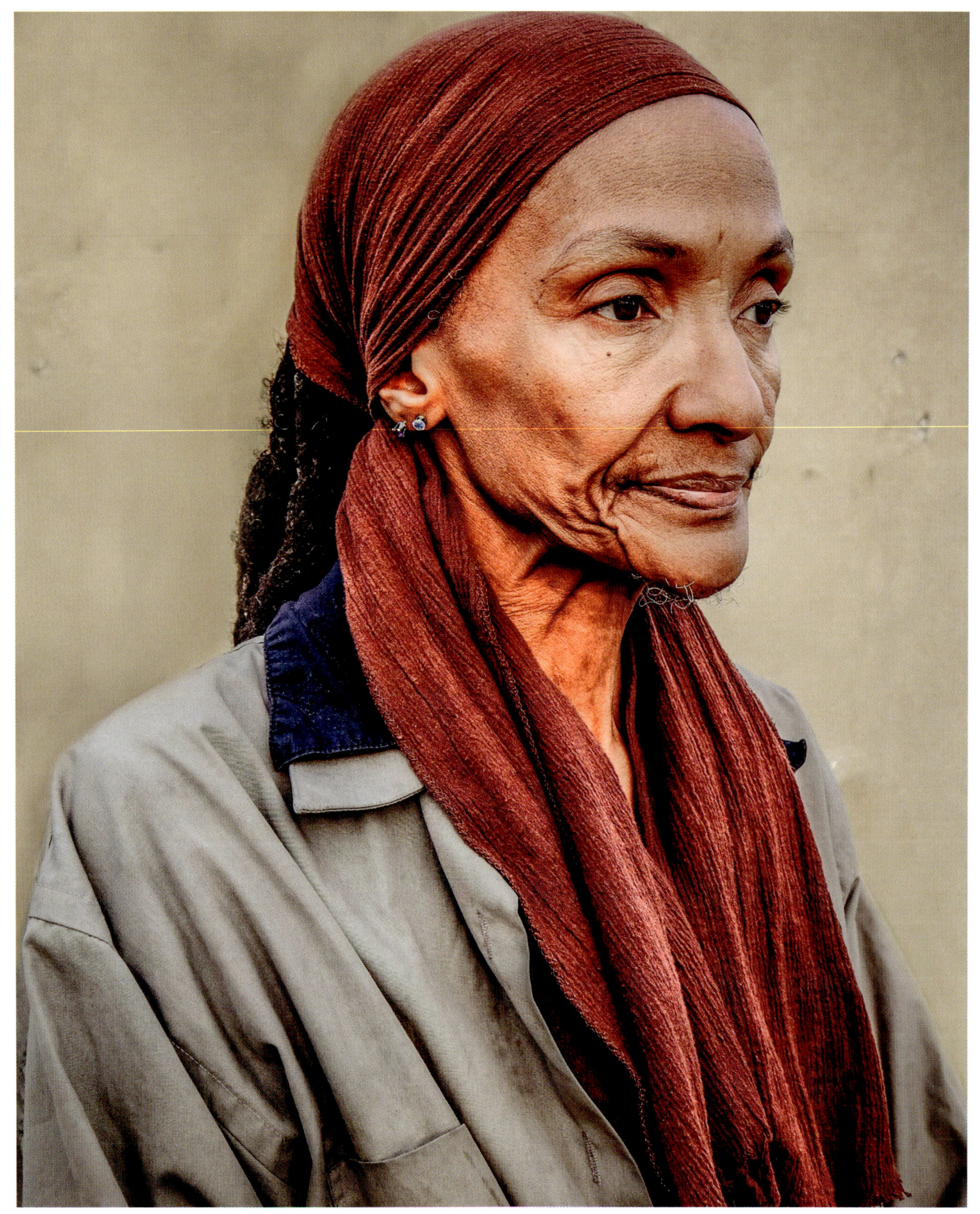

TUSKEGEE, ALABAMA — 2015-03-18

Valeeta: I'm usually a very private person, but today I'll talk to you. My husband of forty years is at home right now smashing up and destroying everything in my house. I'm not even able to go home and lay down.

BW: Is he mentally ill?

Valeeta: It's quite possible. I've put him in Gateway [hospital] before, but they wound up almost killing him. They had him in the mental ward, and somehow he got pneumonia. He's an asshole, anyway, so I guess being there he was even more of an asshole. They had him so drugged up that it almost killed him. They took him off the IV and had the county take him home. So I'm not too quick to have him sent there again.

The kids were supposed to come get him out of the house, but they didn't, so I have to endure another week of this. My daughter is supposed to make it in from Baton Rouge, and I'm trying to hold on.

BW: Have you ever left before?

Valeeta: No. I get away; I don't leave. I just give him space till things get better. This particular time I have to. He's threatened to kill me. It's gonna go my way if he tries, and I don't want to hurt him. The kids keep asking me to be the sensible one. It's really hard. Especially after what he did yesterday. If I would have had a gun, I would have shot him.

BW: What did he do?

Valeeta: He shit on my bed.

BW: No way . . . Why did he do that?

Valeeta: I don't know why. He was bragging he did it. All I know is that if I would have had a gun, I would have shot him myself.

FAIRBURN, GA – 2015-08-05

Linda: I didn't speak for two years. I just sat in [Alcoholics Anonymous] meetings. I didn't think I had anything worth saying. I'm not sure I do even now. [Laughing.] I just have a story.

BW: What brought you into recovery? Was there a particular event that happened or . . .

Linda: There were many. During the period when I was younger, a lot of girls experienced the same things I did that they didn't talk about. There was a lot of sexual abuse. I don't think that we thought we were as important as we are. Somewhere in your mind, when these things happen to you as a young girl, you think that you had a part in it. Parents, particularly mothers, were very much in denial that this was going on. My dad did not abuse me, but there were other people around me who did, and I think my mother knew. She didn't acknowledge it because it's that same old thing: if you acknowledge it, then you've got to take action, and she didn't know how to take action. So I think that was the start of it.

The first man I got involved with, I married. He was an alcoholic. He didn't drink daily, but when he drank, he was gonna get drunk. And when he got drunk, he wasn't gonna be the nicest person. That led to a lot of insanity. When I was twenty-six years old, I came in one night, and he verbally attacked me because I wasn't there when he got home. Things escalated from there, and I shot and killed him.

BW: Can you tell me about that night?

Linda: I sure can. A week before, he had taken me out, and he had shown me how to use the gun because he traveled and I was at home a lot by myself. He said to me, "There will always be a missing bullet in the first chamber, so you'll always have to pull the trigger twice."

David was the type of person that, if he was two or three hours late, you would know he was going to be two to three days late. I wouldn't know where he was, and I'd be worried about him. I'd get hysterical, and then twenty minutes later, you're so mad you want to hit him on the head when he comes in. That day, he'd gone out and didn't come back. I went out in the evening, and he was asleep on the sofa when I got home. I was just going to come in and go to bed. He got up, and he chased me around the kitchen table. He'd never done that before. Then he chased me into the bedroom, into the corner where the gun was, and I pulled it out . . . When you tell it this way, it sounds so cold and so unemotional . . . but you're backed into a corner, and you know you're about to take all hell. When I pulled the trigger that first time, boom, he was gone. He walked around the bed and dropped on the floor.

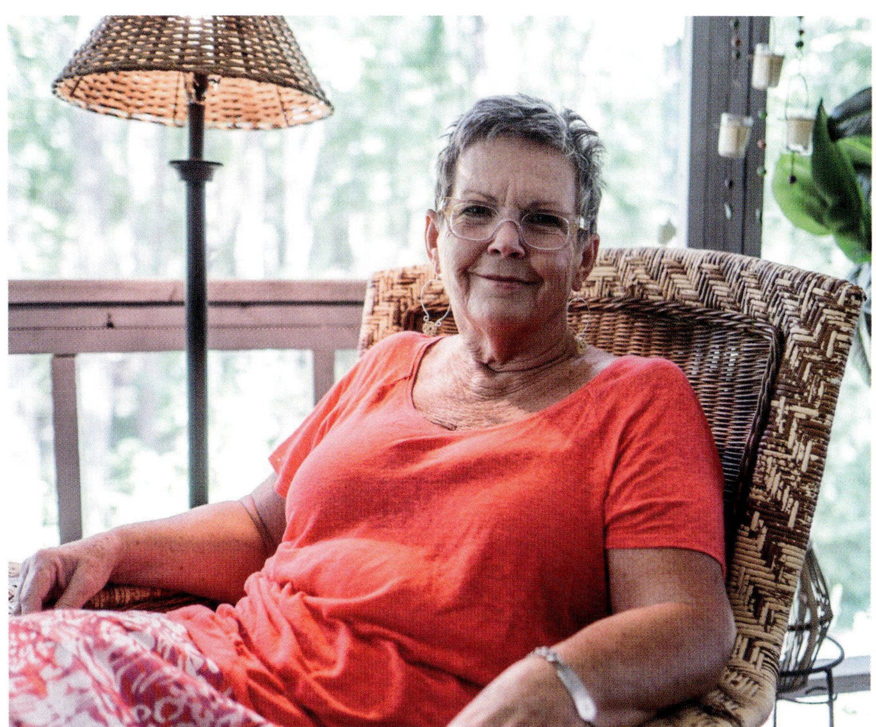

I thought he was still alive, so I called for people to come. Fortunately, the homicide detective who came was an active coroner. He said, "I've always trusted my gut when I walk into a crime scene." If it weren't for him, I'd probably have been in jail.

BW: Had he beaten you before?

Linda: Yes, many times. In fact, he had hit me that night. My face was all beat up. They took me to the hospital and photographed me, and they let me go home. That afternoon, I had to go down and make a statement. They never bothered me again.

I didn't know how to deal with something like that. I had no skills. My daddy was an alcoholic. Most of his family was alcoholic. I do remember my mother telling me later in life that my daddy said I would never be right until I forgave myself. And boy, did he hit that nail on the head. But I didn't know that at twenty-six years old. So I started running, and I ran hard and fast.

Before, I didn't drink when my husband drank because I didn't want to contribute to him getting angry. But when I started, I started hard, and I didn't let up for twelve years. If they had sent me to jail, I don't think I'd have suffered any more than I suffered on the streets. What I did to myself was above and beyond anything they could have done to me in jail. It was brutal.

Part 2 of Linda's story can be found on p. 142.

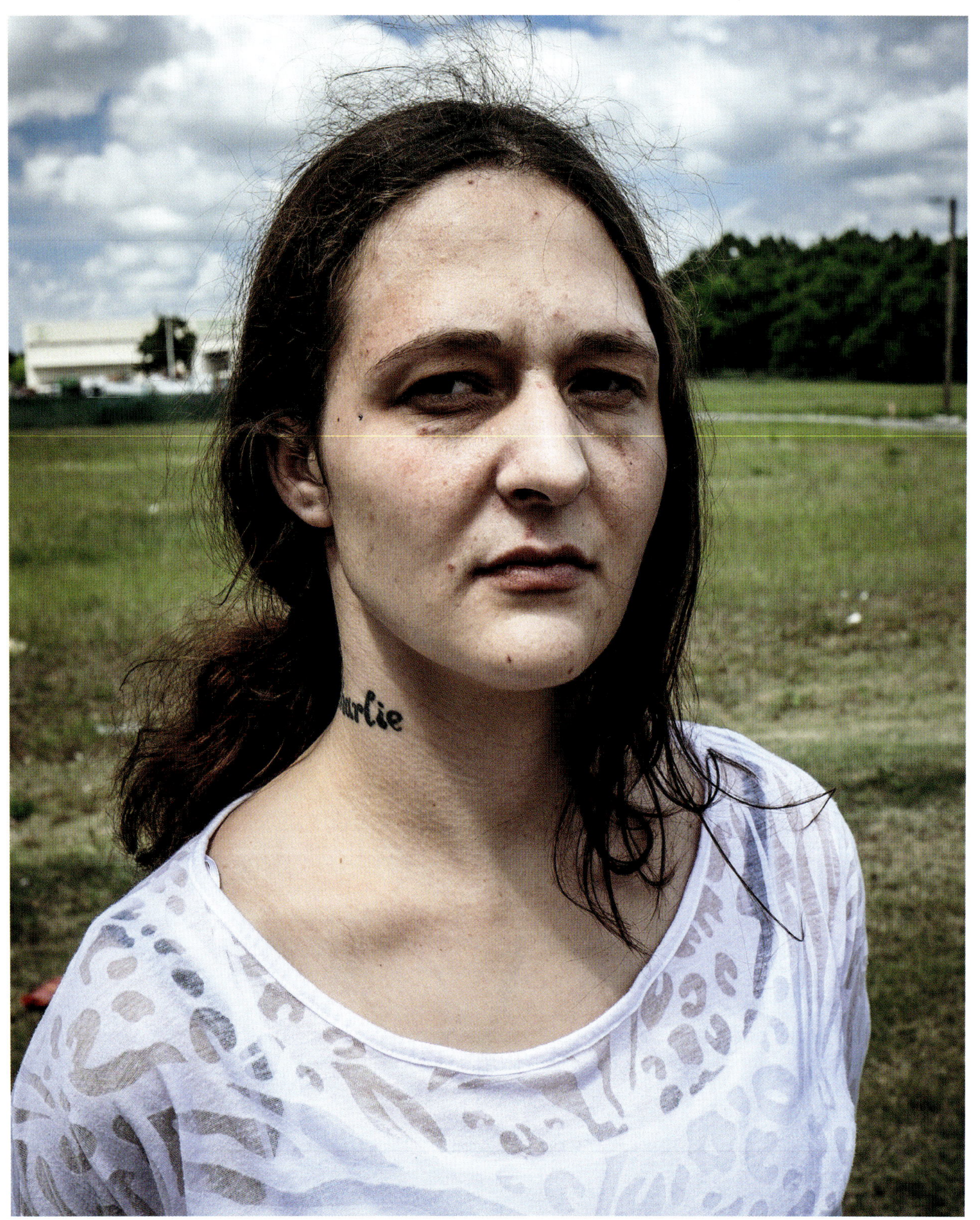

SAVANNAH, GA – 2015-05-24

I stopped at a discount store in Savannah and noticed that the cashier seemed to be recovering from being hit in the face. I asked her if she could come outside and talk to me for a few minutes.

BW: What happened to your eyes?

Brittany: My daughter's daddy. He beat me.

BW: Why did it happen?

Brittany: He was on coke for three days, mixing that with Molly. My daughter walked outside to the garage. She came back in, and as I was going through the laundry room, he just stopped me right there. No reason, really.

BW: How long have you been with him?

Brittany: Two and a half years.

BW: Has he done it before?

Brittany: Yes.

BW: Do you want to leave?

Brittany: I'm in the process. I have a friend who's trying to help me out. But see . . . he's not gonna let me leave and take my baby.

BW: Have other people beat up on you in the past?

Brittany: Yeah.

BW: What do you think is up with that?

Brittany: Well, the guy I'm with now, I told him about my previous relationships, and that was probably my downfall. I shouldn't have told him.

BW: Why? You think he hits you because you've been hit by other guys before?

Brittany: Yeah, because I've been through it already.

NEW ORLEANS, LA – 2015-05-11

Ashley: I got involved with a man. I thought he was the best man I'd ever met in my entire life, so I left home at sixteen. We were together seven years. I had two of his kids. This is not my favorite thing to talk about, but . . . he is a heroin addict, and I figured, all this time, I could change him. And there was no changing him.

He brought me here [New Orleans] about two months ago. I'm pregnant again, as you can see—about five months. Recently he up and just disappeared. So this is the position I'm in at this point.

BW: Did he have a heroin problem from the beginning?

Ashley: He did, but I didn't know that. It seemed like the perfect-whirlwind, sweep-you-off-your-feet, I'm-gonna-show-you-the-world, Aladdin kind of story, and it just didn't turn out that way.

BW: So where are you staying?

Ashley: There's abandoned buildings everywhere here. Basically you can stay in almost any of them, and they don't arrest you, so . . .

BW: Where are you from?

Ashley: Boynton Beach, Florida.

BW: You said you have two kids. How old are they?

Ashley: Two and three.

BW: Where are they?

Ashley: They are currently with my mom in Florida. I gave permanent custody to them because this isn't the position I want them in.

BW: A lot of people I talk to got started using through the person they're with. Did you start using heroin at any point?

Ashley: No. Luckily for me, I'm allergic to heroin. I did have a crack cocaine problem for a while, but recently, because of the baby, I've been off that as well.

BW: What was the hardest day?

Ashley: The day DCF came in and said, "We're taking your kids." The drug test came up dirty, and they literally came in and took the kids by force, with a police warrant. I had to watch them take my two babies out of my life.

BW: What are your plans? Do you want to make it back to Florida?

Ashley: I can't go back because of the DCF restraining order with my kids. I can't be within the same county, so if I went back, I'd be in the same position as here.

Your parents tell you when you're younger, "This isn't what you think it's gonna be. He's not who you think he is." And you think, "No, I know everything. I'm young. I can do anything." You can't.

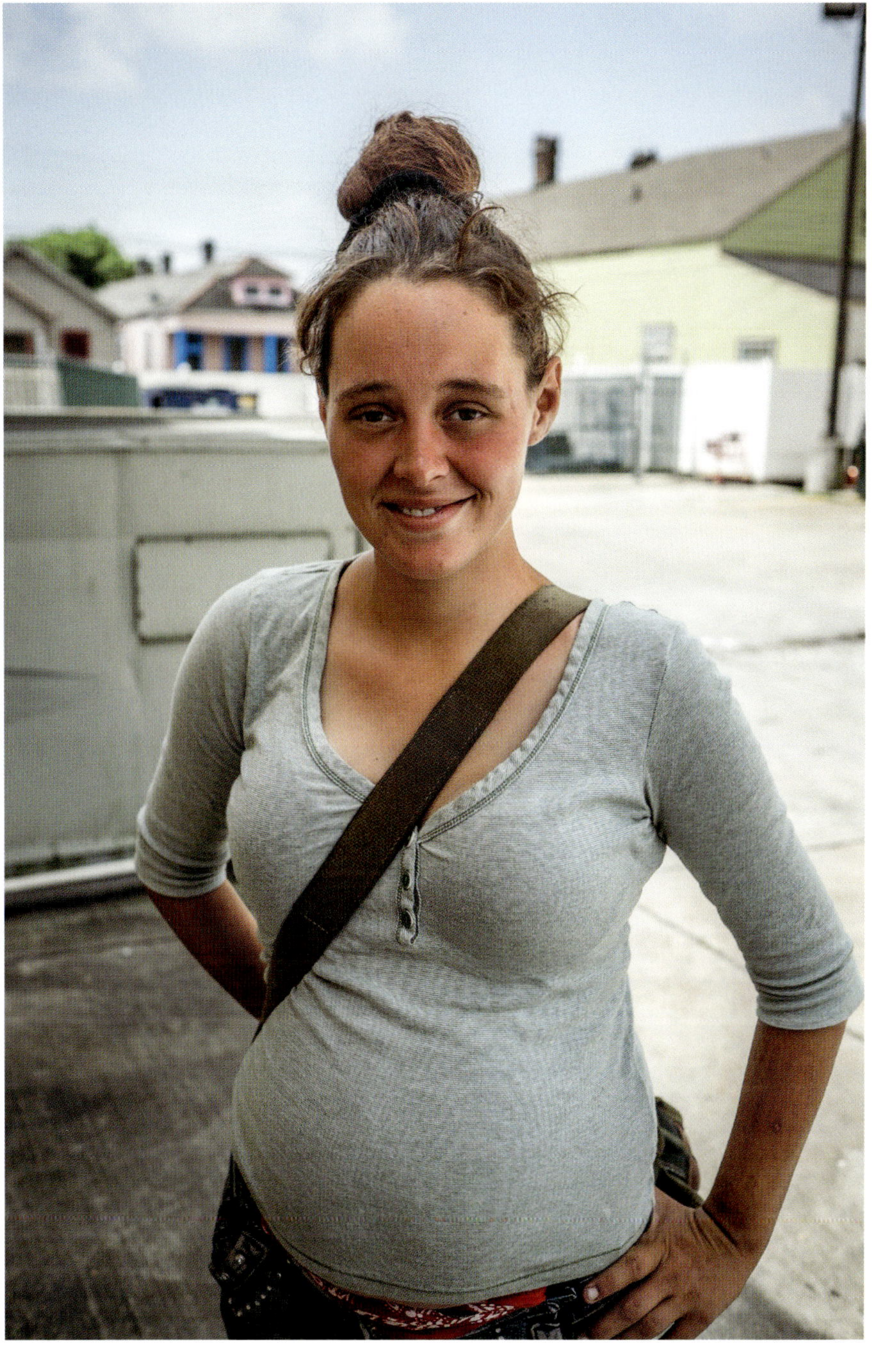

My biggest regret is not listening to my parents. Not taking their advice when they said, "If you do this, you will regret it someday."

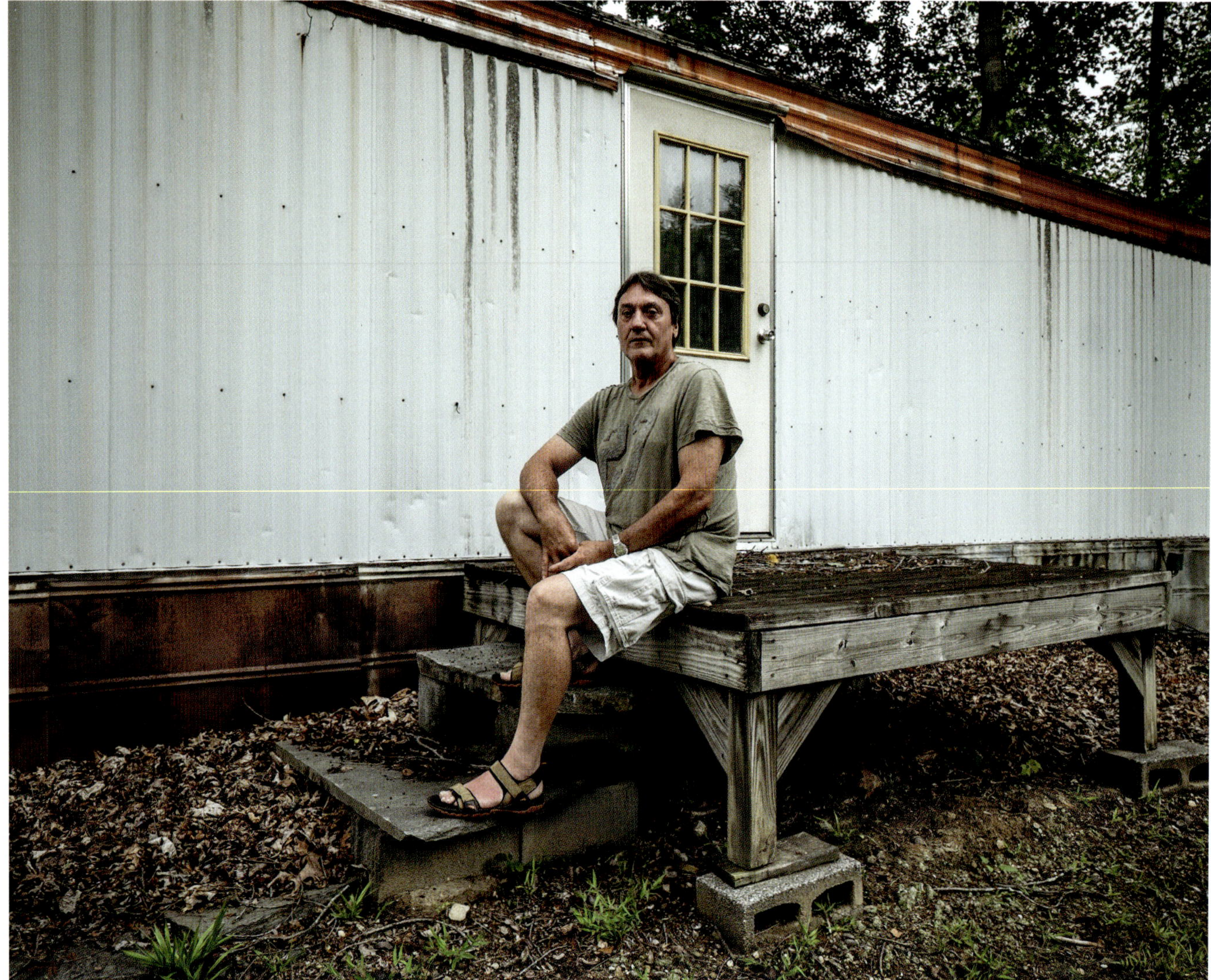

MORGANTON, NC – 2015-06-05

Vance: In 1989, me and my brother stayed in this trailer. I was in my early twenties. There weren't any real good ways to make a living or anything up here in the mountains. We was selling drugs and moonshine and stuff. It was always a dangerous game. That's when the Reagan drug laws came into effect.

A cop I knew that worked with detectives in Morganton kept telling me, "They're watching you. You need to get out of here and go do something with your life. They're gonna bust you."

I passed the word on to my brother, Johnny. He didn't believe it much. But I decided I would take his advice. If an opportunity came up, I'd move away from here and disappear for a while.

There was this guy named Dallas who bought this land across the street. He was a home builder in Wilmington, North Carolina. I went to work for him over here, and he seen that I was a pretty good builder, so he asked me if I wanted a job in Wilmington. He said he was about to start a large project with four hundred homes in February. I accepted, but it was eight months away.

During that time, we kept doing our thing, doing what we could to make a living. February came along, and I moved to Wilmington and started earning an honest living. One morning I got a phone call, and it was my mother. She said, "They got Johnny." They busted him for delivering a Schedule II narcotic: cocaine.

They'd been watching my brother and sixty-five other people in Burke County here. Fortunately, I heeded that warning to get out of town and start a new life. My brother went and did four years in federal prison.

For a couple of years down there, I was always looking over my shoulder. Every time I'd see a cop, I thought maybe they were coming for me.

I always wanted to be a builder. My grandfather was a carpenter. So I learned a trade, but it was more about the guy that gave me a break. Dallas seen potential. He believed in me when nobody else would give me a chance. Once I was out there for a while, he bought me the tools I needed to start my own business.

When we were dealing drugs and moonshine, I don't know how many times I had a gun pulled on me or a knife held to my throat. It was a terrible life. Dallas saved my life. He really did.

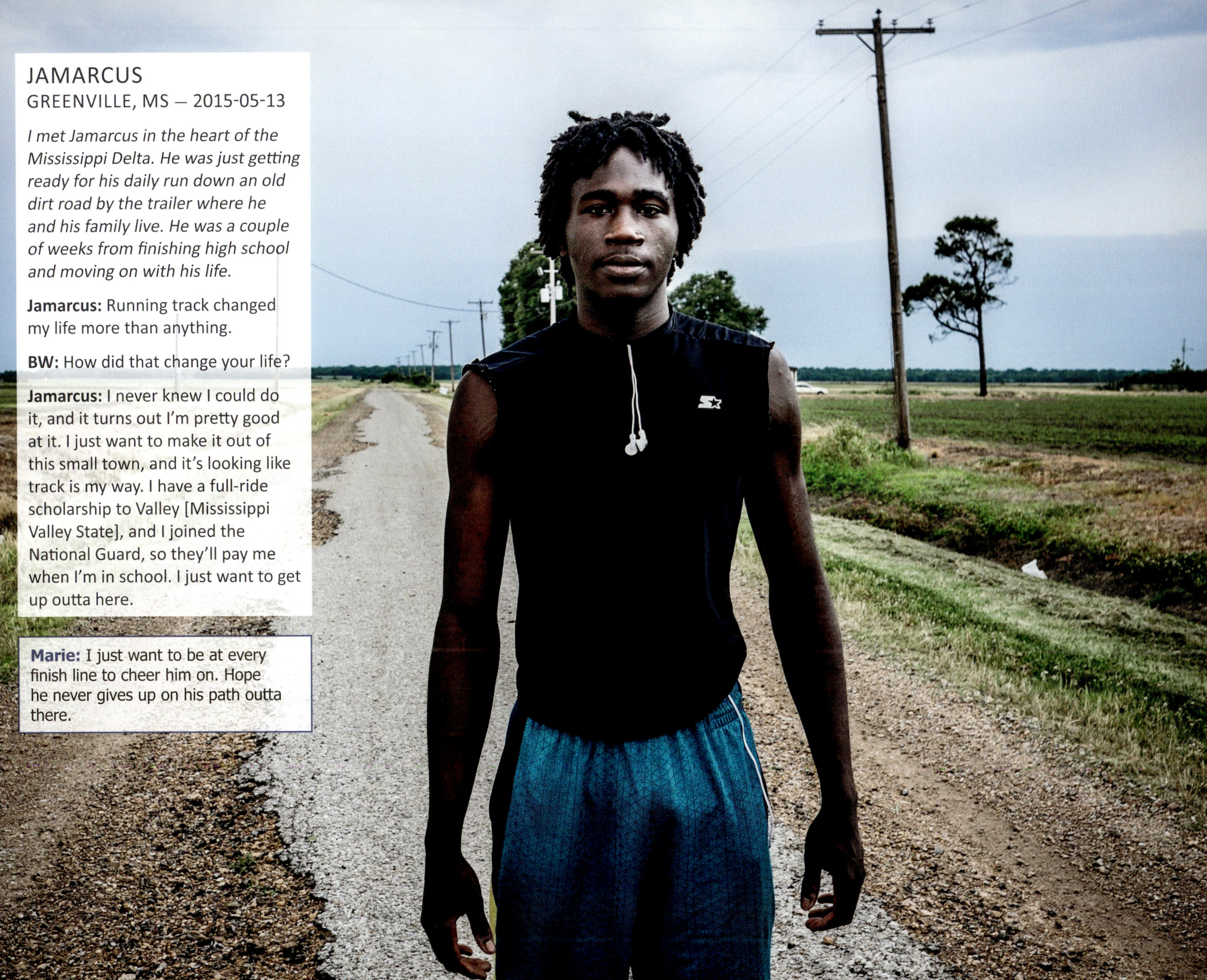

JAMARCUS

GREENVILLE, MS – 2015-05-13

I met Jamarcus in the heart of the Mississippi Delta. He was just getting ready for his daily run down an old dirt road by the trailer where he and his family live. He was a couple of weeks from finishing high school and moving on with his life.

Jamarcus: Running track changed my life more than anything.

BW: How did that change your life?

Jamarcus: I never knew I could do it, and it turns out I'm pretty good at it. I just want to make it out of this small town, and it's looking like track is my way. I have a full-ride scholarship to Valley [Mississippi Valley State], and I joined the National Guard, so they'll pay me when I'm in school. I just want to get up outta here.

Marie: I just want to be at every finish line to cheer him on. Hope he never gives up on his path outta there.

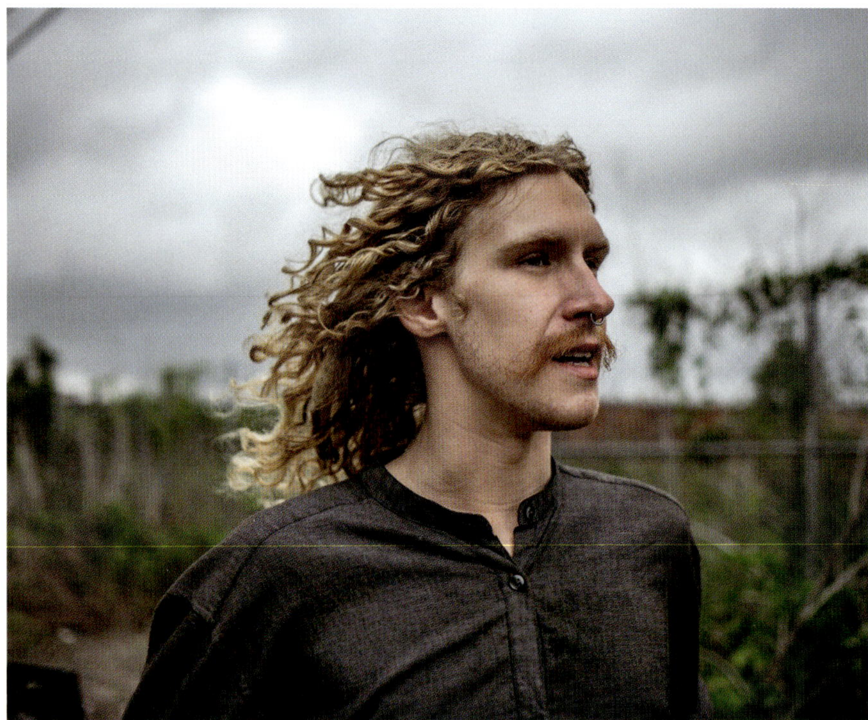

NEW ORLEANS, LA – 2015-05-11

Taylor: At the time, I was young and stupid, traveling with my girlfriend, who was a little older than me but just as naive as I was.

So we were hitchhiking through Arizona, right through the Four Corners. We wanted to go through Navajo land to see what it was like. We were already there, anyway, and that seemed to be where the ride was leading us. We were going down, and we got to a bridge, or maybe it was just a little gap in the earth. Right down there, you could see the town. It was just shacks. It looked like a third world country, not like any part of America I'd ever seen. It was literally just plywood and two-by-fours nailed together, no paint. Just little tiny shacks all over.

There was this Native American guy talking to another Native American guy in a pickup truck backed up to a long string of handmade staffs and flutes and other random things. The truck was leaving as we approached the guy. I saw the staffs, and I don't know why I did it, but I reached out for this one. Right before I grabbed it, he said, "It's yours." I told him I didn't have anything to trade, no money, nothing to offer. He said, "Take it—it's yours." I still resisted. He looked me in the eyes and said "Take it. You might need it to fend off the wolves" in this really deep voice, so I took it.

We went down into this little town. We were walking through, and everyone was sitting down in alleys, babbling. People kept coming up to us, asking us for change. We knew the drill because we did the same shit. But they were kind of following us around. It had a real zombie feel to it—you know, out of their minds. So we were uncomfortable. We said, "Let's get out of here."

We were walking down this dirt road, and we'd been walking for a couple of hours, picking up really beautiful stones off the side of the road that I'd never seen before. A small pickup truck pulls up to us with three Native American boys about twenty-five or twenty-six. They didn't say anything. They just stopped right next to us. We jumped right in the back.

They started driving down the road, and they never looked back at us. Never said hey or anything. We were like, "Whatever. We're getting a ride." We needed it. We were dying out there.

So eventually they turn down this dirt road that goes up a mountain, and they start speeding up. I start knocking on the window and saying, "Let us out!" But they weren't looking. I caught the guy's eyes in the rear mirror, and I was like, "Oh shit." I saw his eyes, and they were fucked up. They looked soulless and black. It was almost like they knew that I noticed. The two in the passenger seat turned around and started mocking me. I was like, "These motherfuckers are crazy." Their eyes were black too. They were laughing and cackling.

My girlfriend starts freaking out, "What are we gonna do? What are we gonna do?" And I didn't know. They just kept driving and driving. I noticed his window was cracked just a little—just enough for the staff that the guy had given me to fit through. When I saw the crack, I heard the dude's voice say to me, "You might need it to fend off the wolves." I looked at it laying in the bed of the truck, and I said, "All right. I guess I'm gonna do this."

I stood up, and I propped it right up to the hole. I was aiming for his eye, and I was about to jam it in his eye when he noticed in the rearview mirror what I was doing. He slammed on the brakes, and I fell forward. [My girlfriend] threw the gear out of the truck, and we started running. The guy leaned his head out of the car and screamed, "Come on—let's go smoke some weed!" I yelled back, "Fuck you!" Then he yelled again, "We're gonna go get a gun!"

We were still running when all this was going down. They came back like five minutes later, so we hid in the grass. They looked for us for a good hour. Every time they'd go around, we'd sneak a little farther off. Finally we got back to the road. As soon as we got to the road, this dude was flying in a nice SUV. I jumped out in front, waving my hands. He stopped. We got in. He didn't say nothing. He just drove us to the next town.

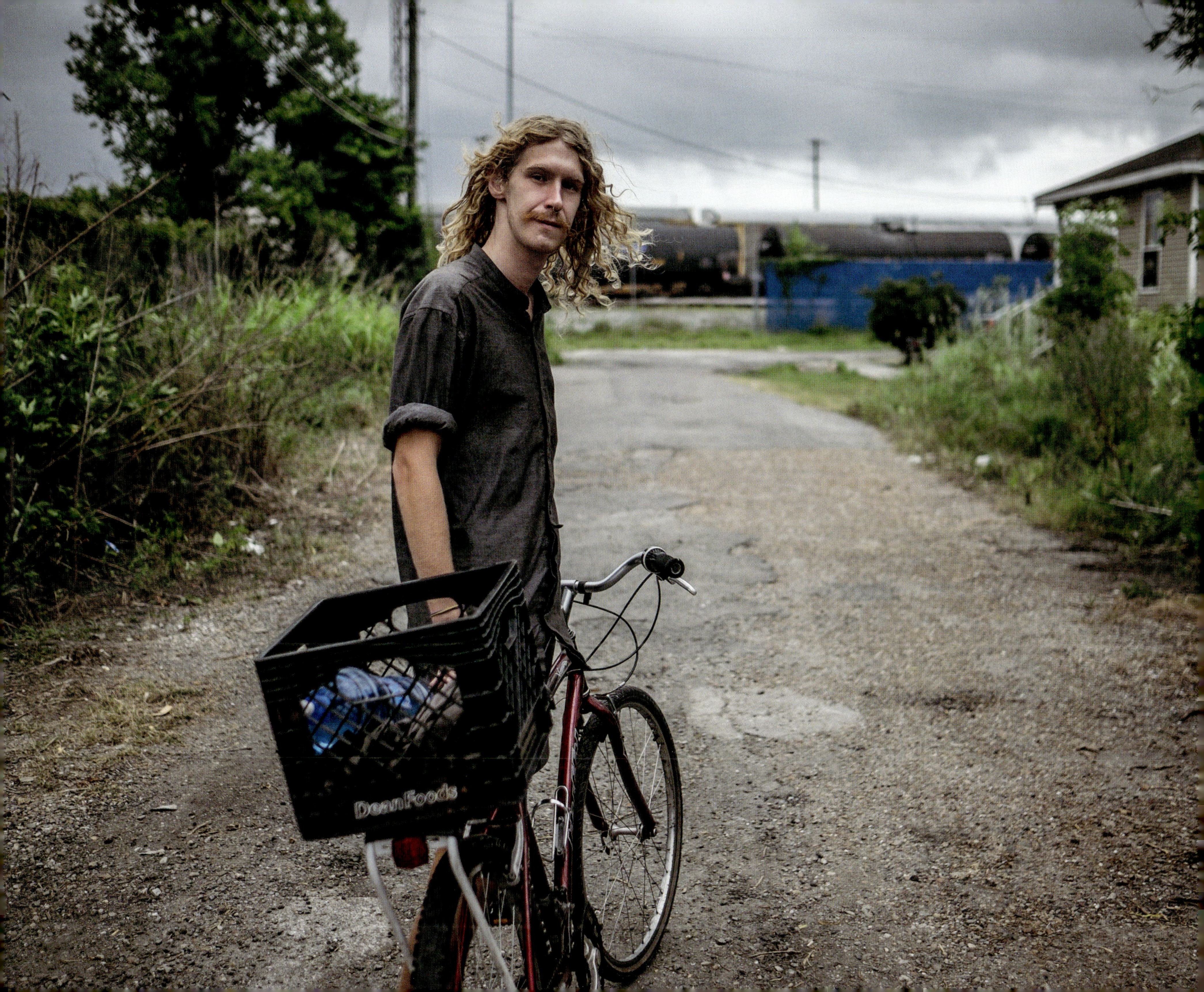
DeanFoods

I can tell by the way you lookin' that you feel sorry for me. That's
why I don't tell people that shit. I don't need nobody's pity.

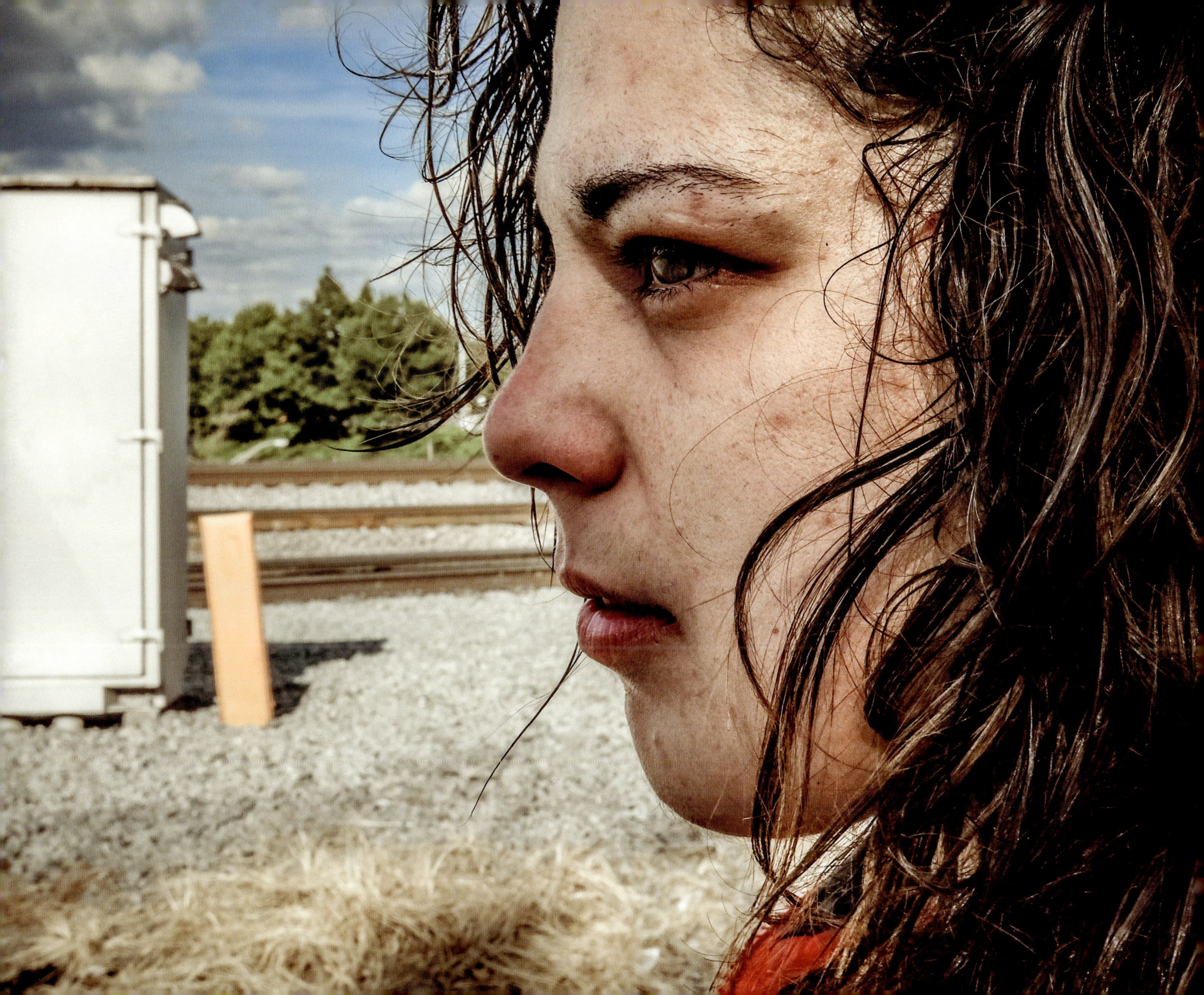

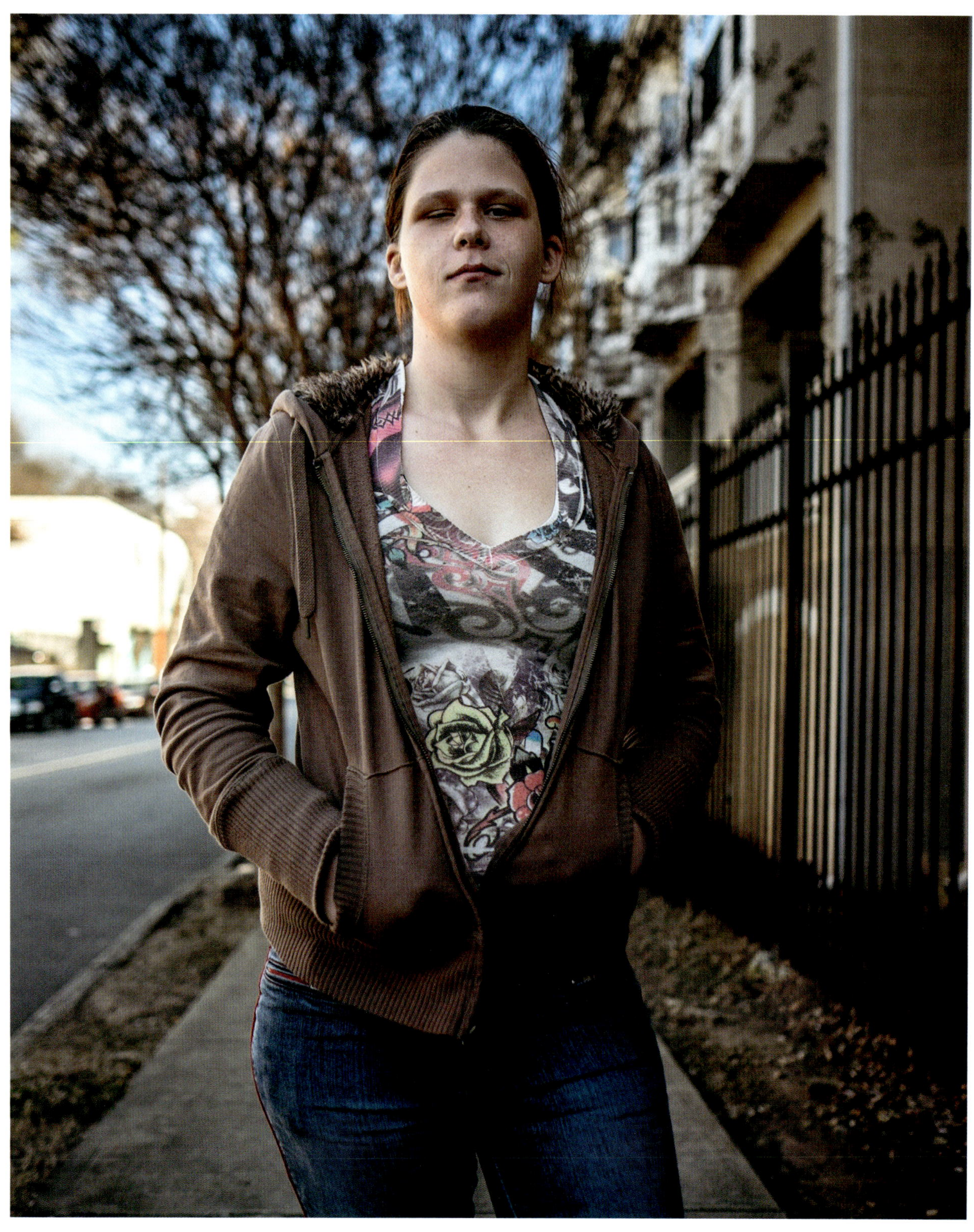

ATLANTA, GA – 2015-02-10

By the time I was twelve years old, I got the courage to tell my folks. My family didn't believe me, so they didn't do anything about it.

BW: How long have you been on the streets?

Brittany: I've been on the streets for about a year now. I'm down on my luck. I had my kids taken away from me. People think you can do it all by yourself, but you can't.

I've had a hard life. I've been beaten, had a gun pointed to my head, I been tied up, and I've been raped. My dad went to prison when I was thirteen, and my mom left us at the same time.

BW: Damn. I'm sorry. Can you tell me a story about something that really impacted your life?

Brittany: Me and my family moved to Panama City Beach, Florida. We moved in with people they barely knew, and they would watch me when my parents weren't home. The family had two other kids. The step-daddy would come in my room at night and would touch on me and feel on me. I was ten years old when he raped me. He told me that if I told my parents, he'd kill them and me. He continued to rape me for two years. By the time I was twelve years old, I got the courage to tell my folks. My family didn't believe me, so they didn't do anything about it. It continued for another year and didn't stop till we moved from Panama City to Daytona.

BW: So the guy never got charged with anything?

Brittany: No, he's still running around. I forgave the man, but . . . some days I'm like, why me? I was just a little kid. What did I do? I couldn't of done nothing that bad to be treated like that.

ATLANTA, GA – 2015-02-11

Denes: I was born into foster care. My foster mama would take us to the country every year in Georgia for a couple of weeks during watermelon season. My foster dad's brother would come over from Jamaica to help pick watermelon, and that's when he would molest me.

BW: How old were you when this happened?

Denes: It started when I was seven or eight, and it ended when I was thirteen. We would always stay in hotel rooms when we went to Georgia, and I would always stay in a room with my foster mama. He would tell me to come to his room. And me being a kid, I didn't really realize that's what it was, because he'd say I was pretty, and I thought it's what I was supposed to do.

He was on top of me when my mom knocked on the door to his motel room. When she came in, I was sitting there with a sheet covering me. She asked me why I was there, and I told her that he was my boyfriend, because secretly, that's what he'd always tell me.

BW: What did she do?

Denes: What *didn't* she do? She beat him up bad—with a cane and everything. She ended up telling my foster dad, and my dad beat him up. Then my stepbrothers beat him up. Then they called the cops. He went to jail for ten years. But that's really what led up to me working on the street.

BW: What was the best day of your life?

Denes: Every day, really. I've done died six times and came back. When I was born, my mom was on crack cocaine, weed, alcohol, heroin, and meth. The only thing I've ever done was powder, weed, and drink, and I don't do those things like I used to. Living every day—knowing that I didn't go as far as my mother did and knowing that I'm still alive—is good enough for me.

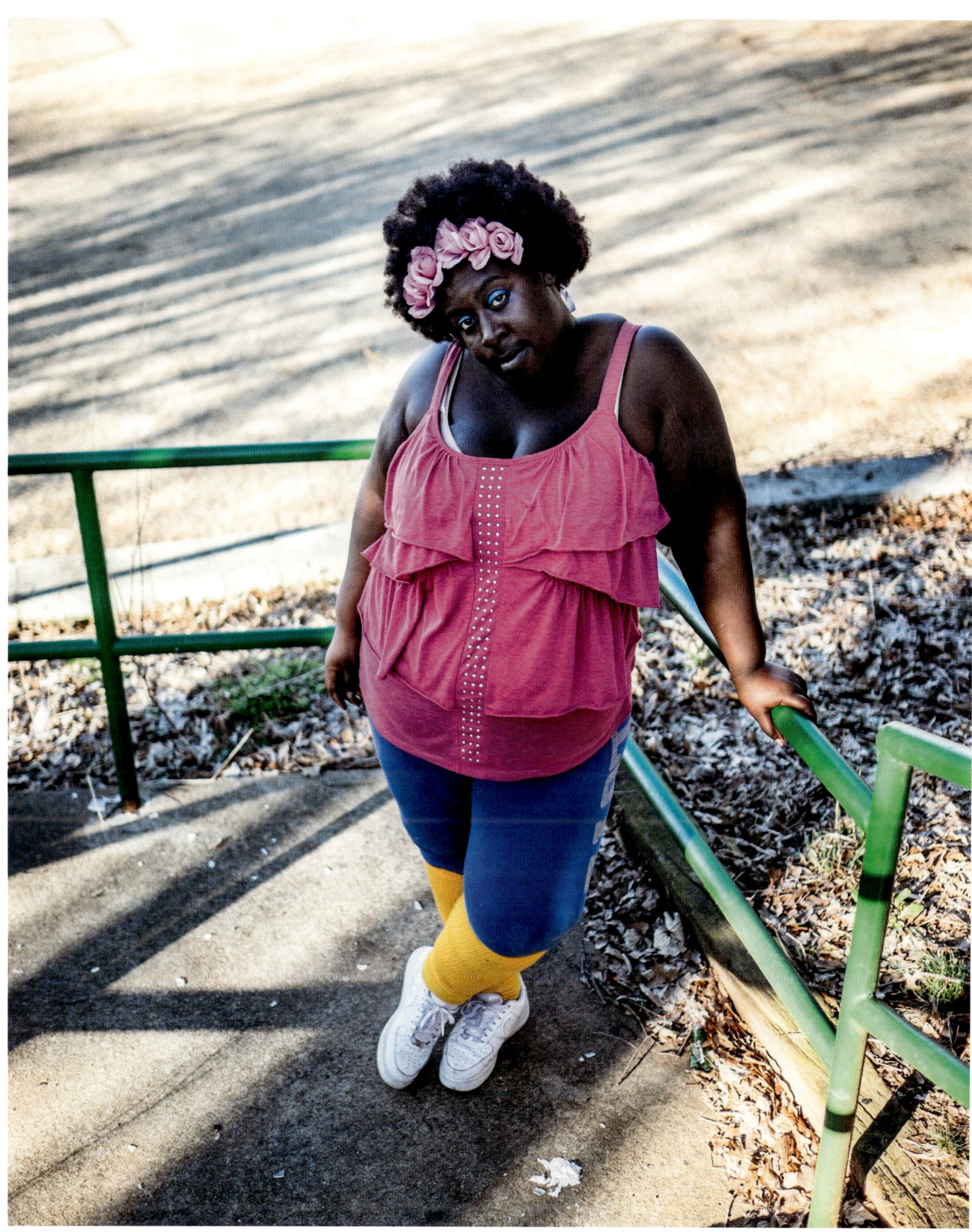

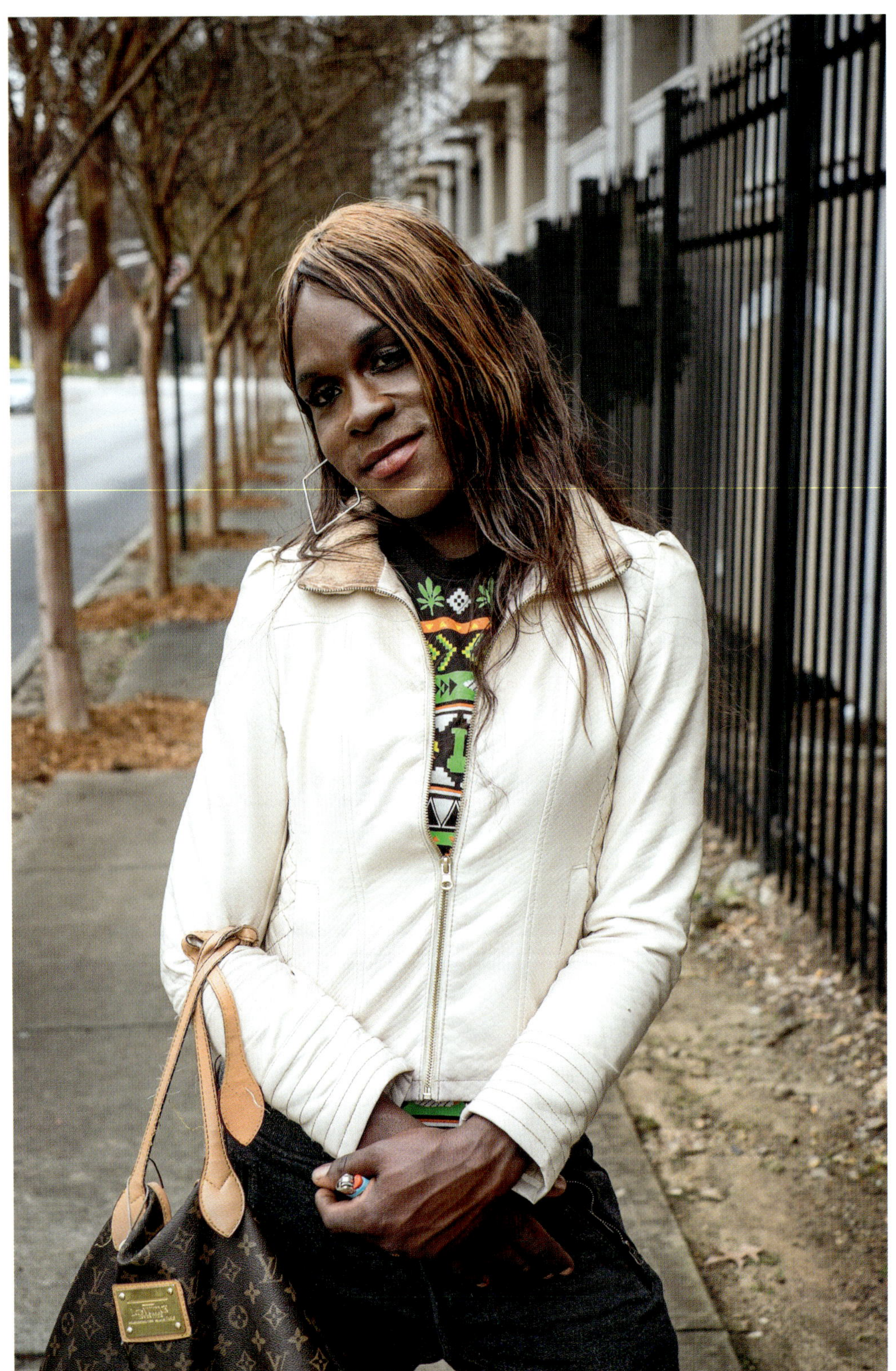

ATLANTA, GA – 2015-03-10

Eunique: My name is Eunique.

BW: That's . . . unique. How'd you get that name?

Eunique: My friend used to tell me I had a unique aura about myself. I used to do things out of the ordinary, and I know I'm different from a lot of folks, so that's why I came up with the name Eunique.

I'm originally from Chicago, Illinois. I'm the middle child of nine. I became a transsexual at the age of thirteen or fourteen. Going to school was hard because I had to fight all the time. I was always suspended. My father never approved of me being the woman that I am. So I got emancipated at the age of sixteen. It was basically my father's idea. He didn't want my younger siblings to think it was okay for them to be like me, a transsexual, or that it was okay to date the same sex.

When I was younger, I used to try on my sister's clothing. I used to get beat—you know, a whupping—for that. If I was hanging around with my sister and playing Barbie dolls and makeup and stuff like that, I'd get a whupping for that. And I was like . . . I'm being me.

My mom tried to be supportive and wanted me to feel comfortable in my skin, but I felt like I didn't belong in my house in a way. My father would call me names, and my brothers would take suit and follow. It really hurt me. It made me think about suicide and hurting my family.

BW: What was it like being punished for being yourself?

Eunique: How would I feel? You are just acting like yourself, and you get a goddamn whupping? Of course it's gonna make you feel like you don't belong. They called me faggot, and I'd cry at night. My dad would come in my room and say, "Shut up, sissy. You supposed to be a man. You ain't supposed to be crying." It just made me want to be me even more.

They sent me to a group home named Saint Joe's for kids in Minnesota because I didn't want to dress like a man in their house. That's when I really felt like I didn't have a family.

Before my father passed, we had talks. He asked me why I wanted to do this. I told him, "I know God don't make no mistakes, and I believe that God made me this way." He just shook his head and said, "Jehovah did not make you this way." I said, "Well, it's genetics." He said, "So what are you saying?" I reminded him that he was a beautician and my grandfather was a beautician. He ended that conversation quick.

He did say, "I love you no matter what you do in your life," and he apologized for the things he said and did to me when I was younger.

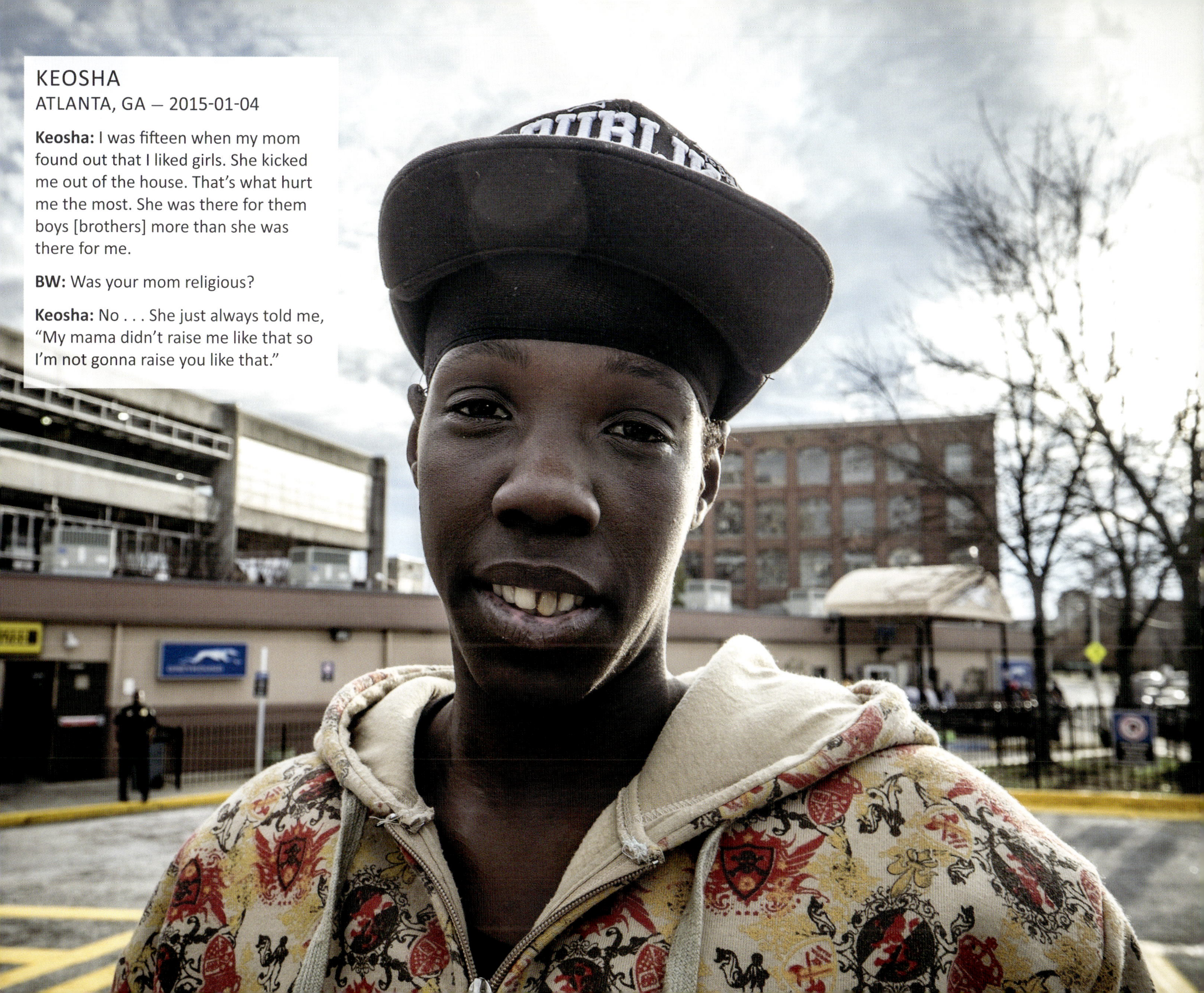

KEOSHA

ATLANTA, GA — 2015-01-04

Keosha: I was fifteen when my mom found out that I liked girls. She kicked me out of the house. That's what hurt me the most. She was there for them boys [brothers] more than she was there for me.

BW: Was your mom religious?

Keosha: No . . . She just always told me, "My mama didn't raise me like that so I'm not gonna raise you like that."

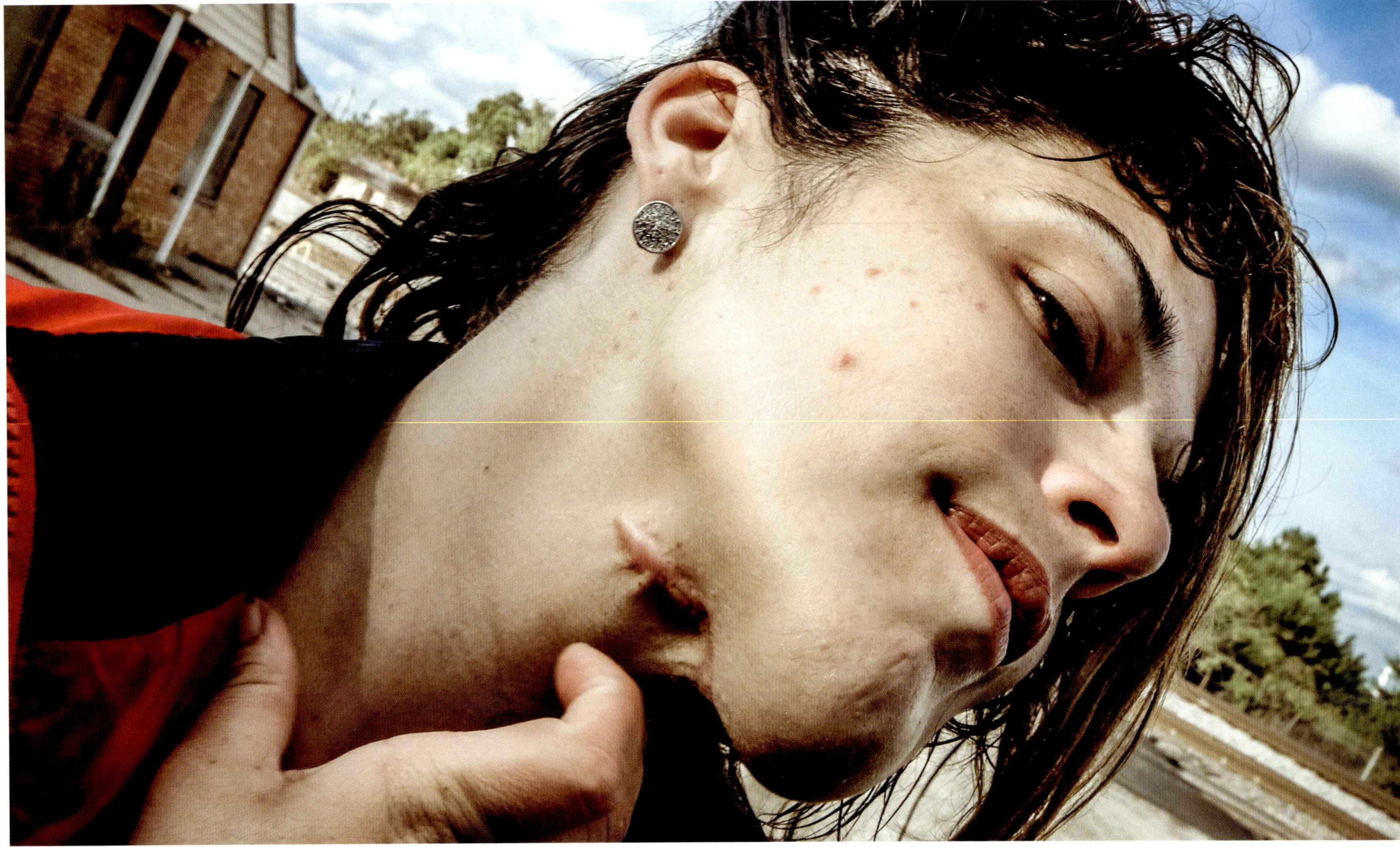

ATLANTA, GA – 2014-10-10

Brittany: All right—you want a story? I'll tell you a fuckin' story about this and this and this. [Points to fresh scars and swelling.] My ex tried to kill me 'cause I was with some other guy.

BW: Damn . . . Where's he at now?

Brittany: Jail. Hate that motherfucker. That's not all he done either. He used to hide under people's porches and wait for me. Run through people's houses looking for me. Crazy shit.

I used to be pretty . . . It's not really healing 'cause I drink too much. They want me to quit, but fuck dat. No way I'm quitin'.

BW: Why?

Brittany: I dunno. I been hospitalized for it five times . . .

See over there in those woods? Had a guy drag me down there one night.

BW: What did he do?

Brittany: Whatever the fuck he wanted to, I guess.

I can tell by the way you lookin' that you feel sorry for me. That's why I don't tell people that shit. I don't need nobody's pity.

ATLANTA, GA – 2015-04-10

I saw Brittany on the same South Atlanta corner where I had originally met her months earlier. I always kept an eye open for her because her condition seemed pretty grave the last time we had talked.

Brittany: I don't got no more stories to tell. It's self-explanatory when you look at me, goddammit.

[Yells at man walking by.] What the fuck you lookin' at? You said what? Fuck me? I asked you what you was lookin' at!

I look more fucked up than I did last time, right?

BW: I think so. The last time we talked, you told me your face wouldn't get better because you couldn't stop drinking.

Brittany: Actually, it had gone down 'cause I had gone and got my antibiotics and was taking them. But me and him [ex-boyfriend] got into some shit, and this wasn't healed all the way, so it fractured this side. But now he's in jail 'cause he shot the motherfucker I was living with three times.

BW: So he got out of jail after we talked the last time?

Brittany: Yeah, he got out. His mom or somebody paid for his bond. I was only renting a room from the guy I was living with. I seen him [ex-boyfriend] coming down the street. When he ran in there, I got away and climbed out the window and went to the bus stop. Later on, I seen it on the news, and people called me and told me. It was true. He had shot the man three times. Someone else came in the house, and he shot them too.

BW: So he shot two people, and that's what he's back in jail for now? And he still hasn't gone to trial for the shit he did to you?

Brittany: Yeah.

> **Pauline:** The reality is Brittany is someone's daughter, sister, cousin, and maybe even mother. She is going to die on the streets and almost seems accepting of her fate. My wish for her is that she can love herself enough to break free of the hold her addiction has on her.

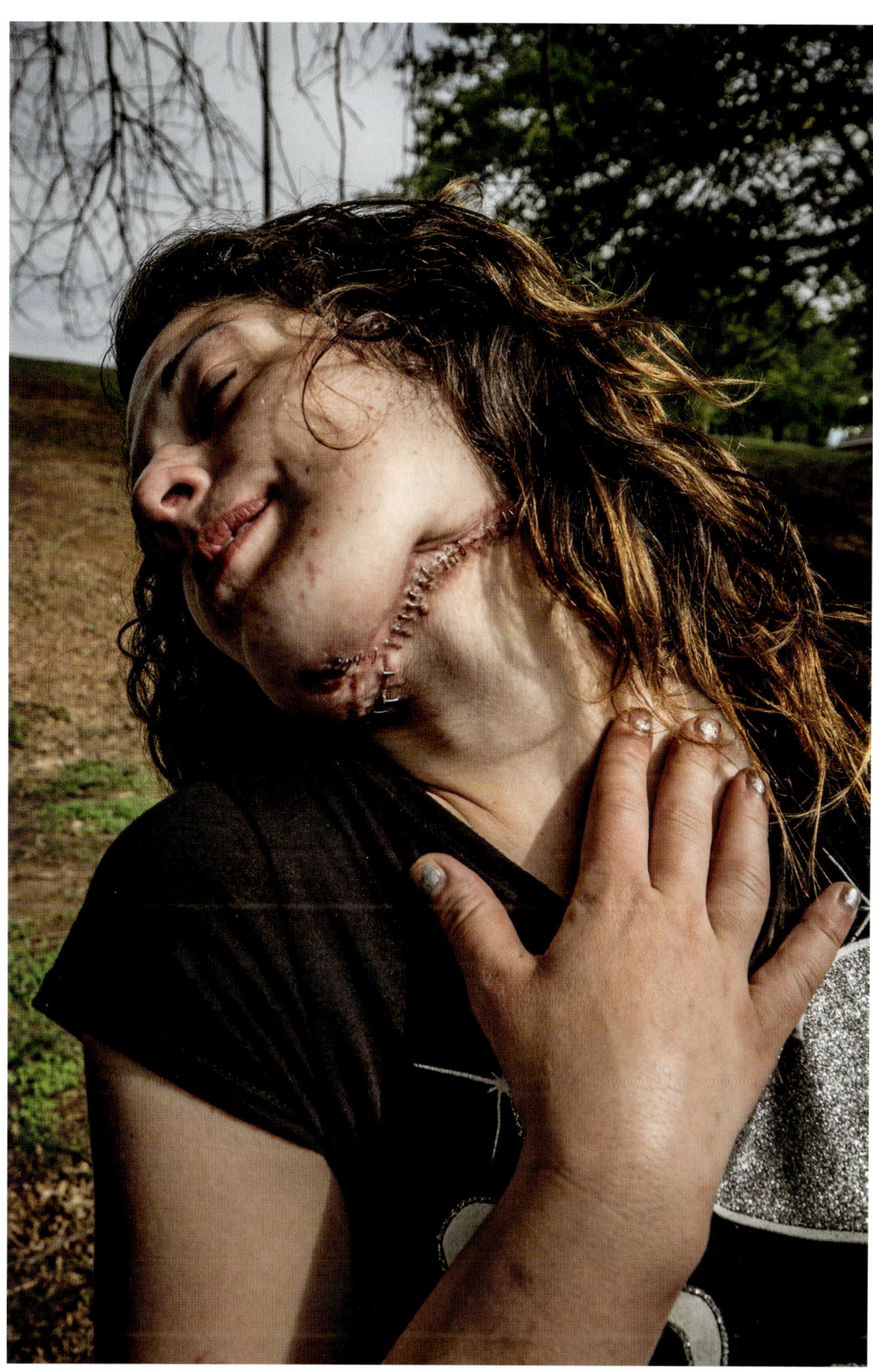

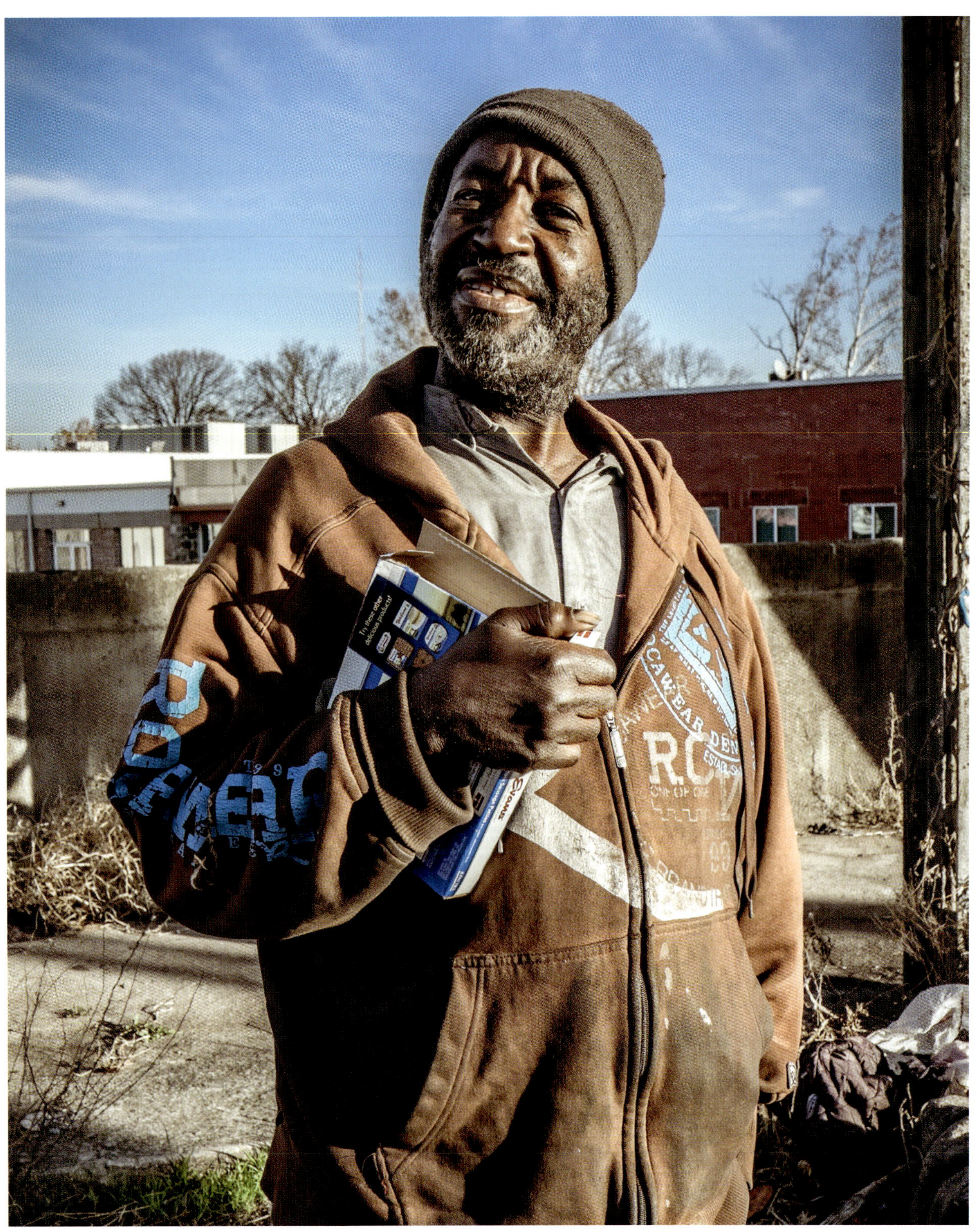

ATLANTA, GA – 2014-12-07

BW: How long have you been on the streets?

Otis: Oh man . . . Whoo, it's been a while. Yeah . . . it's been a while.

BW: Have you ever tried the shelters?

Otis: Yeah, I have tried them. But you know, they're closing a lot of them down. I tried them. I really don't like sleeping with a whole bunch of people.

BW: I've been to Peachtree and Pine. Man, that place is a mess.

Otis: I had to stay there one night. That's when the police would come and lock us up, just for being under the bridge. Just sleeping down there, they would lock you up. So I stayed at Peachtree and Pine one night. Never been back.

BW: What are your plans for the future?

Otis: I'd like to get into a small business. Get me a couple of mowers and grass-cutting equipment. I'm working with this guy now, and I've learned as much as I can. There's a little money in it.

I have a girlfriend. You know what I'm saying? She was on drugs too. Her family came and got her and took her back to California. She's doing good now. I've been thinking about getting cleaned up and getting back with her.

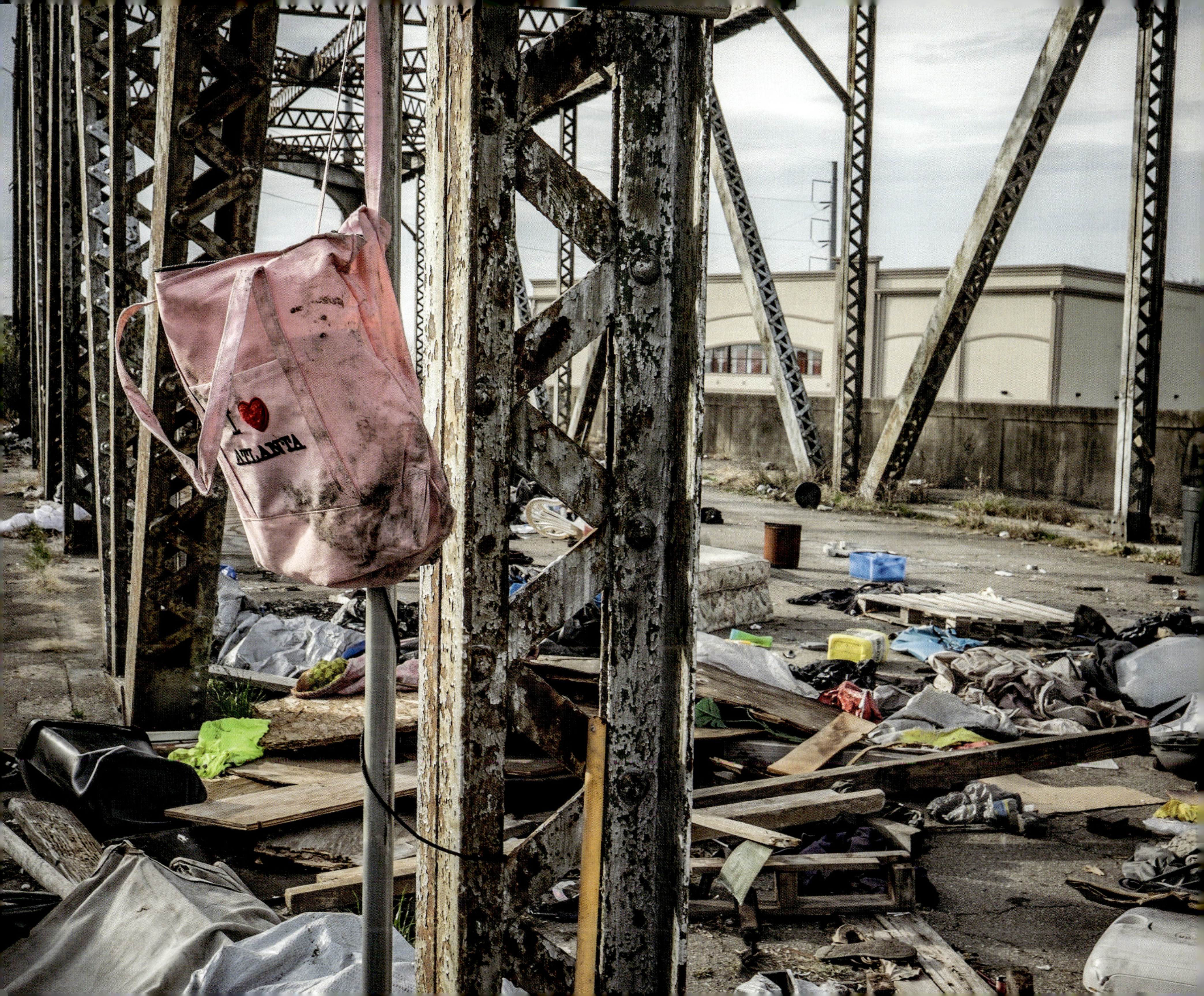

I
ATLANTA

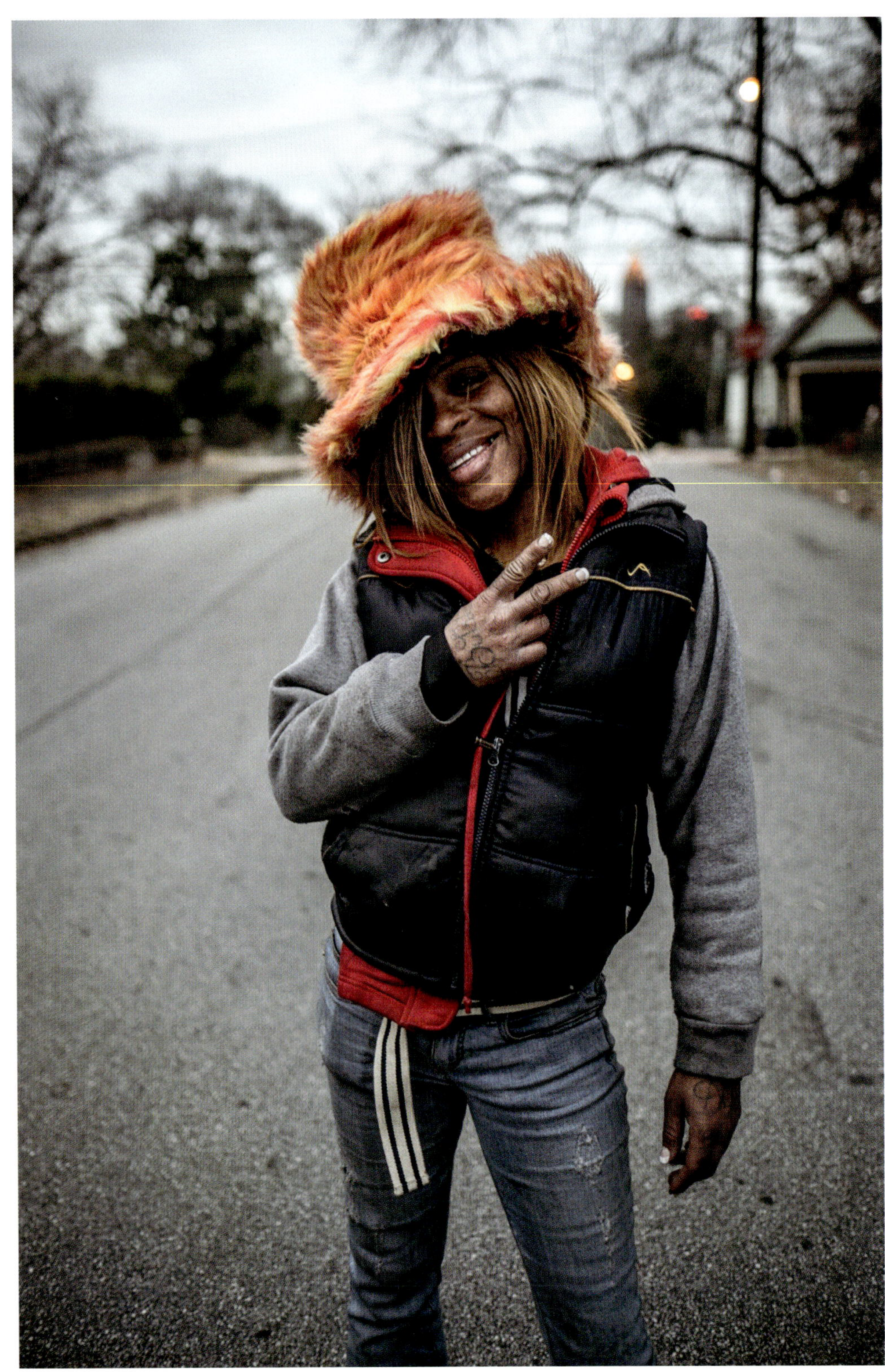

ATLANTA, GA – 2015-01-22

The question was, "Where will you be in ten years?" First she got literal; then she got Pentecostal.

Tootie: Now, that is the best question I've ever read.

BW: Well, give me the best answer I ever heard.

Tootie: I can't tell you until after the tenth year and a day.

BW: Then where do you *think* you'll be in ten years?

Tootie: It doesn't say that. It says, "Where will you be?"

BW: [Laughing.] It doesn't matter.

Tootie: Yes, it does!

BW: It's not about the question. It's about the—

Tootie: Listen, I have to answer what's read.

BW: No, you don't.

Tootie: I take the words that come out of people's mouths very serious. I haven't the slightest idea. But in eleven years from now, I can tell you where I was in ten years.

BW: That's true.

Tootie: 'Cause God, in the name of Jesus, he will lead and guide me, and I hope to live to see a longer life.

BW: [Sighing.] All right. Let me just get a release. . . .

Tootie: And may we pray right quick?

BW: Oh . . . yeah, absolutely.

Tootie: Father God—right now in the name of Jesus, father God—I just thank you right now, father God. I praise you. I glorify your name right now in the name of Jesus, father God. Father God, right now I just want to ask you to please forgive us of all our sins, father God. Father God, all things that are not of you, Father God, I ask that you throw them back into the pits of hell from which it belongs, father God. Because you did say that no weapon formed against us will prosper, father God. Guide our footsteps *right now*, father God. Give us the guidance, give us the strength and the courage, father God. Help us, father God, and please continue to send your angels to protect us from all evil. In the name of Jesus, I pray. Amen and amen.

BW: Amen.

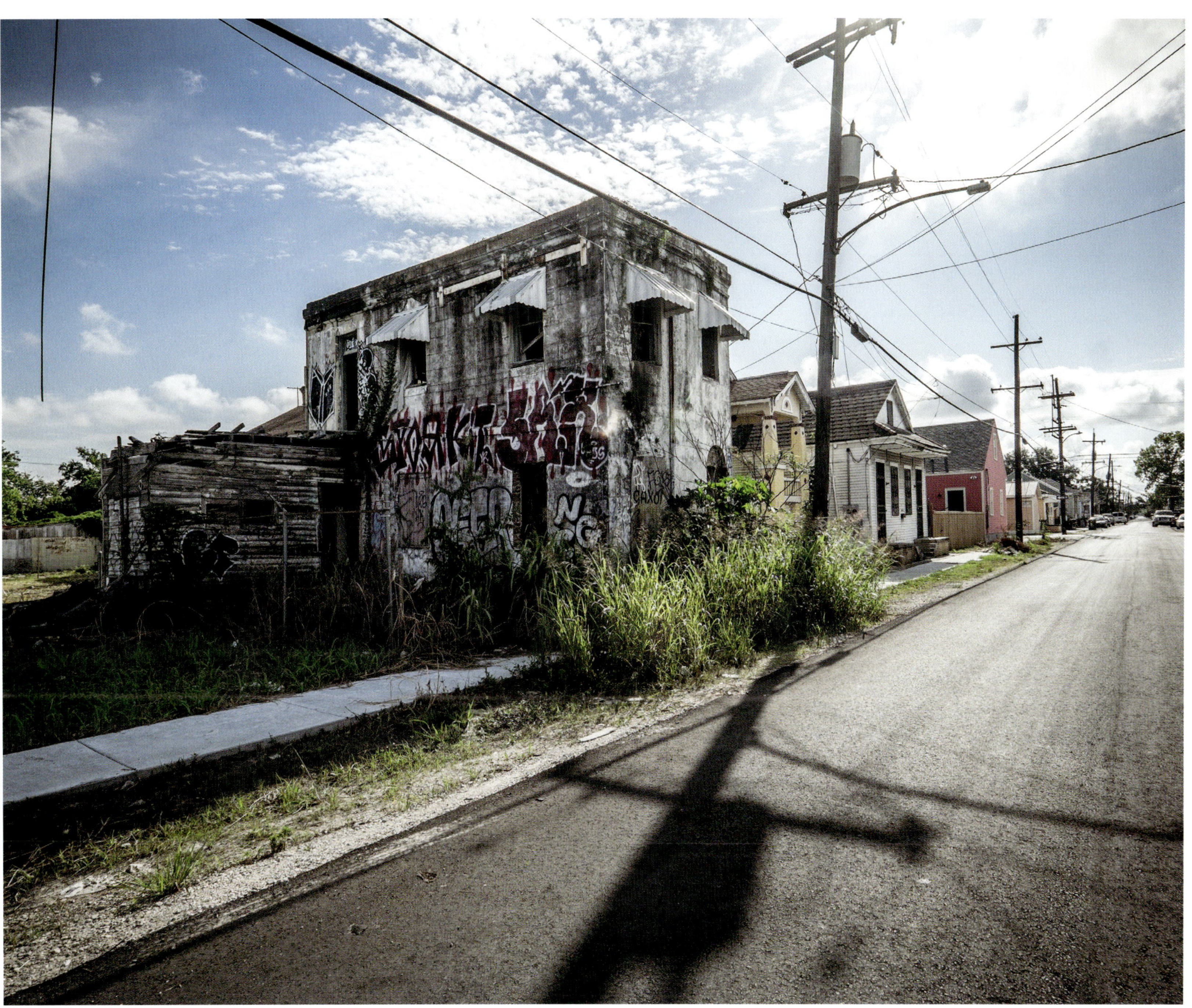

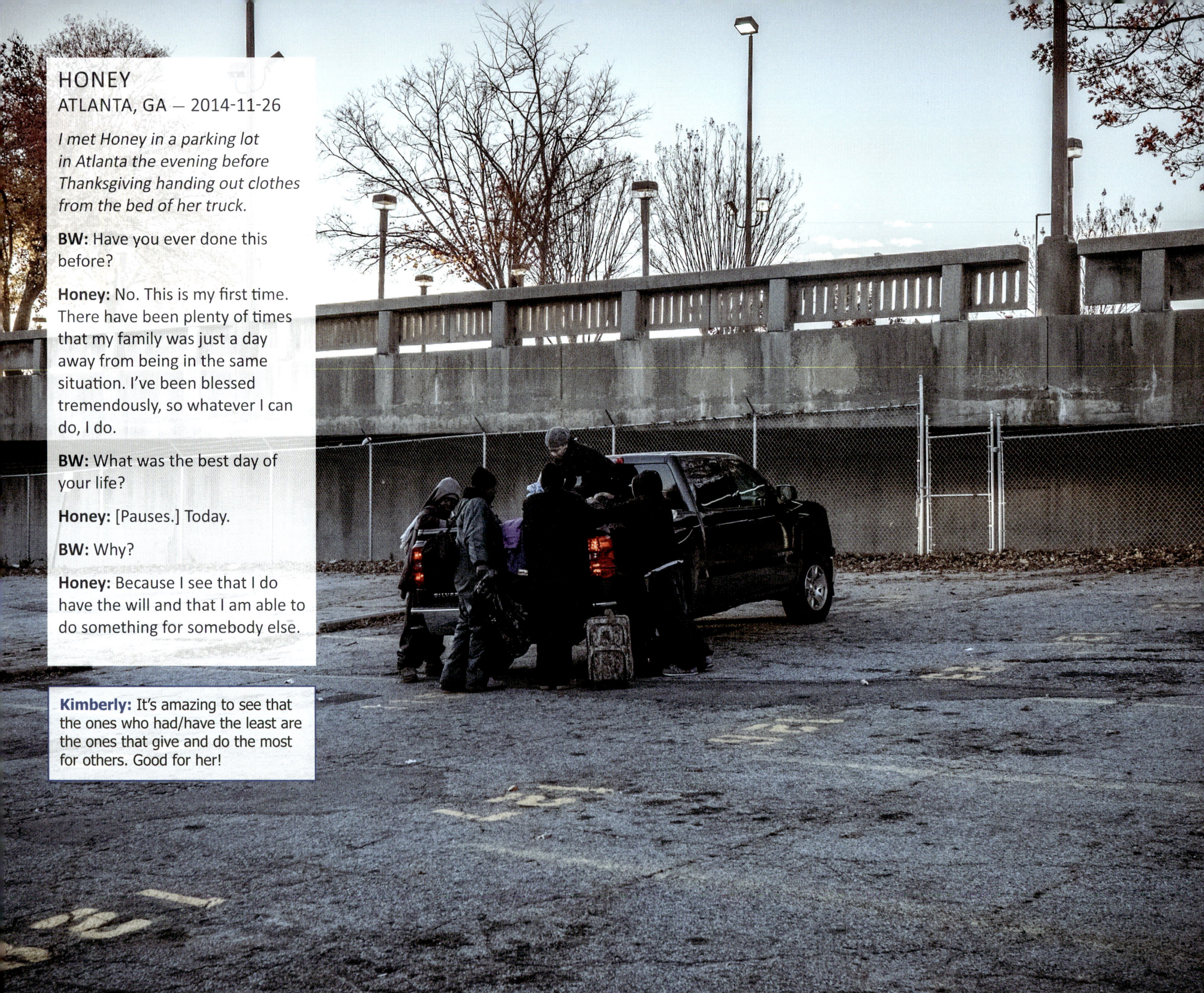

HONEY

ATLANTA, GA — 2014-11-26

I met Honey in a parking lot in Atlanta the evening before Thanksgiving handing out clothes from the bed of her truck.

BW: Have you ever done this before?

Honey: No. This is my first time. There have been plenty of times that my family was just a day away from being in the same situation. I've been blessed tremendously, so whatever I can do, I do.

BW: What was the best day of your life?

Honey: [Pauses.] Today.

BW: Why?

Honey: Because I see that I do have the will and that I am able to do something for somebody else.

Kimberly: It's amazing to see that the ones who had/have the least are the ones that give and do the most for others. Good for her!

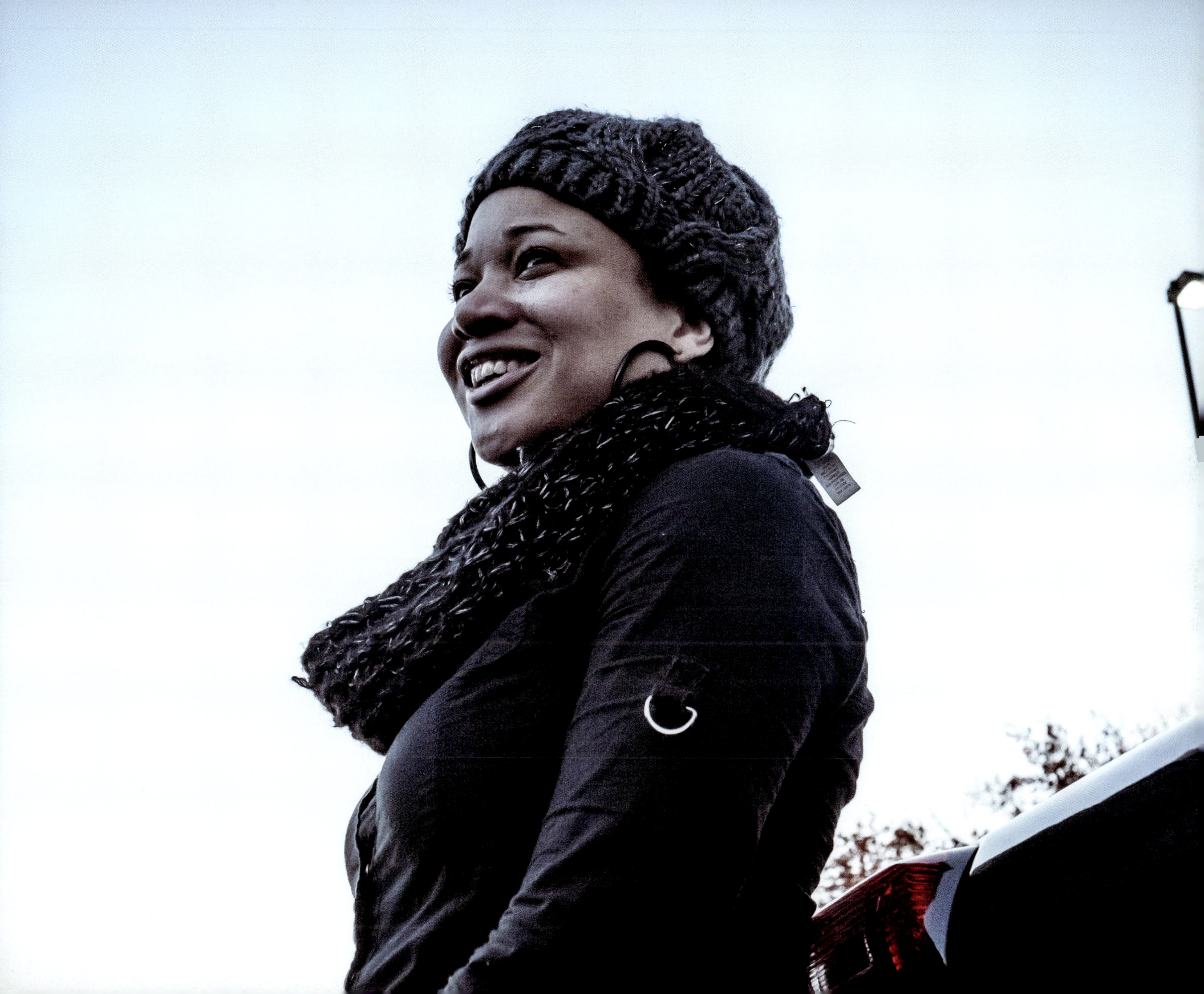

Ready for love
Ready for life
Ready for no more strife
Smiling through all the fights
Only one love, one life, one dream
Lost in a dream, trying not to scream
Broken but not bleeding
Lost but not leaving
Ready for love
Ready for life
Ready for no more strife

—*Manie (p. 123)*

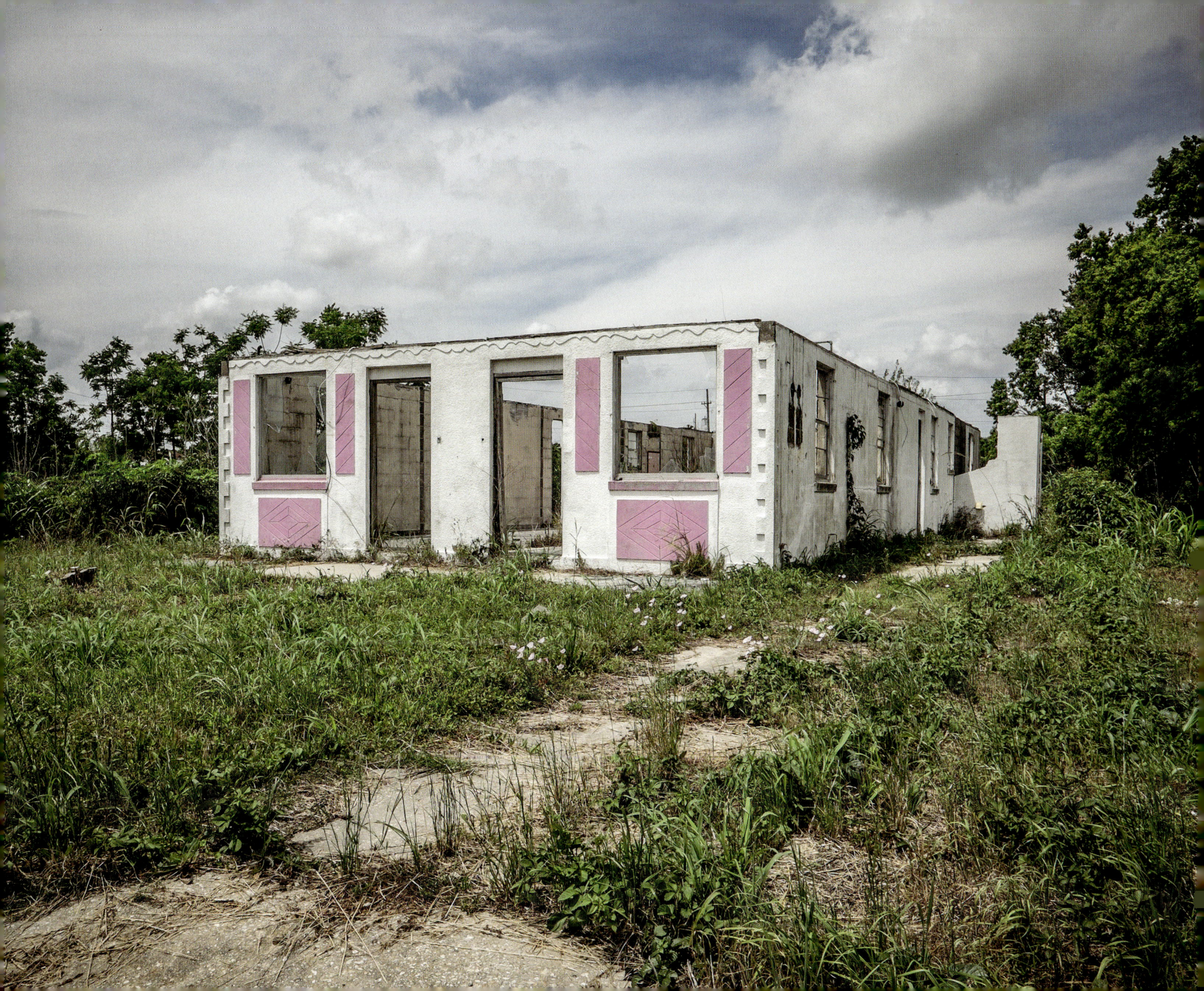

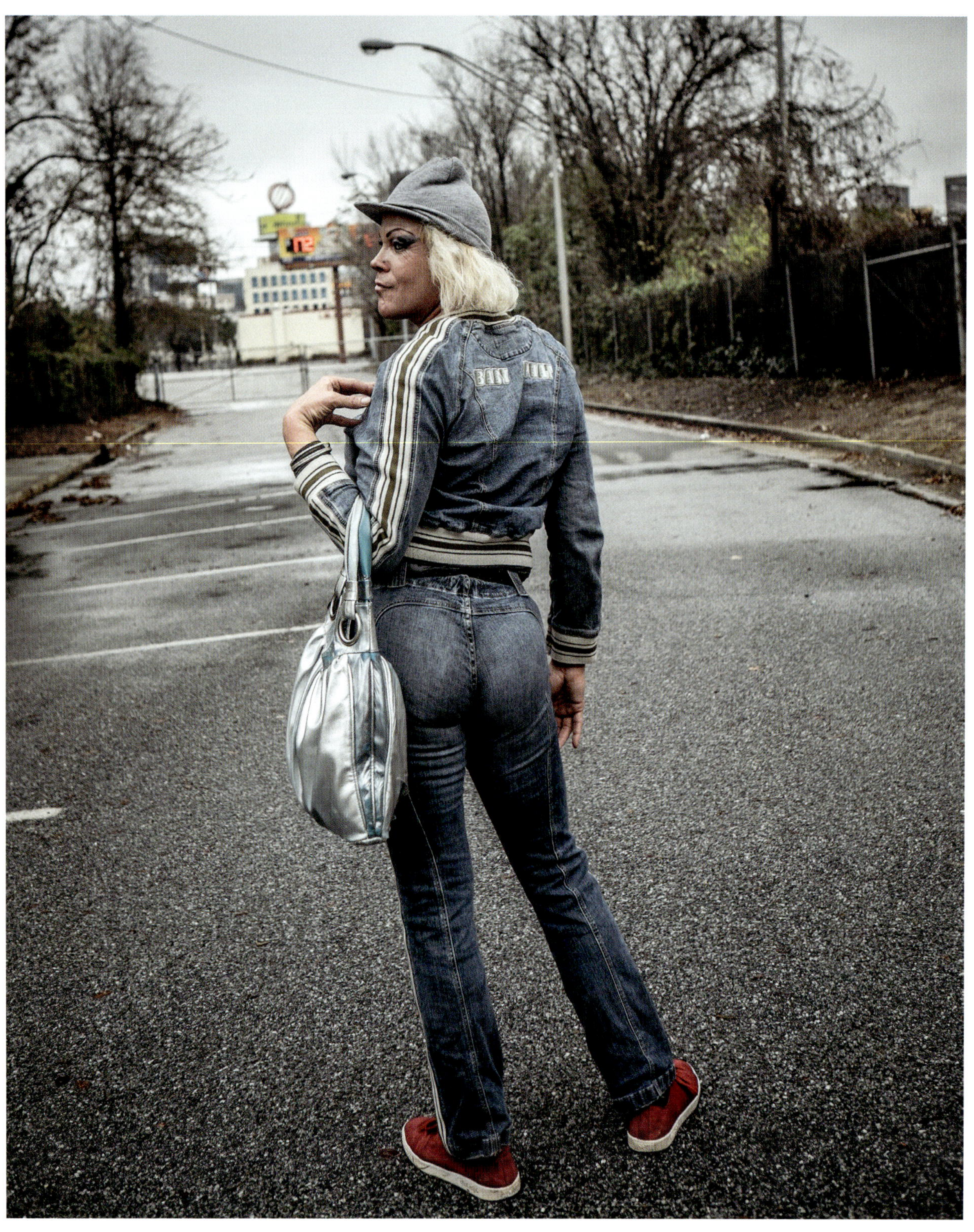

ATLANTA, GA – 2014-12-28

Jenna: I had a very turbulent childhood. My dad was murdered when I was twelve in Charlotte, North Carolina. It was very traumatic. He worked at a beverage store. It was a robbery. The dude had escaped from a Tennessee prison. Shot my dad three times in the head and once in the chest, for like $200.

I learned how to prostitute at a very young age. I was sixteen. It was bad, but you learn how to work it, honey. I got my teeth veneered . . . I did a lot. I worked it. I caught a boyfriend that I was with for many years.

I'm getting older. I'm forty-four now. The street life is fascinating to me. It's vicious. It's the devil. It's scary. But God puts a bubble of protection around you.

BW: Around everybody or just you?

Jenna: Around everybody. At least the people I'm involved with. 'Cause if you're my friend, I will pray for you. What's your name?

BW: Brent.

Jenna: Okay, I'll pray for you.

BW: Good. I can use all the help I can get.

Christy: BW, do you hug them after they tell you their stories? So much of what I see here is a cry for love. These people have had their humanity stolen from them, beaten out of them, smothered. And with a simple interview, you give it.

BW: I hug often and am able to experience more genuinely loving and healing moments than most humans ever get to experience. Truly grateful.

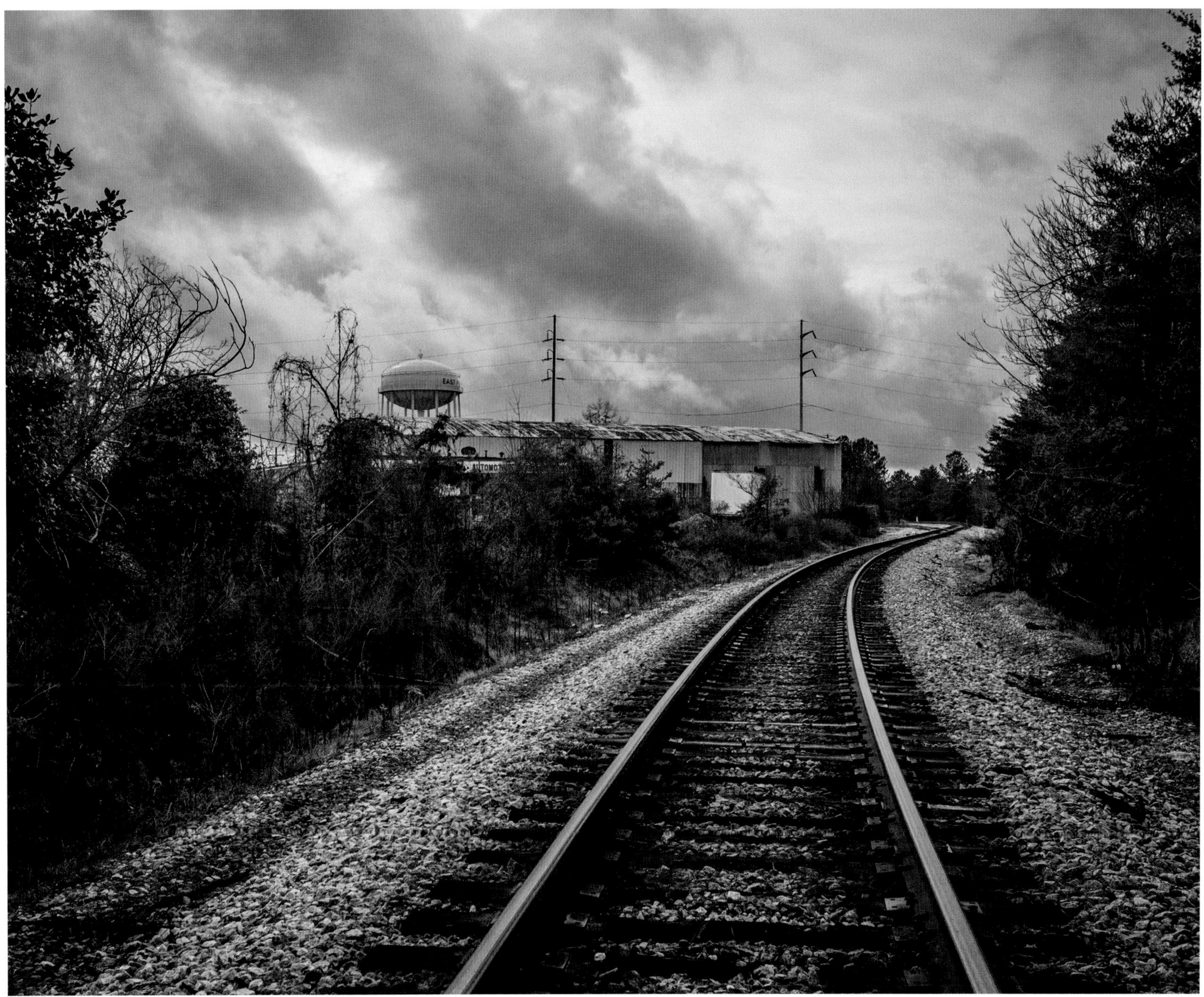

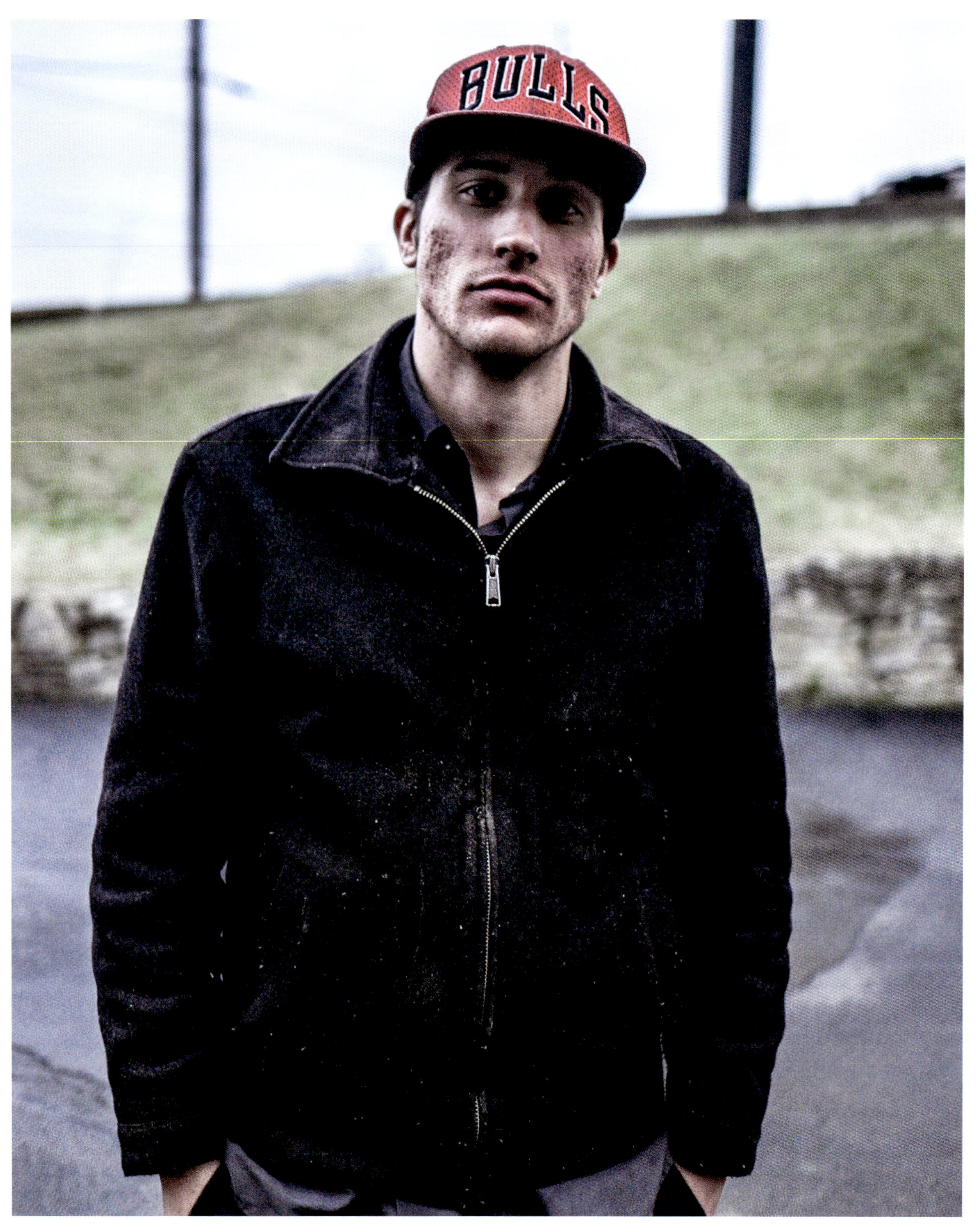

NASHVILLE, TN – 2015-01-11

Tony: My mom was mentally ill, and my dad used to flush her medication down the toilet. He was cruel. He went to prison when I was five years old for raping my three sisters. After that, I was separated from my sisters and sent to live in foster care. While I was in foster care, I was molested by three different people. There was one that it happened the most with. His name was David. He was around fourteen, and I was much younger.

BW: How do you think that affected you?

Tony: Well, when I went to live at another foster home, I did the same thing as what was done to me. I was a teen, and the kid I messed around with was a lot younger. I honestly didn't know it was wrong. I thought it was completely normal.

BW: What about as an adult?

Tony: I don't know . . . I've been in several porn movies. Gay, straight, bi . . .

BW: Did you ever see your dad again?

Tony: Yeah, once. He tried to apologize and all that. Never saw him again.

Alan: Maybe his father had been abused. When and how does the cycle ever end?

BW: In my opinion, the only way for it to end is by being open and honest. However, in order to do that, we have to put judgment and punishment on the back burner and bring compassion, empathy, and healing to the forefront. A tall order.

ATLANTA, GA – 2014-12-10

Star: My nephew, who was about five years older than me, used to molest me.

BW: How old were you?

Star: I had to have been between three and six. It happened for a year or two.

BW: Do you remember it?

Star: Yeah . . . It's kind of like a dream—at the time it was happening and even after. When I was younger, I didn't realize what it was or that it was bad. As I got older and saw TV shows about it and stuff like that, I started to remember, and everything came back. I was like, "Wow, that's what was going on." It affected me . . .

My father passed away when I was seven. I was at the house when it happened. He had a heart attack. [Tears.]

He was watching the race, and he called me in there and told me that he loved me and that I'd always be his baby girl. Later that day, he had a heart attack. It was like he knew. Like he felt something was gonna happen.

You know what they say about females who have dad issues when they don't have a father figure: they are always looking for a man, for that love. It's very true.

> Victims of child sexual abuse report more substance abuse problems: 70–80% of sexual abuse survivors report excessive drug and alcohol use.[12]

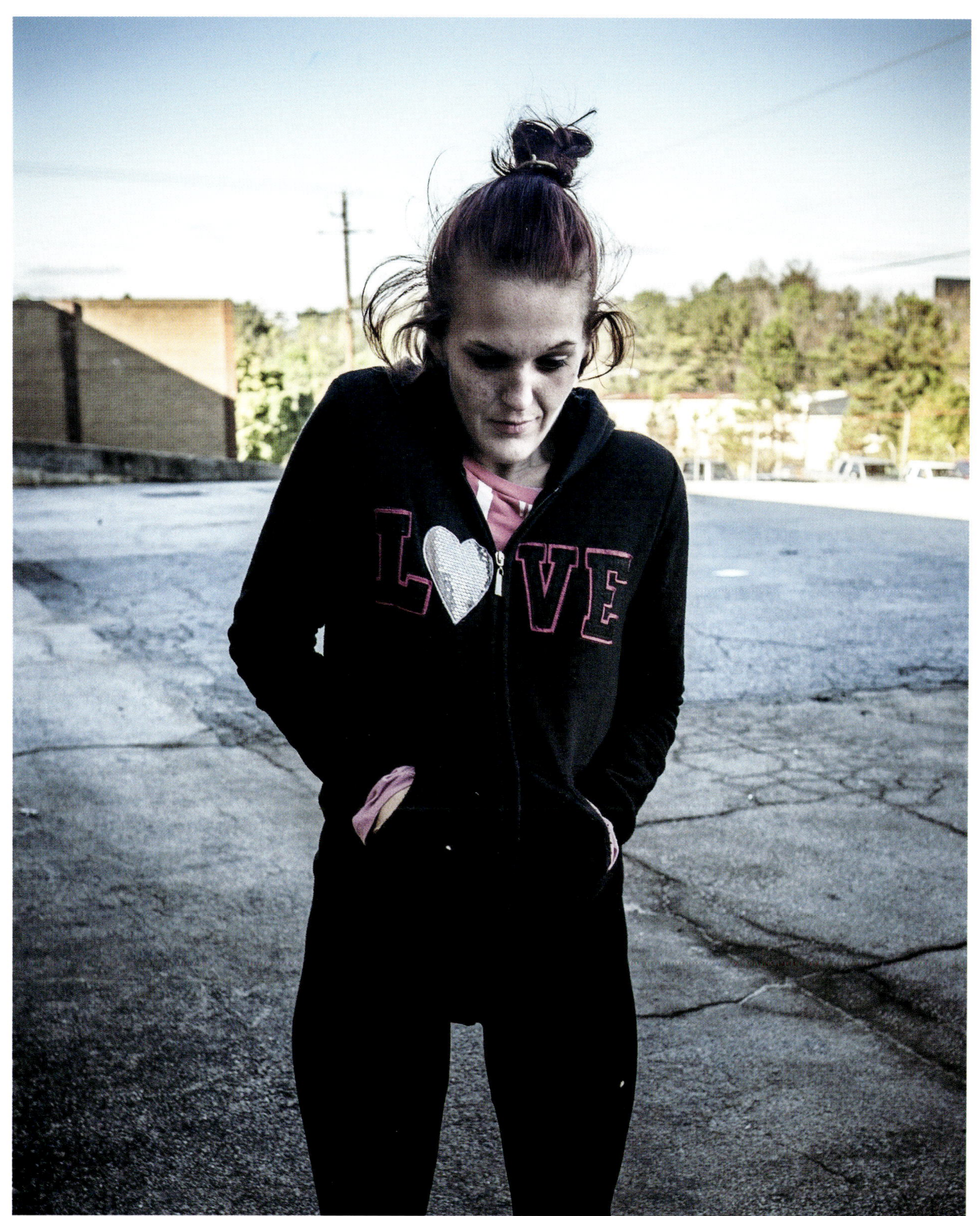

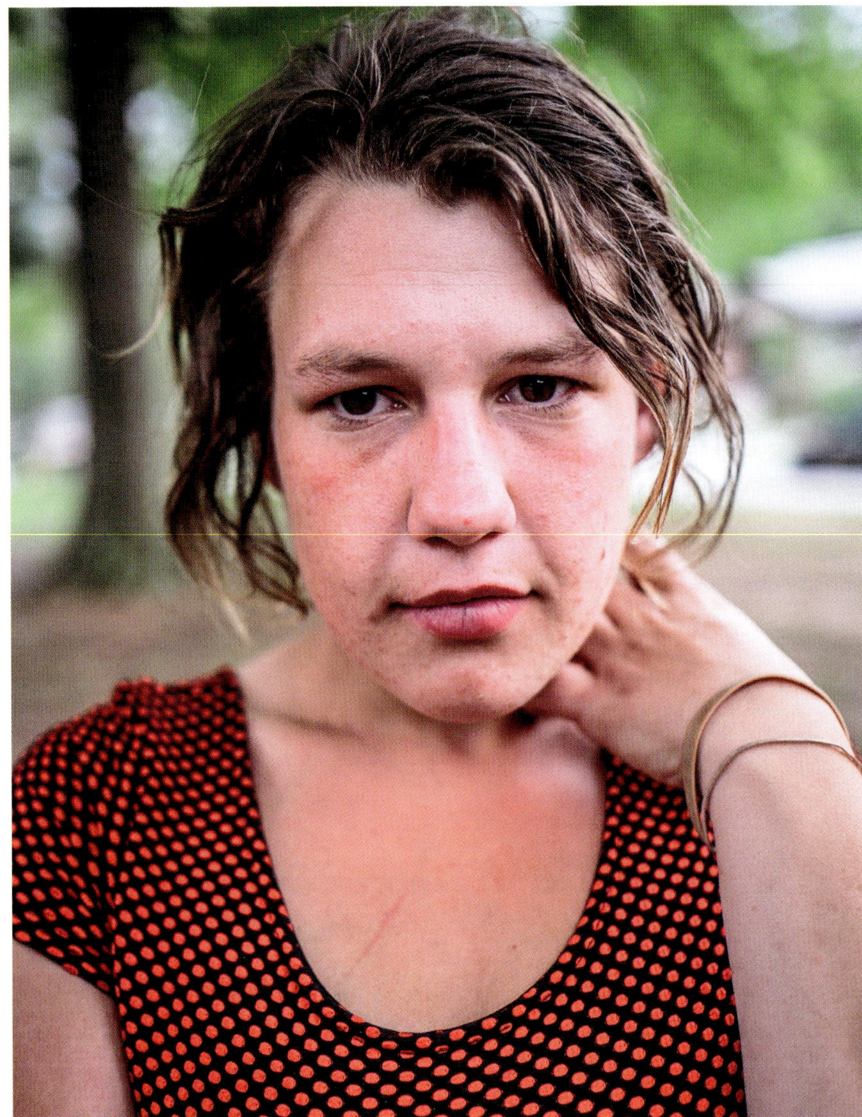

ATLANTA, GA – 2015-04-14

Manie: I don't speak too much. I have PTSD, so . . .

BW: PTSD from what?

Manie: When I grew up, there was a lot of stuff goin' on. My mama did drugs and stuff, so she always had all kinda people over. Everybody. Anybody. A lot of slammin' doors. A lot of yellin'. In and out. Bein' little, that messes with you. Put you on edge. Especially when you by yourself.

They didn't diagnose me until I was nineteen years old, 'cause my son passed away at two years old.

BW: How did it happen?

Manie: My baby daddy beat me up and set the house on fire. My son died of smoke inhalation. It took a week or two for him to pass.

BW: Damn. Why did he do it?

Manie: He was crazy. I was like seventeen [when the fire happened]. I was fifteen when I had him. My baby daddy was twenty-six. He'd always get drunk and think I was cheatin' on him.

BW: Tell me about the day it happened.

Manie: I don't remember too much about it. I blacked out. I was in my bed, and my son was in his crib. He higher up than me. He [the father] gets out in three years.

BW: He's getting out? Did he go to prison for manslaughter?

Manie: Involuntary manslaughter of a minor.

BW: Are you worried about him getting out?

Manie: He write me and tell me he sorry. I'm more worried about what I'm gonna do, but I don't think I go that far. My heart too good.

Manie: I'm gonna be an artist too. I wrote a poem.
BW: What'd you write?
Manie: You want to hear it?
BW: I'd love to hear it.

Ready for love
Ready for life
Ready for no more strife
Smiling through all the fights
Only one love, one life, one dream
Lost in a dream, trying not to scream
Broken but not bleeding
Lost but not leaving
Ready for love
Ready for life
Ready for no more strife

BW: That's awesome!
Manie: I know! [Giddy and laughing.]
BW: [Laughing.] What does that mean to you?
Manie: Keep my head up, because no matter what . . . I'm ready for something different.

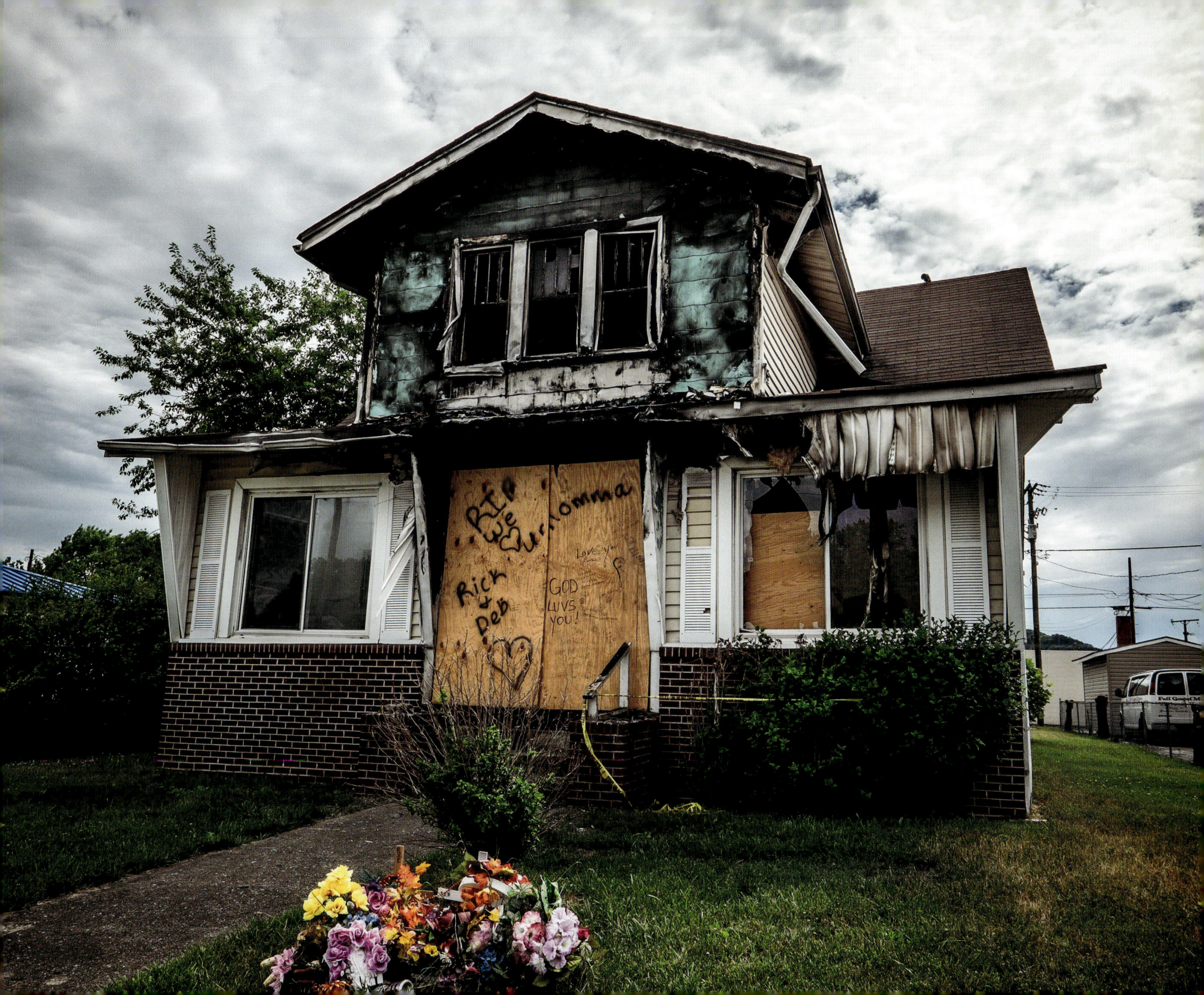
RIP
We ♥ Ur momma
Rick & Deb
Love you
GOD LUVS YOU!

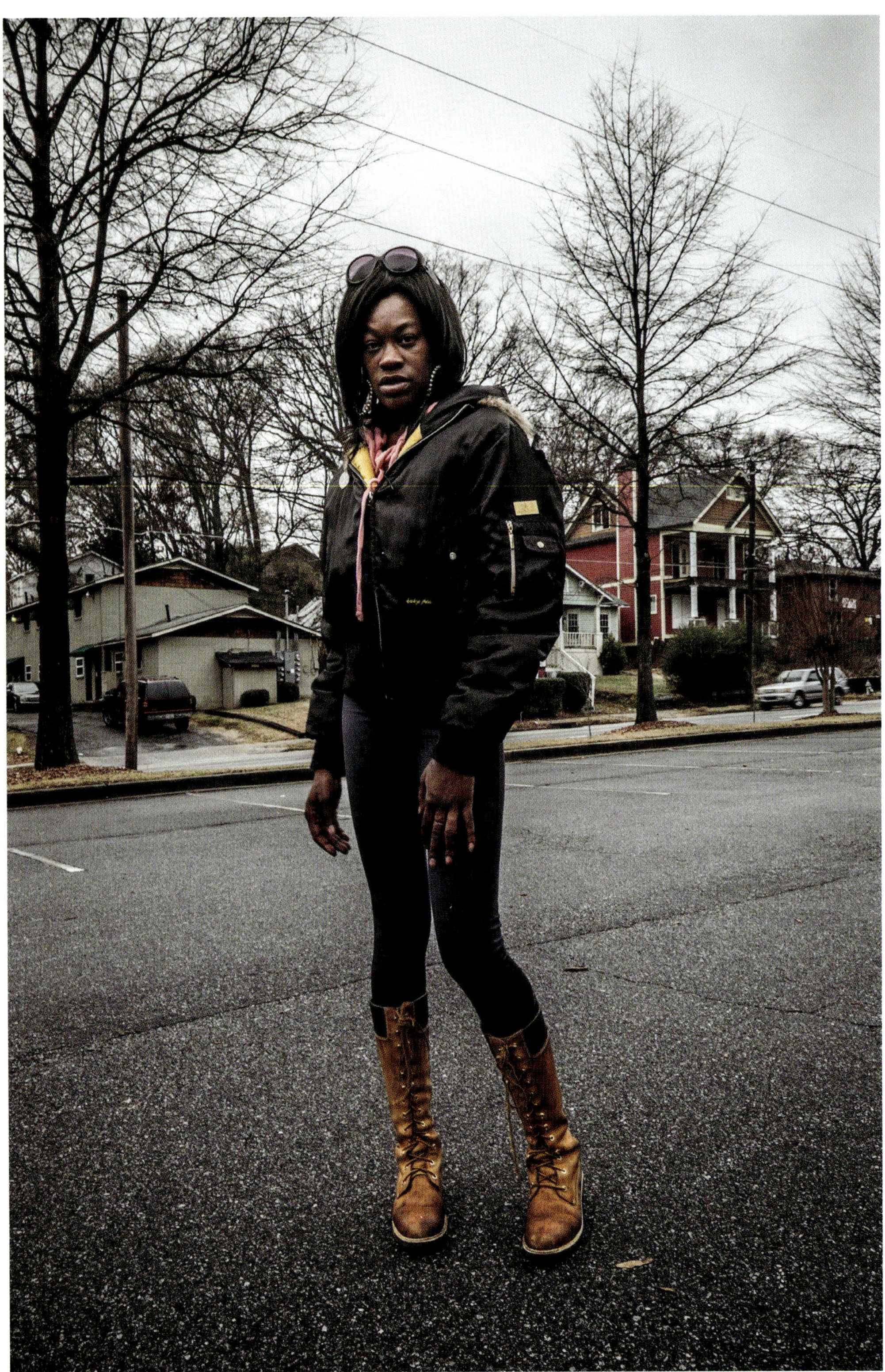

ATLANTA, GA – 2014-12-28

Mecca: My dad was an addict. He spent ten years of my life in prison. I used to go see him and stuff. We never really had a relationship. I always wanted one, but we never really had a solid father-daughter relationship. That's why I was always looking for a sugar daddy, someone to take care of me and stuff. So I started dancing when I was seventeen. I'd hop the train and go to Jersey and dance.

I ended up moving to Atlanta to go to college. I didn't finish 'cause I found the club life so fascinating. It was awesome. I was eighteen or nineteen, getting into all the best clubs in Atlanta. My boyfriend was a headhunter by day, but by night he sold drugs.

It came out that he was an intravenous drug user. I started doing it because I wanted to be close to him. I couldn't let go of our relationship 'cause I guess I was that insecure. You know, I thought that nobody would ever love me.

Our addiction got so bad that we started fighting. Physical and mental abuse. He committed suicide when I was twenty-two.

BW: Do you know why he killed himself?

Mecca: He had a lot of emotional turmoil within himself. He always felt like he was in some sort of prison. That's kind of how drugs are—a prison of the mind. No matter what, you're gonna do it because you're addicted.

I was on and off drugs for a long time, then it got so bad that they sent me to prison. I did two years and was a model prisoner. I finished this program and won awards and stuff.

I got out and was doing good, and then my mom got cancer. I became overwhelmed, so I started using drugs again. While I was using, she passed away. [Tears.] My grandma died first, and then my mom in the same year. I was all alone down here, and I started using drugs real bad.

I got my settlement [see note below] from the case, and I went to rehab. After rehab, I got out, got an apartment. I was a student again. Got all these awards, and honestly it was too much for me . . .

It started again.

Note: After Mecca finished her two-year prison sentence, it was discovered that she should have been sentenced only to probation. Because of that, she received a settlement.

ATLANTA, GA – 2015-01-22

I met Mami while she was walking the streets in a neighborhood in Atlanta known for prostitution and drugs. I had a sense before I even approached her that she carried a heavy burden. She was beautiful but had the same look in her eyes as a soldier returning from the front lines of war. She was hesitant to talk to me at first, but she eventually told me the story of how she was forced to grow up too fast and the search for her family that brought her and her sister to Atlanta.

Mami: I'm from Puerto Rico. When I was thirteen, my mom saved my life from an eighteen-wheeler, but she got killed. She was a single mom, so after she died, I raised my sister who was eight and a half. We stayed at my mom's house because it was paid for, but they cut the lights and water off. The neighbors would sometimes give us food and stuff like that. I would steal food from the supermarket, and then I started selling drugs when I was fifteen. That's how I took care of us.

BW: How long have you been in Atlanta?

Mami: I've been in Atlanta eighteen years. We came here looking for my dad when I was twenty-one. He left us when I was four years old. We found him, but he ain't shit.

BW: When you found your dad, what did he say?

Mami: He opened the door, and the only thing he told us was, "Why didn't y'all tell me you was coming?" That's it. He don't love us. He don't care about us. He looked at us like we were strangers. He had another family, and he just kicked us to the curb.

> **Misty:** So many times we see someone on the streets and judge them for their station in life. People will never understand it's not weakness that helped her survive, it is her utter strength. She is no less because of her profession, she makes her own way in this world. Her beauty isn't in her skin, but the unstoppable spirit.

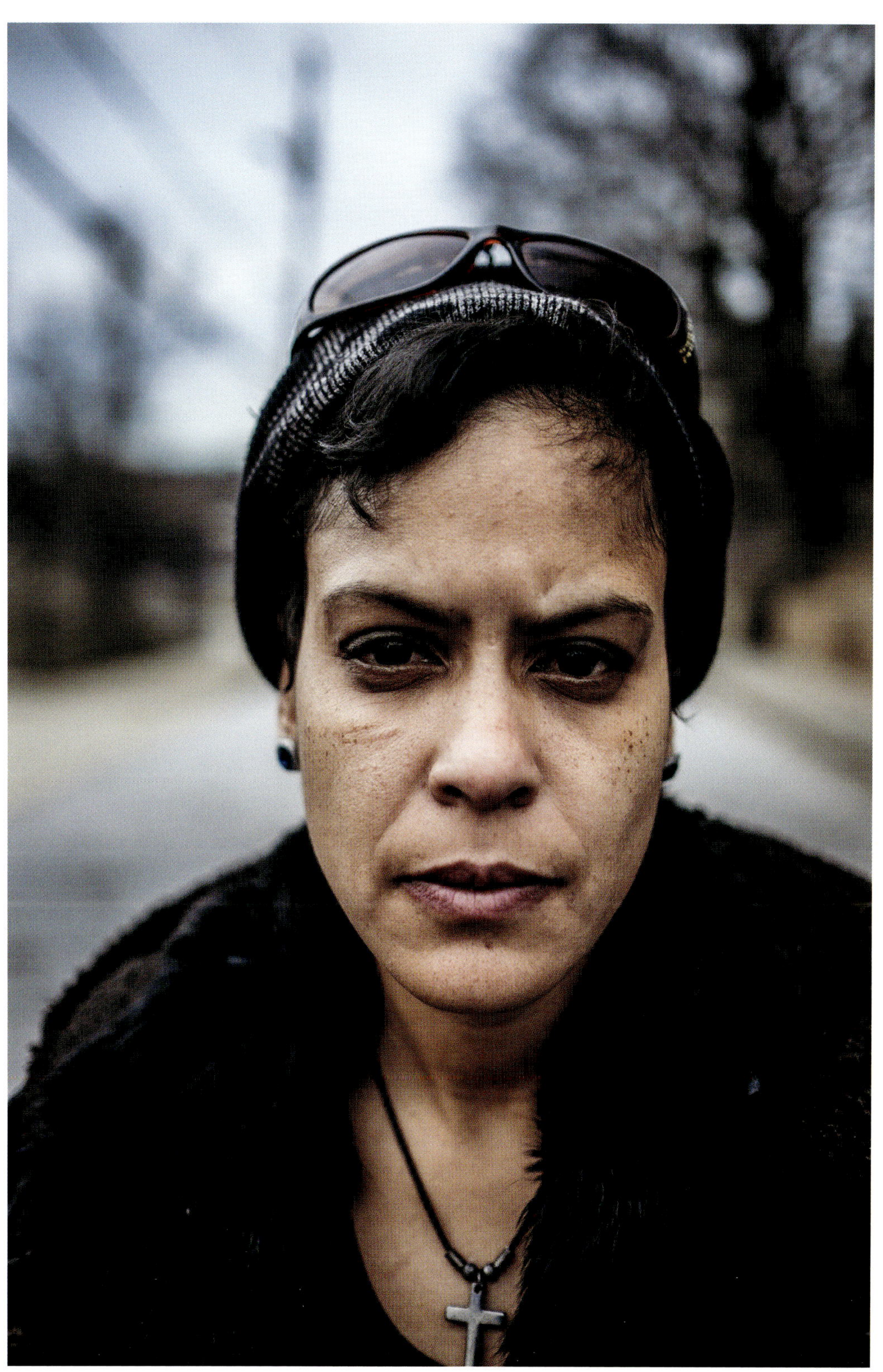

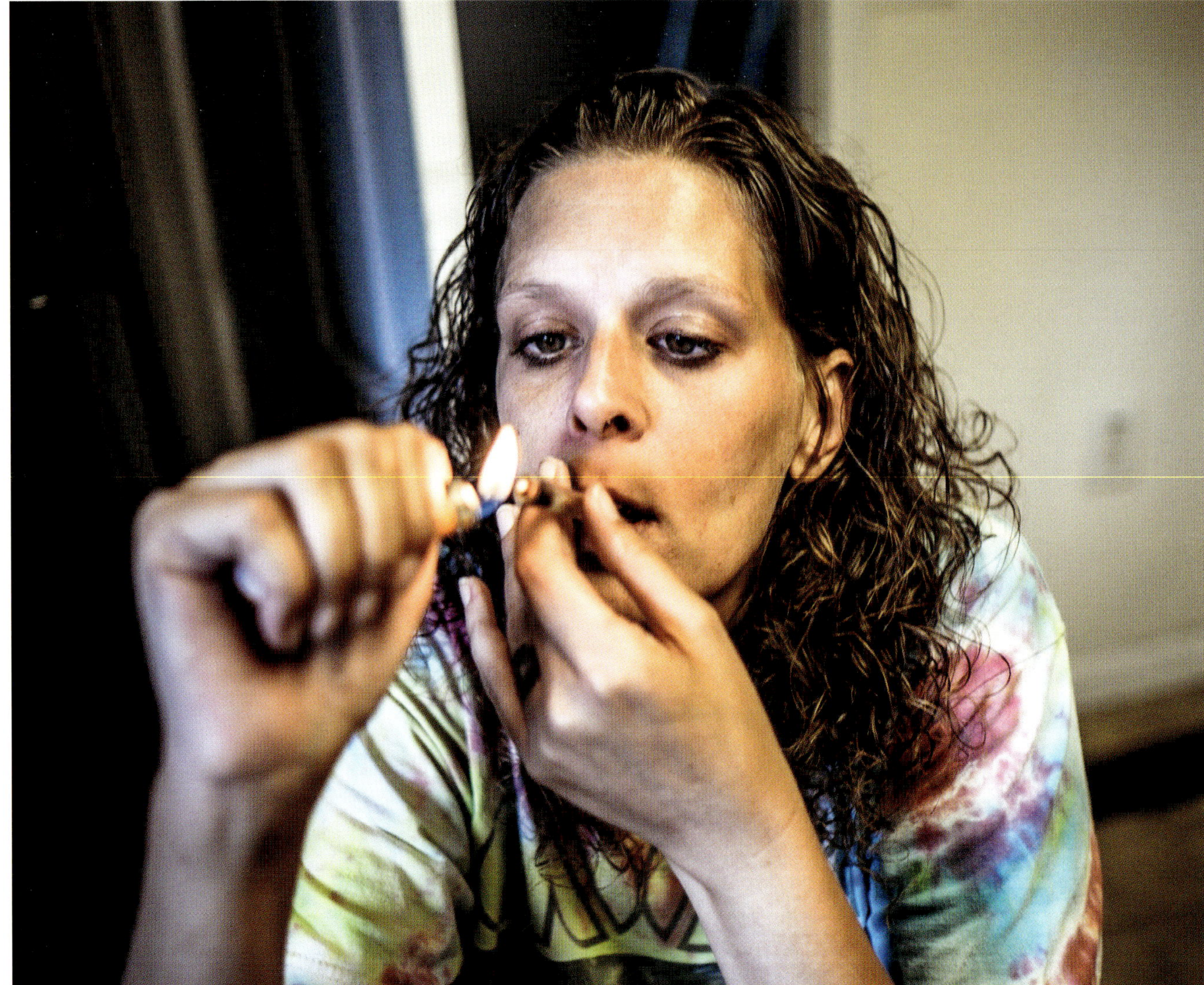

KINGSPORT, TN – 2015-06-03

Heather: My old man works at Eastman, and he makes pretty good money, but he can't afford me with my habit. My habit's pretty bad.

BW: Does he know you're working?

Heather: Yeah. He don't like it. I even charge him. I don't have sex for free. Sometimes I'll do him for free, but usually I'll say, "Hey, I'll do a little of this if you'll do a little of that." But this is the best relationship I've ever been in. Been with him for eight years. He don't drink. He don't do dope. I'm fucked up enough. I need someone with a level head around me to watch my back.

BW: Do you think you could have a relationship where money wasn't involved?

Heather: I don't know . . . I don't know.

BW: Why do you think it's like that?

Heather: 'Cause I'm sick and fuckin' twisted. I think somethin' done snapped inside my head that relates money to sex and sex to money. I think I started at such a young age that there's something in my head that correlates the two.

BW: How old were you?

Heather: I started out at seventeen as a Bottoms Up showgirl. They trained me pretty well. They taught me how to take advantage of little ole men and run through their bank accounts real quick. Now I'm thirty-five. I'm too old to dance, so I'm walking the street, and that's where I'm at.

BW: What's the hardest part about working on the street?

Heather: The law, man. The fucking narcotics officers always hounding me, wanting my dope dealer, wanting this, wanting that. I don't tell them anything. They busted me two years ago, and I gave them just enough information to get them off my ass. You know what I'm saying? I didn't really give them anything they could sink their teeth into.

Now here it is two years later, and I'm walkin' up the street. I just took a big shot of gravel [Flakka]. If you've ever done gravel, you know that when you shoot that shit, you hallucinate and you get a little crazy for a few minutes. This undercover officer comes up and pulls me to the side and says, "I'm the police, and I know who you are and I know what you do." He said, "I don't want you. I want your damn dope dealer." I started flippin' the fuck out on him. I started yelling,

"You're the police! You're an undercover cop!" Started settin' him out right there in the middle of the street. Everybody knowin' who I am, and now everybody knows who he is. He starts running. I ran the other way. It was just a really bad deal. I don't know if they're gonna bother me again or if now they know not to. [Laughs.] I just flipped the fuck out. I haven't seen that guy since.

BW: What is gravel? I've never come across it.

Heather: God, it's a chemical, and it's horrible for you, but it's really good shit. It doesn't last as long as meth, but it definitely lasts longer than crack and a little bit more severe than crack. If you like crack, you'll really love gravel 'cause it will last longer and the rush is stronger.

BW: Have you ever stayed sober for any length of time?

Heather: Yeah. The longest I ever made it was fifteen months. Had to go to meetings like twice a day. I got this whole group of friends that don't use from Narcotics Anonymous. The most fun I ever had in my life was at a damn convention. It is so much fuckin' fun, man. There was like a thousand Narcotics Anonymous members there saying the Serenity Prayer at the same time. I just get chills thinking about it.

Asher: I can relate to this. It scares me . . . Hope she does well, and fuck the haters. True struggle is something most people have the fortune not to know.

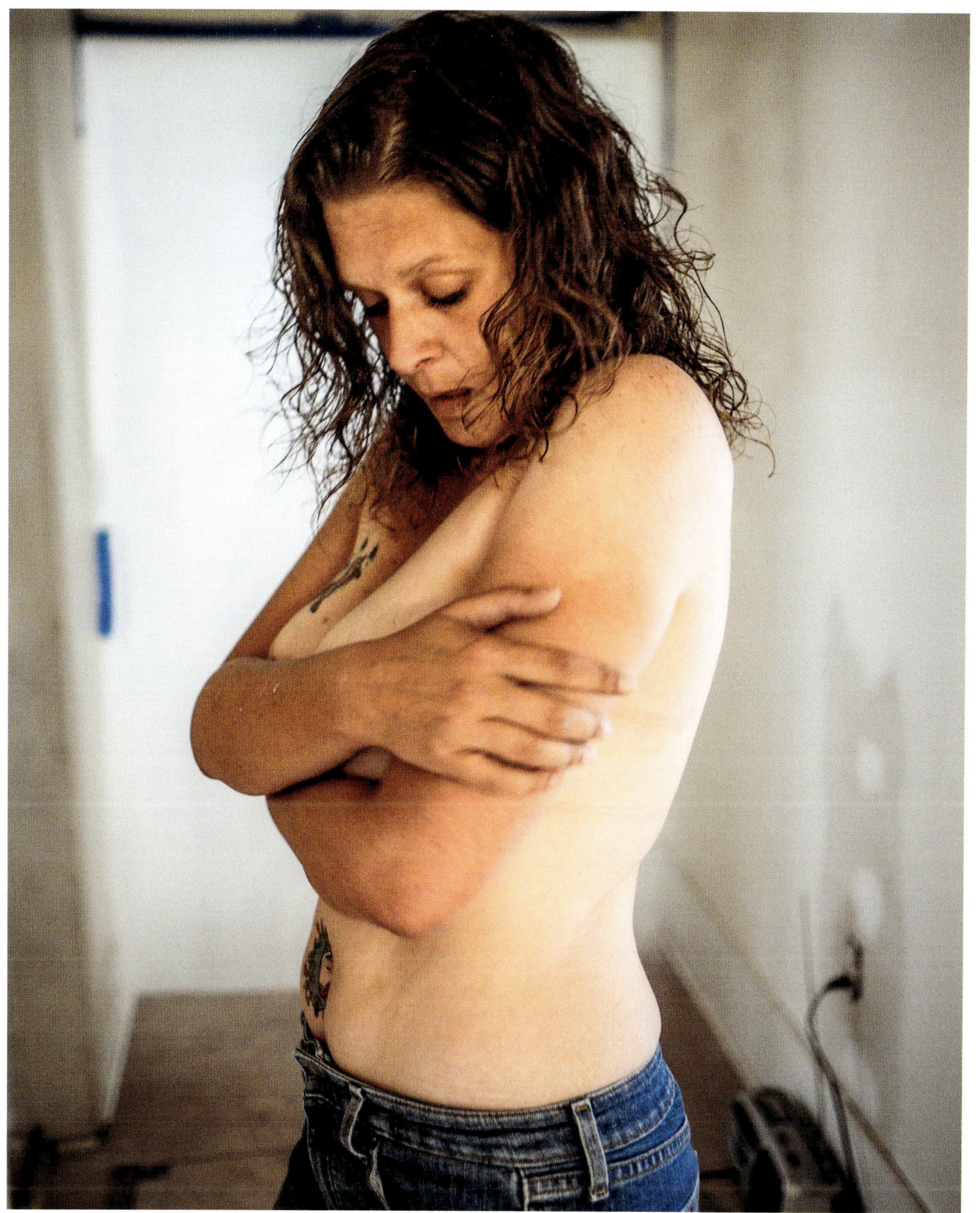

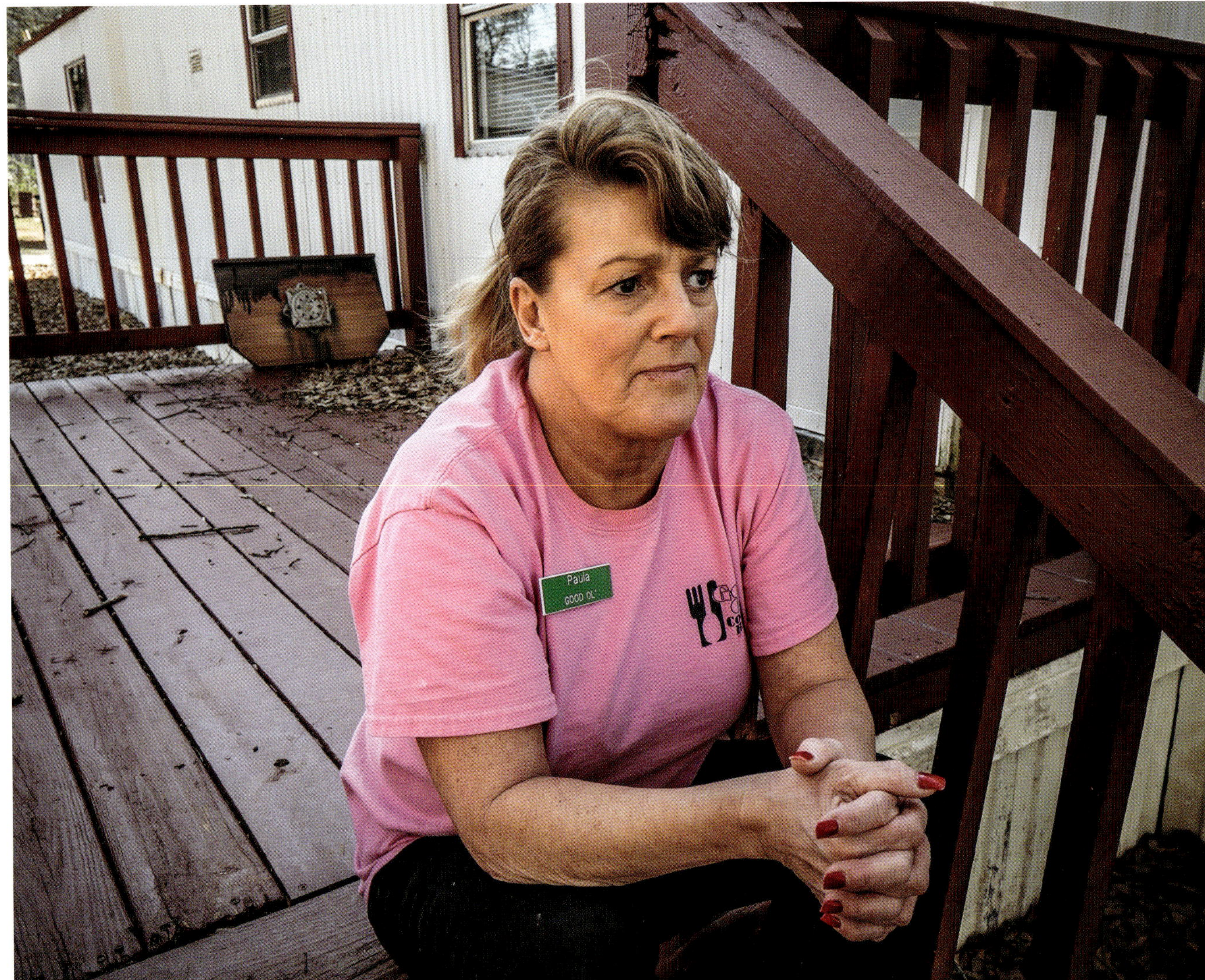

LAGRANGE, GA – 2015-02-14

Paula: I took my first drink when I was twelve years old. I had a very bad, abusive childhood, and alcohol made me feel like an adult . . . like I was bulletproof. I've been in treatment twice, and I've been in and out of Twelve Step programs for the last twenty-six years. I just can't seem to maintain any period of sobriety. I've been sober for two years now, but these last six months have been hell. I quit going to meetings when I got involved with somebody. Last Sunday, I threw him out. I always fall back into drinking when I stop going to meetings. I isolate myself really, really bad. I'm kinda isolating now, ya know? I've been in that trailer since Sunday. I said to myself, "If one more person tells me, 'Happy Valentine's Day,' I'm gonna slap the shit out of them."

BW: [Laughing.] I hear ya.

Paula: I stopped drinking two years ago on Valentine's Day. My husband was with another woman. I told myself that if I drank that day, then I would have gone over there and killed him, because I'm a violent drunk.

Here I am, two years later, upset because my boyfriend left me for another woman. But nothing is as bad as how it was. This pain is nothing compared to what I went through getting sober. I'm not going to let this asshole take me back to that. I'm better off without him. I didn't get sober to be miserable.

BW: I know what you mean. There's nothing more painful than going back to that. So, what are you grateful for?

Paula: I'm grateful for that roof over my head. I got a comfortable bed, food to eat, and a job. I'm really grateful for my friends.

I think I'm going to wash my hair, put on too much makeup and some nice clothes, and go to a meeting.

Charlene: Hey, Paula. From the first day I met you, I knew you were a very special lady. We've all had hard times at one time or another in our life. The hero is the one who pulls up her bootstraps, holds her head up high, and keeps moving on. Paula, happiness comes from within us. People or things can't make us happy. Truly you are a hero. Your friend, Charlene.

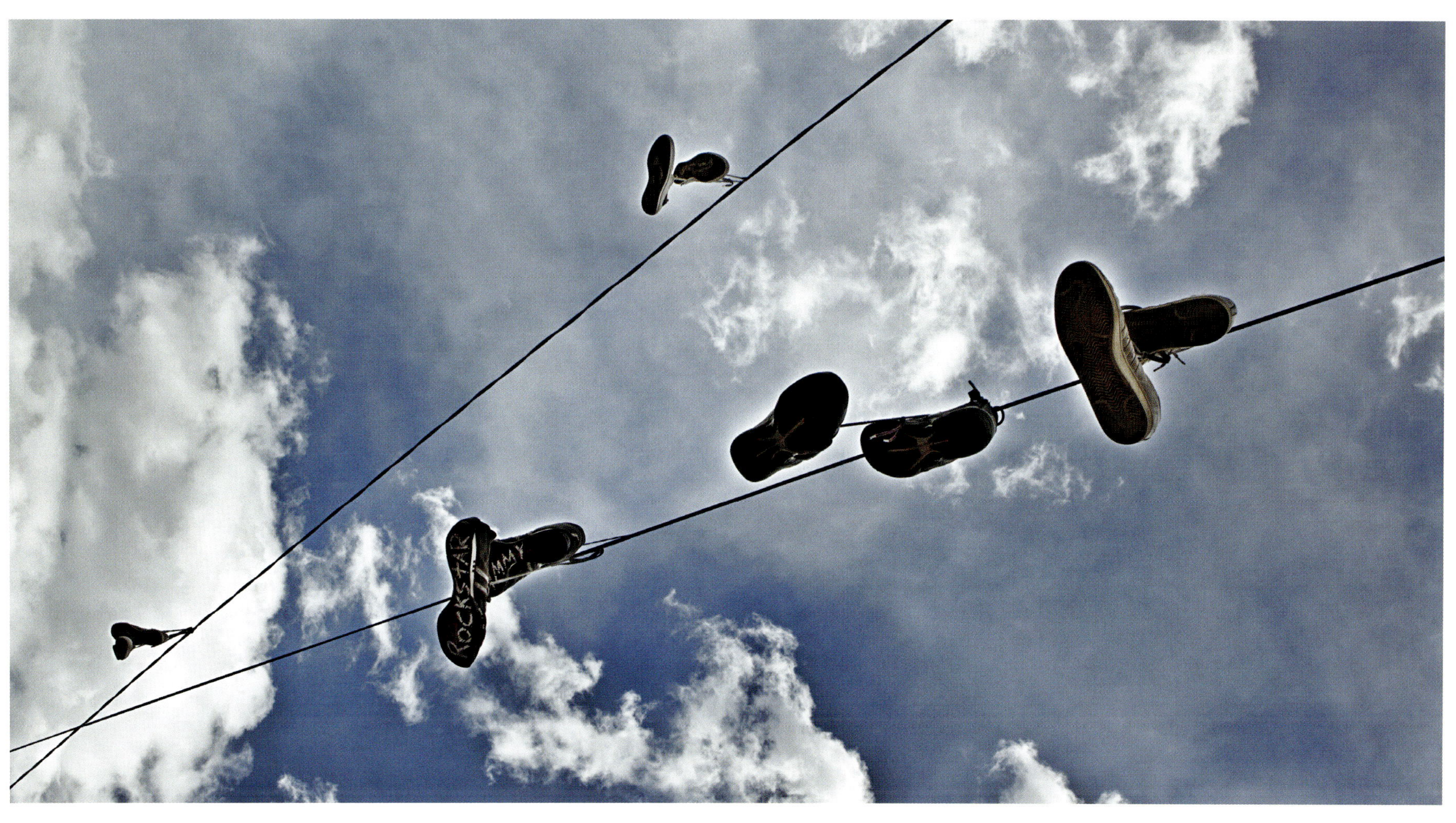

If we are painstaking about this phase of our development, we will be amazed before we are half way through. We are going to know a new freedom and a new happiness. We will not regret the past nor wish to shut the door on it. We will comprehend the word serenity and we will know peace. No matter how far down the scale we have gone, we will see how our experience can benefit others. That feeling of uselessness and self pity will disappear. We will lose interest in selfish things and gain interest in our fellows. Self-seeking will slip away. Our whole attitude and outlook upon life will change. Fear of people and of economic insecurity will leave us. We will intuitively know how to handle situations which used to baffle us. We will suddenly realize that God is doing for us what we could not do for ourselves.

Are these extravagant promises? We think not. They are being fulfilled among us—sometimes quickly, sometimes slowly. They will always materialize if we work for them.

The Promises of A.A. - The Big Book of Alcoholics Anonymous, 2nd edition

People I meet often describe the act of chasing their addiction as the attempt to fill a void or replace something that was lost. In Twelve Step programs, this is sometimes described as having a God-shaped hole in our soul.

—BW

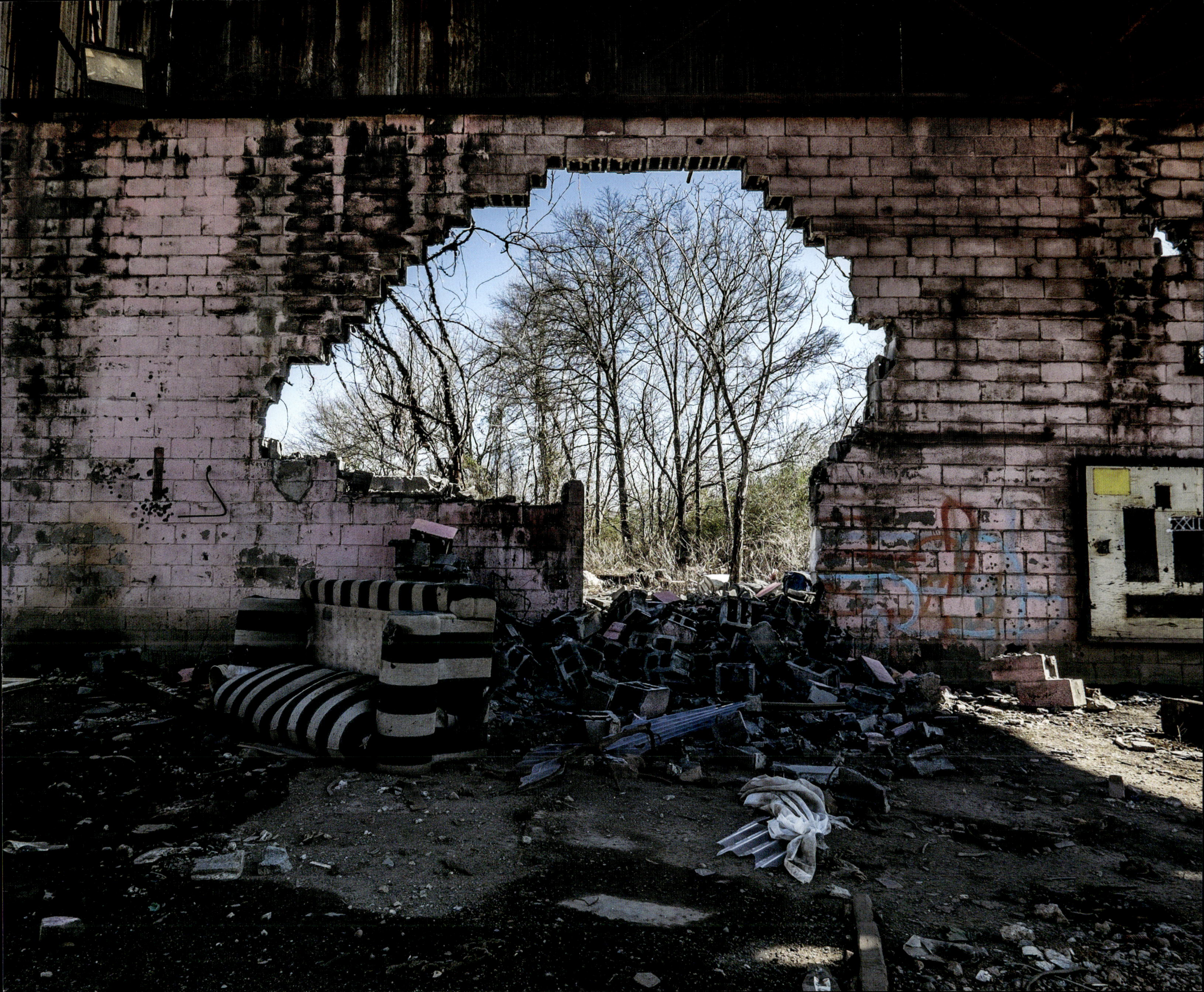

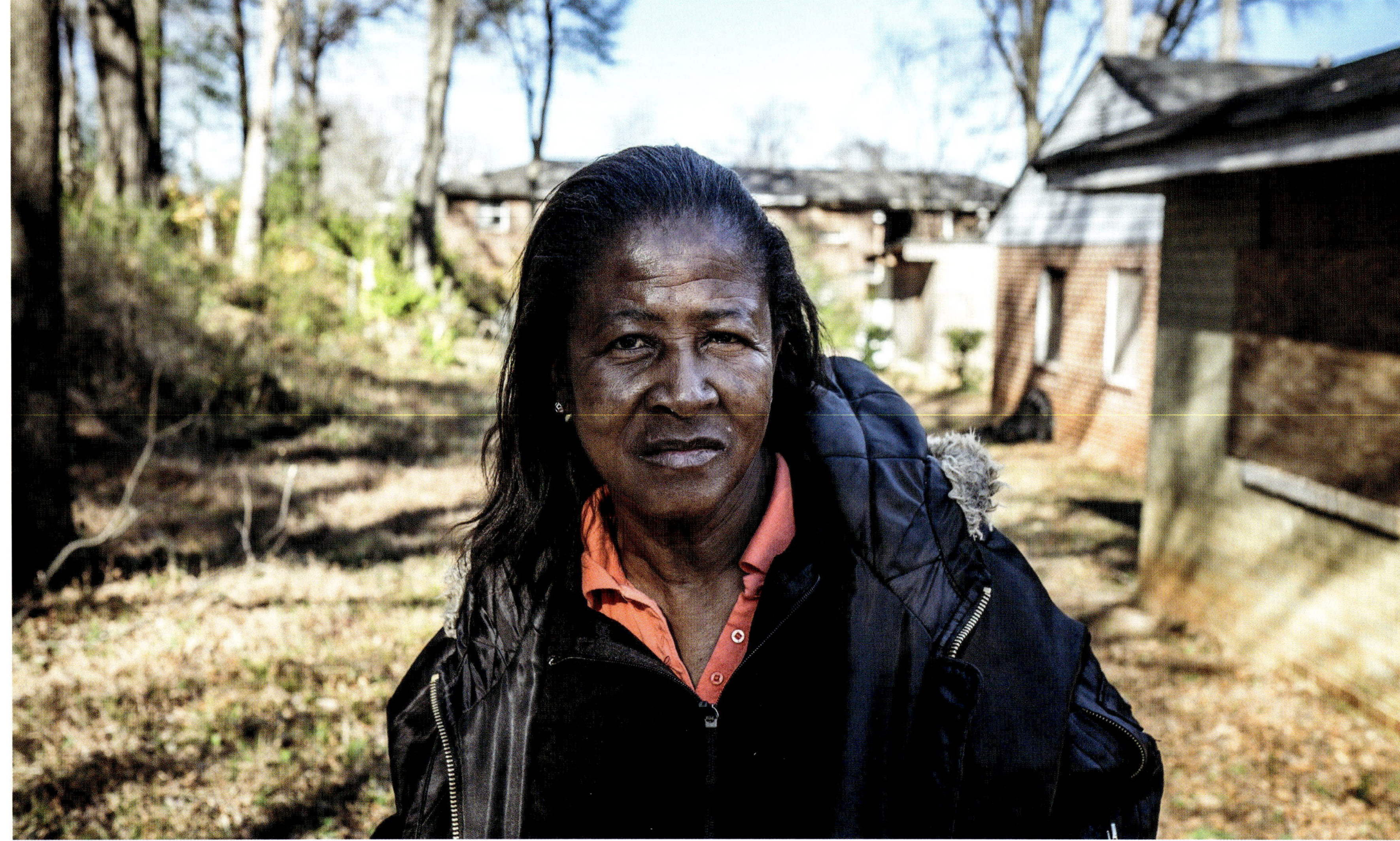

ATLANTA, GA – 2014-12-12

Estelle: I was molested as a child, by my stepfather.

BW: How old were you?

Estelle: Ten . . . I was ten.

He took me to the store all the time and would buy me candy and stuff. I was just a little girl, you know? He started playing with me. Rubbin' on me and stuff. Tellin' me I had to do these things to him.

BW: How long did that go on?

Estelle: Till I was fourteen.

BW: Do you remember how you felt about it?

Estelle: No . . . I knew it wasn't supposed to be happening. I went along with it 'cause he'd give me candy and money and stuff. All kids like that . . .

BW: Did you ever tell your mom or anything?

Estelle: I told my aunt, and my aunt told me to tell my mom. I did, and my mom said she didn't believe me. You know how that crushed me, right? She chose him over me so I was, like, hurt.

BW: How do you think it changed you?

Estelle: I think it's the reason I started doing drugs. When I get high, it takes it away. I don't have to think about it. I think that people doing drugs has a lot to do with hiding stuff. Know what I mean?

BW: Yeah, I do. That's kind of what this project is all about.

SAVANNAH, GA – 2015-05-22

Danielle: I moved to Savannah in '98. I've battled with addiction for thirty years. Crack is my drug of choice. I do good for a little while, and then I do bad for a little while. And then an intervention takes place, and that usually involves the Chatham County police department.

BW: That's no fun.

Danielle: No, it's not. But there's something about total admission, when you reach that point. Everything comes out, and then it gets better.

BW: That's true. There's a saying in the rooms, "You're only as sick as your secrets." This project was started based on that one line and on the belief that there's freedom and healing in sharing those things that we perceive have so much power over us. So what are those things for you? What led up to the last thirty years of using?

Danielle: When I was three, my stepfather started molesting me. He did it until I was about fifteen. I think that played a part. My mother hated him so much because of his own addictions [alcohol and crack], that I don't think she noticed what was going on.

It wasn't an everyday thing, but then again, it was. When I'd go to bed at night, I'd barricade my door. It didn't keep him out, but it made noise where I could wake up. Or I'd sleep under my bed and leave my window open so it looked like I snuck out. I'd rather take the whipping for sneaking out . . .

BW: Did you ever tell anyone about getting molested?

Danielle: It was me and my older sister. I was fifteen, and we told my mom together. She didn't want to believe us at first, and I thought, "Why would I make up a lie like that?"

But apparently she believed something about it because she left Dad after that and took the three younger children with her.

BW: Do you think he molested a lot of the girls in his path?

Danielle: I know he got in trouble many times for touching women's breasts in public. I would bring girlfriends home, and he would just not leave them alone. I could tell how uncomfortable they were, so I quit bringing friends home 'cause I didn't want them to start talking about me at school.

BW: Have you ever stayed sober for any length of time?

Danielle: Yes. Three and a half years. I got my CDL and became a long-haul truck driver. I did very well with that. I was a trainer.

BW: What do you think keeps you out here?

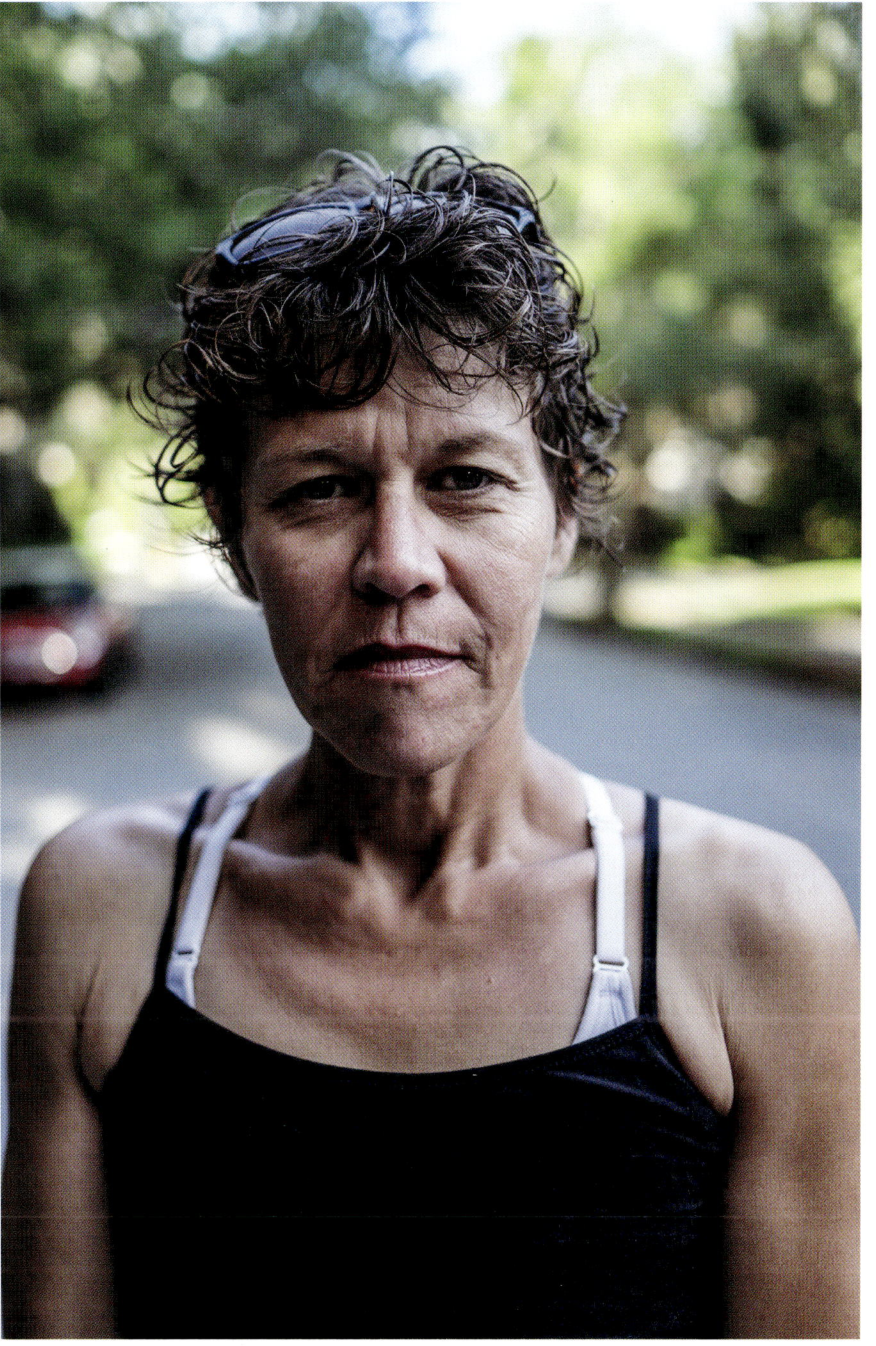

Danielle: The reason I continue is because when reality starts hitting, it's very uncomfortable. It's like my mind says, "I want to smoke," and my body follows. I guess I figure trying to fight it is a losing battle, so why try?

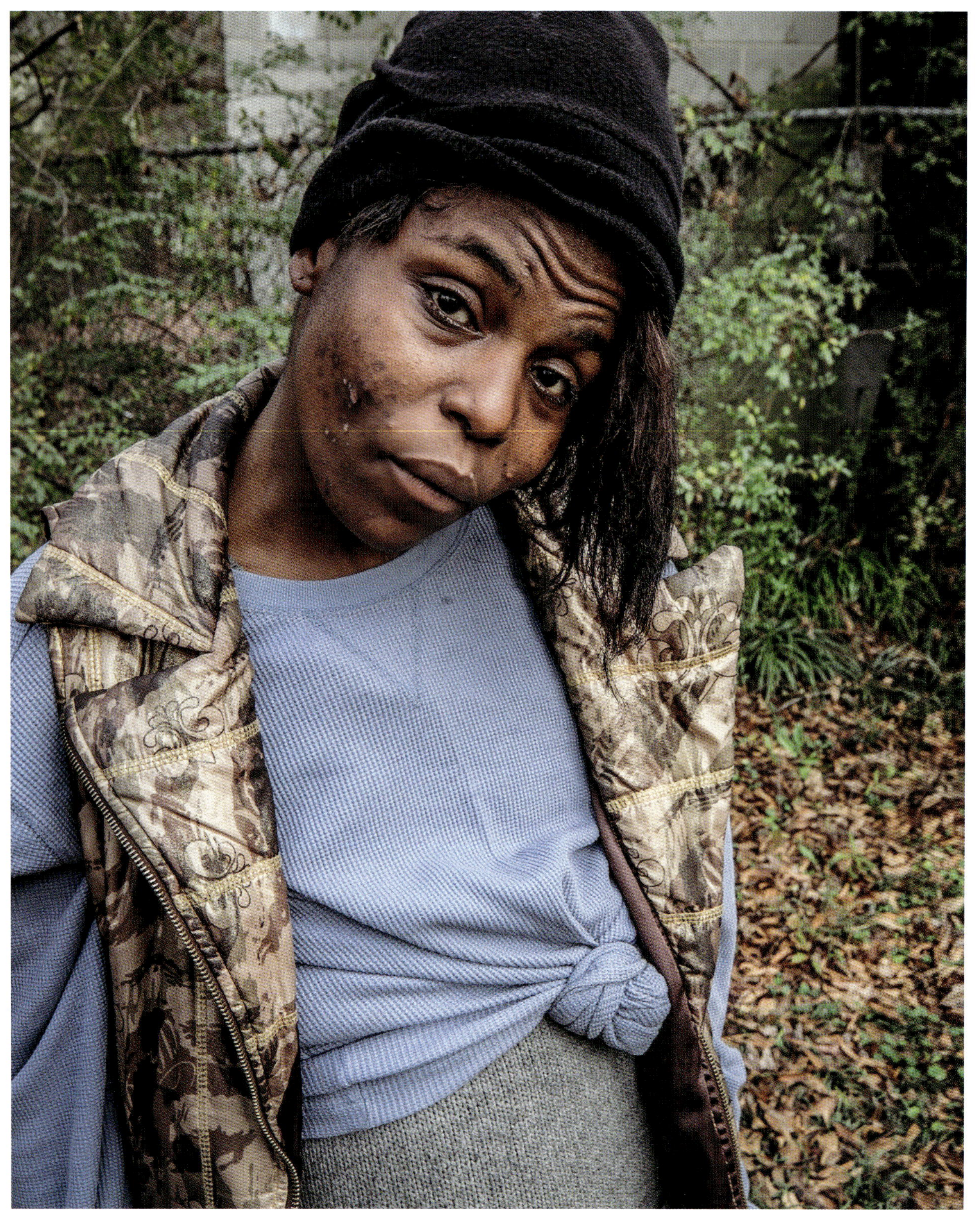

ATLANTA, GA – 2014-12-28

I think the prostitution for me is like more of an addiction because I feel like somebody loves me. I know I'm not being loved, but I've already told myself for that two minutes I'm being loved.

Skittles: My mom died on my birthday last year. I woke up, and she was dead. My dad died on Mother's Day. [Tears.]

BW: I'm really sorry. You said you were sober before they died?

Skittles: Yes. I'd been sober since I was eighteen. I'm twenty-five now.

BW: When did you start doing drugs?

Skittles: I was twelve. My older sister was doing heroin, and I sniffed it. Been liking it ever since.

BW: What's the plan for the future?

Skittles: [Pausing.] Just to wake up.

BW: What do you mean wake up?

Skittles: Just to wake up. The crack isn't even that good. I don't do it all the time. I think the prostitution for me is like more of an addiction because I feel like somebody loves me. I know I'm not being loved, but I've already told myself for that two minutes I'm being loved.

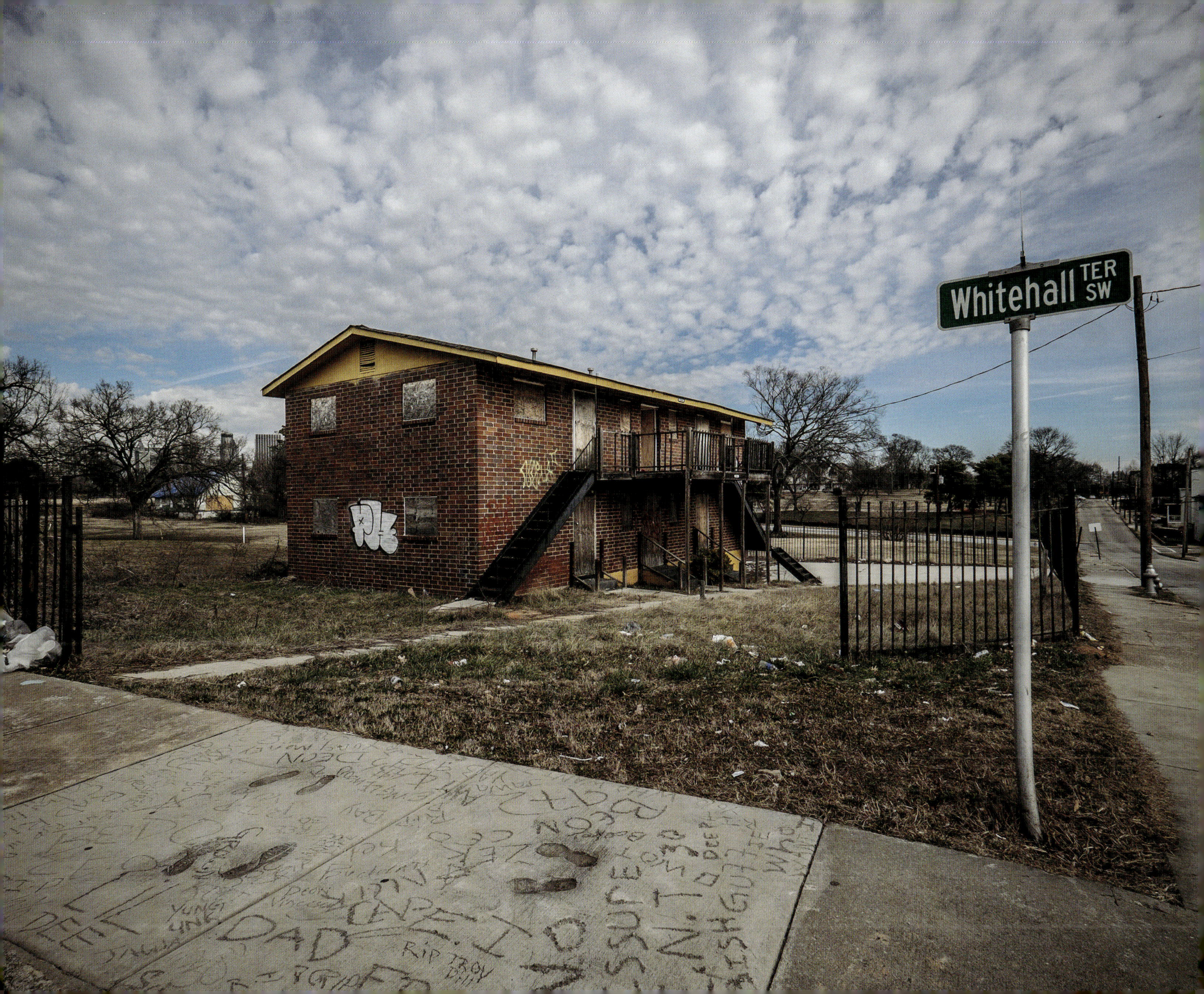
Whitehall TER SW

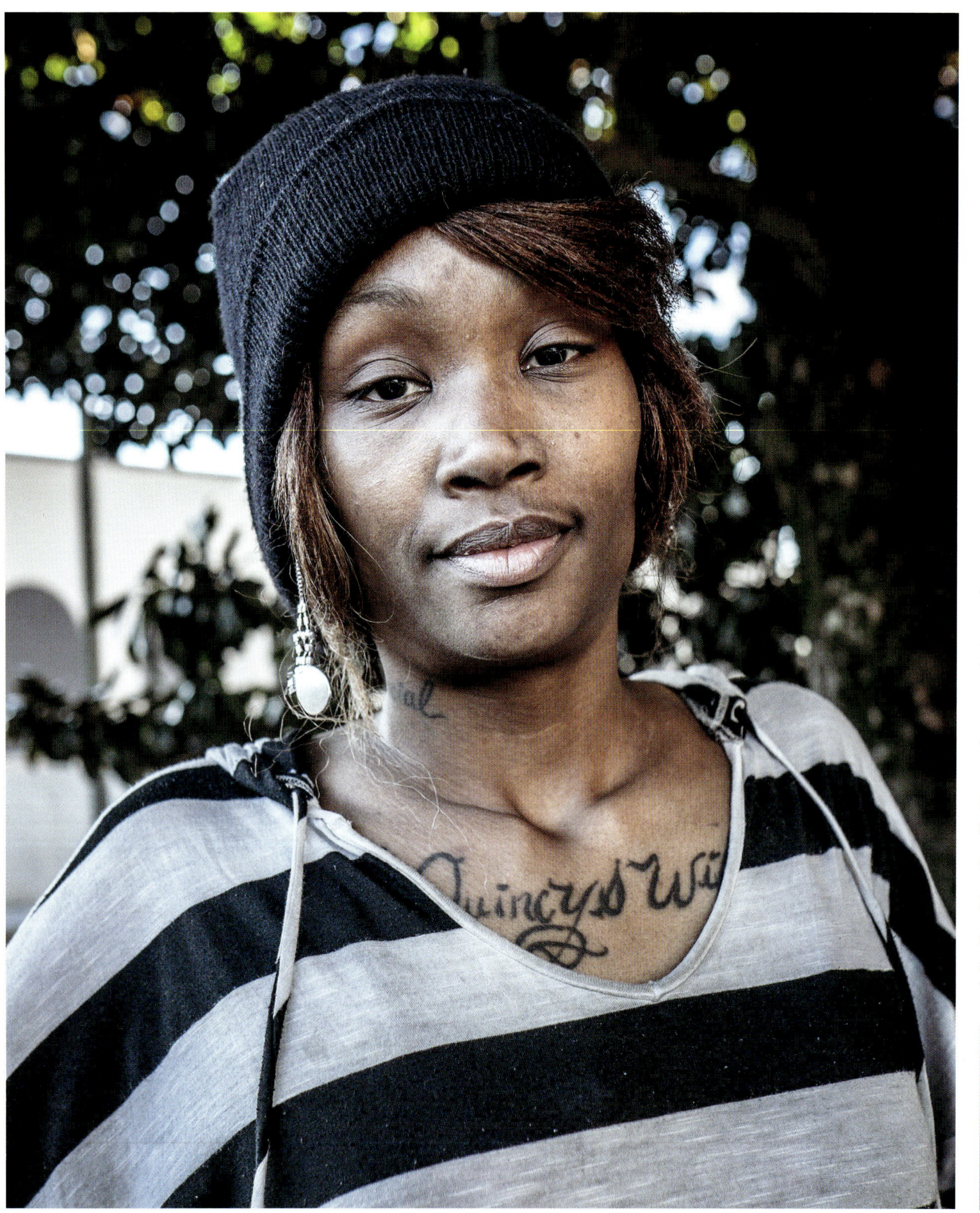

ATLANTA, GA – 2015-01-25

Read part 1 of Queen's story on p. 13.

Queen: My addiction is heroin. It brings me down. I can't move or operate without it. My body has become dependent on it. I've been doing it for eight years.

BW: How did you get started?

Queen: I was in a car accident in Miami, and I started getting Roxys for the pain. When I moved to Atlanta, I couldn't get the Roxys anymore, so I switched to heroin. Basically they are the same thing.

BW: What's the longest you've gone without heroin in the last eight years?

Queen: Two weeks, when I was in jail.

BW: What was that like, coming off that stuff in jail? It must have been hell.

Queen: Well, yeah. But they can't not help you in jail now 'cause someone died. So now it's a law that if you have a heroin or alcohol addiction, they have to detox you the right way. They eventually got me on methadone, but the first two days were hell because they had to get it approved by a doctor. I was sick as a dog. The third day, they gave me the methadone, and I stopped hurting instantly.

BW: I've never taken methadone. Do you still get high?

Queen: Yes, exactly. It's just another drug.

BW: I don't understand. What's the point?

Queen: I don't even know, baby, 'cause there's a lot of people addicted to methadone now. They're still opiates.

Sunshine: The ability for her and others in this project to be so open and so raw with their stories shows so much strength! If more of us were not afraid to be open about our stories, there would be more awareness and compassion.

ATLANTA, GA – 2014-12-03

Alex: I have a terrible little heroin addiction going on right now. It's sort of jumbled up life a bit.

BW: How did you get started on heroin?

Alex: Like most people [who are heroin addicts], I started messing around with pills in high school. By the time I tried heroin, I was already a full-blown opiate addict. Heroin was just a cheaper alternative.

BW: I hear that from a lot of people.

Alex: Yeah, that's how 90 percent of the people I know got started. I mean, in this day and age, everyone knows heroin is terrible. Nobody wakes up one day and says, "I want to shoot heroin." By the time they get to that point, they usually have a pretty bad opiate addiction going already.

The addiction is obviously not something I enjoy. It's kind of like a love affair. I love it and I hate it at the same time. When you're high, it's the best feeling ever, you know? It's better than sex. Better than anything on the planet! At the same time, I know it's ruining my life.

Back when I was living kind of a normal life, honestly it wasn't all that great. But the worse my life got, it's like the better [heroin] made things for me. I don't know . . . It's so weird.

Andrea: I always have an internal struggle with panhandlers. On one hand, I know most of them aren't just down on their luck, can't find a job . . . They have very real addiction and/or mental health problems. On the other hand, I feel guilty for supporting their addiction by giving money.

Julie: Another way I personally look at it is, who are we to judge whether someone "deserves" help? I just give and leave the burden on their shoulders.

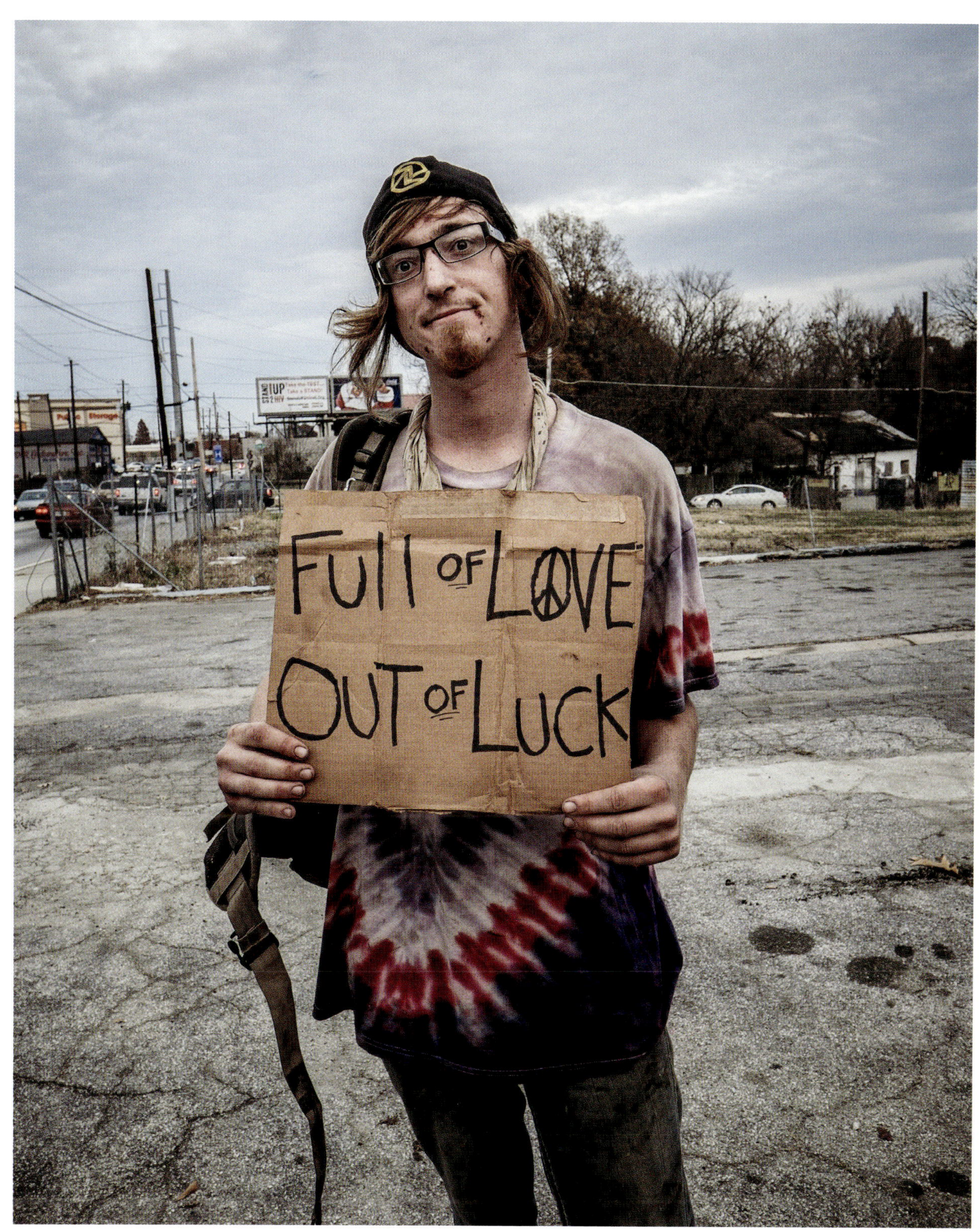

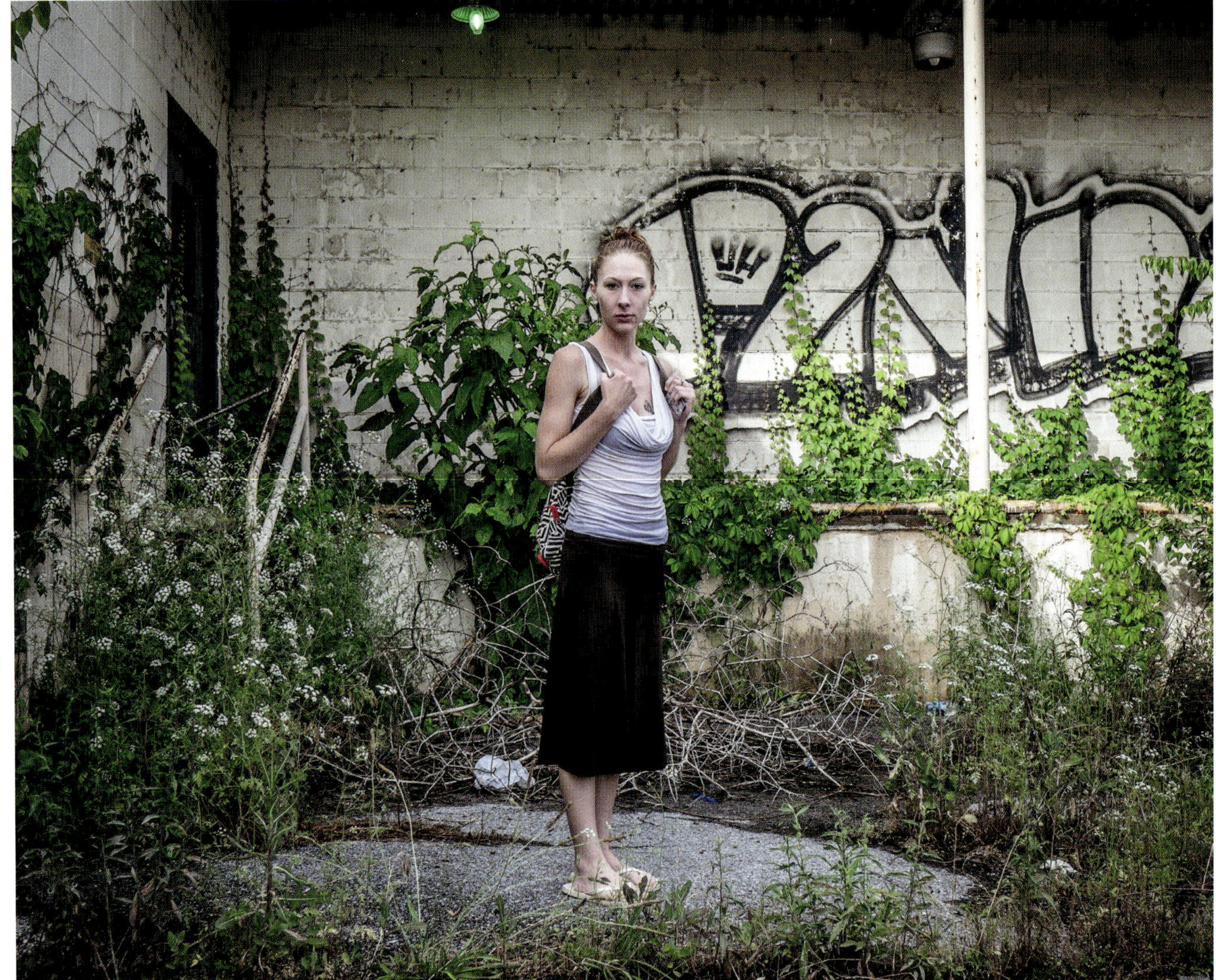

KNOXVILLE, TN – 2015-05-29

Chelsey: I've definitely had better times than what I'm having right now. I went to Kentucky and stayed with my sister for a couple of months. I wasn't supposed to be there that long, but she wouldn't bring me back. Couldn't afford it.

I live in KCDC [Knoxville's Community Development Corporation] housing, so they can kick you out once your lights get shut off. So I just know it's coming. It's not come yet, but . . .

BW: Do you have kids?

Chelsey: Yes, I have two. They got taken away because I was on drugs. I was addicted to opiates. I've been sober for four days. It's not much, but it's something.

BW: It's a start. Where are your kids now?

Chelsey: A lady adopted them. I have a boy and a girl. One and two. It hurts that I lost them, but I know [tears] they're in better hands right now. They're more taken care of than I could have done right now. So . . . I've got to look at it the best way I can.

BW: Do you get updates on them or anything?

Chelsey: We have a private Facebook account set up so I can see pictures and find out how they're doing. I think once I get my life straightened out and really get on my feet good, then I'll maybe get to be around them a little bit. She said so, but you never know.

BW: How do you think you'll get there? Have you ever had any length of time sober?

Chelsey: Oh yeah, and I love it.

BW: How did you do it before?

Chelsey: God.

BW: Did you go to meetings? Work the steps?

Chelsey: No, I've never done the steps. Just because, my dad—he used to be a preacher. So I feel like, if you really want to quit, you'll just quit.

BW: What's the longest you've stayed sober?

Chelsey: Like, three months.

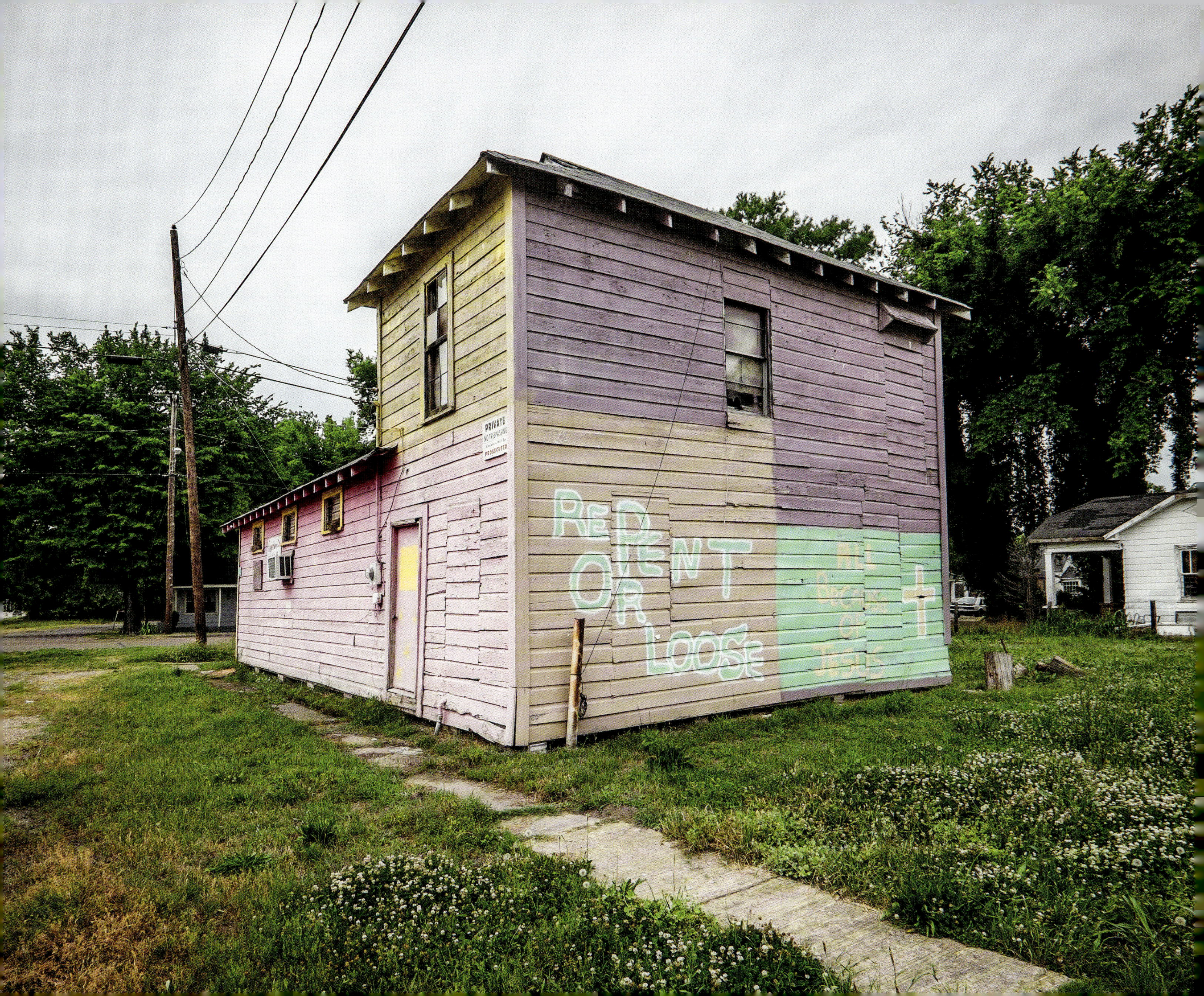
PRIVATE
NO TRESPASSING
PROSECUTED
REPENT
OR
LOOSE
ALL
BECAUSE
OF
JESUS

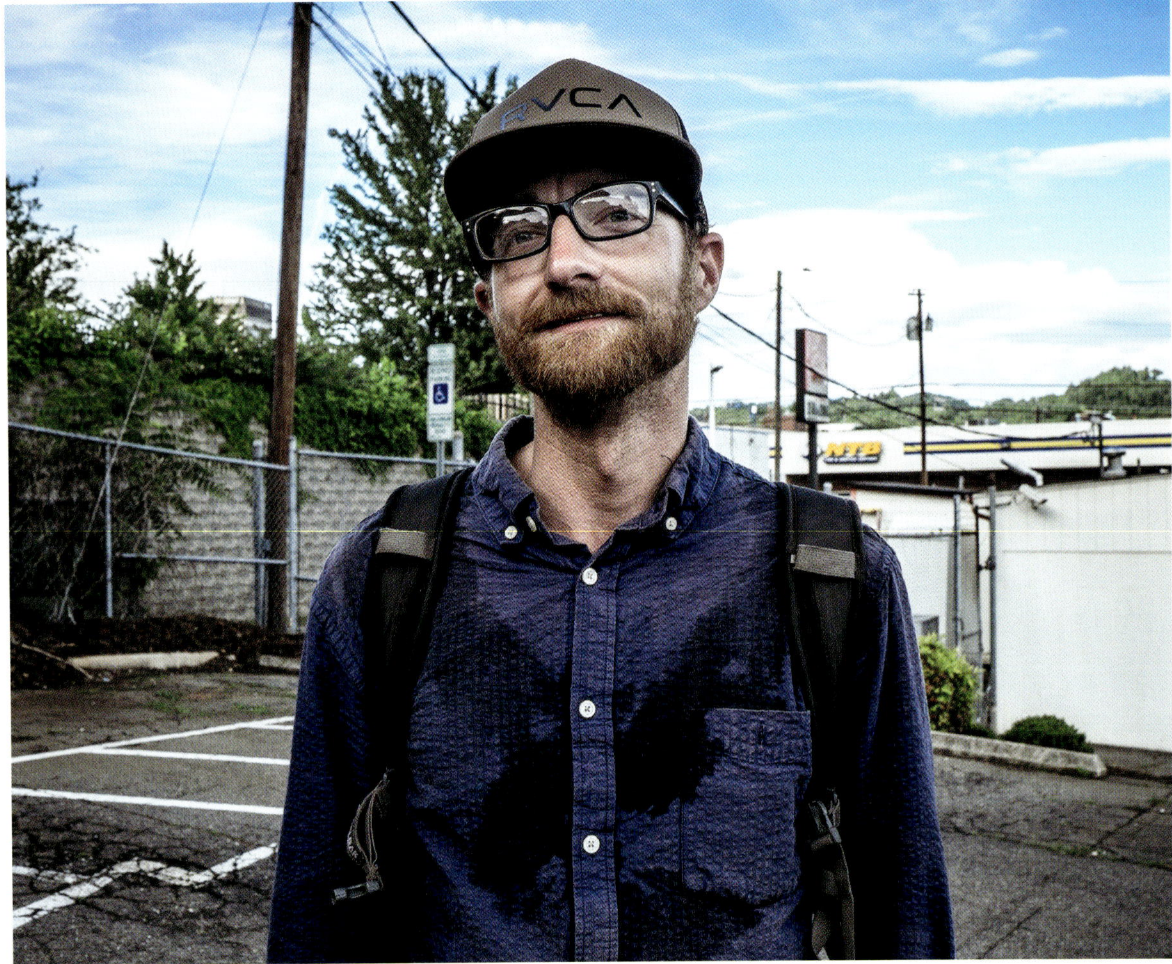

ASHEVILLE, NC – 2015-06-01

Patrick: I was born in southeast Texas in the swamps. When I was ten, we moved to Saudi Arabia. All my relatives lived in double-wides and stuff, so it was a really big change. It was a good thing because I got a really good education over there, and I got to experience a multicultural environment.

I went to college in Austin. Right after I graduated from college, I started using heroin, which didn't pan out too well, as you can imagine.

BW: How did you get started using heroin?

Patrick: You know, I got my wisdom teeth out when I was seventeen in Saudi. They gave me codeine to start out with, and it didn't do anything. I was in so much pain. So my dad golfed with a doctor there and got some Percocet, which is Oxycodone. I should have known at that point that I needed to be very careful with opiates 'cause that stuff worked well for me.

I kind of ran the gamut of the whole drug thing. But starting to use heroin was a big turning point for me. I was on a path to success, and my life quickly became this downward spiral of failure. It's such a terrible thing to get into.

BW: I can relate. I sabotaged myself for years. Deep down, I didn't feel like I deserved anything good, so I'd screw everything up. Why do you think you chose that path?

Patrick: Yeah, I get that. I get that. You know . . . I'm gay. I kind of tried to come out when I was ten years old. This was right before we moved to Saudi, and they weren't having it. They told me, "No. Don't act like that. You're just going through this phase." So I've kind of had that feeling deep down inside of me for a long time, that it's not acceptable. Even though since that time period I've experienced nothing but acceptance. I think that might be part of the self-loathing, which is ridiculous to me. I don't understand it.

But, man, I'm happy now. My life is pretty dang good. I just moved to Asheville about a month ago, and I just got a job today, actually. It's at the Goodwill, but it's a job.

BW: I'm glad you got a job. They aren't easy to come by in this town, from what I hear. Are you still using heroin?

Patrick: No, absolutely not. I haven't done heroin in six months, so it's been a while.

BW: How did you kick it? Cold turkey?

Patrick: Yeah, I actually ended up going to jail in Austin. I had no choice but to go cold turkey. When I was in jail, I made the decision that I needed to leave Austin. It's not like I can run from drugs. There's drugs everywhere. But everybody in my life who cared about me had been telling me I needed to get out. I ignored them for five years, but I finally listened. It's been really positive, man.

I'll tell you what—it's great to wake up in the morning and not feel sick and not have to worry about where I'm going to get money to get well again. Every morning I wake up and thank God I'm not addicted to that stuff anymore.

FAIRBURN, GA – 2015-08-05

Read part 1 of Linda's story on p. 96.

Linda: I tried for the next twelve years [after her husband's death] to see how much I could harm myself. I had some money when I started out, and by the end, I had none. I was sleeping on the floor in an empty bedroom at my girlfriend's house. I was just trying to run.

So when I decided to get sober, I tried all the geographical cures. I came to Atlanta with two suitcases, a box of shoes, a tool chest, and a Waterpik shower head. When you move, you think it's gonna be different. I left all the people I drank with. Well, you just find other people to drink with.

I thought I was one of those people who was just gonna have the hard knocks in life and that I just needed to square my shoulders up and keep walking. One day, however, I had this light bulb moment, and I said, "Maybe I'm participating in this."

When I did get sober, I just wanted to purge everything, and I didn't know how until I had a sponsor that walked me through it. After six months, we went into a little room at 8111 (A.A. clubhouse). I dumped a bunch of stuff on her and thought to myself, "She's gonna fix me." All she did after I was done was say, "Okay, let's go to the meeting." But it was the start of healing. That old A.A. saying about how your secrets keep you sick—it's true. They'll bury you.

BW: It is true. There are so many reasons for this project now, but the original thought was around that idea that "you're only as sick as your secrets." I thought that if I was able to give people a platform to share their secrets, it could be freeing for them.

For me, keeping shame-based secrets was toxic. I finally released a lot of that in my early thirties. And while it didn't fix everything, it was a jumping-off point to recover. I didn't have to carry the weight of silence on my shoulders anymore. Now it just doesn't have power, but for so many years I allowed it to have so much fucking power.

Linda: I think it's very hard for a man to say what you said.

BW: It is hard, but why is it hard? I didn't do anything wrong. I was a kid, and some guy took me in the bathroom at the park and molested me. I didn't ask for it.

Linda: When I look at the work you're doing, I look at the ladies and their stories, and I think what heavy burdens they must be carrying around.

BW: Horrible shame in most cases. You have whatever baggage from

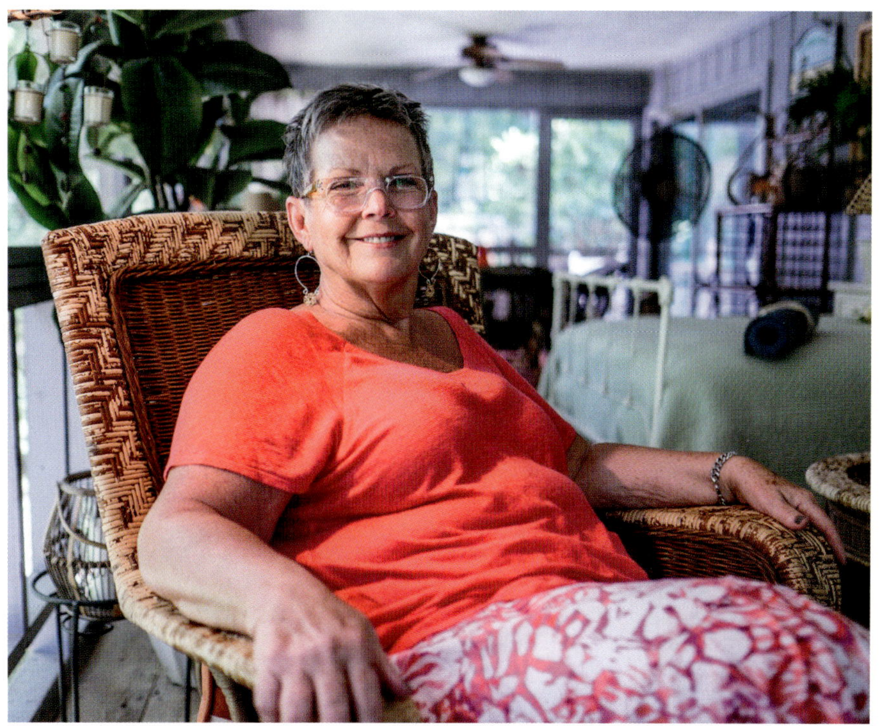

your past that weights you down, and then, for me, I'd have this cycle. I would get really fucked up and wake up feeling that shame and guilt and promising never to do it again. And then, by the end of the day, the shame would win, and the only way to drown out the pain was to do it all over again.

Linda: And we'd wake up every day saying, "I'll never do that again."

One of the reasons A.A. works is because when you go into meetings, you stay familiar with what it was like. You hear other people's insanity, and you work with another person, and you stay close to that. When you stay close to it, you stay in a state of gratitude.

BW: It's true. Imagine how much gratitude I get from working on this project.

> Guilt motivates you to want to correct or repair the error. In contrast, shame is an intense global feeling of inadequacy, inferiority, or self-loathing. You want to hide or disappear . . . You don't believe that you matter or are worthy of love, respect, success, or happiness.[13]

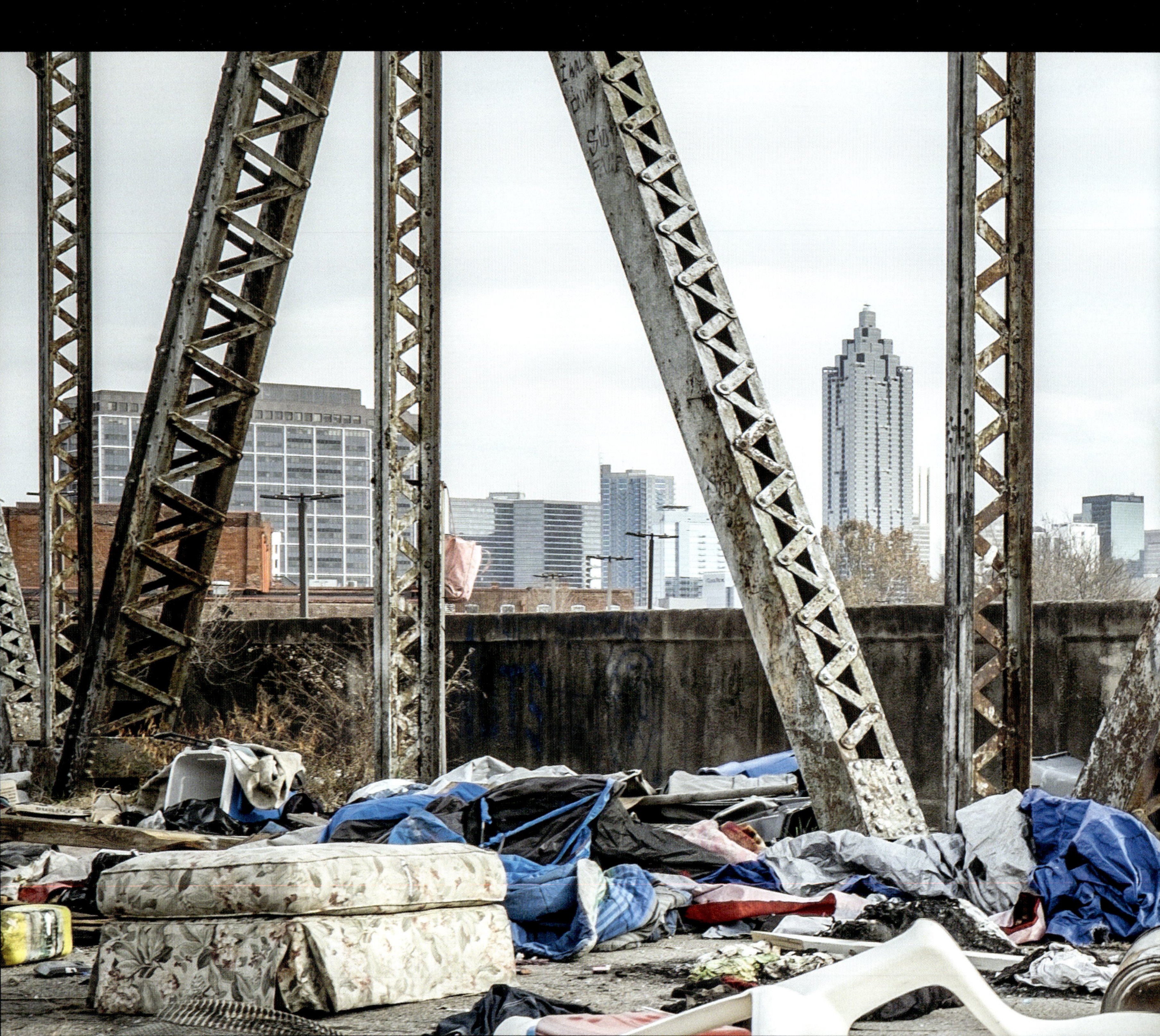

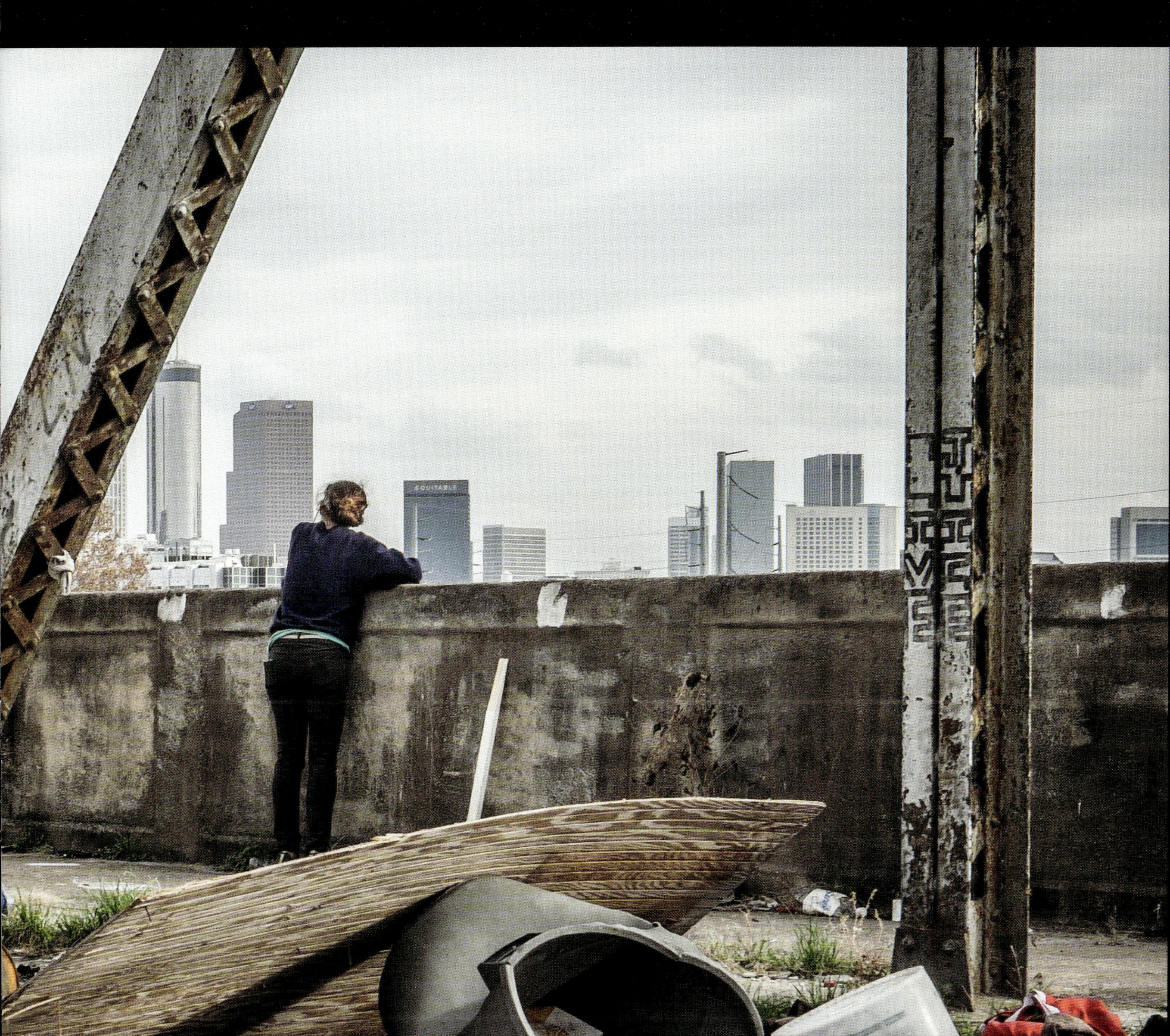
EQUITABLE

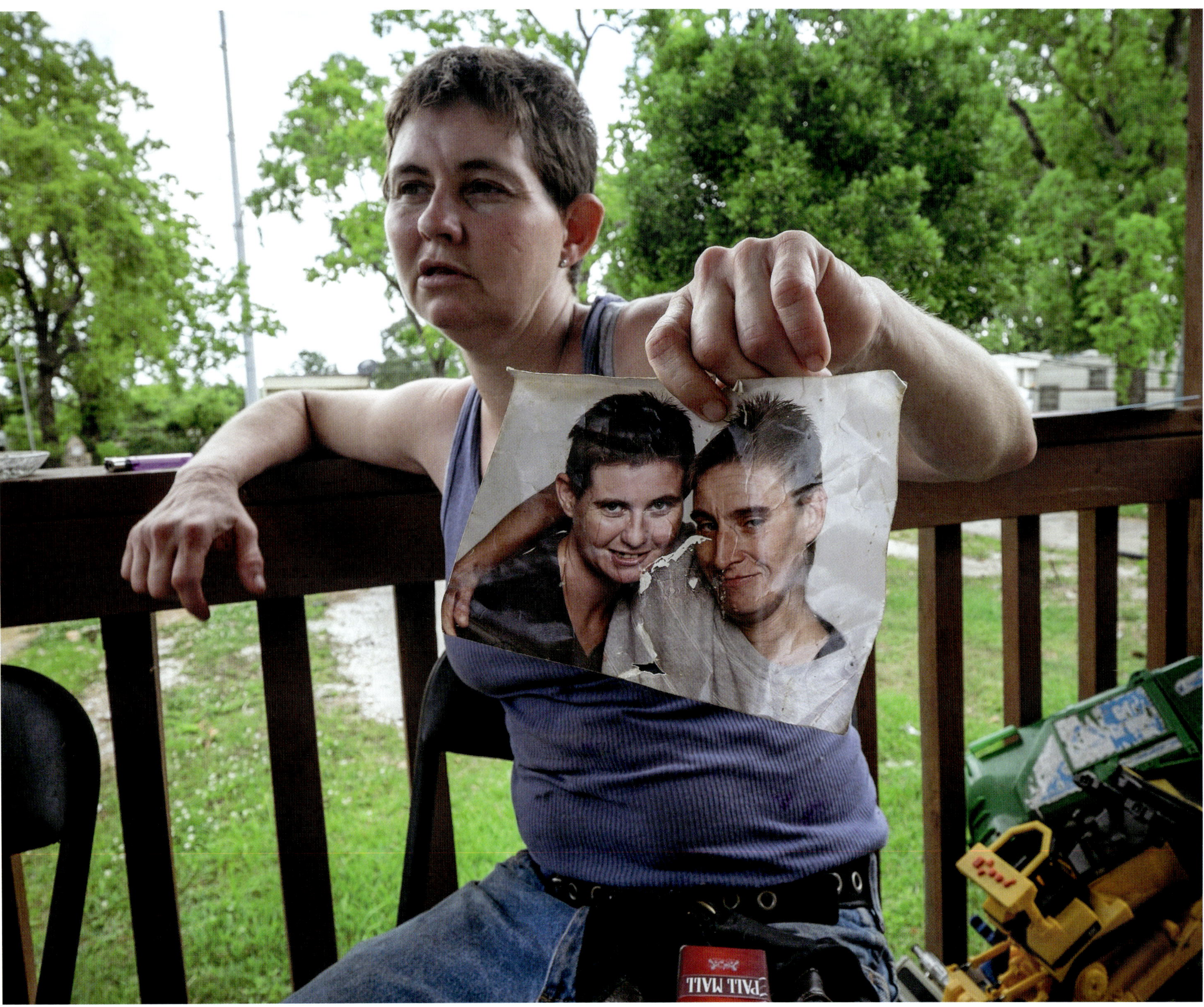
PALL MALL

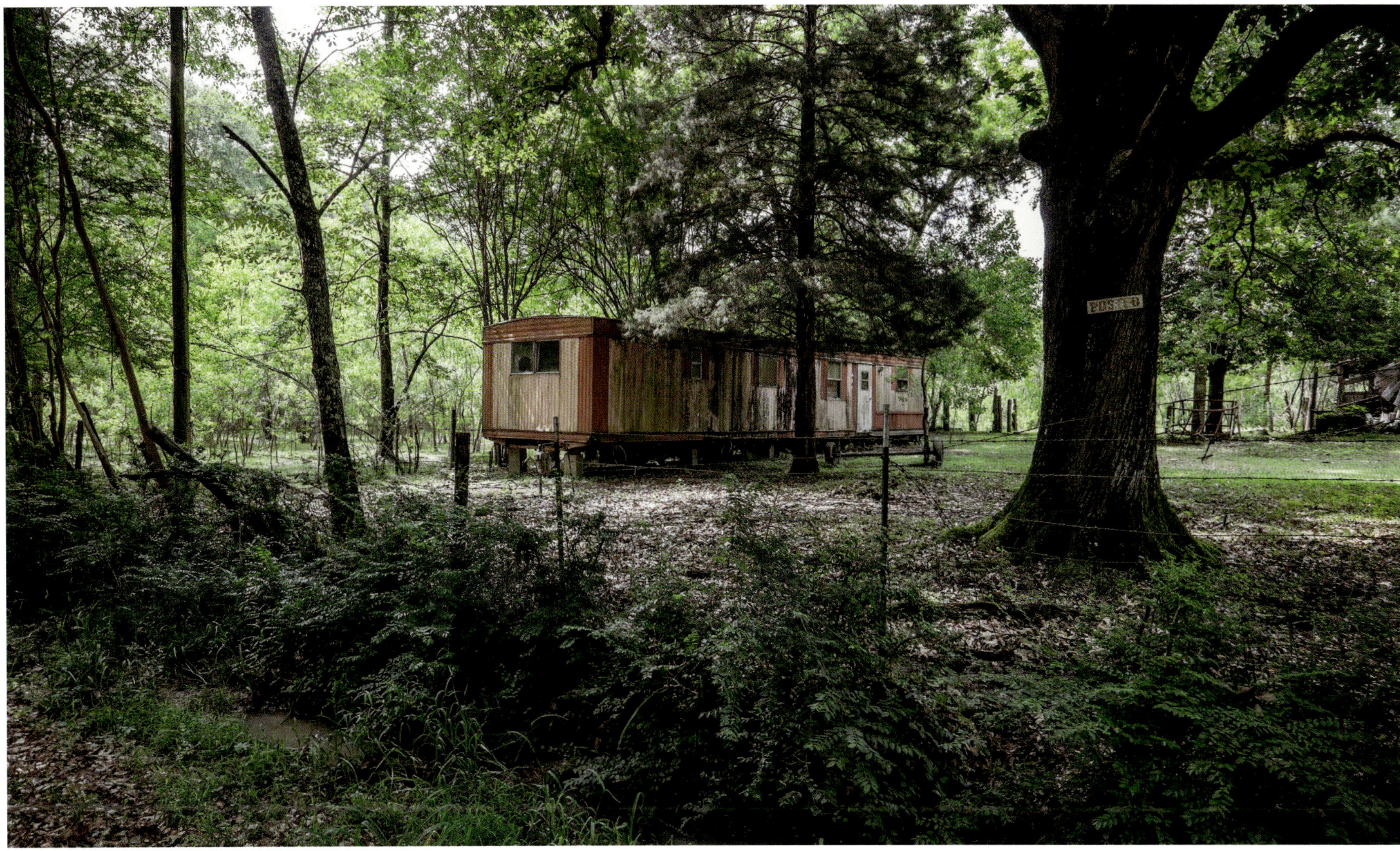

NEW ORLEANS, LA – 2015-05-10

Read part 1 of Tina's story on p. 78.

Tina: I lost my best friend and partner three years ago. I miss her, and so do the kids. She passed away thirteen days before our anniversary. It was tragic. Everyone called us Ike and Mike. Said we looked alike. We was crazy together. We loved each other. There's no doubt about it—she was my soul mate.

BW: I'm sorry. How did she die?

Tina: Her ex old man pushed her out of the truck. It was a real high truck, and her head hit the concrete. He laid her on the sofa to die. Didn't even take her to the hospital. When she finally did get to the hospital, they took an X-ray of her brain and said she shouldn't even be alive. Said she was living on unconditional love.

She told me, she says, "I don't never regret being with you. Even though we put each other through a lot of bad times, we had so many great times too." And she was right. We had started to work through things and get right. And just like that, she was gone.

It's not easy to find your soul mate, but I did and I lost her.

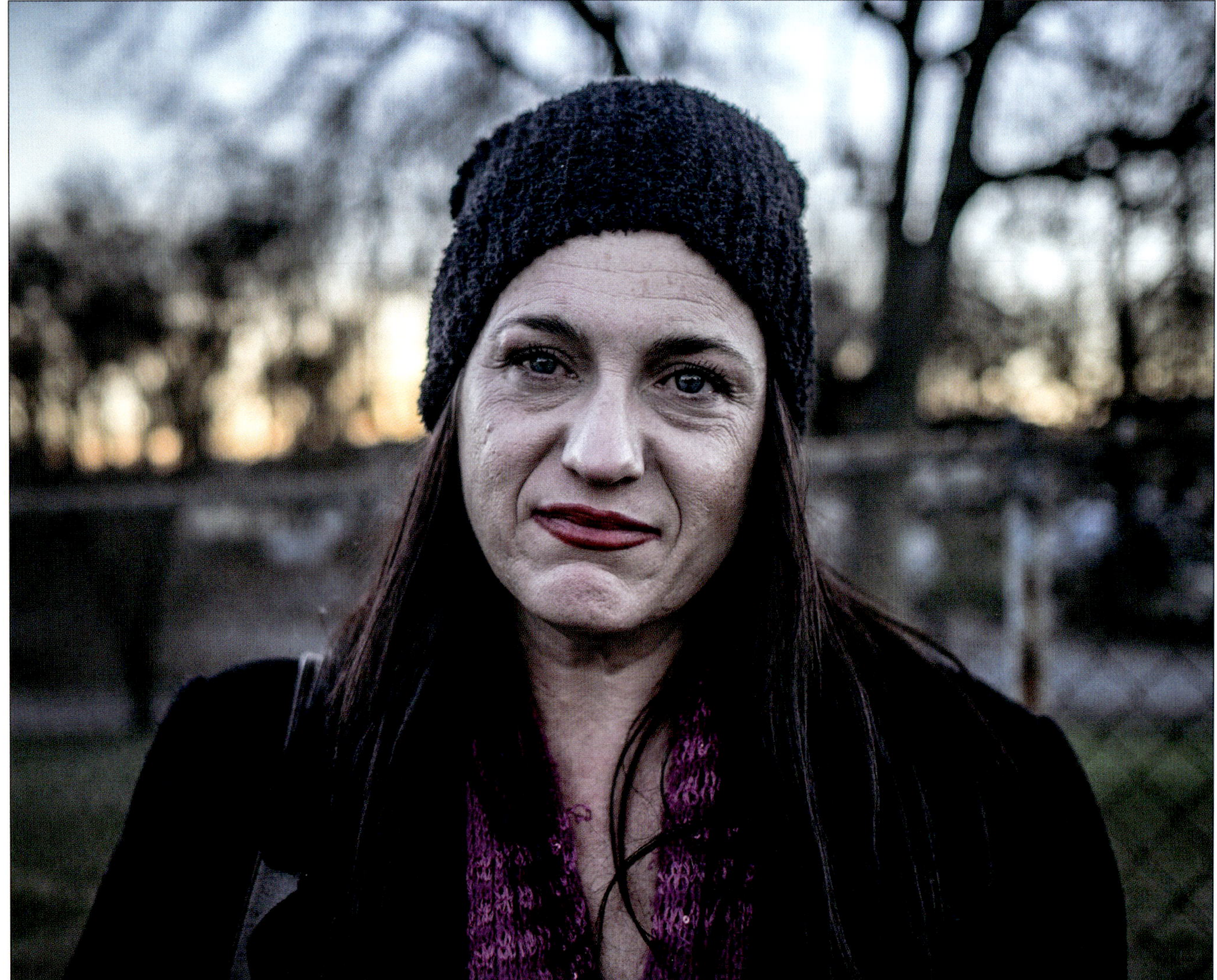

NASHVILLE, TN – 2015-01-10

Michelle: I was married for twenty years to my second husband. It was an abusive relationship that I stayed in. I found him hanging in my garage two years ago. It devastated me. I had a house in Hendersonville, but I lost it all because insurance didn't pay. So I've just been trying to survive. Every time I trust someone, they just want something from me, and I end up having nowhere to go.

BW: What led up to his suicide?

Michelle: The economy messed us up. Our house was an adjustable rate, and our mortgage almost doubled. At the same time, we had a small business, and we were losing business. He dealt with depression for a couple of years. He wouldn't ask for help. His pride got in the way. My husband was a carpentry contractor. He did beautiful work, but it wasn't necessary, so people held their money. So we lost a lot.

He was from an abusive background, and I think that, when it happened, he just wasn't equipped to deal with it.

BW: You said he was abusive? Physically?

Michelle: Yeah. I didn't tell anyone. That was the biggest secret. I didn't want to ruin his reputation. I was a substitute teacher, and we ran a business, and people knew us. I didn't want to be the one to ruin it. I didn't want to break the family up. But in doing that, I became such a caretaker. So when he checked out on me the way he did, it just devastated me because of all that I had I put into him for so long. It left me feeling lost.

When you're in a home like that, and there is so much verbal abuse to everyone, it affects you. I suppressed so much that I quit hurting just to survive. You keep telling yourself everything is fine until you believe it. When he died, there was this big release, but it wasn't all good. Everything came back at me quite a bit. So I'm dealing with all that. I'm kind of alone right now.

My biggest regret [tears] is that I wasn't strong enough to change things before my kids grew up, you know?

I'm forty-five, and I'll be forty-six next week. I've lost so much.

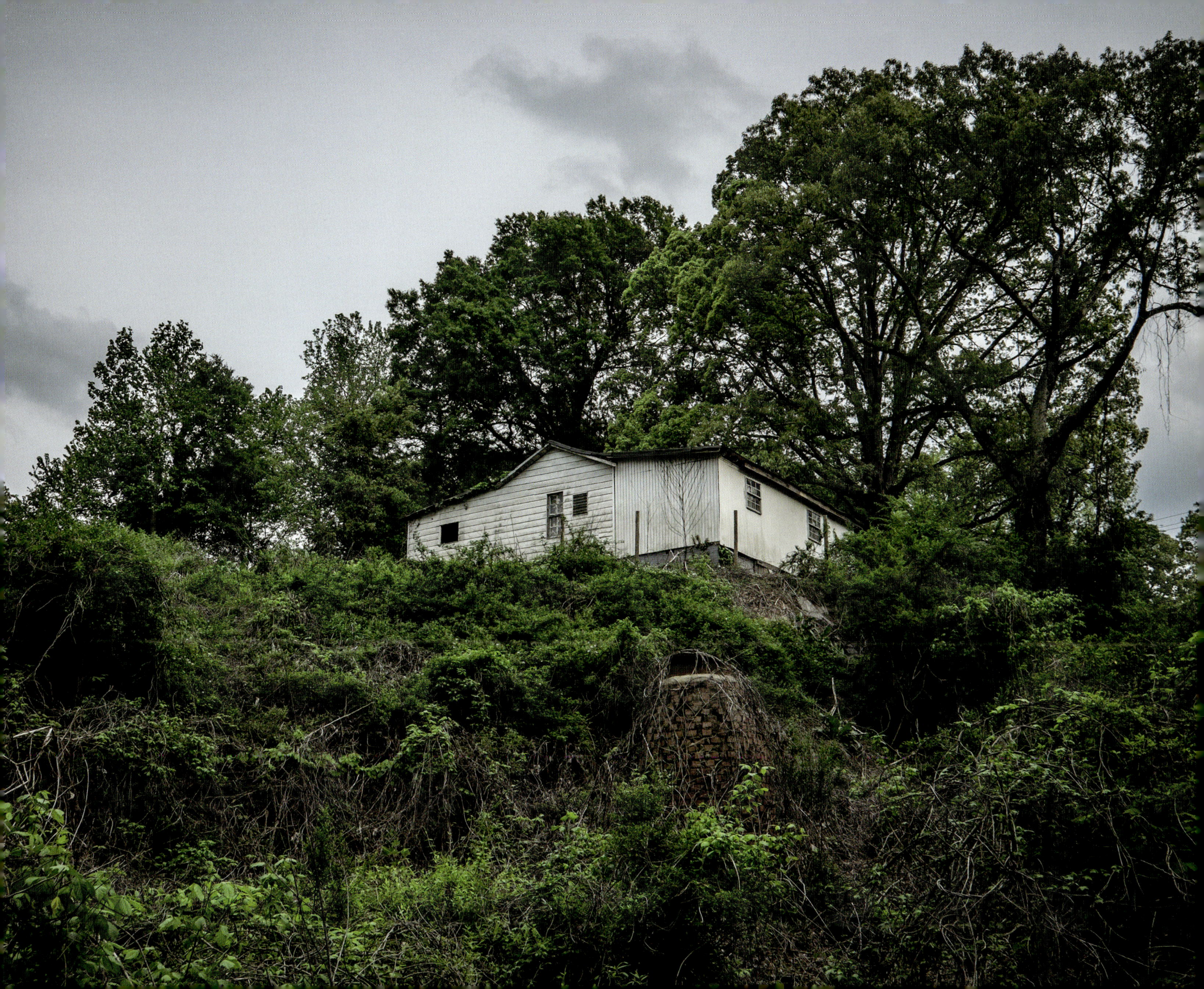

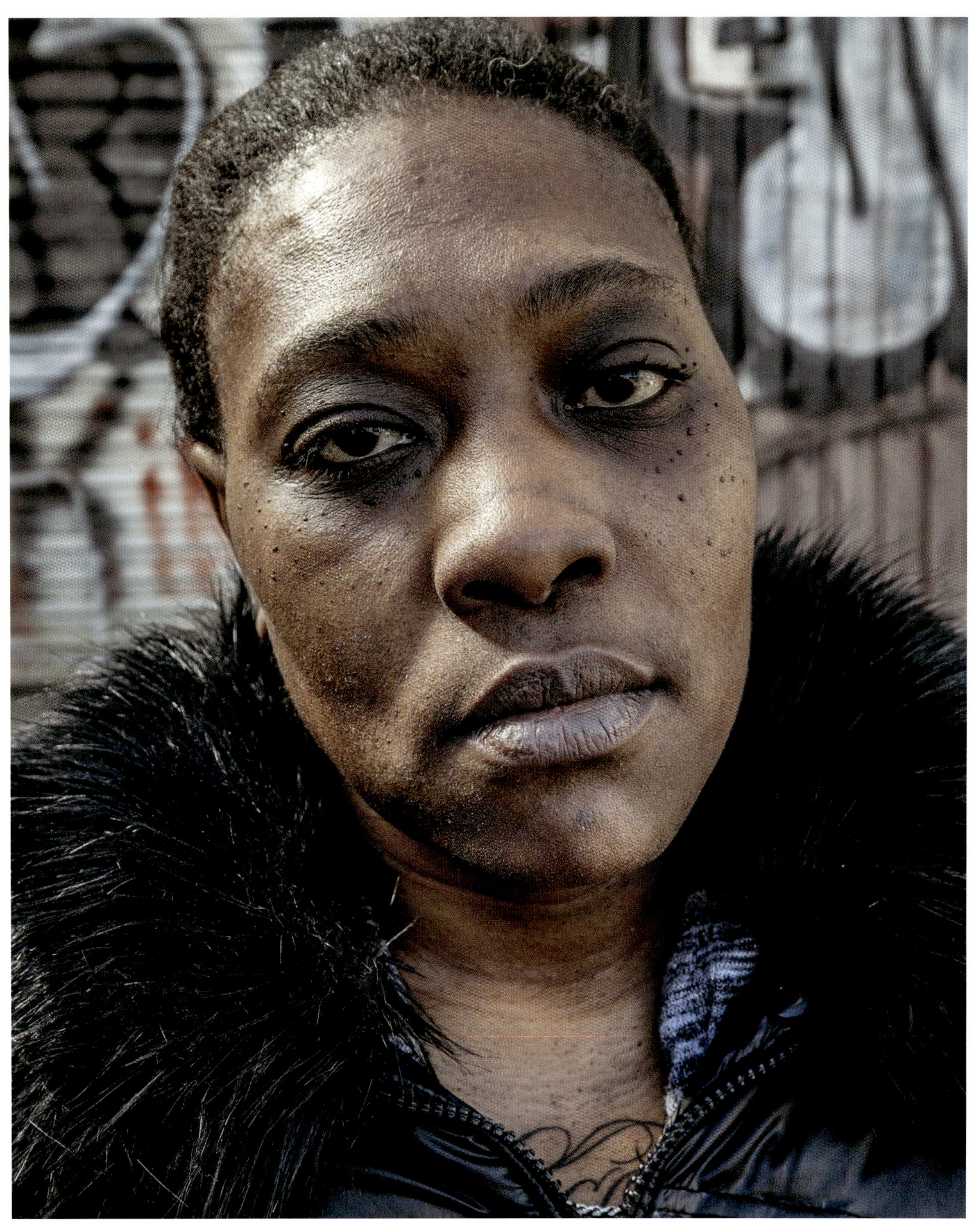

ATLANTA, GA – 2015-02-06

Shawn: About two years ago, I was in a bad, abusive relationship. Him and his friend had kidnapped me and held me hostage at a hotel on Cleveland Avenue for three weeks.

BW: Did they hurt you?

Shawn: They didn't rape me or do nothing like that. He jumped on me and broke my nose. Both my eyes were black, and my face was swollen real big. They made me play Russian roulette. Thanks to the good Lord that the gun didn't ever go off.

BW: How'd you get away?

Shawn: Well, the boy was on heroin. He had fell asleep, and that's how I got away. I called the police, and I took warrants out on both of them. They got twenty years and are still in prison right to this day.

BW: I bet that was scary as shit.

Shawn: Yeah, it was very scary. He kept telling me, if he can't have me, can't nobody have me. That's why I tell these young girls, when a nigga says he gonna do something, he's gonna do it. I tell them be careful who you talk to and don't be with no nigga because of his money. There's something behind that money. You just gotta be careful out in these streets because it's very dangerous.

ATLANTA, GA – 2015-04-14

Read part 1 of Meshell's story on p. 42.

Meshell: I've been working with a psychiatrist. I can't remember anything before I was thirteen. We just can't get it to come up. We're thinking something traumatic happened and my brain blocked it. She said, "What if you find out what it is, and you don't want to remember it?" So I figured I would leave well enough alone.

BW: Did they diagnose you with something?

Meshell: Yeah, manic depression and PTSD—post-traumatic stress disorder.

BW: Do they know what the PTSD is from?

Meshell: Yeah. I got attacked in 2006. I was at the Underground in Atlanta and went through the garage to get out the other side. Three guys jumped me in the garage. They took me to a house for three days. They did everything you could ever even imagine to a woman, everywhere.

I don't remember getting out, but the neighbor told the detective she called because I was in the yard crying and saying I had just crawled out the bathroom window. I don't remember it. They said my body was in such shock from all the pain and trauma that it had basically just shut down.

BW: How do you think it impacts you now?

Meshell: I have a lot of nightmares from it. And then I seen a guy the other day that looked a lot like the guy who picked me up. I literally flipped because it was like I had a flashback right there.

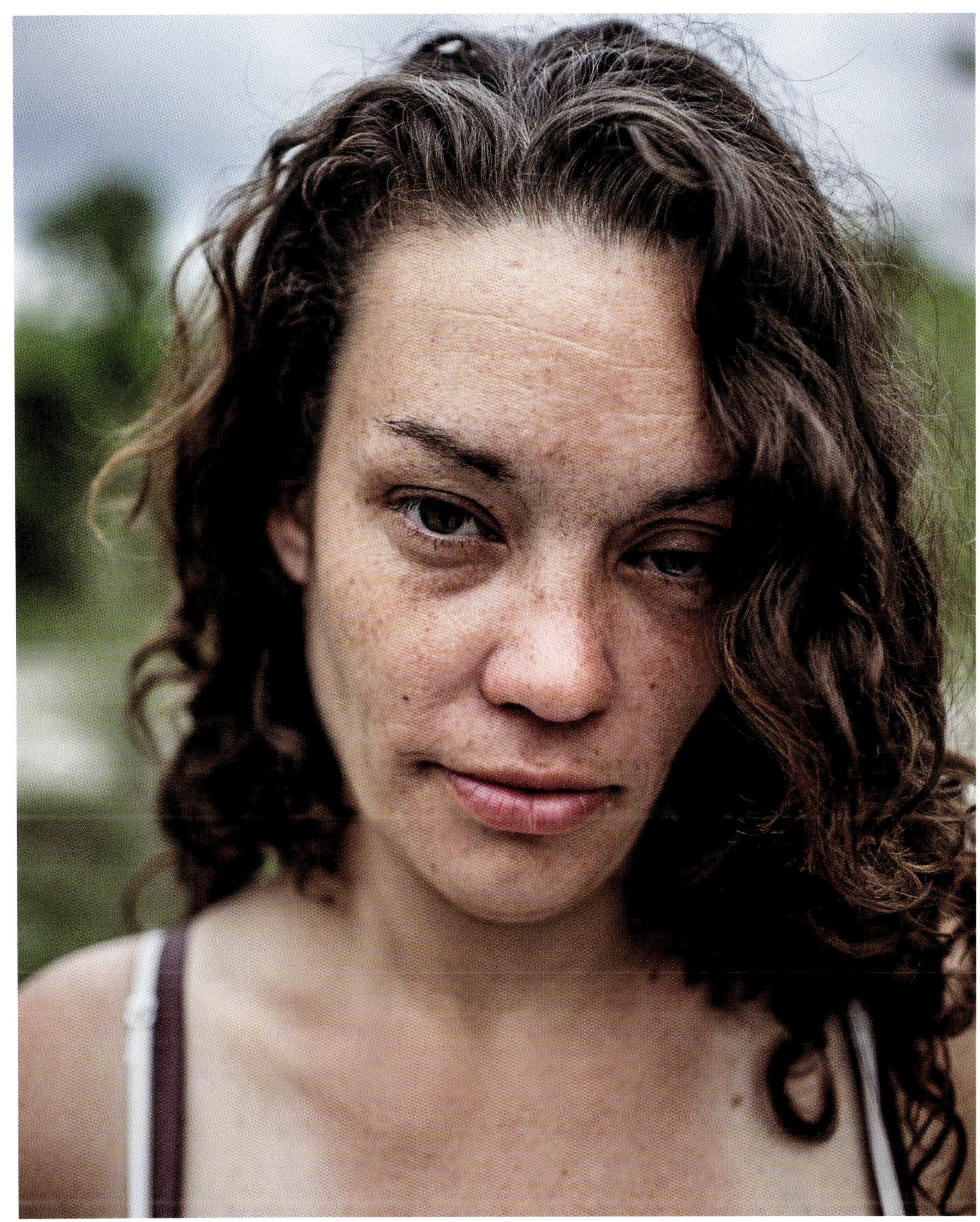

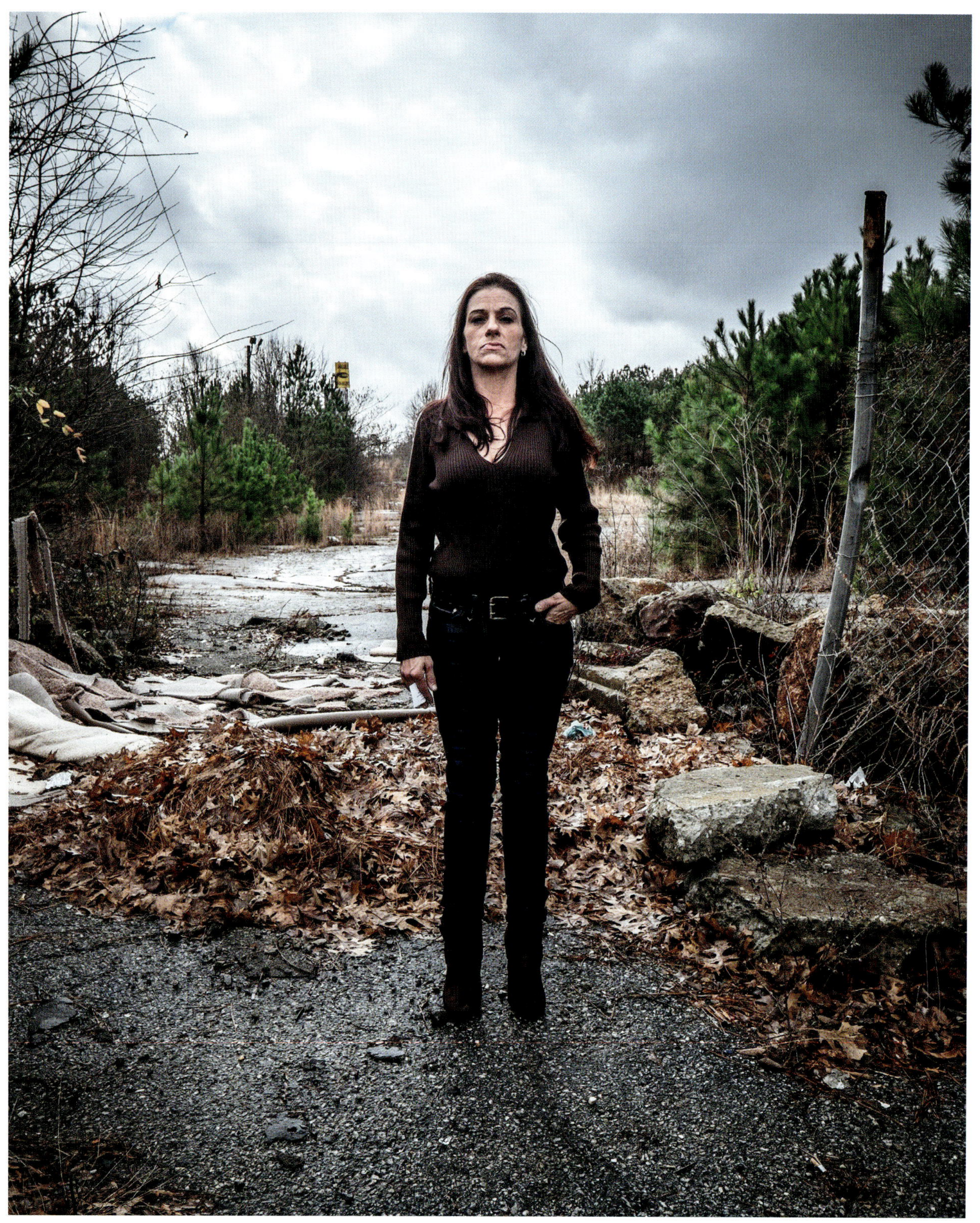

ATLANTA, GA – 2014-12-24

Nicki: I was at a drug house. I had been getting high. It started raining. A guy that had been there many times asked me for a ride home. He only lived a street over, so I said okay. I went to take a right to take him home, and he pulled out a knife and grabbed me by the hair. He drove me to Glenwood Road and took me down a dead-end street.

When we parked, he grabbed me by my throat. I thought it was the last breath I was gonna take. I thought, "This is it." He was trying to get into my pants. I don't think I'd ever been that scared.

I guess out of fear came strength, 'cause somehow I got away from him. I ran to a house, and a man came to the door. I was screaming all the way to his house. He called the police, and they brought out the crime lab and investigators and took pictures. My neck was red for days from where he'd choked me.

BW: Did they ever catch the guy?

Nicki: No, they didn't. That's what made me get a gun, really. I felt like, if anyone tried to hurt me again in that way, I promise you I'd have been able to pull it out and kill them. At that point in my life, I became very hard.

I already had a felony on my record. I got caught about a year later in Clayton County with the gun. They gave me five years to the door for being a felon and carrying a concealed weapon.

I'd been in jail for little stuff before, like fifteen days for prostitution. But five years in prison—that really threw me.

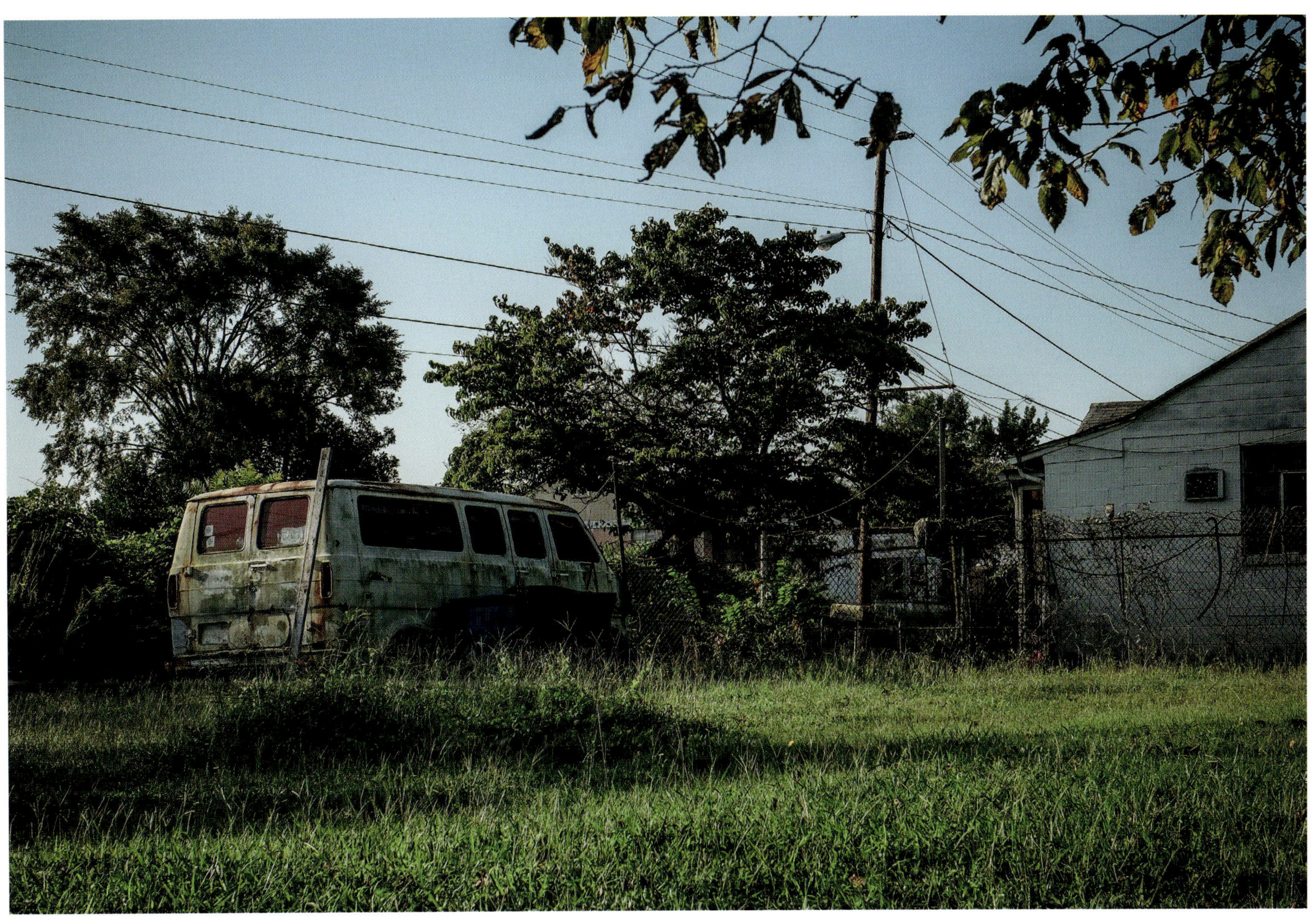

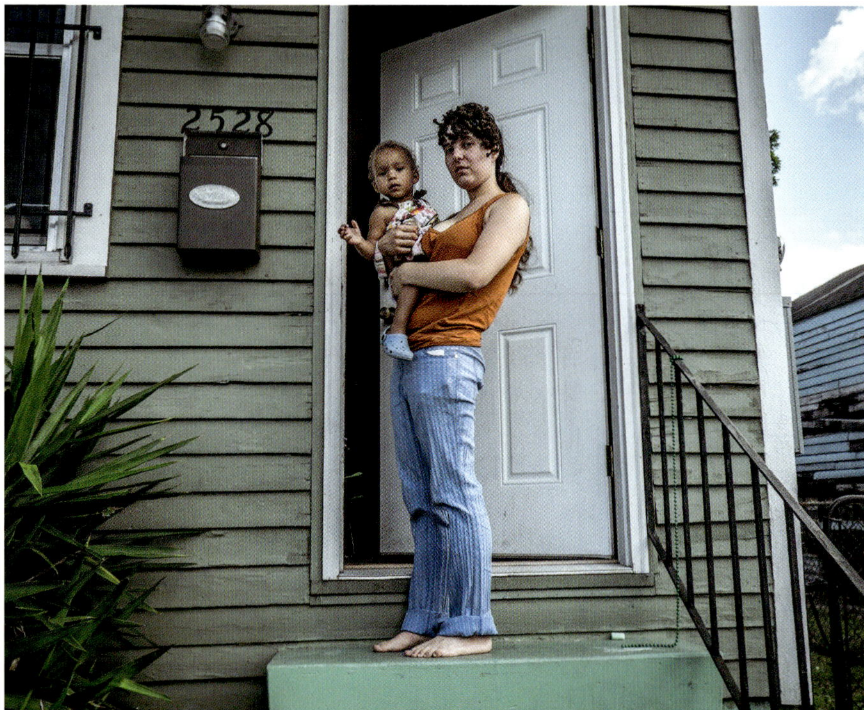

NEW ORLEANS, LA – 2015-05-08

Frenchie Moe: Music is my life. It's all I ever wanted to do. I'm from France, in the countryside. People there didn't get the music I was playing. Like I told my band yesterday, the reason why I wanted to be here in the States and here in New Orleans was because I wanted to be in a place where people had an understanding of soulful music. Soulful music is my life. I couldn't be in a place where people don't understand blues and jazz. So the little town I'm from, people can't relate to the music like they relate to it here.

BW: Sure, but why do you think you related to the music, seeing you came from that same place they did?

Frenchie Moe: Yeah, it's very weird. Actually my dad loved music, and he would go see live music. Basically my dad never really worked much. He hung out in bars and would take me with him.

BW: Was your dad a musician at all?

Frenchie Moe: Not at all. He just liked to hang out and drink. [Laughs.] In the area we were from, there weren't any bars with music, so we would drive to the next town, and every now and then there would be a band. One day we were in this bar and there was this English musician named Victor Brox. My dad became friends with him. One thing led to another, and he ended up mentoring me when I was just a little girl, so I was really blessed.

It's the story of my life, being mentored by so many people that are really great artists. A few years ago, I hooked up with her dad [referring to her baby] and fell in love with him. I had been a fan of his for several years. He was my hero. I just wanted to play like him. He was a god.

BW: What happened with your relationship?

Frenchie Moe: I think we're still in love, but he doesn't want to make a commitment. I can't say I'm totally through with him because I'm still in love with him. I think he still loves me too. The fact that he's married doesn't help. [Laughs.] No . . . he's separated from his wife because we had the baby. The thing is, she's pretty sick, so he's around to help her out.

You know, musicians here who are well known, even if they aren't known nationally, are like gods in New Orleans. They eat and drink for free. So I think he's worried about his reputation too. If he were to live with us while his wife is sick and something were to happen to her . . .

BW: Do you understand?

Frenchie Moe: No, not really. It's been heartbreaking. There's this side of him that's an artist and a free spirit and this other side that worries about his reputation. What I've realized being around these famous people is that there are really two sides to that coin. It's kind of a curse in a way. To the point of not wanting to be famous myself. I mean, I want people to hear my music. But you have so many people watching you all the time.

BW: You came into the relationship being his fan. Now, obviously you have a different relationship, but how has it changed? Do you still look up to him?

Frenchie Moe: I look up to him musically, and I always will. When I met him, I feel like he changed my life philosophically 'cause he's a very spiritual person. We used to talk about things like how every day is a new beginning and how material things aren't important. So that is what he was preaching, but when I got to know him further . . . I'm not saying he doesn't believe in all that stuff, but there's a whole other side to him that's a player and likes to gamble and party.

I forgot to tell you that he's seventy-one years old and I'm twenty-nine.

BW: Wow . . . that's a big difference. Have you always been attracted to older men?

Frenchie Moe: Yeah, I have. But not that old. I never thought I'd be involved with someone that old. But I can't compare him to other people who are that age. He's not like that. His personality is very dynamic. He doesn't talk about the past all the time. He's very much about the present, and that's what I fell in love with. It's all about now, and I just love that. His mind is wide open. I would say he is the grooviest person I've ever met.

INDEPENDENCE, LOUISIANA – 2015-05-12

Ronnie: See, I just have a thing for bad boys.

BW: Why are you attracted to bad boys?

Ronnie: I guess because of they badness. It's a challenge to me.

BW: What was it like growing up in a small town like this, being gay?

Ronnie: My mom loved'ed me, and that's all that mattered. It was irrelevant [to the rest of my family]. Society didn't clothe me or house me or feed me. As long as my mom accepted me, who cared what the world thought?

BW: Was it hard at school? Were you out of the closet?

Ronnie: I was always me. The boys always liked'ed me. [Laughing with BW.] I never had no problems with the boys. It was always the girls I had problems with. They had envy of me 'cause all the boys liked'ed me, and I didn't give a hoot. I had this thing about me, and that was it. They didn't like me because their boyfriends did.

BW: [Laughing hard.] So you got a lot of action in school?

Ronnie: In high school, college, nursing school. I've never, ever, ever had a problem in that department. Even right now . . . It was never who chose me; it was who I chose to be with.

BW: So tell me about one of your relationships.

Ronnie: Me and my lover, we lived'ed together, but he was a bad boy. He was a thug. He wanted me and everybody else too. He ended up getting killed because he was running around.

I was working, and he wasn't. That wasn't a problem for me, but when you using my car all day, I expect you to be sitting there when I get off work at three. He started being late more and more.

This one day I got in my car. I would always leave my driver's license in the console, and I kept noticing he would move it to the visor, where it couldn't be seen. So I get in my car this one day, and the first thing I see in the ashtray is purple lipstick. So I said, "Who been in my car with purple lipstick? I don't wear purple lipstick or any lipstick, period."

So the day afterwards, I pretend to go to work. I didn't have to work, but he didn't know that. So right after he dropped me off, there was my mom to pick me up. I told her I wanted to borrow her car for a while. So I go where he's supposed to be, and he's riding somebody around in my damn car. I said, "Oh hell no."

So I left him. But like I say, he was a bad boy. He went to prison. He would write me, and I'd write him back when I felt like it. But you know how they got the pen pals with the girlfriends and stuff? Well, he ended up marrying this schoolteacher.

I didn't even know he'd gotten out. I was in the grocery store one day, and I hear somebody calling my name. I turned around to look, and there was

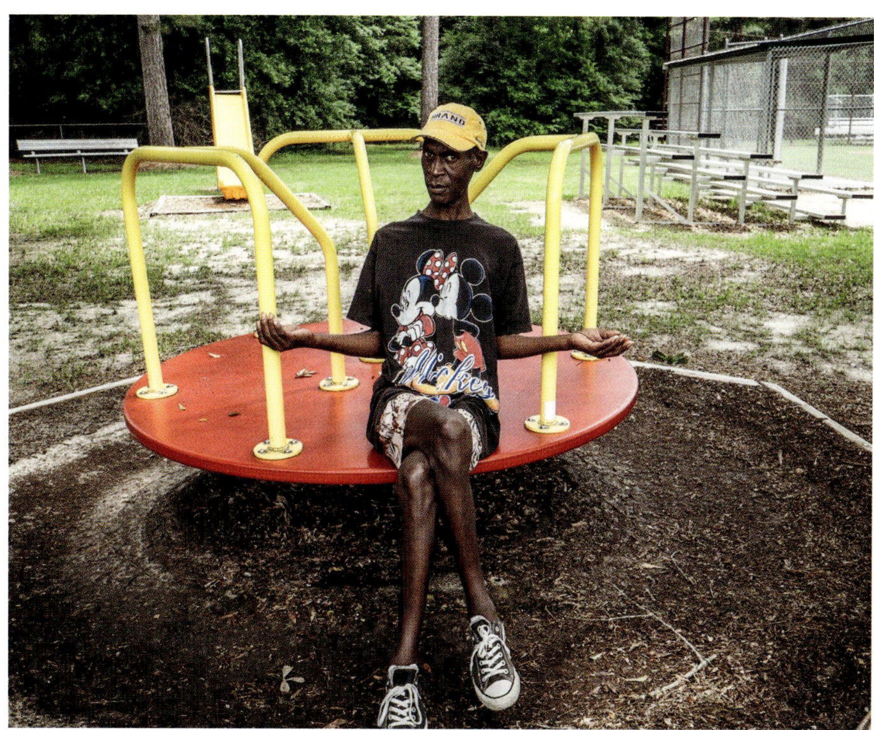

him. So we talked, and he said he wanted to see me for old time sake. You know what I'm saying? We hadn't seen each other for a long time and just wanted to see if it was still what it used to be.

Now, I didn't know he'd gotten married. We were supposed to go out that Friday. On Thursday, my sister calls me and says, "Ronnie, guess who got killed last night?" She said, "Dado got killed." He had died in a car crash. Broke his neck. I pick up a copy of the *Daily Star* [Hammond, Louisiana, newspaper]. It shows that he married to this white woman, and he was driving around with this black woman when he died.

BW: I'm sorry. Do you think you'll ever forgive him?

Ronnie: Hell no. 'Cause when I went to the goddamn funeral home, I spit in his face, in his casket! I did that. Honestly and truly.

BW: Did it make you feel better?

Ronnie: I don't know . . . It didn't make me feel better, but I told him, "You lied to me. You just no good, even in your grave." And I left.

But I do miss him in some ways. He was everything I wanted, but he was a thug. He was a bad boy!

BW: Did anything positive come out of it?

Ronnie: He was dead, and I know where he at. That was a positive thing that came out of it.

BW: [Laughing.] No. I mean, like, did you learn anything from it?

Ronnie: Yeah . . . Not to trust bad boys!

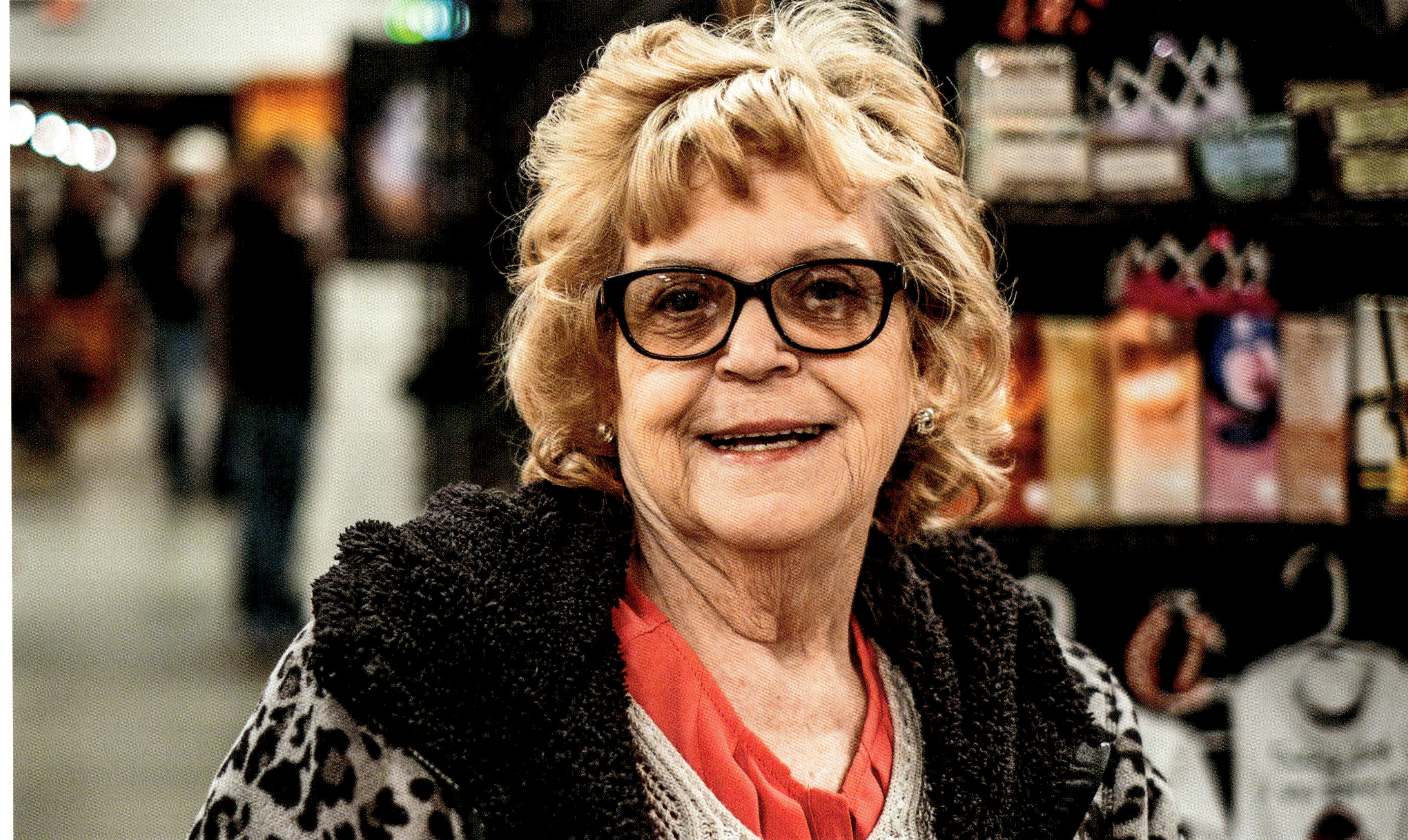

MCDONOUGH, GA – 2014-11-15

Beverly: I got saved because I couldn't find an answer to my son's drug habit. I was thirty-five years old.

BW: How old was your son when he was having drug problems?

Beverly: He was about fourteen or fifteen then.

BW: Did he get straightened out?

Beverly: He did get straightened out and went in the military, but he ended up getting back on drugs and committing suicide at thirty-five. But that ended up being good too.

BW: How was your son's death good?

Beverly: Oh, because he was saved, so he went to heaven. His journey is over. I just celebrate his home-going, not my poor self-pity here.

I just knew I wasn't gonna get stuck. I've seen too many people who, when things happen to them in life, get stuck, and they can't go on. Well, that's selfish to me. Always thinking about self, self, self. This whole life is about bringing people to the Lord.

BW: Why do you think God requires you to bring people to him?

Beverly: 'Cause I think that's why Jesus came—for salvation and a lot of other things.

BW: What was your son's name?

Beverly: Robbie. In fact, today was his birthday. He would have been fifty-five.

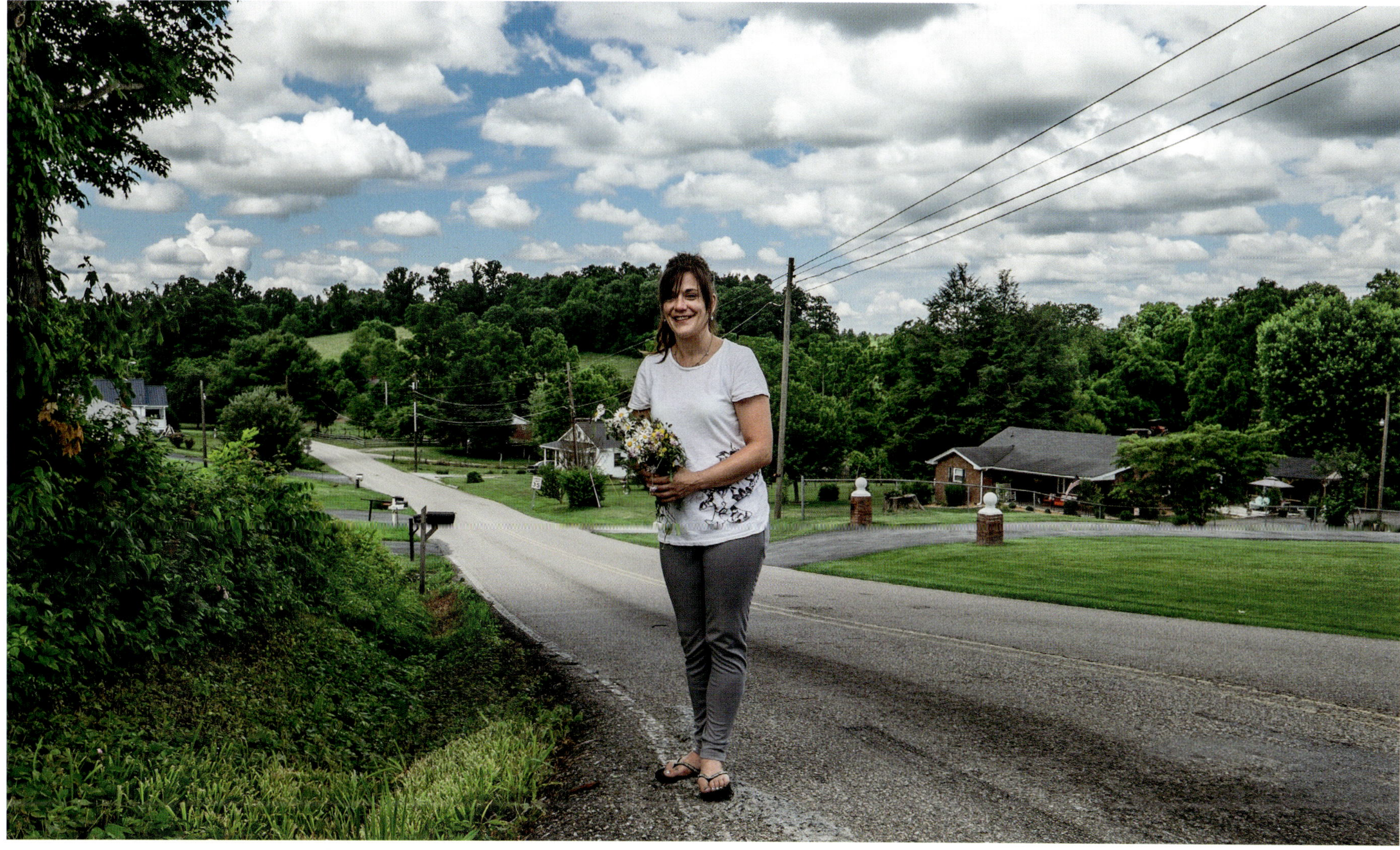

KINGSPORT, TN – 2015-06-04

Melissa: I grew up on this road. Today is the anniversary of my mother's death. I only have five memories of her, and one of them is walking up and down this road, picking flowers with her. So this is what I do instead of going to a graveyard and crying. I try to make it a happy thing.

BW: How did she die?

Melissa: She died of breast cancer right before I turned six.

BW: What are your other memories of her?

Melissa: Well, one time I remember I had made her a bowl of chicken noodle soup and a glass of Pepsi with ice cubes and took it to her. It was the weekend she died. She was like, "Don't you want to stay here and make Mommy another glass of Pepsi?" But I had this awesome aunt Becky who had lots and lots of money. They had horses for me down there. Know what I'm saying? Everything my heart desired. So I left, and that was the last time I saw her.

BW: Did you feel guilty about that?

Melissa: I did. For a long time, I did.

Angela: As a girl who lost her mother at a young age, and now a mother myself, I cannot imagine a more honest and beautiful way to honor and remember her on the anniversary.

I was sitting on a stone, and I was like, "God, I never asked anything of you, but what am I supposed to do?" In my head, I heard this voice say, "Walk up the hill." So I walked up the hill, and this big guy came across the street. And he said, "Let me help you 'cause that looks heavy." I said, "It is, but this is my burden." He says, "Where are you going?" I said, "I have no idea. I'm not from here."

—Deborah (pp. 165-166)

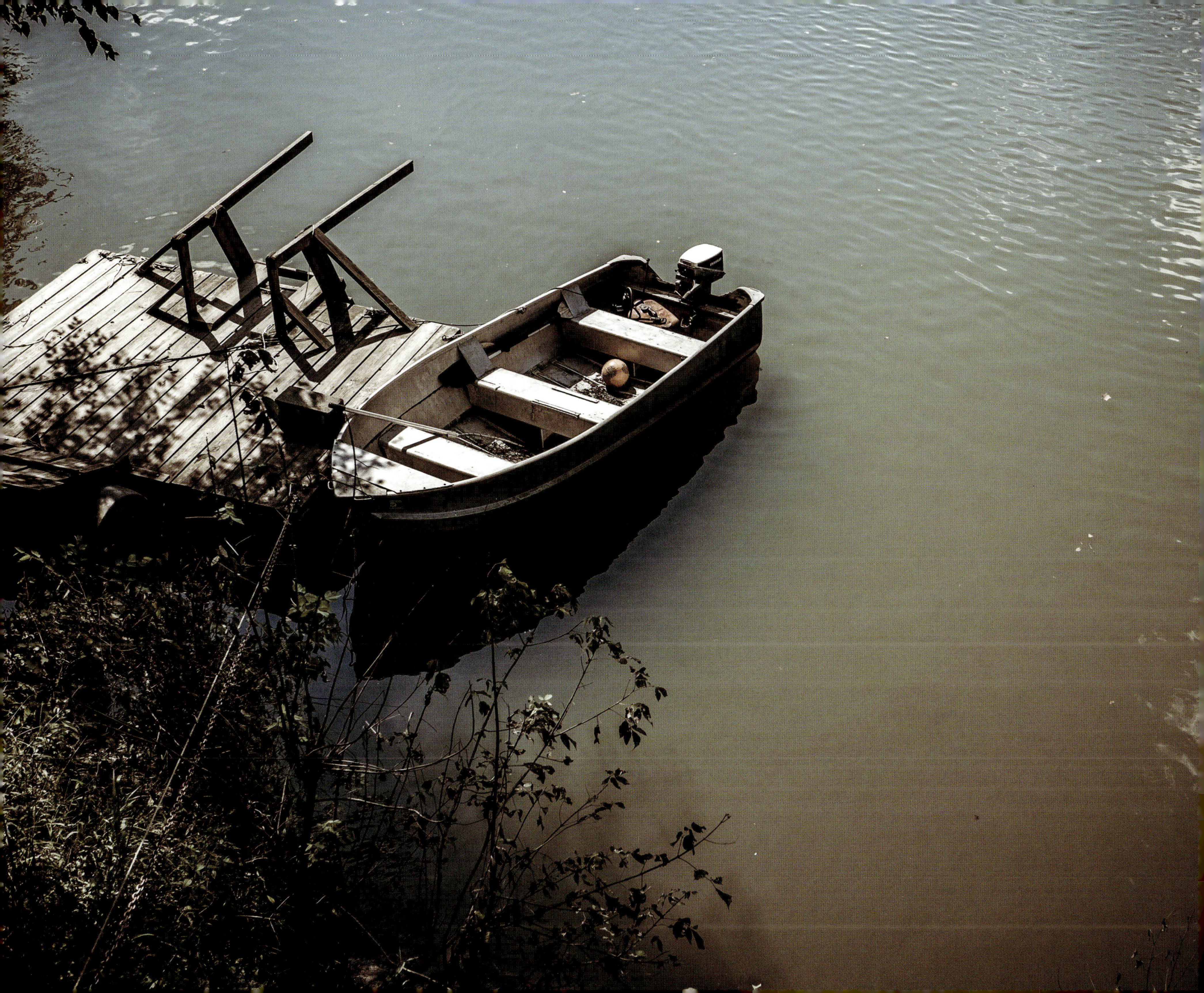

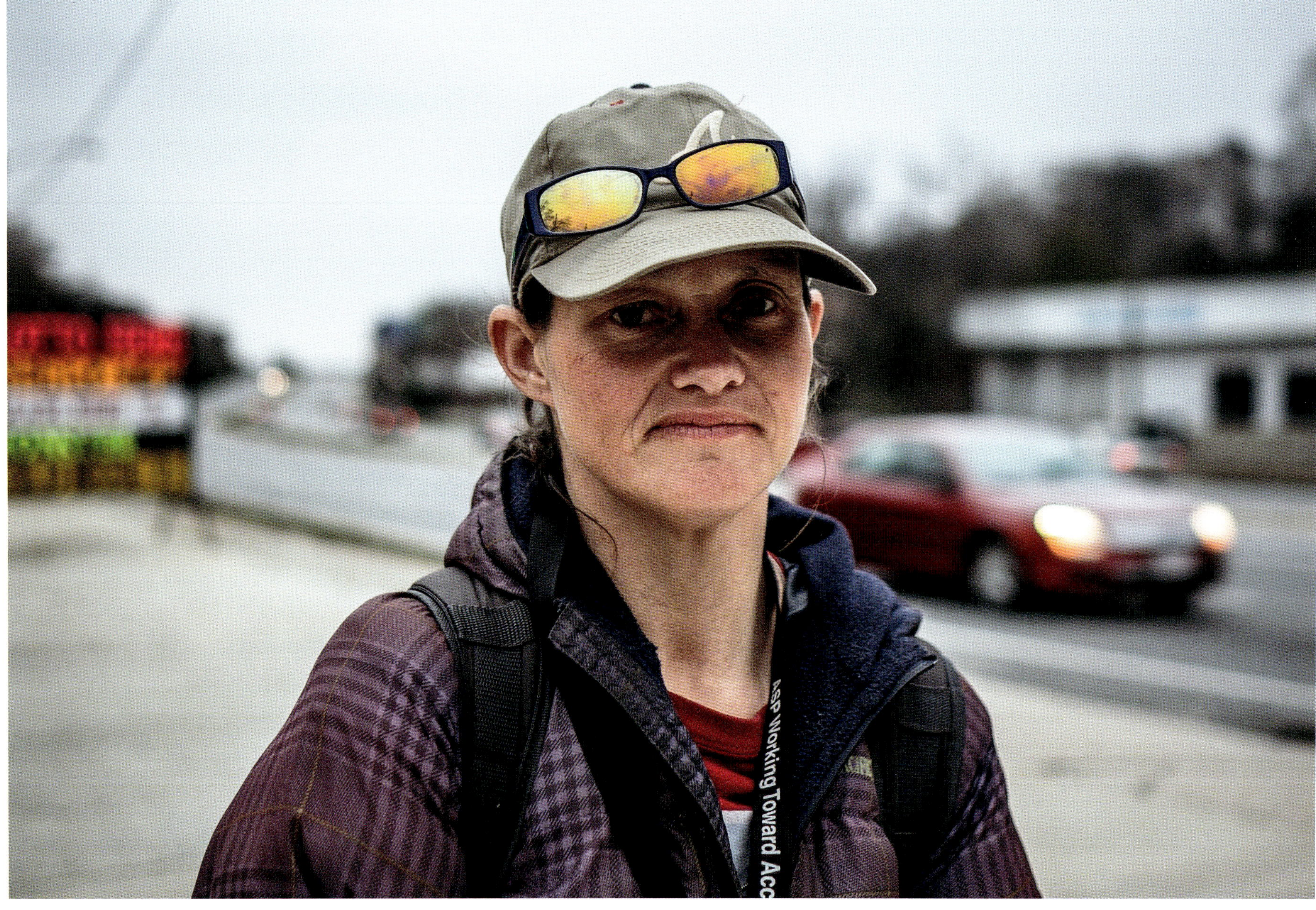

COLUMBUS, GA – 2015-03-01

I met April walking down the road in Columbus, Georgia. She came to Columbus to get away from her problems back home in Orlando, Florida, and make a fresh start.

April: I was raped a couple times when I was younger. The first time when I was seven, and the second when I was sixteen by my grandma's boyfriend. Life is hard. Even now at thirty-five years old, it's hard to get over. I'm not a bad person. I just have a lot of anger inside of me.

BW: Do you think you'll ever forgive the men who raped you?

April: To be honest with you, I don't know . . . I really don't know. The hardest thing is when your own mother doesn't believe you. That's the hardest part right there.

[Tears.] Either way, it's not gonna answer why they did it. I just don't understand why.

ATLANTA, GA – 2014-12-16

Debbie: My mom's best friend molested me when I was eight years old. It really affects my adult life.

BW: Did it happen more than once?

Debbie: Yeah. My mom used to let her babysit us.

BW: Did you tell your mom about it?

Debbie: My mom knew about it because she took me to the doctor. She got me checked out. She [the mother's friend] was using objects, so my mom knew 'cause I got injured. It was irritable, and I complained about it.

BW: What did your mom do when she found out?

Debbie: Well **. . .** her friend who did it lived next door to us, and I never saw her again. I think my mom did away with her. My mom went to jail, and I went to stay with my grandma.

I still have nightmares about it. It affected my sex life in my marriage. The way he had sex with me would remind me of the way she did it. It tore my marriage apart. I tried to get over the hump and not think about the abuse as a child, but things started going downhill.

BW: If you could have one wish, what would it be?

Debbie: To have my family back.

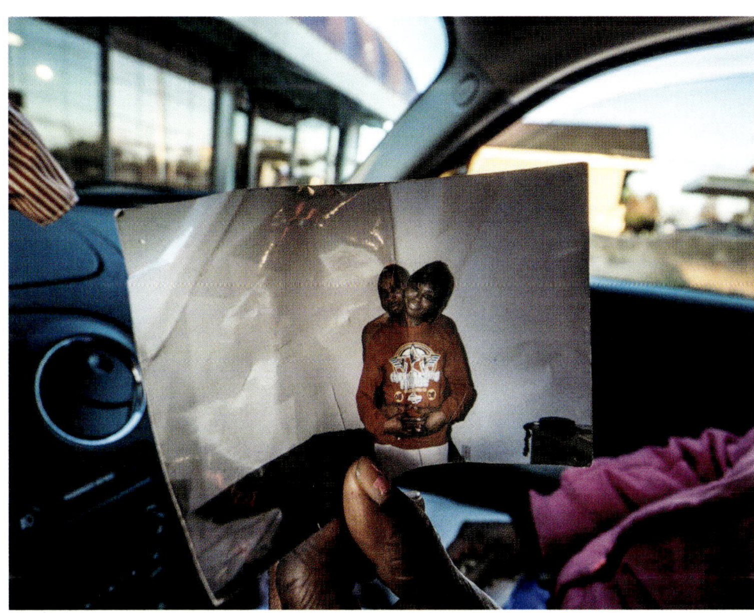

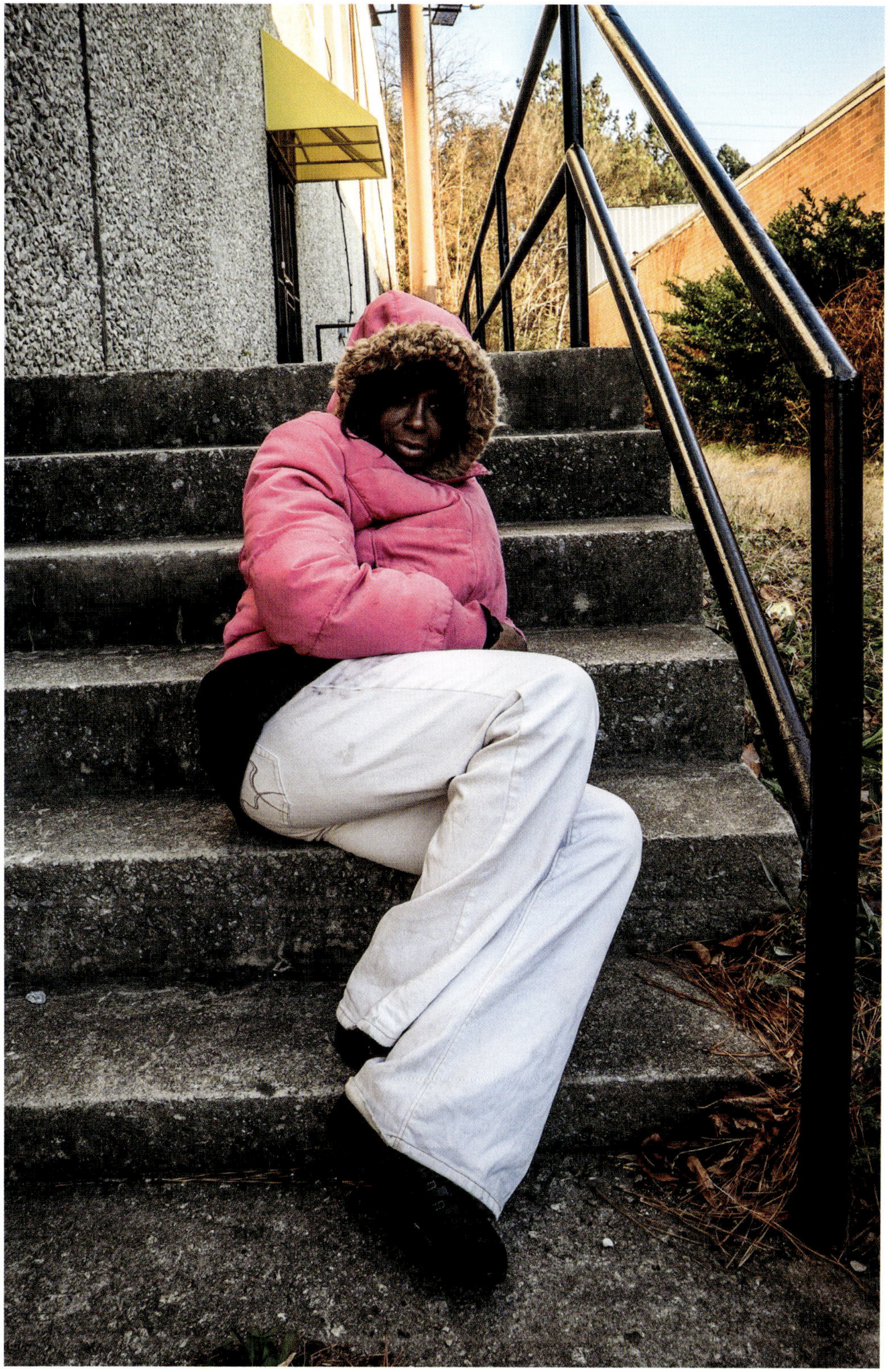

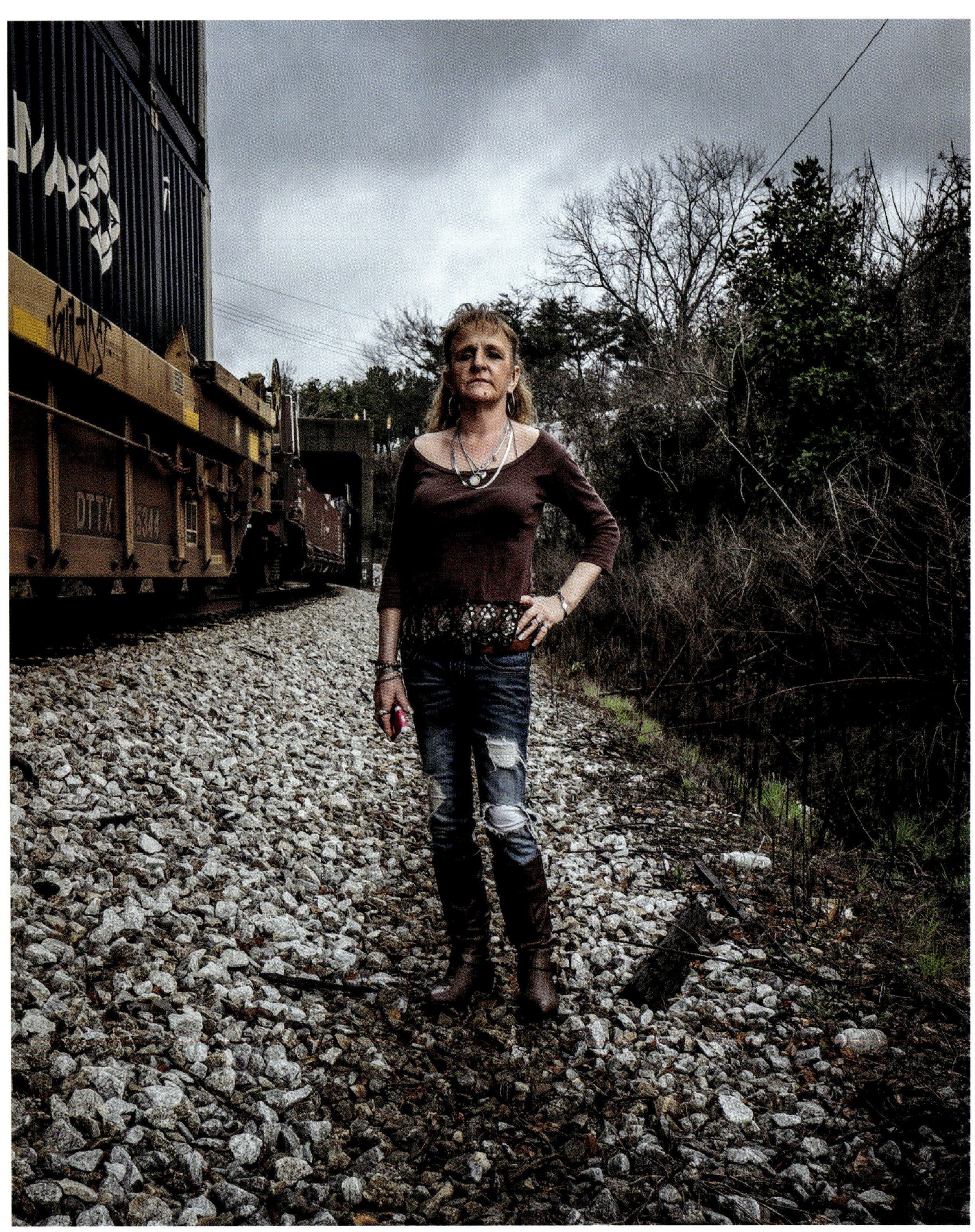

EAST POINT, GA – 2015-01-04

When I met Cathy, she was walking down Cleveland Avenue, not far from where she grew up, in East Point. We immediately hit it off despite her fear that I was going to kill her. She'd spent most of her adult life as a prostitute and, as a result, had more than a few colorful tales. I asked her to tell me about a customer who left a distinct impression on her.

Cathy: Let me tell ya, this one time I met this dude. When I got in the car, he had on panties, a bra, and high heels. I'm like, "*Okaaaay.* I think I need to get out right here." He says, "Oh no, no, no." He said he'd come from a family of magicians, like Houdini. Then he hands me these panties, bra, and high heels. He had a brand new fuckin' saw. A wood-handled saw that had a deer on it. I was like, "Whoa!" He had rope and everything. I said, "Look, man—I need to get the fuck out!"

He says, "No, no, no. I don't want to cut you. I want you to do it to me." He showed me his legs, and he had scars all over them where he'd been cut. I said, "Okay, man. I can do that."

So we get down there, and he lays down on the tracks. And I'm bending down, and I started, and I was like, "You know what? I can't do this!" So I took the saw and I slung that motherfucker as far as I could sling it! I already had my $100, so I said, "I'm ready to go home!"

He said, "Okay, okay, okay." So he goes over to the other side of the bridge. His clothes were folded perfectly. He knew exactly what he was gonna do. He put them on, and we left.

I told him when he got in the car, "You know, you owe me more than this." I told him I wanted to go get my sister. He rented us a motel for four days, took us out to eat, and left. But I think he was really gonna kill me. He already had his clothes there. He already knew he was gonna take me there.

I can take you to the spot, if you promise not to kill me.

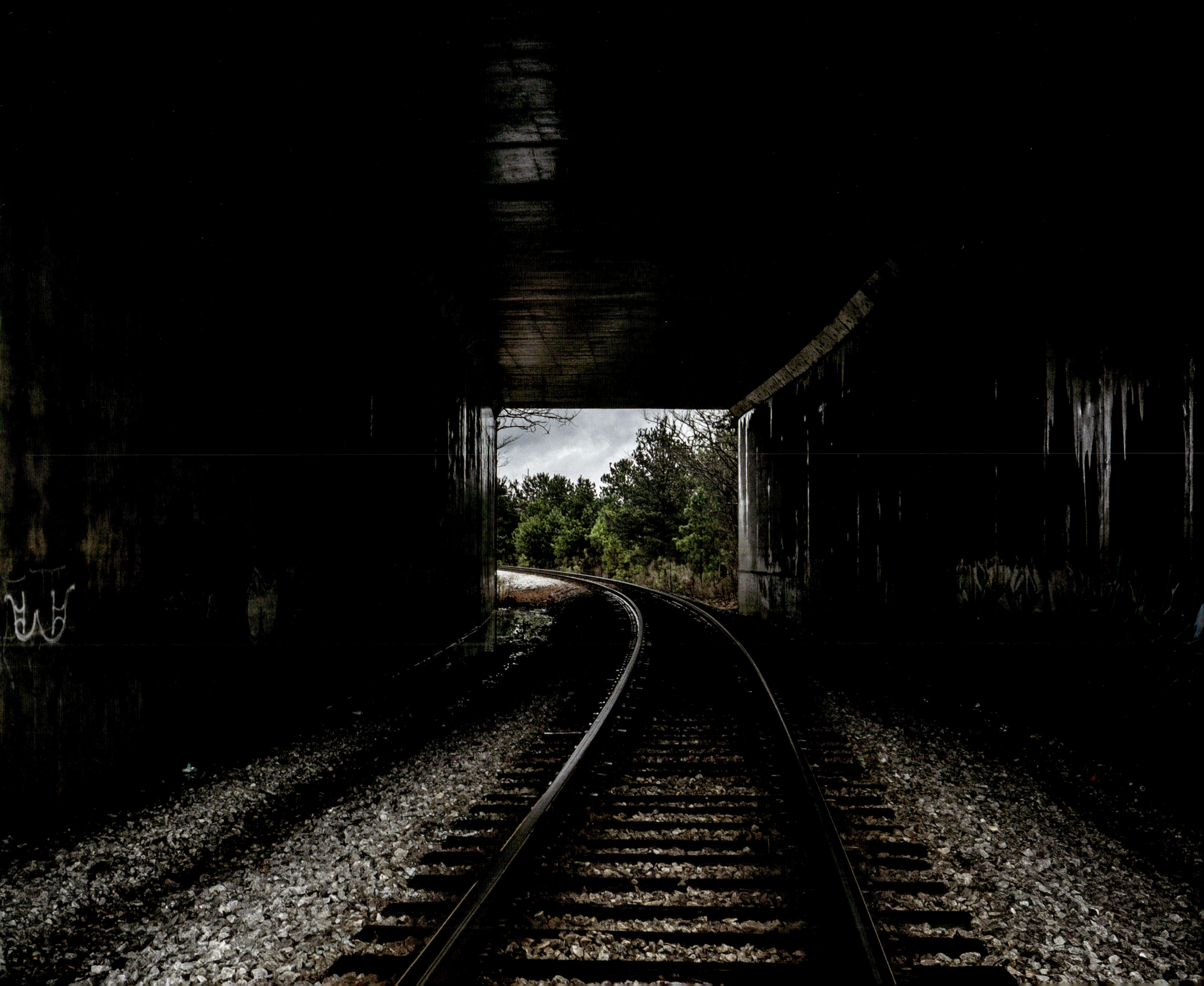

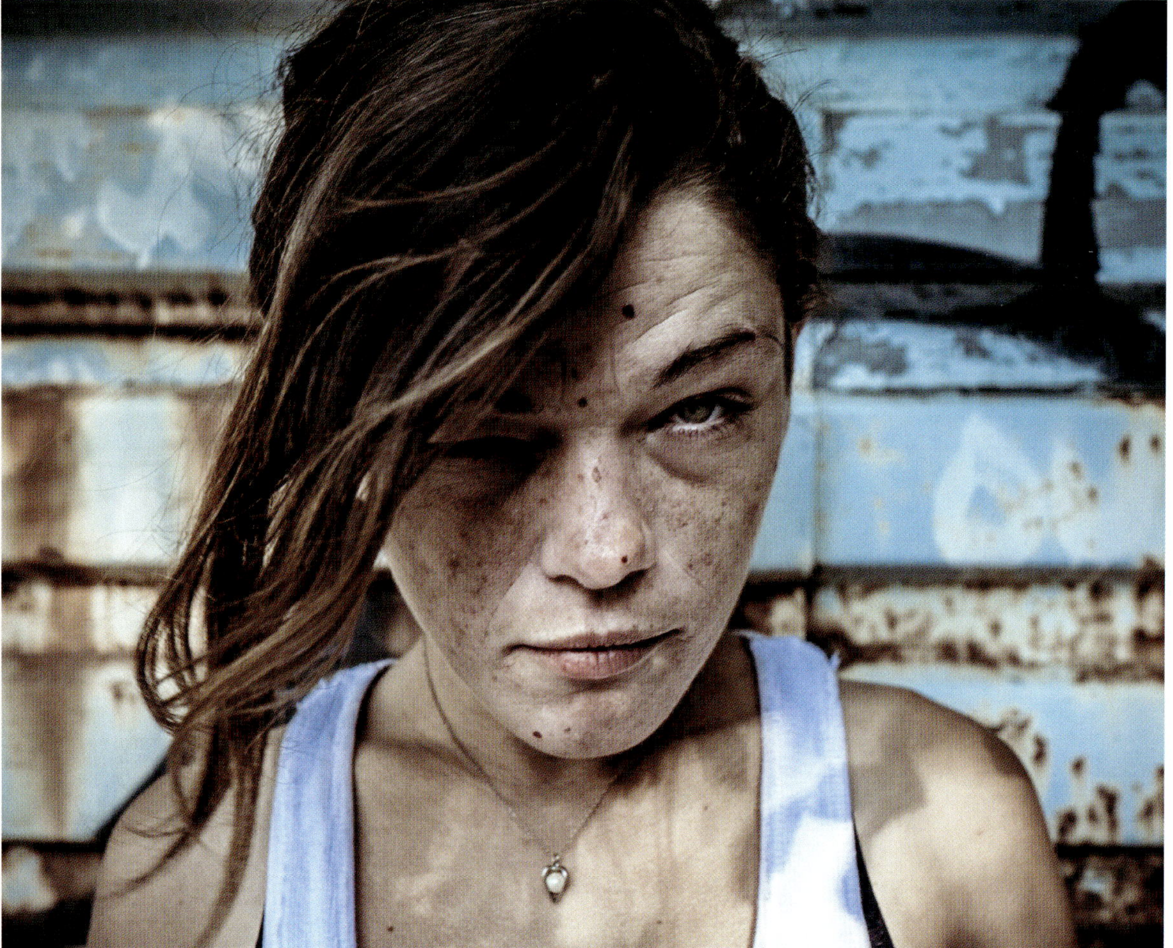

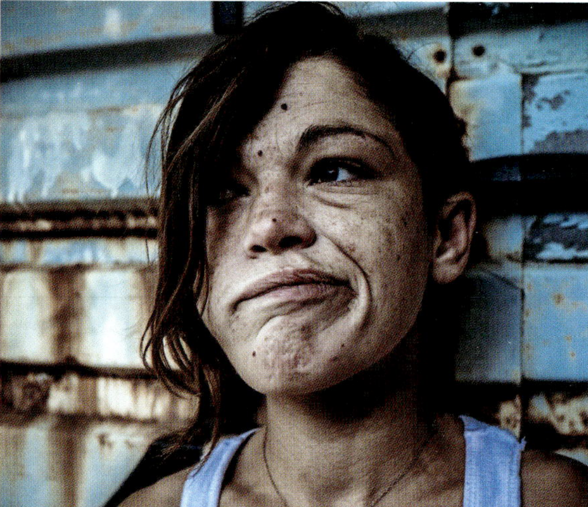

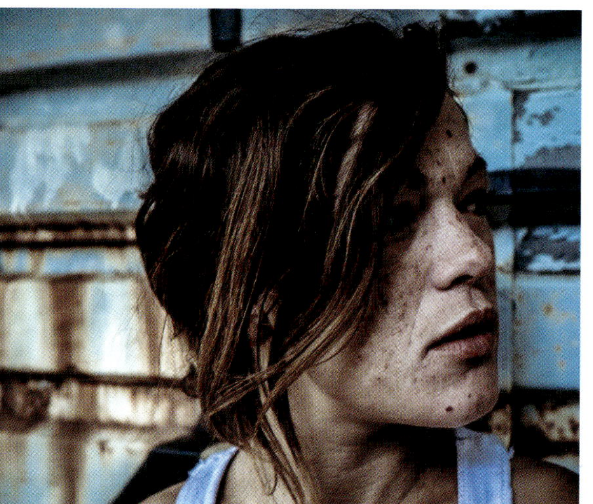

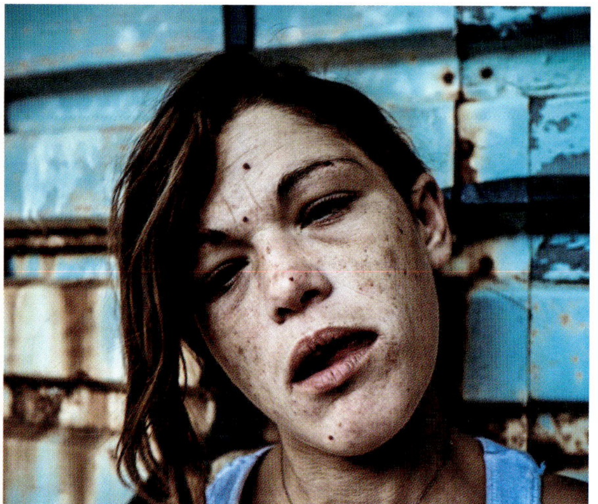

ATLANTA, GA – 2014-09-24

BW: What was the best day of your life?

Ela: The day my son was born.

BW: How old is he now?

Ela: Twelve. He lives with my parents 'cause I'm so fucked up. How long have you been clean?

BW: It's been seven years since I've had a drink or any of the hard stuff.

Ela: That's a long time. I can't imagine . . . I probably won't get sober till he [son] is grown and the damage is done.

BW: You really think you'll make it that long?

Ela: Wow . . . I look that rough?

BW: [Pausing.] Honestly, it's not looking good from here.

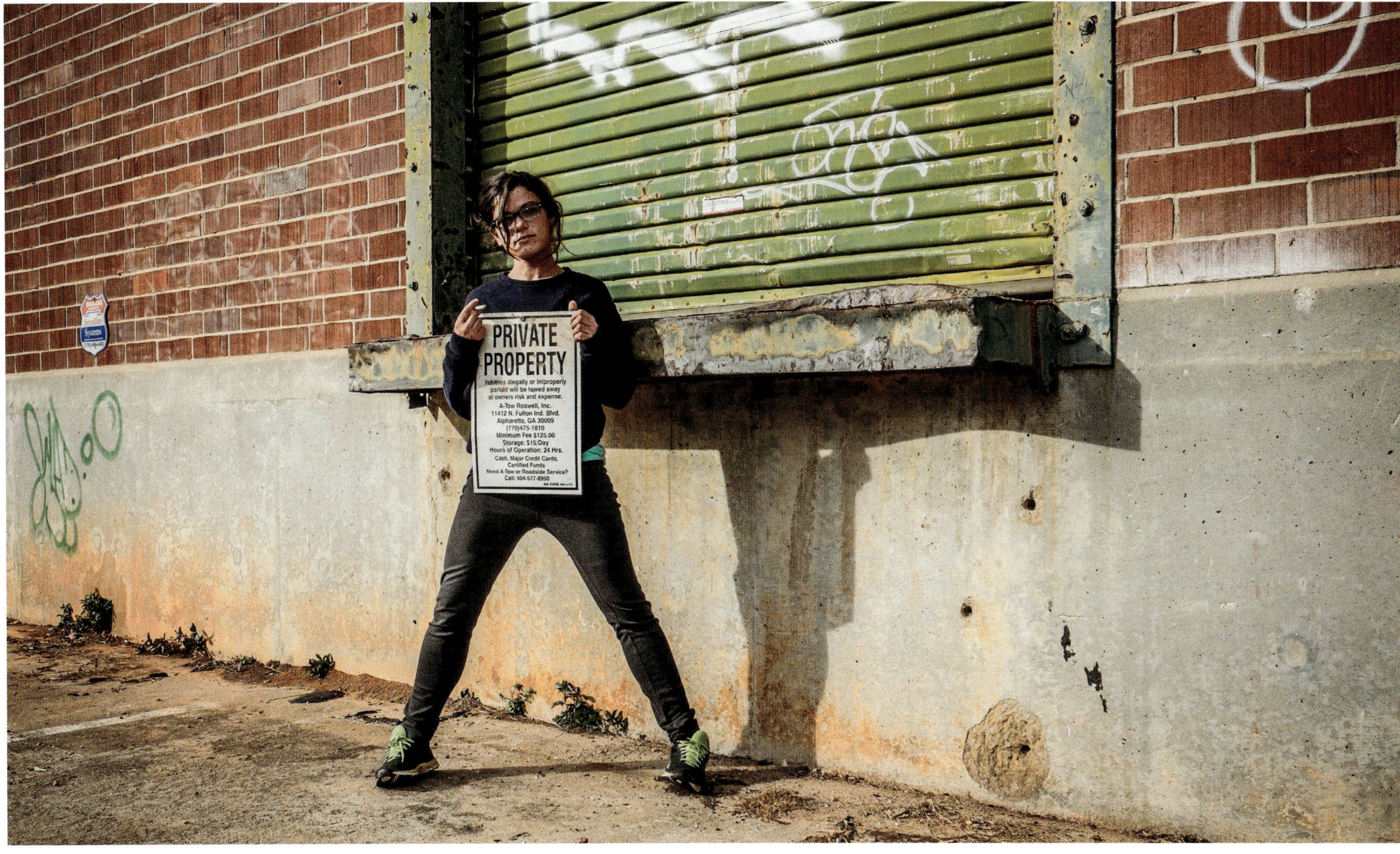

ATLANTA, GA – 2014-12-03

Every time I go back to the neighborhood where I first met Ela, I'm on the lookout for her. It'd been a while, so I figured she'd moved on. But then we met again.

BW: Where are you staying?

Ela: On the street. I have blankets and a sweater and a jacket.

BW: Are you always outdoors?

Ela: I usually sleep in a stairwell because it's like half closed and kind of warm. One night it was so cold that I had to start a little fire with a magazine. It was just that cold. I couldn't get warm.

BW: Well, look . . . I'm not trying to freak you out, but they were talking about someone on the news that's killing homeless people.

Ela: [Groans.] Here in Georgia? No! It's true?

BW: Yeah. There's only been two victims, but they think it's the same killer.

Ela: Well, say it: What happened? How'd he kill them?

BW: Sounds like he just walked up and shot them while they were sleeping.

Ela: That's really scary, dude. I'm walking around until all hours of the morning because I'm too scared to sleep at night, and now this.

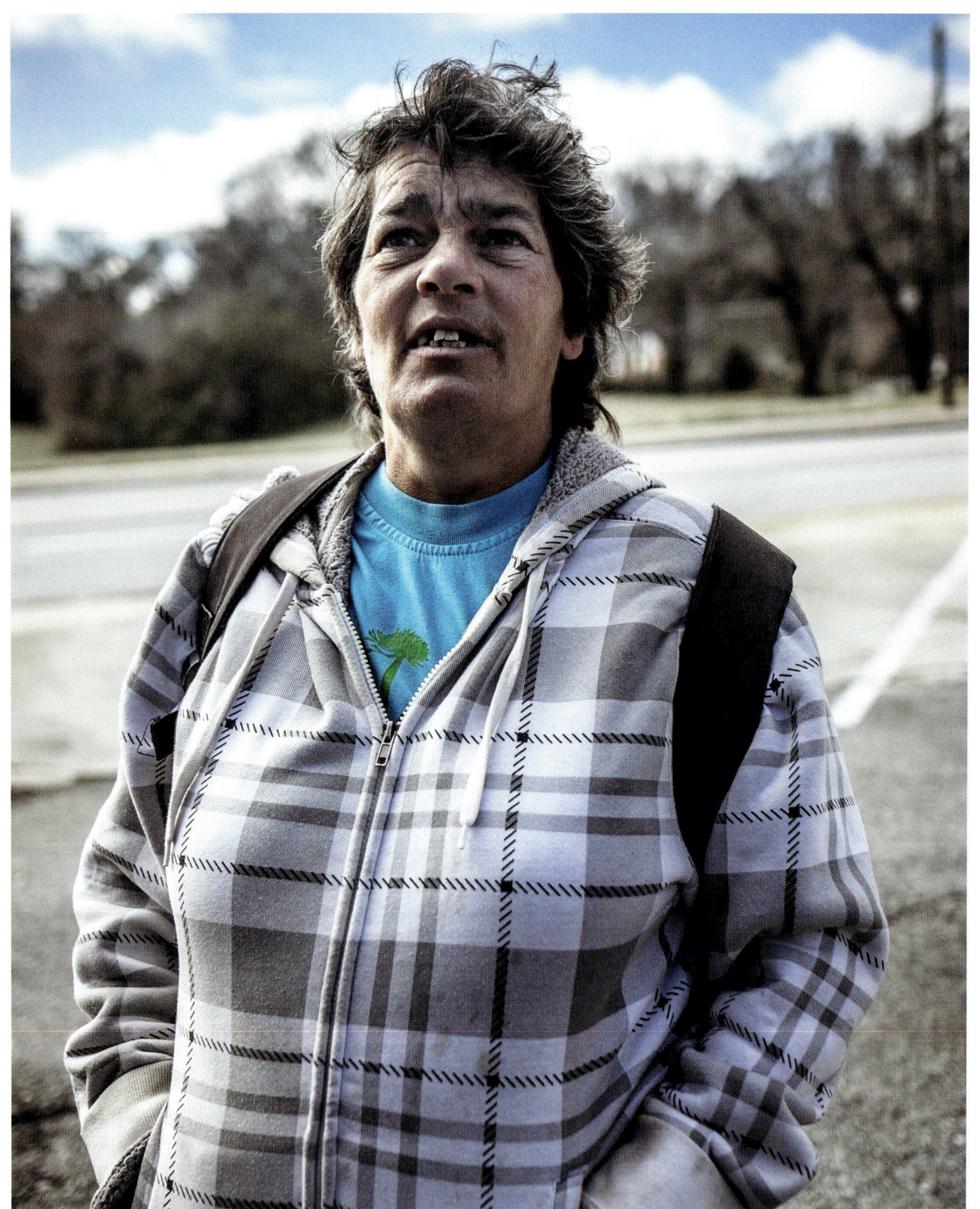

ATLANTA, GA – 2014-12-30

Deborah: Boston ain't as beautiful as people think. I think it's a little worse than the South as far as deviousness, cruelty, and all that. When I came here and people would say, "Good morning," I was shocked. That was a good thing 'cause it kind of brought me out of my shell. 'Cause where I come from, you don't even ask for the time of day. Here, it's totally different. It's given me the strength to actually be who I am.

I actually found God here. I had been thrown out, and I was sitting on the street corner in front of the mission for men. They told me they couldn't help me and all that. They told me to go sleep in the airport, and I was like, "Man, this sounds like something from back home."

I was sitting on a stone, and I was like, "God, I never asked anything of you, but what am I supposed to do?" In my head, I heard this voice say, "Walk up the hill." So I walked up the hill, and this big guy came across the street. And he said, "Let me help you 'cause that looks heavy." I said, "It is, but this is my burden." He says, "Where are you going?" I said, "I have no idea. I'm not from here." And he's like, "Have you ever heard of the Salvation Army?" I said, "No, I don't even know what it is." He says, "It's across the street." I turned to look, and when I turned back, he was gone.

So I was like, "I found God." I saw him later. I guess he just didn't want me to thank him or something. He was just trying to do a good deed. So down south here, it is good.

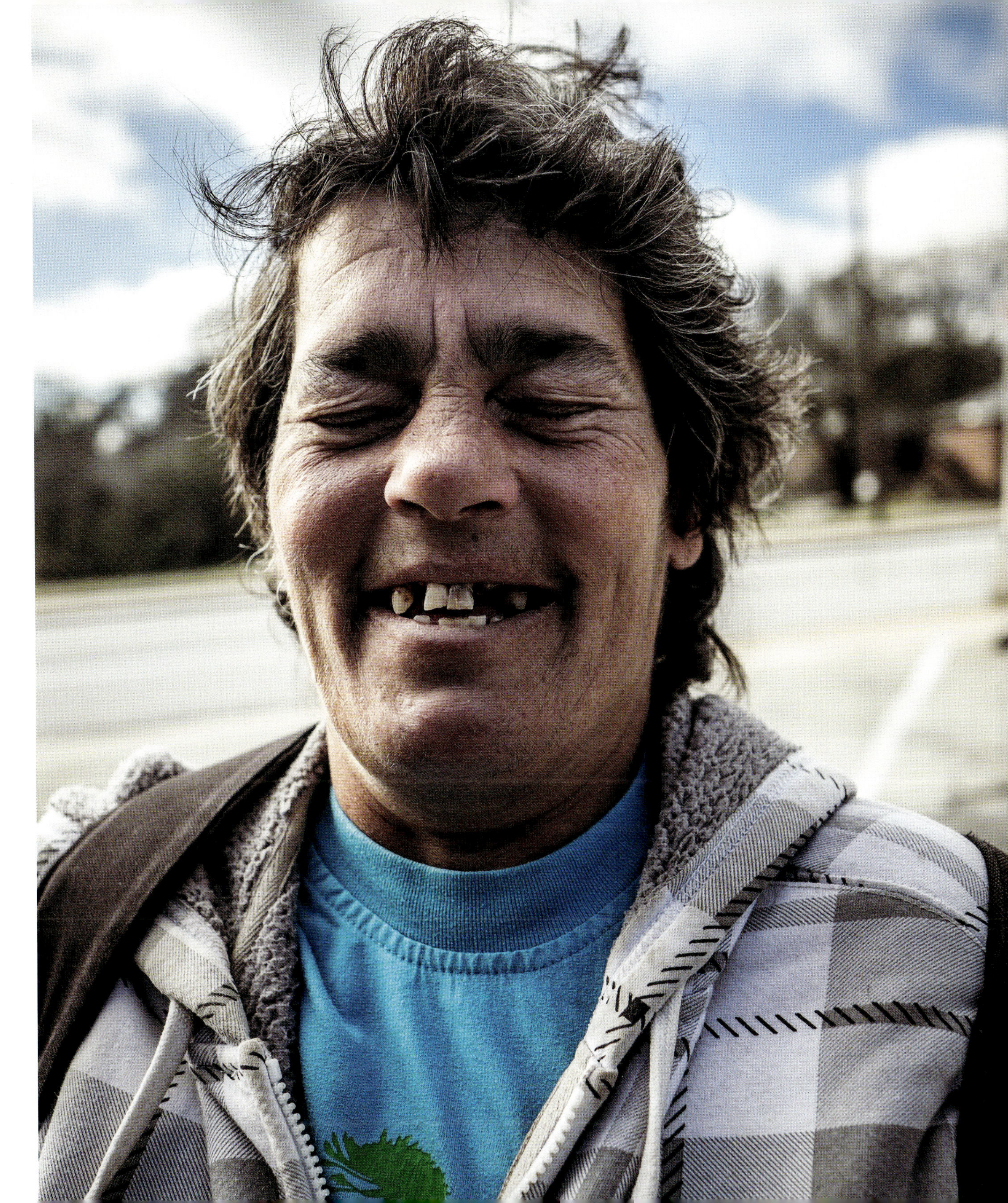

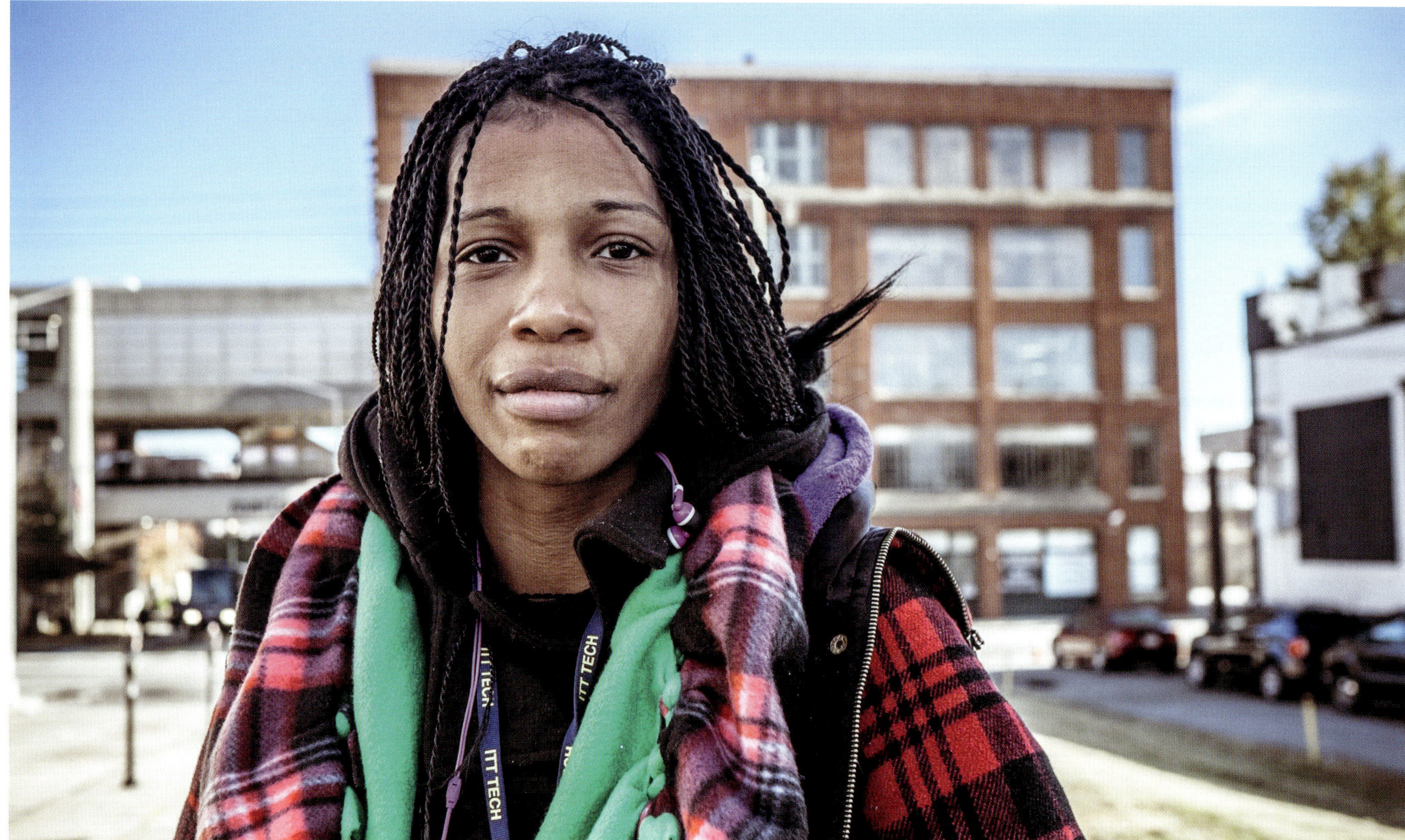

ATLANTA, GA – 2014-11-19

BW: How many kids do you have?

Joann: I have nine lovely children. My oldest is thirteen, and my youngest is nine months.

BW: Do their dads help out much?

Joann: Not really. They're in and out of the picture.

BW: That must be difficult, raising nine kids by yourself. I just can't imagine . . .

Joann: It is hard, but life is hard. Anything worth doing is gonna be hard.

BW: Does it ever get overwhelming?

Joann: It's not the kids that get overwhelming. It's the rest of the world. Their dads and their drama, and I have a boss at work . . . Just all that extra stuff.

BW: What was the best day of your life?

Joann: The day my first child was born. Oh my gosh. I did not understand the love a parent could have for a child. It was like a seed that bloomed into a full-blown flower in a moment.

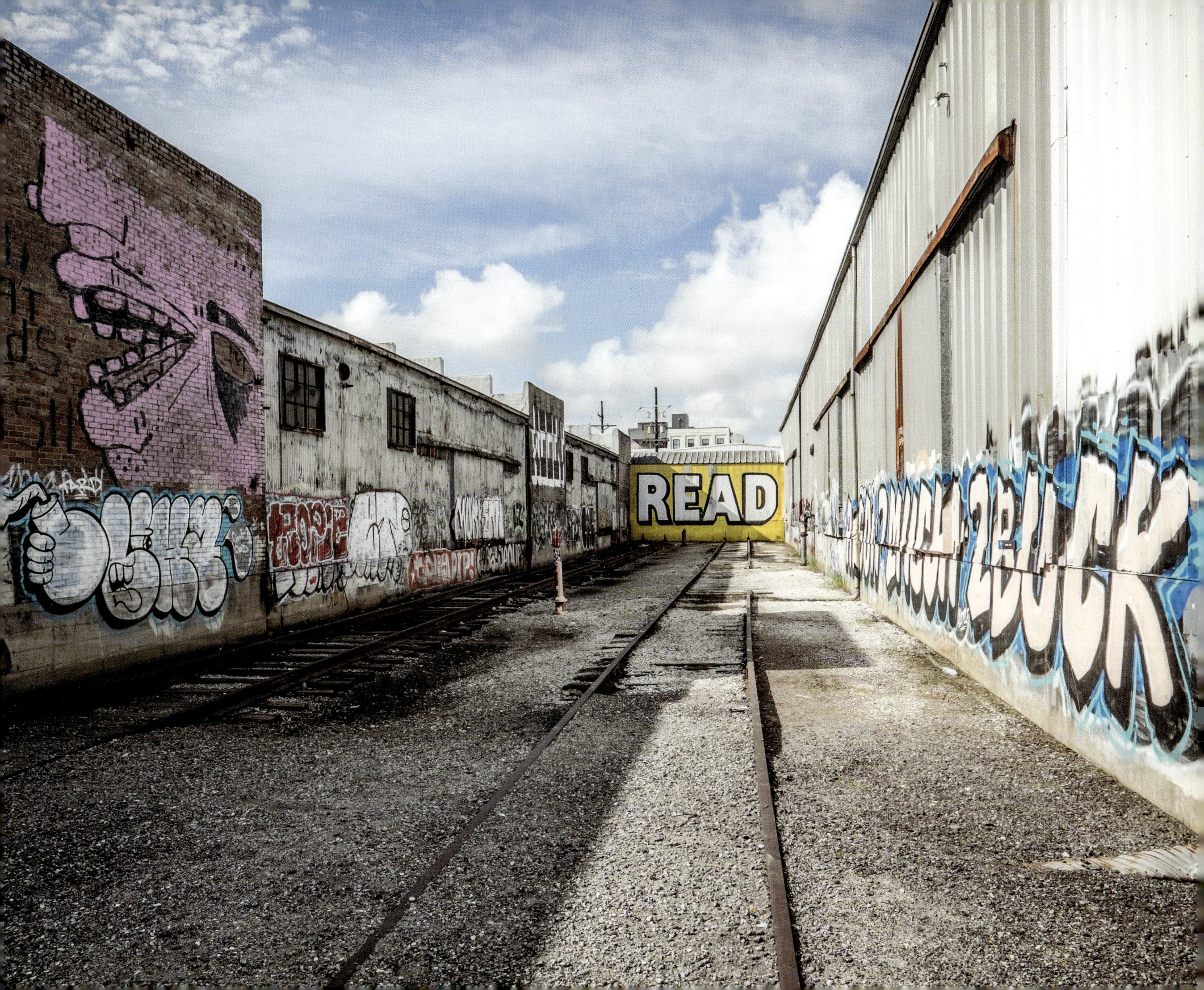
READ

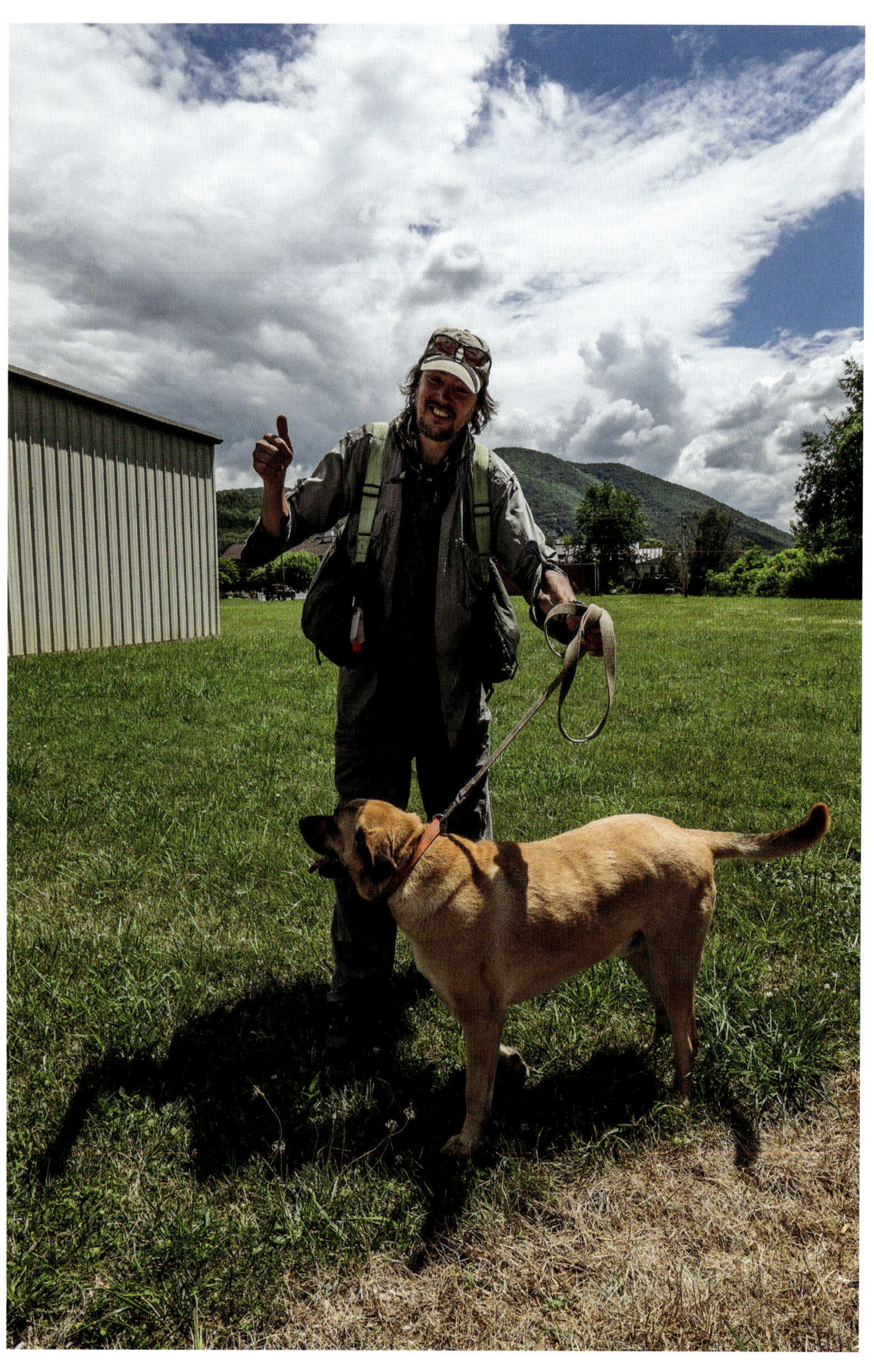

ELIZABETHTON, TN – 2015-06-04

On the way back home from my trip across the Southeast, I met a man and his dog who were on their own journey.

Roman: I grew up on a dairy farm in a place called "God's Thumbprint." That's actually where I'm hiking back to. I have some health issues. I've been diagnosed with leukemia. I went through two surgeries and radiation this past winter. But God provided—know what I mean? I could either sit home and feel sorry for myself or get back out here and experience nature.

BW: I used to dream about hiking the Appalachian Trail. I think a lot of people dream about it, but very few actually do it. What made you do it?

Roman: I grew up around the trail as a kid, and someone in school told me it goes all the way from Georgia to Maine. So I started hiking up on the trail when I was a kid, and I told myself that one day I'd do it. When I got diagnosed with leukemia, I said, "You know what? It's time for me to get out there 'cause life goes by fast." You never know what's gonna happen.

BW: You mentioned receiving radiation to treat the cancer. What was that like?

Roman: It was hell. I'm still recovering. I'm not even back to 50 percent capacity.

BW: You think you'll ever fully recover?

Roman: I don't know. If I keep active the way I'm doing . . . These doctors don't know everything. Sitting around the house all day isn't gonna help me.

BW: Is there anything positive that's come from having leukemia?

Roman: Yes! Actually, in the next two years, I'm going to be working on making Duncan a service dog. He's too young and wild right now.

BW: What's the best thing that's happened since you've been out here?

Roman: I met a terminal cancer patient a couple of weeks ago. The guy was in his late sixties. I told him about my leukemia, and he told me he had about a year to live. He said, "This is the place for me to be. I already have all my affairs in order. There ain't no more time left in my life." Meeting him was powerful. [To BW.] What about you? Where are you headed?

BW: This is the last leg of my journey around the Southeast. I'm taking backroads home to Atlanta. I really don't want it to end.

Roman: Yeah, man. Neither do I.

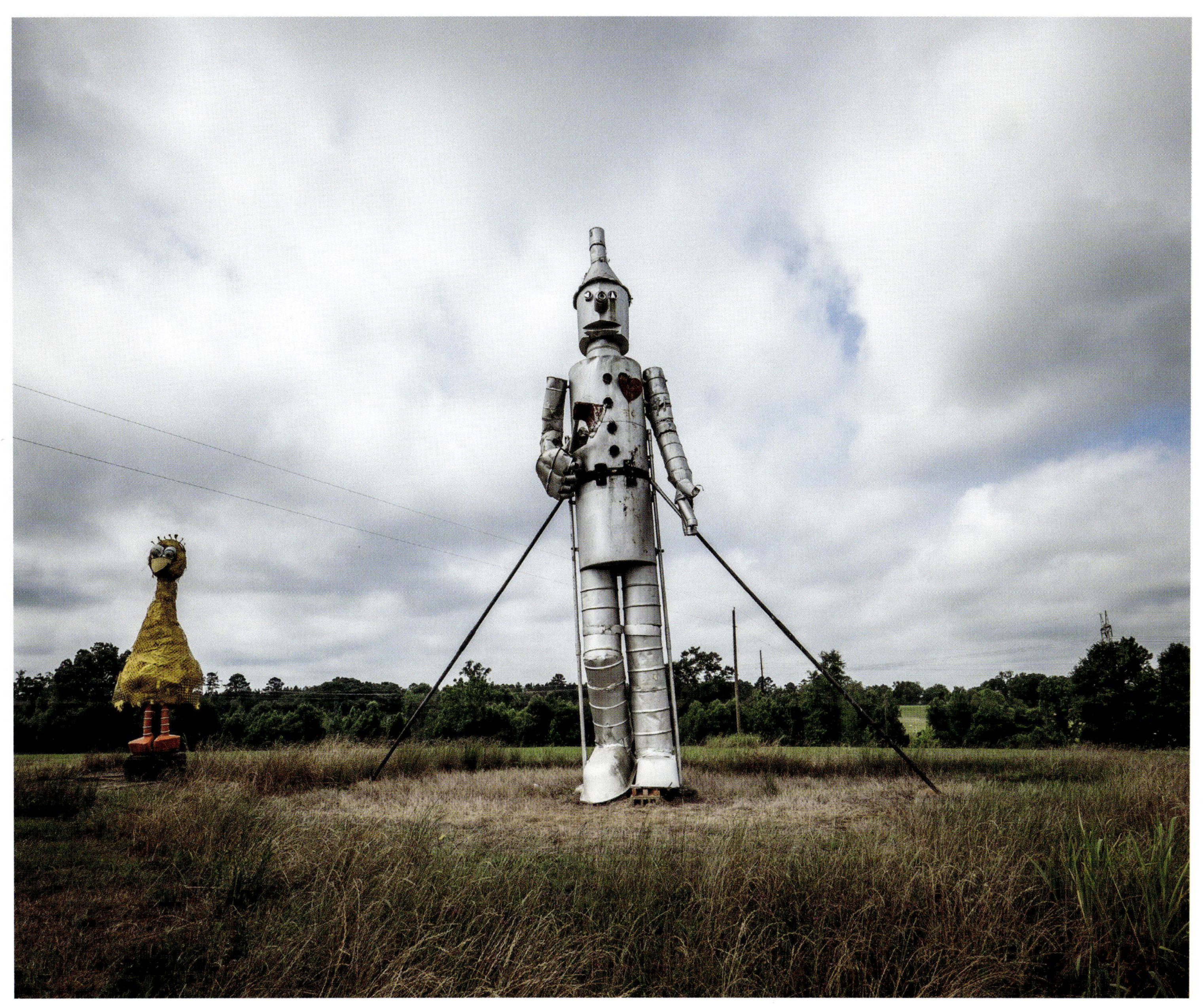

Artist Jim Bird, Forkland, AL

ACKNOWLEDGMENTS

Since the inception of this project, the right people have come along at the right time to help me create this book. These people are like angel investors in the business world, but the only return they want is your project to come to life. They find projects like *The Hidden South* before they have mass appeal and give freely of their time and money to help the project take off.

One of the first people who believed in this project and provided significant help in spreading the good word was Martha Prewitt Levy. Thank you for your guidance and support during the time leading up to successful funding of this book.

The Kickstarter campaign started off with a bang. Supporters gave what they could, and we raised a lot, but it stalled out around the halfway mark. At one point, I began to accept that it simply wouldn't happen because there was too much ground to make up in too few days. Then on Easter Sunday 2015, my brother, Scott, through tears, announced that he and his wife, Paula, wanted to make a significant donation. In return for their contribution, they wanted nothing, not even an acknowledgment here. (I pled my case, and they conceded.) Thank you, Scott and Paula Walker, for your kindness. This book wouldn't exist without you.

Since before I left on my journey around the Southeast, I've been working with a fantastically talented consultant, Christy Cooksey. Christy has spent countless hours helping me on this project, asking nothing in return. During the creation of the book, she's been there to read every word and look at every image. Her honest feedback has been extraordinarily beneficial. During the many long evenings of review, she's also become a close friend. Thank you, my friend, for freely giving your time and knowledge.

I'd like to thank my partner, Suzu Tran, for taking this journey with me and for capturing great video footage along the way. Our life has changed dramatically in the past year, and I'm grateful for your faith in me and the potential of this project.

My father, Wesley Walker, has been gone for some time now. During my formative years, I was fortunate to watch this beautifully flawed man walk the walk by taking in the homeless and helping lifers at Jackson State Prison. I didn't know it at the time, but you were inadvertently teaching me what I needed to know for this journey. I feel your presence often. Thank you.

My daughter, Taylor Walker, interned with me briefly and assisted in writing some of the stories. I'm grateful for the time we spent working together and will cherish it always.

Thank you to the fine folks who volunteered their time to help me create the video for the Kickstarter campaign: Daryl Brown, Richard Paine, and Alex Allgood. I couldn't have done it without you.

Creating this book in a lot of ways was very much like putting a puzzle together. Thank you, Kristen Barwick, for helping me put the pieces together. You're a good friend and a fantastic problem solver.

This project obviously wouldn't exist without the brave people who bared their souls to me. You are the teachers. Your words break us down and put us back together. I'm humbled that you have entrusted me to share your stories. Thank you.

To the people who continue to contribute to the project on a daily basis through comments filled with empathy, compassion, and even judgment—thank you. It's these conversations that can change everything. We don't need preachers or politicians to figure this thing out. We just need to have an honest conversation.

And last, but certainly not least, I want to thank every person who contributed to the successful funding of this book. You just don't know what'll happen when you free-fall into the crowd. Will you be caught, or will you feel the pain of hitting the ground? Well, 237 of you caught me, and I'll forever be grateful.

KICKSTARTER CONTRIBUTORS

Adriane Goff
Afnan Linjawi
Alan Lyons
Alicia Ann Anderson
Alison Proefke
Amber Senter
Amy Jo Bell
Amy Knight
Andrea Weber
Andrew Teebken
Angela Farrell
Anita French
Annalise Kaylor
Anneliese Wirth
Armond Netherly
Ashley Wilson
Avion Charleen Anderson
Benjamin
Bill Stakemann
Brandy McGrady
Breck Prewitt
Brian Barefield
Bubba Hartigan
Carmen
Carmen Ford
Caroline Reese
Carolyn
Carrie Flaspohler
Cassandra Imfeld Jeyaram
Cassie Grove
Cathy Valerio
Celeste
Charlotte Swint
Chris Cenkner
Christina Spencer
Christina White
Christopher Lamp
Christy Cooksey
Christy Fricks
Corrie Phillips
Dan Fox
Dana
Daniel Donaldson
Dave Cartwright
David Bundrick
David Habashy
DeAnne Sasser
Denise Crawley
Dewayne Lawson
Dietmar Leibecke
Dirk Günther
Dustin Twin
Edward Ehler
Eleanor Burden
Elizabeth Donaldson
Elizabeth Erwin
Emily Curtin
Fay Miller Hardy
Finbarr O'Mahony
Frédérique Blanchard
Gail Serauskas
Gardner
Golda Noble
Hannah Lee Cook
Haylee Hunter
Hayley Nelson
Heather Verner
Hightechzombie
Holly
Hostile Living
HugMe and Sara Allman
Hugh Denman
Jackie Smith Kennedy
Jacob Akira Okada
Jacques Thomas
Jaime Marsau
Jake Rudin
James Turnbull
Jamie Callen Sells
Jay
Jenn
Jennifer
Jennifer Beaudette
Jennifer DeSantis
Jennifer Fisher
Jennifer Mesk
Jesse San Nicolas
Jessica
Jessica Jones
Jessica Thomas
Jim Finch
Jim Gaines
Jo E Lewis
Jo Jones
Jon Ouzts
Jonas Nielsen
Jonathan Vang
Jonathan Zufi
Jono and Meghann Ramey
Joseph J Fiore
Joshua Newport
Joy Bala
Karen
Karen Steinberg
Kari Lumme
Karin Haberlin
Kate Brambrut
Katherine Campbell
Katherine Zolman
Kathleen Garcia
Katie B Zander-Flores
Katie Condon
Katie Foster
Katy Kozee
Kayla Jones
Kelley LeMaster
Kelly Corcoran
Kelly Hembree
Kelly Morales
Kenneth Stewart
Kenneth Uzquiano
Kevin Rinker
Kim Lawson
Kim Mross
Kimberly Ramey
Klei Richards
Kristen Buckley
Laura Beth Daws
Laura E. Rogers
Laura Gann
Lauren Daniel Loden
Laurie in Colorado
Laurie Shock
Layton Elliott
Lee Gresham
Lester Samples
Linda Schear
Lindsay Wolfe
Lisa Frenkel
Lisa Porter
Lisa White
Loren D Bruffey Jr
Lori Miller
Lynette Charity
M Cason
Maggie Noonan
Malcolm Lightner
Mara Suttmann-Lea
Maria Dumas
Maria Schuetz
Marlin Hauff
Martha Prewitt Levy
Mary Leslie Hardy
Mary Olsen
Matt J. Duffy
Maxwell
Maya Lorentzen
Melanie Fletcher
Melany
Melissa
Merdek Innovations Ltd. Co.
Michael
Michael Fletcher
Michael K Gremillion
Michael Smith
Michael Theisen
Michael Willis
Michelle Hall
Michelle Neilson
Misty Johnson Jorek
Molly Gollinger
Molly Paschal
Monica A. Cantwell
Monica Flynn
Nate Steiner
Nicholas Ramey
Nicole Acevedo
Nina Samples
Nzmccorm
Oscar
Pamela Dennison
Patrick G. Duffy
Paula Davis
Paula Orman Hall
Paula Ouder
Phyllis Walker
Pilar Ritcherson
Rachel Donovan
Rachel Jackson
Rebecca Mick
Regina Genwright
Reshma Arun
Rhonni
Richard Paine
Richard Shores
Robert Colby Perkins Jr.
Roxanne Marin
Ryan Cardone
Ryan Holbird
Ryan Jarvis
Ryan and Marna Walker
Sal Mannino
Sally & Beau Eadon
Sandra M. Klingler
Sara Brown
Sarah Overcash
Scott and Paula Walker
Sean
Sean Reynolds
Serge "Je suis Charlie" M.
Shana
Shannon Fullen
Sharon Ravert
Sharyn Watson
Shawn Simpson
Shayna Gaspard
Soheil Eshghi
Sterling
Steve Boyd
Stewart C Annis
Susan Lobdell
T. Grant Cobia
Tamara Plasha
Tamaradaniel
Tara Miller
Thomas
Tim Bailen
Tortuga Twins
Trish Doyle Roberts
Valerie Kiser
Vicki Lyn Engel
Vicki Pheil
Victoria Dupree
W!
Walter Ray Davis jr
Wesley Chen
Wesley Lucas
Woody Marshall
Zack Jones

NOTES

1. *The Foster Care Alumni Study*. "Improving Family Foster Care: The Foster Care Alumni Study Findings from the Northwest Foster Care Alumni Study." (Public) Retrieved from http://www.casey.org/media/AlumniStudies_NW_Report_FR.pdf.
2. "In the Midst of It All," written by Kevin Bond and performed by Yolanda Adams.
3. Johann Hari. *The Huffington Post*. "The Likely Cause of Addiction Has Been Discovered, and It Is Not What You Think." (Public) Retrieved from http://www.huffingtonpost.com/johann-hari/the-real-cause-of-addicti_b_6506936.html.
4. *International Centre for Prison Studies*. "World Prison Population List (tenth edition)." (Public) Retrieved from http://www.prisonstudies.org/sites/default/files/resources/downloads/wppl_10.pdf.
5. *U.S. Department of Justice*. "Correctional Populations in the United States, 2013." (Public) Retrieved from http://www.bjs.gov/content/pub/pdf/cpus13.pdf.
6. *CASA Columbia*. "New CASA report finds: 65% of all U.S. inmates meet the medical criteria for substance abuse addiction, only 11% receive any treatment." (Public) Retrieved from http://www.casacolumbia.org/newsroom/press-releases/2010-behind-bars-II.
7. Aviva Shen. *ThinkProgress*. "Private Prisons Spend $45 Million On Lobbying, Rake In $5.1 Billion For Immigrant Detention Alone." (Public) Retrieved from http://thinkprogress.org/justice/2012/08/03/627471/private-prisons-spend-45-million-on-lobbying-rake-in-51-billion-for-immigrant-detention-alone/
8. Tyler Fyfe. *Plaid Zebra*. "This city is using tiny house villages to fight homelessness." (Public). Retrieved at http://www.theplaidzebra.com/the-progressive-pacific-northwest-is-fighting-homelessness-with-tiny-house-villages/
9. Abby Ohlheiser. *The Washington Post*. "Pastor Creflo Dollar might get his $65 million private jet after all." (Public) Retrieved at https://www.washingtonpost.com/news/acts-of-faith/wp/2015/06/03/pastor-creflo-dollar-might-get-his-65-million-private-jet-after-all/.
10. *Georgia Department of Community Affairs*. "State-Wide Homeless Counts." (Public) Retrieved at http://www.dca.state.ga.us/housing/specialneeds/programs/homeless_count.asp.
11. *National Coalition for the Homeless*. "Mental Illness and Homelessness." (Public) Retrieved from http://www.nationalhomeless.org/factsheets/Mental_Illness.pdf.
12. Day, A., Thurlow, K., & Woolliscroft, J. (2003). Working with childhood sexual abuse: A survey of mental health professionals. *Child Abuse & Neglect*, 27, 191–198. Retrieved from https://www.clevelandrapecrisis.org/resources/statistics/about-child-sexual-abuse.
13. Darlene Lancer. *Breaking the Cycles*. "Shame: The Core of Addiction and Codependency." (Public) Retrieved at http://www.breakingthecycles.com/blog/2012/11/02/shame-the-core-of-addiction-and-codependency/.

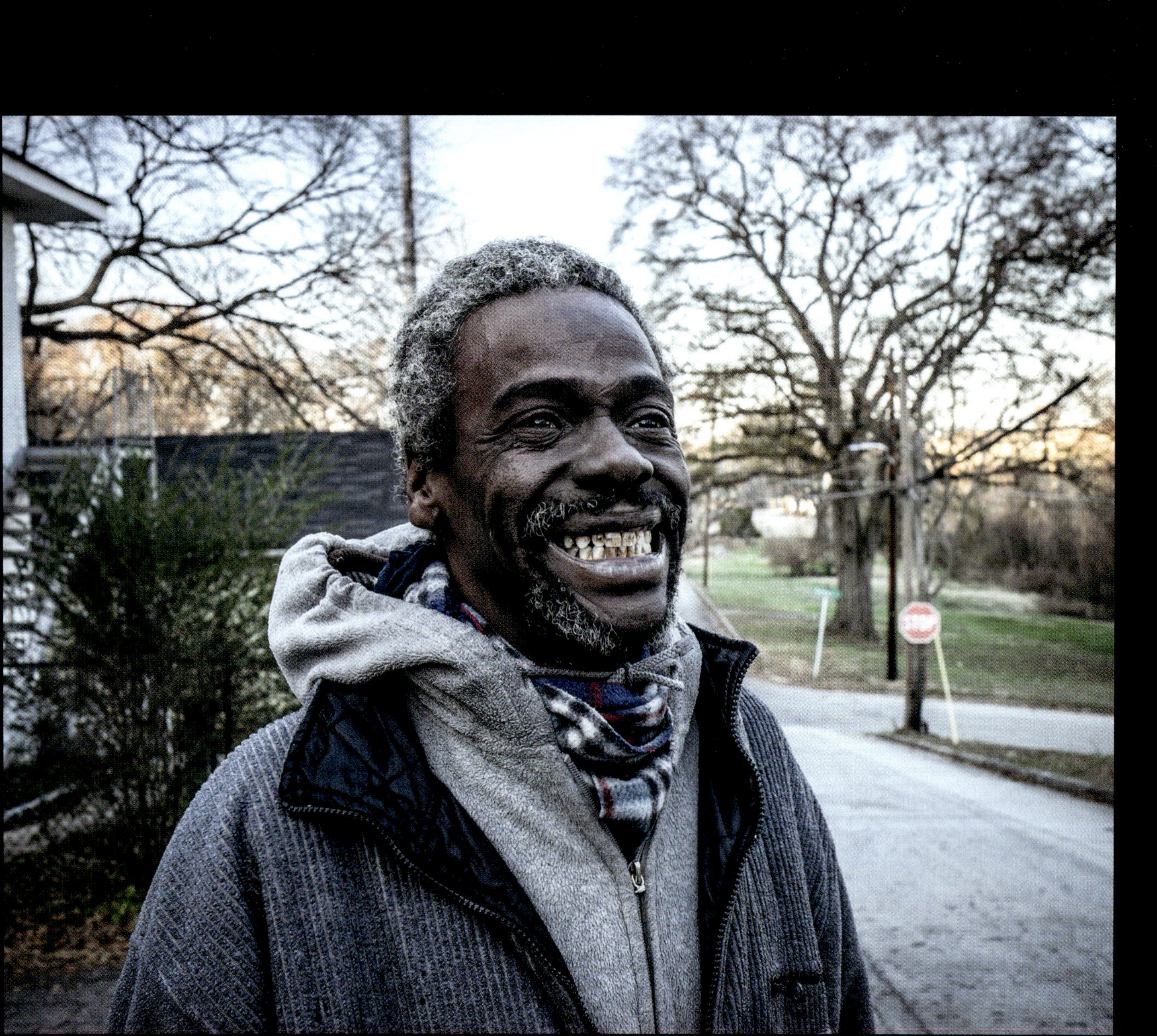